Bridging Multiple Worlds

Bridging Multiple Worlds

Case Studies of Diverse Educational Communities

SECOND EDITION

Lorraine S. Taylor

State University of New York at New Paltz, Emerita

Catharine R. Whittaker

State University of New York at New Paltz

PEARSON

Boston • New York • San Francisco
Mexico City • Montreal • Toronto • London • Madrid • Munich • Paris
Hong Kong • Singapore • Tokyo • Cape Town • Sydney

Series Editor: *Kelly Villella Canton*
Series Editorial Assistant: *Christine Swayne*
Marketing Manager: *Darcy Betts*
Production Editor: *Mary Beth Finch*
Editorial Production Service: *Pine Tree Composition, Inc.*
Composition Buyer: *Linda Cox*
Manufacturing Buyer: *Linda Morris*
Electronic Composition: *Pine Tree Composition, Inc.*
Cover Administrator: *Elena Sidorova*

For related titles and support materials, visit our online catalog at www.pearsonhighered.com

Between the time Website information is gathered and published, some sites may have closed. Also, the transcription of URLs can result in typographical errors. The publisher would appreciate notification where these occur so that they may be corrected in subsequent editions.

Library of Congress Cataloging-in-Publication Data

Taylor, Lorraine S.
  Bridging multiple worlds : case studies of diverse educational communities /
Lorraine S. Taylor, Catharine R. Whittaker.—2nd ed.
     p. cm.
  Includes bibliographical references and index.
  ISBN-13: 978-0-205-58251-8
  ISBN-10: 0-205-58251-6
 1. Multicultural education—United States—Case studies.   2. Multiculturalism—
United States—Case studies.   3. Teachers—Training of—United States.
I. Whittaker, Catharine R.   II. Title.

  LC1099.3.T393 2009
  370.117—dc22

                                                      2008003425

Printed in the United States of America

10   9   8   7   6   5   12   11   10

Allyn & Bacon
is an imprint of

www.pearsonhighered.com

ISBN 10:   0-205-58251-6
ISBN 13: 978-0-205-58251-8

For my grandparents, George and Mary Louise Wesley,
and for my mother, Ida Mae Young

L. S. T.

For my husband, William S. Whittaker

C. R. W.

About the Authors

Lorraine Taylor received a doctorate in special education and educational administration at the University of Minnesota. She recently retired as professor emeritus from the State University of New York at New Paltz where she taught in the special education graduate program for 25 years.

Her research interests have always focused on children who lag behind in public schools where traditionally trained teachers using a traditional curriculum and methods prevail. A disproportionate number of these students come from diverse racial and cultural groups and many depend on education as their only way out of poverty. Her earlier book, *Schools for All*, focused on children in danger of failing in U.S. schools. She continues to write from the perspective that the preparation of effective teachers for an increasingly diverse school-aged population and urgent changes in our nation's schools are critical needs for the future progress and prosperity of the United States.

Catharine Whittaker is a professor of special education at the State University of New York at New Paltz. She was a secondary English and special education teacher in public and private schools before teaching on the university level. She teaches undergraduate courses on inclusive education and graduate level courses on multicultural education and methods for teaching adolescent learners with disabilities. Her research interests include differentiated instruction, issues of diverse student populations and the use of case studies in teacher education.

Contents

Preface

The Purpose and Content of the Book

Our major purpose in writing this book is to help to prepare preservice and in-service teachers to successfully teach students from diverse backgrounds. We are interested, first, in helping teachers to understand the critical issues related to diversity in the society and briefly introducing them to relevant research. However, we expect that instructors will use other sources in multicultural education to supplement our overview. Additionally, we hope to help teachers to become skilled decision makers who reflect on their practices and approach problems from a comprehensive perspective in order to arrive at long-term solutions. We have found that using case studies is an effective vehicle for bridging the gap between the real world of students in classrooms and the university setting. We believe that cases taken from schools and classrooms, involving authentic teachers, students, and their families, provide the most honest and effective learning experiences. Cases that present the complex, multiple worlds of children give preservice and in-service teachers the opportunity to appreciate the complexity of issues that arise and to apply a decision-making approach that ensures long-term solutions. Finally, our third objective is to assist teacher educators in their crucial role in preparing teachers who will commit themselves to equity and equality in their services to students.

We have developed a series of authentic case studies for this textbook that involves real students, teachers, families, and community members from different backgrounds as an effective approach to understanding the issues involved in educating an increasingly diverse student population. The cases raise some of the most urgent issues in diversity that challenge every school system across the country. They will stimulate the processes of reflection and decision making that are central for those who will successfully teach our school-aged children and adolescents. Although we do not provide solutions to the problems or issues in the cases, we believe that they reflect guiding principles that lead to comprehensive, long-term solutions to the complex situations.

In addition to the cases, we have included background information on important aspects of the issues involved in each case. Chapter 1 discusses immigration trends, our meaning of diversity, and the new metaphors for the American society. Chapter 2 outlines the current state of education as it relates to diverse student populations, discusses various approaches to multicultural education, and describes the preparation of teachers for diverse students. Chapter 3 discusses the multiple worlds of school, home, and community that students must negotiate and offers suggestions for helping students and teachers to bridge these worlds in the classroom. Chapter 4 details the benefits of using cases in teacher education programs and presents a decision-making scaffold that can be used as a guide when reading and discussing the cases in class, and Chapter 5 presents a model case and the process for using the decision-making scaffold. Thirteen individual cases then follow in Chapters 6 through 12, each preceded by essential background information. The cases are placed in chapters that indicate the major issue that each chapter addresses. However, most cases involve more than one of the diversity topics described in these chapters. The matrix on pages xv–xvi provides an overview of the cases and provides information about the topic, schools level, and community represented (see Matrix).

The cases that we present represent difficult and complex issues that educators, families, and community members have had to confront in the educational arena. Our purpose in sharing these cases is to offer specific situations in which attitudes, understandings, approaches, and policies must be radically altered in order for the students involved to have positive educational experiences. In reviewing these cases, you should not in any way infer that because we present problematic cases we sanction all the attitudes and actions of those we describe. Rather, we hope that by carefully moving through the decision-making process described in Chapter 4 you will learn how to identify alternative values and actions in working with students and their families. Such alternative values and actions are clearly delineated in a comprehensive view of multicultural education. Sleeter and Grant (2006) and Banks and Banks (2003), among other researchers, have contributed immensely to our understanding of multicultural education by synthesizing the research and theory related to diversity and schooling and delineating the various approaches to multicultural education. We will address these approaches in Chapter 2.

Supplements

Instructor's Manual

An instructor's manual to accompany this textbook has been developed by the authors to guide teacher educators in using this book for their courses. It can be downloaded in PDF from the Instructor Resource Center at the Pearson Higher Education website (www.pearsonhighered.com/educator). Your local Pearson sales representative can help you locate and set up a password for the Instructor Resource Center.

Acknowledgments

Writing a book of authentic case studies is a process that involves the expertise, cooperation, goodwill, patience, and time of many individuals. First, we want to acknowledge the kindness of many colleagues who offered their professional wisdom. Laurel Garrick Duhaney, Laura Dull, Gowri Parameswaran, Judith Rance-Roney, Michael Smith, Robin Smith, and Spencer Salend were generous in offering resources and

Matrix of Cases

Topic Areas, School Level and Community

Cases by Chapter	Race	Culture	Language	Socio-economic Status	Exceptionality	Gender	Sexual Orientation	Religion	Elementary	Secondary	Urban	Suburban/Rural
Chapter 4												
Jesus Gonzalez	x	x	x						x			x
Chapter 6 Race and Ethnicity												
Jim Peterson	x				x	x				x		
Lisa Golden	x	x				x				x	x	
Chapter 7 Culture and Language												
Onteora Indian	x	x							x	x		x
Fome Qureshi	x	x	x			x		x		x	x	
Chapter 8 Poverty												
Maria Ramirez	x	x	x	x	x	x			x		x	
Sue Wilson				x	x				x		x	x
Chapter 9 Exceptionality												
Selina James	x			x	x	x			x		x	
Matthew Simpson	x			x	x	x			x		x	

Cases by Chapter	Race	Culture	Language	Socio-economic Status	Exceptionality	Gender	Sexual Orientation	Religion	Elementary	Secondary	Urban	Suburban/ Rural
Chapter 10 Gender												
Cassie	x					x				x	x	
Brown												
Justin				x		x				x		x
Healy												
Chapter 11 Gender Orientation												
Renee							x	x		x	x	
Fischer												
Sam							x	x	x			x
Meyers												
Chapter 12 Religion												
The Higher Ground Academy	x		x			x		x	x	x	x	

support. Second, we welcome our colleagues at SUNY New Paltz, Terry Murray and Jane Sileo, who co-authored Chapters 10 and 11, respectively. Furthermore, we are deeply indebted to the many individual teachers, administrators, staff, and families who welcomed us into their schools, communities, and lives so that we could tell their stories. In particular, we want to acknowledge Denise Bernstein, Carl Cotrell, Maureen DeHaan, Aida DeQuarto, Ann Marie DiBella, Jane Eakins, Cecily S. Frazier, Rosibel Gonzalez, Francis Gorleski, Raka Gulati, Liaquat Ali Khan, Cyndy Knapp, Erin McGurgen, Ted W. Petersen, Christopher Schuon, Linda Stevens, Lyn Umble, Mana Watsky, Bill Wilson at Higher Ground Academy, and Dennis Yerry. The help of our graduate assistant Phil Myers was invaluable. In addition, it is important to recognize the many students in the SUNY New Paltz School of Education who have taught us the value of using teaching cases in teacher preparation and who have given us the opportunity to refine the process of writing and discussing cases. We are extremely grateful for the encouragement and expertise of our reviewers. We would like to thank the reviewers of the current edition, Michaela W. Columbo, University of Massachusetts, Lowell; Dr. Yoko Mogi-Hein, St. Norbert College; and Dr. Joy L. Wiggins, University of Texas at Arlington. We would also like to thank reviewers of the first edition, Dr. Blidi Stemm, Northeastern University; Pamela Taylor, University of Southern Indiana; and Michelle Vandervelde Woodfork, University of Washington, Seattle. Our thanks also go to our editor, Kelly Villela Canton. Finally, we would like to thank our families for their continual support, encouragement, and sustenance throughout the writing of this book.

Introduction

We write the second edition of this book at a time of tremendous controversy in our country regarding the policies adopted and implemented since September 11, 2001, when the threat of terrorism became a horrific reality within the United States. The victims of this tragedy came from more than forty nations, included members of every social class and economic status, represented all major religious groups, and encompassed both genders and all age categories. While the initial, gut-wrenching response has abated for many, the questions about how to respond wisely and reasonably remain.

It is clear that the shift in national priorities to a continual military presence in Iraq and Afghanistan has resulted in an escalating national debt accompanied by negative economic consequences for many U.S. citizens. The number of individuals living in poverty continues to grow as does the number living without healthcare. Controversy over No Child Left Behind focuses on the increase in requirements for standardized assessment without adequate funding to improve programs. Increasingly, public policy has limited the personal rights of citizens and aliens alike. Hard-won battles for desegregation of public schools are being reversed. Immigrants are facing intolerance because of their country of origin, skin color, language, culture, or religion. Therefore, the focus of this casebook, understanding diversity, will only become more important as we all seek to make wise decisions for ourselves and for future generations on Earth.

In times like these we cling to the hope that we have learned from the past, that we value high moral principles, and that we have the wisdom to make good decisions for the future of the United States and the world. This book suggests a decision-making process that includes understanding, tolerance, clarification, and deliberation and that ultimately leads to social action. As we listen to the questions that permeate our society and declarations about what should be done, it seems that we no longer have the luxury of talking about what *they* should do to address the political, racial, educational, medical, religious, and economic problems of this century. We must ask ourselves what *we* are willing to do or, if we lack the ability, what we can in good conscience ask those we love and respect to do. Our commitment to a just, peaceful, and inclusive society and world will determine the direction, degree, and extent to which "this changes everything."

One of the greatest challenges facing U.S. schools today is the ability of educators to successfully teach students from a wider variety of backgrounds that differ from their own. The knowledge, attitudes, and skills required of teachers as we enter the twenty-first century will include understanding the important issues associated with diversity in race and ethnicity, culture and language, socioeconomic status, gender, ability, and religion. Although the United States has always been a diverse nation in which immigrants from many different origins have settled, the character of this diversity has changed. In addition to new patterns of immigration, changes in society's values and customs have intensified the presence of previously oppressed groups who, inspired by the civil rights movement, also demand inclusion in the mainstream. These groups include persons who are not heterosexual, persons with disabilities, and females. Although the country was founded by those fleeing religious persecution, the increasing diversity of religious groups is also challenging organizational norms in the society.

The Meaning of Diversity

A standard dictionary defines the term *diversity* as "the state or fact of being diverse; difference; unlikeness; variety" (*Webster's New Universal Unabridged Dictionary*, 1994). However, researchers in the area of multicultural education have chosen to focus on areas of diversity depending on their views of the importance of each area. In this text, we discuss diversity in race and ethnicity or skin color, socioeconomic level, culture and language, exceptionalities, gender, sexual orientation, and religion, since these areas are associated with important issues for students and their teachers in the public schools. These issues are involved in the case studies that follow. Knowledgeable teachers with appropriate skills and attitudes can help all students to bridge their multiple worlds of home, school, and community and successfully engage in essential learning experiences (Phelan & Davidson, 1995).

The New Metaphor

Most immigrants to the United States have historically assimilated into the mainstream society, replacing their language and culture of origin with the English language and Eurocentric culture of White America (Novak, 1972). According to Spindler and Spindler (1990), this culture has been characterized by fluency in English with a native-like oral skill and internalization of the values traditionally viewed as American. Thus, fluency in English and the adoption of values such as equality, honesty, and the work ethic, coupled with clear goals and meaningful participation in U.S. society, have been assumed by immigrants who wish to assimilate (Novak, 1972).

However, changes in the national rhetoric as well as more recent emphasis by educators on intercultural and multicultural education have resulted in "a context ostensibly more accommodating of cultural diversity than the contexts of the past" (Fuchs, 1995, p. 313). Certainly, this view is far from universal in U.S. society. Nevertheless, the encouragement of ethnic consciousness and diversity has contributed to the rise of cultural pluralism, and new metaphors are replacing the "melting pot." *Salad bowl*, *mosaic*, and *tapestry* are examples of new terms to describe a population in which one's culture and language of origin are maintained and valued, adding to the overall richness of the society, while the individual also participates in the mainstream culture. Ideally, the immigrant becomes bicultural and is able to enjoy both the culture of origin and the mainstream culture of the United States.

We prefer the metaphor of a *kaleidoscope*, an image that is enduring, yet constantly changing. Each piece is self-contained, colorful, and unique, yet contributes to the overall beauty and richness of the whole. Pieces are not permanently placed as in a mosaic, but are constantly reconstituting themselves. A kaleidoscope changes its configuration each time it is moved, just as individuals can change their attitudes and beliefs as they come in contact with new cultural groups. Thus, we view the many diverse cultures that make up the society like a kaleidoscope.

Authors' Statement of Philosophy

It is important to understand the authors' belief system regarding the approach that teachers and the broader society should take regarding educating students from diverse backgrounds. First, we believe that immigrants can and should be able to live biculturally. Many immigrant groups have successfully maintained their core values at home and in their communities while also learning to negotiate the mainstream culture. Living biculturally should be viewed as a positive contribution to society, not as a threat to national unity. Furthermore, our schools should be places where we are willing to redesign policies and procedures in order to respect the cultures of all students. This is an ongoing and sometimes complex process. Therefore, teachers must receive an education that provides the necessary knowledge about issues of diversity, challenges attitudes that support the status quo, and offers the skills that are crucial for change.

Second, we believe that both teachers and students need to discuss issues involving interpersonal relations and to come to an awareness of their own identity and an understanding of their commonality with one another, regardless of personal characteristics. Racism, classism, homophobia, and other prejudices threaten the very fabric of our society and must be decried. However, many prejudices remain at the unconscious level. Educators must help students to know and experience the dissonance inherent in becoming aware of the privileges that some groups enjoy, often at the expense of other groups. Because of age and background, some people are much further along in this process than others, so we must be patient with one another while promoting such awareness.

Third, we believe there is a need to continually examine the school curriculum so that all racial and ethnic, gender, language, socioeconomic, ability, and religious groups in our pluralistic society are included and affirmed. Authentic voices of representatives of these groups must be heard. Such a curriculum should allow students to recognize that, at times, intragroup differences can be greater than intergroup differences.

Fourth, we believe that instruction should be designed with multiple learning preferences and multiple intelligences in mind, with high and equitable expectations for all students and with consideration of students' prior knowledge and the development of cooperative and social skills as well as academic skills.

Fifth, we firmly believe that positive school–home–community partnerships are critical to all successful educational programs. An understanding of the multiple worlds of students' homes, school, and community and the possible dissonance that occurs as they move among these worlds is necessary for all educators. Families must be welcomed, listened to, and involved in the schools.

Sixth, we believe that the underrepresentation of teachers of color in the teaching profession is a serious problem that must be corrected. Likewise, both genders should be equitably represented on the elementary and secondary levels and in administrative positions. Teachers should be treated equitably, regardless of sexual orientation. Students need role models from their own groups who will understand their particular backgrounds. This is a complex problem that will involve the joint efforts of government, teacher education institutions, public schools, and community groups.

Finally, we believe that schools should prepare citizens to work toward social justice, equity, and equal opportunity. Teachers can accomplish this by organizing curricula around issues such as the meaning of democracy, justice, compassion, and community. Furthermore, teaching critical and reflective thinking and social action skills must be accomplished in collaboration with parents and the community.

In many schools, teachers will need to assume leadership in schoolwide reform where major changes are needed in curriculum and school organization. They will need to "speak up about conditions that limit their effectiveness and policies that restrain positive momentum. This means engaging in continuous professional developmental [and] comporting themselves as professional educators who know what is best for students" (Baumgartner, 2000, p. 24). Other researchers support this view: "School wide reform requires a new vision of professionalism, where teachers assume a major role and responsibility for the schools"(Bodilly cited in Desimone, 2000, p. 24). And, in the words of Muncey and McQuillan (1996), "professional development is at the heart of school change efforts" (p. 1).

There is agreement among many educators that "it is no longer viable for one person to act as the school-level authority" (Vasquez-Levy & Timmerman, 2000, p. 363). Teachers are a vital agent in schoolwide reform and can provide important leadership in the identification and solution of schoolwide problems. Others have noted that teachers can "navigate the structure of schools, nurture relationships, model professional growth, help others with change and challenge the status quo by raising students' voices as well" (Silva, Gimbert, & Nolan, 2000, p. 78).

However, principals must play a major role in developing teacher leadership. They must identify, develop, and support the teacher leaders in their schools, define teacher leadership, be comfortable with teachers as leaders, and encourage teachers to become leaders and develop their leadership skills (Buckner & McDowelle, 2000). In addition, principals will need to provide feedback that is constructive and limited. In other words, principals must "create the infrastructure to support teacher-leadership roles" (Childs-Bowen, Moller, & Scrivner, 2000, p. 28). Principals need to create opportunities for teacher leadership, build professional learning communities, and celebrate innovation and teacher expertise (Childs-Bowen et al., 2000).

For social actions to be successful, there must be a consensus among those involved regarding values held in common. Stakeholders involved in schools must take the time to clearly establish which goals are possible, given mutually shared values. Working for justice is a long and arduous path, and many have faltered along the way once they understood the implications for their own lives of the values that they claim to espouse.

Furthermore, even when values are held in common, the time, resources, and emotional skills that each person brings are limited. Given the immensity of the task, there is a need to develop and nurture patience, perseverance, personal responsibility, understanding, forgiveness, and caring as educators thoughtfully make decisions about individuals and the collective action to be undertaken.

Finally, we must recognize that teaching is a moral endeavor. Educators must learn to identify their own spiritual values and ethics before they can understand or guide others. While it may not be possible to agree as a society on one rigid and extended set of values, it is worthwhile to try to agree on an essential set of values to which we can ascribe. The culture of the United States espouses a commitment to the development of a life of justice, freedom, and equality based on a democratic process. Such a society can only be established and sustained through love, compassion, and unselfishness based on an understanding that these qualities refer more to actions performed on the basis of what is right than to feelings of the moment. This essential set of values will be the foundation on which we can build as we undertake the difficult decisions involving multiple worlds and diverse backgrounds.

Use of Terminology Related to Diversity

As Nieto (2003) points out, language is always changing because it mirrors social, economic, and political events. Consequently, the terms used to refer to various individuals in this book will inevitably change over time and represent different meanings to our readers, depending on their own experience. Our attempt has been to use terminology that the individuals themselves use in the case studies. However, much of our discussion in the opening chapters relates to the U.S. Census and, therefore, it seems most accurate to use those terms.

Census 2000 defined race categories as follows:

- *White* refers to people having origins in any of the original peoples of Europe, the Middle East, or North Africa. It includes people who indicated their race or races as "white" or wrote in entries such as Irish, German, Italian, Lebanese, Near Easterner, Arab, or Polish.
- *Black or African American* refers to people having origins in any of the black racial groups of Africa. It includes people who indicated their race or races as "Black, African Am., or Negro" or wrote in entries such as African American, Afro American, Nigerian, or Haitian.
- *American Indian and Alaska Native* refers to people having origins in any of the original peoples of North and South America (including Central America) and who maintain tribal affiliation of community attachment. It includes people who indicated their race or races by marking this category or writing in their principal or enrolled tribe, such as Rosebud Sioux, Chippewa, or Navajo.
- *Asian* refers to people having origins in any of the original peoples of the Far East, Southeast Asia, or the Indian subcontinent. It includes people who indicated their race or races as "Asian Indian," "Chinese," "Filipino," "Korean,"

"Japanese," "Vietnamese," or "Other Asian," or wrote in entries such as Burmese, Hmong, Pakistani, or Thai.
- *Native Hawaiian and Other Pacific Islander* refers to people having origins in any of the original peoples of Hawaii, Guam, Samoa, or other Pacific islands. It includes people who indicated their race or races as "Native Hawaiian," "Guamanian or Chamorro," "Samoan," or "Other Pacific Islander," or wrote in entries such as Tahitian, Mariana Islander, or Chuukese.
- *Some other race* was included in Census 2000 for respondents who were unable to identify with the five Office of Management and Budget (OMB) race categories. Respondents who provided write-in entries such as Moroccan, South African, Belizean, or a Hispanic origin (for example, Mexican, Puerto Rican, or Cuban) are included in the "some other race" category.

The federal government considers race and Hispanic origin to be two separate and distinct concepts, and Census 2000 asks respondents a separate question about whether they are Spanish, Hispanic, or Latino. Hispanic or Latino is defined as a person of Cuban, Mexican, Puerto Rican, South or Central American, or other Spanish culture or origin regardless of race (Grieco & Cassidy, 2001).

Given the above parameters, we also recognize that there are personal and political reasons that individuals and groups may resist these terms and prefer others. For example, many people who fit the above definition of Hispanic prefer not to use that term, believing that Hispanics–Latinos are not a race, but a heterogeneous group in terms of ethnicity, language, national origin, religious beliefs, and cultural assimilation (Davila, 1997). *Latino* is more acceptable to many who reject bureaucratic and colonial imposition on the part of the U.S. government. The term includes all Latin Americans, especially those born in the United States, without regard to language, nationality, or ethnic affiliation. Similarly, some individuals prefer the terms *Indigenous Peoples* and *First Nations People* to *American Indian*, *Indian*, and *Native American*, seeing the use of the former terms as an act of intellectual liberation and a rejection of the "discovery and progress" narrative maintained by European Americans (Pewewardy, 1999).

The terms *minority* and *people of color* are often used synonymously. However, these terms, too, have been somewhat politicized. In general, we have tried to remain true to the terms used by people in the case studies, the literature cited, and current general usage, such as African American to designate people of African ancestry. We have attempted to use the most appropriate word given the context. For example, the case study about the Onteora Indian in Chapter 7 uses the term Indian because of the name given to the team mascot and the term Native American because it is used locally in the setting of the case. Nevertheless, we affirm the need to dispute the dominant mind-set that Indigenous Peoples obtained status only in relation to their "discovery" by "explorers." We also try to use a more specific term when appropriate, such as Mexican American, rather than Hispanic, or Hmong, rather than Asian.

Finally, we support the idea that individuals with disabilities are people who happen to have a disability and thus have tried to use "people first" language.

References

Banks, J., & Banks, C. A. McGee (Eds.). (2003). *Handbook of research on multicultural education (2nd ed.)* San Francisco, CA: Jossey-Bass.

Baumgartner, A. (2000). Teachers as leaders: Notes from a leader who never planned to become one. *NASSP Bulletin, 84*(616), 23–26.

Buckner, K., & McDowelle, J. (2000). Developing teacher leaders: Providing encouragement, opportunities, and support. *NASSP Bulletin, 84*(616), 35–41.

Childs-Bowen, D., Moller, G., & Scrivner, J. (2000). Principals: Leader of leaders. *NASSP Bulletin, 84*(616), 27–34.

Davila, E. (1997, Spring). Hispanic/Latino: What is in the name? *Diversity.* New Paltz, NY: Academic Senate Task Force on Cultural Diversity.

Desimone, L. (2000). *The role of teachers in urban school reform.* New York: ERIC Clearinghouse on Urban Education (ERIC Document Reproduction No. ED 442 912).

Fuchs, L. (1995). The American civic culture and an inclusivist immigration policy. In James A. Banks & Cherry A. McGee Banks (Eds.), *Handbook of research in multicultural education* (pp. 293–309). New York: Macmillan.

Grieco, E. M., & Cassidy, R. C. (2001). *Overview of race and Hispanic origin: Census 2000 brief.* Washington, DC: U.S. Census Bureau.

Muncey, D. E., & McQuillan, P. J. (1996). *Reform and resistance in schools and classrooms: An ethnographic view of the Coalition of Essential Schools.* New Haven, CT: Yale University Press (ERIC Document Reproduction No. ED 399 345).

Nieto, S. (2003). *Affirming diversity: The sociopolitical context of multicultural education* (4th ed.). New York: Allyn & Bacon.

Novak, M. (1972). *The rise of the unmeltable ethnics.* New York: Macmillan.

Pewewardy, C. (1999). From enemy to mascot: The deculturation of Indian mascots in sports culture. *Canadian Journal of Native Education, 23*(2), 176–189.

Phelan, P., & Davidson, A. (Eds.). (1995). *Renegotiating cultural diversity in American schools.* New York: Teachers College Press.

Silva, D. Y, Gimbert, B., & Nolan, J. (2000). Sliding the doors: Locking and unlocking possibilities for teacher leadership. *Teachers College Record, 102*(4), 779–804.

Sleeter, C. E., & Grant, C. A. (2006). *Making choices for multicultural education: Five approaches to race, class, and gender* (5th ed.). Upper Saddle River, NJ: Prentice Hall.

Spindler, G., & Spindler, L. with Trueba, H. & Williams, M. D. (1990). *The American cultural dialogue and its transmission.* London: Falmer Press.

Vasquez-Levy, D., & Timmerman, M. (2000). Beyond the classroom: Connecting and empowering teachers as leaders. *Teaching and Change, 7*(4), 363–371.

Webster's New Universal Unabridged Dictionary. (1994). New York: Barnes and Noble.

Bridging Multiple Worlds

1

The Changing Pattern of Immigration

Immigrants have been a primary source of population growth and cultural changes throughout our history. They have come to enjoy political freedom, religious tolerance, economic opportunities, and family reunification. They came through forced immigration in the case of slavery. Recent data on immigration show consistent trends and new patterns. One consistent trend is that of immigration from Mexico, which became one of the top five countries of origin for immigrants to the United States in 1921 (U.S. Department of Justice, 1994). It became the leading country in 1961 and that trend continued until 2005, the most recent data available (Tables 1.1 and 1.2).

The recent patterns have contributed to the increasing diversity of our population. Immigrants from Asia, Africa, and Central and South America have largely replaced those of Western Europe. As we continue to receive immigrants whose cultures, languages, races and ethnicities, and religions differ from those of the dominant U.S. mainstream, it will be essential to help all children acquire the knowledge, understanding, attitudes, and skills to live and work together for the common good. We hope that the content of this text will aid teachers and others who work with children in achieving these goals.

TABLE 1.1 *Immigrants by Continent of Origin 1961–2000*

	1961–1970	*1971–1980*	*1981–1990*	*1991–2000*
Europe	1,238,600	801,300	705,601	1,309,106
Asia	445,300	1,633,800	2,817,381	2,890,153
Africa	39,300	91,500	192,293	382,520
Oceania	NA	NA	NA	47,926
North America	1,351,100	1,645,000	3,124,958	3,910,082
Mexico	443,300	637,200	1,653,268	2,250,497
South America	228,300	284,400	455,919	539,330

Source: U.S. Department of Homeland Security, Office of Immigration Statistics, *2005 Yearbook of Immigration Statistics.*

TABLE 1.2   *Immigrants by Continent of Origin 2000–2005*

	2000	2001	2002	2003	2004	2005
Europe	130,996	174,411	173,524	100,434	133,181	176,569
Asia	264,413	348,256	340,494	243,918	334,540	400,135
Africa	44,534	53,731	60,101	48,642	66,422	85,102
Oceania	5,105	6,071	5,515	4,351	5,985	6,546
North America	338,959	405,638	402,049	249,968	342,468	345,575
Mexico	173,493	205,560	218,822	115,585	175,411	161,445
South America	55,823	68,484	74,151	55,028	72,060	103,243

Source: U.S. Department of Homeland Security, Office of Immigration Statistics, *2005 Yearbook of Immigration Statistics.*

Historical Overview

Although Mexico has been one of the major sources of immigrants to the United States since 1920, in every decade between 1880 and 1924, 13 million immigrants from Southern Europe, on average, came to the United States (U.S. Department of Justice, 1994). This massive, predominantly European immigration ended in the mid-1920s during an isolationist period of anti-Jewish, anti-Catholic sentiment when laws restricting immigration were passed (Jacobson, 1996).

Quotas restricted the numbers and were lowest for those from countries labeled "undesirable," a category in which the countries change periodically depending on U.S. attitudes regarding race and social class. For example, the Chinese Exclusion Act of 1882 reduced the number of Chinese immigrants to the United States. Chinese laborers had been imported to build the transcontinental railroad that would connect San Francisco to the Atlantic states and cultivate the rich soil of California (Takaki, 1989). Palmer commented in 1848, "No people in all the East are so well adapted for clearing wild lands and raising every species of agricultural products as the Chinese" (cited in Takaki, 1989, p. 22). Although the Chinese constituted only 0.002 percent of the U.S. population in 1880, the passage of the act was a response to the class tensions and conflict within white society during a time of economic crisis (Takaki, 1989). Thus, "Congress voted to make it unlawful for Chinese laborers to enter the United States for the next ten years and denied naturalized citizenship to the Chinese already here" (Takaki, 1989, p. 111). The prohibition that was initially directed at Chinese laborers was broadened to include all Chinese in 1888 (Takaki, 1989).

Changes in the immigrant population also occurred from 1841 to 1861 when France, Canada, Norway, and Sweden were added to the list of dominant sending countries and from 1901 to 1920 when Italy moved to the top of the list, followed by Austria-Hungary, the Soviet Union, Canada, and England. Important changes were seen again from 1921 to 1940 when Mexico became one of the top sending countries. In fact, during the 1920s, immigration from Mexico increased significantly when both families and single men crossed the border in search of work and in 1942 when an emergency wartime agreement between the United States and Mexico allowed the legal entry of temporary agricultural workers known as the *braceros*. This arrangement lasted for twenty-two years until 1964.

Amendments to the U.S. immigration laws in 1965 resulted in higher immigration rates than at any time since the early 1920s (Jacobson, 1996). During the 1960s, Asia, Central and South America, and Mexico became the predominant countries of origin for the majority of immigrants. By 1994 the top five sending countries were Mexico, the Philippines, China, Korea, and Vietnam, and from 1995 to 1998 Mexico continued to lead all countries in the number of immigrants to the United States, followed by China, India, and the Philippines.

The dominance of Asians and Latin Americans in the recent immigrant population is due to family unity–based selection priorities, which favor newer immigrant groups, and a shift in the demand for immigration to the less developed regions of the world (Meissner, Hormats, Walker, & Ogata, 1993). As Pastor (1983) noted, people of the Caribbean Basin, for example, pull up their roots for a new land for two "of the elemental human instincts, hope or fear, and in some cases, both" (p. 98).

The 1990s revealed an economic gap between "relatively few, but mostly very rich, developed countries of Europe, North America, Australia and Japan on the one hand, and on the other, the very many countries, mostly, but by no means all, poor, developing countries of the Third World, where more than three quarters of the world's population live" (Gould & Findlay, 1994, p. 23). Large, economic disparities among countries are the root cause of most international migration (United Nations, 1999). However, migration is also driven by (1) internal and international conflicts, (2) the failure of governments to respect the rights of minorities, (3) the lack of good governance, which includes the collapse of the state, and (4) the lack of security in terms of basic necessities, the environment, or human rights (United Nations, 1999). To some extent, the interaction of race and the push to emigrate is another factor. Citizens of Cuba and Haiti, for example, who have attempted to flee poverty and persecution have not received equal treatment in their pleas. The "asylum" explanation has apparently worked for Cubans fleeing Castro's communist regime, while it has not worked for Haitians.

Other incentives for migration have arisen from the advent of global media and multinational corporations that initiate international transfers of employees, as well as from the collapse of internal controls in former Eastern Bloc countries, more accessible means for migration, and "brain drain" migration from countries where young, well-educated persons cannot find suitable employment. Calls for temporary labor in agriculture have also contributed to the intense pressure for migration in developing countries in the 1990s (Gould & Findlay, 1994).

The United Nations has been very involved in human rights and other issues regarding international migration. Thus, international protection for those who emigrate from one country to another is embodied in certain agreements and conventions of the United Nations. For example, the 1975 Helsinki Accords required countries to lower the barriers to free movement of people and ideas, and the Refugee Act of 1980 made countries more open to the claims of refugees (Sassen, 1996). Second, The

International Convention, adopted by the United Nations in December 1990, protects the rights of all migrant workers and members of their families. Courts have blocked the attempts by several countries to limit family reunification based upon that Convention (Sassen, 1996). The Programme of Action of the International Conference on Population and Development in 1999 called for cooperation between governments of origin and countries of destination. In response, the governments of Canada, Mexico, the United States, and each of the Central American countries have set up a consultation mechanism known as the Puebla Process (United Nations, 1999). This process involves a multilateral mechanism to coordinate the policies, actions, and objectives agreed to by participating countries. This process, also known as the Regional Conference on Migration, is important, because it provides a focus on effective responses to problems arising in the area of migration (International Organization for Migration, 1999). Countries participating in the process include Belize, Canada, Costa Rica, Dominican Republic, El Salvador, Guatemala, Honduras, Mexico, Nicaragua, Panama, and the United States.

Finally, the 1999 United Nations Conference on Population and Development focused on the need to ensure protection against racism, ethnocentrism, xenophobia, and physical harm for both documented, or legal, immigrants and undocumented, or illegal, immigrants (United Nations, 1999). In fact, Sassen (1996) has noted that "there is a shift to the rights of the individual regardless of nationality, and respect for international human rights codes" (p. 95).

Legislation

Important national legislation has also affected the flow of immigrants to the United States. Immigration law in the United States began with World War I when fears regarding the arrival of enemy spies encouraged Congress to pass a law in 1917 that introduced literacy requirements, banned "Asiatic" immigrants, and required all arrivals to have a passport (Harris, 1995). This law was superseded by legislation in 1921 and 1924, which introduced immigrant quotas in proportion to the national origins of the U.S. population (Harris, 1995).

After World War II, the U.S. Congress conducted a review of the country's immigration policies and passed new legislation, the Immigration and Nationality Act, also known as the McCarran–Walter Act. This legislation, in effect since 1952, continues as the basic immigration law (United Nations, 1998). The McCarran–Walter Act eliminated previous racial exclusions, but retained the national origins formula of the Quota Act of 1924 (United Nations, 1998). It allocated visas according to nationalities already represented in the U.S. population. The McCarran–Walter Act also gave preference to relatives of American citizens and skilled workers.

As mentioned earlier, in 1965, during the Kennedy administration, Amendments to the Quota Act abolished quotas based on national origins, fixed a ceiling on Western Hemisphere immigration, and devised a preference system favoring close relatives of U.S. residents and citizens; those with needed occupational skills, abilities, or training; and refugees (Fuchs, 2000). Other aspects of the amendments allocated visas on a first-come, first-served basis and placed no numerical limit on immediate relatives of U.S. citizens (Fuchs, 2000). The 1965 legislation resulted in a great shift in the nationality of immigrants and, by 1985, 46.4 percent of immigrants to the United States came from Asia (United Nations, 1998).

The Refugee Act of 1980 provided that refugee admissions would be a permanent component of immigration. In addition, the Immigration Reform and Control Act (IRCA) of 1986 legalized the status of many illegal aliens, most of whom were from Mexico and had lived in the United States continuously since 1982. In the amendments of the IRCA, family reunification is a high priority, which has led to a tremendous increase in immigration and a change in the ethnic composition of the immigrant population. Nevertheless, the number of illegal immigrants has continued to increase due to both regional and global changes.

Subsequently, the Immigration Act of 1990, which provided the first major change in immigration legislation in twenty-five years, changed the quota preference system to allow an increase in skilled workers, reduce the delay in the admission of immigration-eligible family members, and provide greater diversity in the sending countries (Meissner et al., 1993; United Nations, 1998). The IMMACT (Immigration Act of 1990), in fact, established annual overall limits on total legal immigration; created a guaranteed minimum number of visas for close family members; increased the number of persons admitted for employment reasons, with higher priority for professionals and highly skilled persons; and created a diversity class of admissions for persons from nations that had not recently sent many immigrants to the United States (U.S. Commission on Immigration Reform, 1997). Diversity admissions refers to provisions in the IMMACT to increase national diversity in the immigrant population by widening access for immigrants from underrepresented countries whose citizens have neither strong family nor job ties to the United States (U.S. Commission on Immigration Reform, 1997).

Thus, in recent years the percentage of foreign-born persons in the general U.S. population increased from a total of 5.4 percent in 1960 to 86 percent in 1993. About 68 percent of immigrants in 1993 came from only fifteen countries (Jacobson, 1996), and immigrants are most concentrated in six states: California, New York, Texas, Florida, New Jersey, and Illinois (U.S. Department of Homeland Security, 2004).

BOX 1.1 • *Illegal Immigrants: Facts*

- Only a small percentage work in agriculture.
- About 20 percent work in construction.
- About 17 percent work in leisure and hospitality industries.
- About 14 percent work in manufacturing.
- About 11 percent work in the wholesale and retail trades.

- Pay rates are commonly in the range of $10 to $20 per hour.
- It seems likely that there are about 8 million illegal immigrants with jobs now. (Based upon the Center's figures).

Source: Passel, Pew Hispanic Research Center, 2005.

The Illegal Immigration Reform and Immigrant Responsibility Act of 1996 is the most recent U.S. legislation. This act was designed to provide increased funds to apprehend, detain, and deport illegal aliens. Rules were severely tightened for those claiming asylum and for illegal aliens who tried to prevent their deportation to avoid severe hardship (Fuchs, 2000).

Illegal Immigration

The aftermath of 9/11, in addition to the marked increase in international acts of terrorism, has caused a renewed national interest in immigration, particularly illegal immigration. The economic, social, and political aspects of immigration have created controversy in the Congress and across the country. Similarly, the impact of population growth in view of the current rate is a concern of environmentalists and others. The population is projected to increase from 288 million in 1996 to 400 million in 2050 (Center for Immigration Studies, 2006). The question is whether a population of 350 or 400 million will be beneficial or harmful to the future of the country (Bouvier, 2007).

Illegal immigration has dominated the national debate, although the exact number of illegal immigrants can only be estimated. The U.S. Government Accountability Office (GAO) (2006) estimates that between 400,000 and 700,000 illegal immigrants have entered the United States each year since 1992. From Pew Hispanic Center Report 20, Mexicans make up about 57 percent of illegal immigrants, Latin and Central Americans about 25 percent, about 9 percent from Asia, 6 percent from Europe and Canada combined, and 4 percent from the rest of the world (Passel, 2005).

Immigrants can become illegal when they (1) cross the U.S. borders without authorization or inspection, (2) stay beyond the authorized period after they enter legally, and (3) violate terms of their legal entry. A substantial portion of the estimated 400,000 to 700,000 who enter illegally do so by crossing the U.S.-Mexico border or the U.S.-Canada border (U.S. GAO, 2006). In fact, border control has become a major issue throughout the country, especially in those states and cities close to our borders.

Some immigrants overstay the amount of time permitted by their visas after entering the United States legally. In other cases, immigrants enter the United States using a Border Crossing Card and then violate the restrictions imposed on the cardholders. The Border Crossing Card is a laminated, credit-card type document with many security features and a ten-year validity (U.S. Department of State, 2002). In order to track visa overstayers, the new U.S. Visit program collects and retains biographic, travel, and biometric information, such as photographs and fingerprints of foreign nationals seeking entry into the United States (Passel, 2005). The third type of illegal immigration into the United States involves violation of the terms of legal entry. Accepting unauthorized employment is an example of violating terms of entry. Another example is coming to the United States on a student visa and not attending school or not leaving after finishing school. The introduction of the Student and Exchange Visitor Information System (SEVIS) by which universities are required to report electronically any "no-shows" or irregularities to the U.S. Immigration and Customs Enforcement (ICE), has somewhat curtailed the student visa problem.

Current Issues

Current issues include the problem of what is to be done with illegal immigrants already in this country. One of the most controversial solutions suggested is granting amnesty or "guest worker" status. While many employers who need low-wage workers are in favor of this solution, many citizens and members of Congress are opposed. In fact, the President proposed a guest worker program in 2004 that failed to be enacted by Congress.

Another issue involves "birthright citizenship." The Fourteenth Amendment has been interpreted by the U.S. Supreme Court to grant citizenship to nearly every child born in the United States, regardless of the citizenship of the parents, with the exception of children of diplomats and children born to enemy forces in hostile occupation of the United States. Thus, children of illegal immigrants have the same rights to a free, public education as other U.S. children (Mexican American Legal Defense and Education Fund, 2007).

The Supreme Court ruled in 1982, in the case of *Plyer v. Doe*, that undocumented children have the same right as U.S. citizens and legal permanent residents to receive a free, public education. The underlying rationale is that deprivation of public education punishes a class of individuals not responsible for their legal status. However, legal custody and residence within the school district are required.

The issue of border control has been equally divisive. Falfurrias, a small town in Texas, has one of the traffic checkpoints that serves as a "strategic enforcement lay" of the approach by the Customs and Border patrol (PCB) for border security. Agents check the immigration status of the occupants of every car. When they spot something, or if a canine alerts, they send the vehicle to a secondary site for more complete inspection (Kane, 2007). At the Falfurrias checkpoint, the highest rate of seizure exists (Kane, 2007). In 2006 the Falfurrias checkpoint apprehended almost four times as many illegal aliens as residents (Kane, 2007). In this area, which includes some of the largest ranches in the country, ranchers help by providing extra eyes and ears for the agents.

In Cochise County, Arizona, agents have reported that not only Mexicans are involved in the smuggling traffic. Central and South Americans, Asians, and Middle Easterners attempt to enter the United States by crossing the border there. Even illegal immigrants from countries such as Egypt and Yemen have been caught. The San Diego *Tribune* reported that after 9/11 attacks, an anonymous caller led Mexican immigration agents to forty-one undocumented Iraqis waiting to cross into the United States. Thus, potential terrorists are well aware that the 4,000-mile border between the United States and Mexico is easy to cross, with vast, unmonitored stretches (Walley, 2007). The possibility of potential terrorists illegally crossing the border had been predicted before 9/11.

Proposed Legislation

In both the U.S. House and Senate, a significant amount of legislation has been introduced to reform immigration laws. Legislation has been proposed by the 109th (2005–2006) and the 110th (2007) Congresses. Bills in the Senate have included legislation designed to increase border control, organize illegal immigrants in a three-tiered system, develop a temporary worker program, and offer legal residence to children of illegal immigrants. Similar bills have been introduced in the House of Representatives. Bills to increase the screening and tracking of aliens; to remove alien terrorists, criminals, and human rights violators; and to expedite removal proceedings have been proposed in the House (Republican National Hispanic Assembly, 2007).

Other bills introduced have proposed more drastic changes: a moratorium on immigration until the government can effectively reduce illegal immigration, a reduction in the quota of family-sponsored immigrants to zero, the ending of birthright citizenship, elimination of the Visa Lottery Program, lowering all levels of legal immigration, repealing some visa categories, and creating a massive agricultural guest worker amnesty (Republication National Hispanic Assembly, 2007).

A comprehensive immigration bill that received the agreement of a bipartisan group was recently introduced in the Senate. Although the bill addressed all of the previously identified issues, it was defeated in the final Senate vote.

On a recent White House website, a series of possible reforms that the President will pursue are listed. The reforms address a broad range of current issues including those of immigration (The White House, 2007).

Assimilation and Acculturation

Immigrants to the United States have historically assimilated, adopting the new culture and language as their own. In fact, according to Horace Mann (cited in Salins, 1997), public schools were necessary, above all, to ensure the assimilation of immigrants. Salins (1997) has described assimilation "American style":

> Assimilation American style set out a simple contract between the existing settlers and all newcomers. Immigrants would be welcome as full members of the American family if they agreed to abide by three simple precepts: First, they had to accept English as the national language. Second, they were expected to take pride in their American identity and believe in America's liberal democratic and egalitarian principles. Third, they were expected to live by the protestant ethic—to be self-reliant, hardworking, and morally upright (Salins, 1997, p. 6).

Assimilation occurs when an individual or group does not maintain its own culture when in contact with other cultures or social environments. Mrs. Lee, for example, emigrated from Taiwan 50 years ago. She commented to one of the authors that she had been so eager to "fit in" the mainstream that she never taught her children the language or the culture of Taiwan. She wanted them to learn only English. When her daughter was 18 years old, she bitterly complained that she "really didn't know who she was." She wanted to go to Taiwan to learn about her background and language (S. Tung, personal communication, 1995).

A somewhat different perspective appeared in a campus memo at San Francisco State University where Linda Juang (2003) wrote about the cultural differences that sometimes created differences in the family. She had to explain to her friends that a young woman would never keep late hours in the culture of her Taiwanese parents, even at 21. She also noted that "in many Chinese American homes with parents who grew up with traditional Chinese values and behaviors, children are often pulled in two directions—being Chinese and being American" (Juang, 2003, p. 1).

Thus, assimilation in the twenty-first century has become a controversial concept. In the view of Renshon (2005),

> it carries with it the implication that there is a national American identity and culture. It also carries the implication that immigrants choosing to come here should, in good faith, try to embrace it. (p. 84)

Renshon also points out that assimilation is now being contested by many multiculturists as "stripping immigrants of their identity" (p. 84). For Renshon, as for many who oppose *multiculturalism*, immigrants come to the United States not to express their ethnicity but to seek political and economic freedom.

Yet, when we listen to people like Mrs. Lee's daughter above, it is easy to appreciate her longing for the identity to be found in knowledge of Taiwan, its history, language, and culture. However, in his book, *The 50% American*, Renshon (2005) disagrees with the view of many people that "we can encourage and integrate millions of new immigrants who have come to our country by encouraging their emotional, political, and economic ties to their home country" (p. 1).

He describes national identity and the need for elements that constitute the "core foundations of American society—our psychology, emotional attachments to our country, our values and ideals, and the institutions that reflect and encourage them to fit together" (p. 1). However, Renshon is most concerned about dual citizenship (the meaning of his book's title), which allows a person to have many of the rights and responsibilities inherent in citizenship in each country of which he or she is a citizen. He describes it as "encouraging or resulting in shallower attachments to the American national community." In a world threatened by terrorism, national unity and loyalty are urgently needed, in his view. Many Americans agree, for example, as Katel writes:

> In small communities experiencing unprecedented waves of new immigrants, many residents say that Mexican immigrants—perhaps because they need only walk across the border to return home—stick to themselves and refuse to learn English or to assimilate (Katel, 2005, p. 17).

Support for Renshon's point of view is implied in the following comments expressed by The Center for Immigration Studies (2006):

> Though most immigrants will undergo a superficial assimilation, however broken our immigration policy is, there is more to Americanization than learning English and getting a job. The development of a visceral, emotional attachment to America and its history, or "patriotic assimilation," is increasingly unlikely when the schools and culture at large are skeptical, even hostile to patriotism (p. 1).

In contrast to assimilation, acculturation involves the process of learning a second culture while maintaining one's culture of origin. Indicators of acculturation include language usage, media behavior (television programs watched in the first language, for example), ties to one's country of origin, length of time in the United States, values expressed, and the composition of one's interpersonal network (Korzenny, 1998).

Both behavioral and attitudinal changes that may be superficial, intermediate, or significant occur in the acculturation process (Casas & Pytluk, 1995; Marin, 1992). Whereas superficial changes may only involve learning and forgetting cultural facts and traditions, significant changes involve alterations in one's beliefs, values, and norms (Marin, 1992).

Both assimilation and acculturation are gradual processes, and different individuals may be at different points in the process at any given time (Korzenny, 1998). However, either process can be prevented when immigrants are marginalized as barriers to participation in the new culture are erected.

Acculturation is in practice at a charter school in Minnesota (to be described in Chapter 12) where the cultures of diverse students are respected as they acquire language and customs of the United States. This philosophy is also embodied in multicultural education, which we will discuss in Chapter 2.

Demographic Changes in the Schools

Statistics show that foreign-born immigrants continue to cluster into a handful of metropolitan areas. According to Frey and DeVol (2000), "just 10 metropolitan areas house 58 percent of the U.S. Hispanic population and ten metropolitan areas, led by Los Angeles, New York, and San Francisco, house 61 percent of all U.S. Asians" (p. 3).

The increased number of ethnically and linguistically diverse immigrants in the central cities, which are densely populated centers of a metropolitan area with a concentration of cultural and commercial facilities and a disproportionately high population of disadvantaged persons, and metropolitan areas of major cities has also affected the school population. Furthermore, in many central cities and metropolitan regions, the population of African American and Hispanic students may be close to 100 percent due to hypersegregation (excessive segregation) or resegregation by which a school previously desegregated becomes segregated again through practices such as tracking, bias in the identification and placement of gifted students and those with disabilities, advanced placement courses that screen out certain groups of students, and biased counseling or guidance.

The most recent data on the school-aged population reflects the national, regional, and local changes in the general population. Indian/Alaskan Natives comprise 1.2 percent; Asian/Pacific Islanders, 4.2 percent; Hispanic, 15.4 percent; Black-non-Hispanic, 16.4 percent; and White-non-Hispanic, 63.3 percent (U.S. Census Bureau, 2000).

While the population of culturally diverse students in the schools is changing dramatically, the characteristics of teachers and administrators remain largely homogeneous. From 1971 to 1991, 88.3 to 88.8 percent of public school teachers were

White (National Education Association, 1993). The most recent data show a slight decrease to 80.5 percent for White teachers, 9 percent for African American teachers, and 5 percent for Hispanic teachers (Yasin, 1999). School principals are also predominately White, approximately 84 percent in the 1993–1994 school year and 82.2 percent in 2003–2004 ("Characteristics of Elementary School Principals," 2006).

The implications for teachers are obvious. Even in areas of the country that remain predominately White, it is essential that teachers learn about the cultures and languages of many children who are arriving in greater numbers and entering their schools for the first time. Furthermore, many of the jobs available in the next decade will be in urban areas where the population is likely to be more diverse. All children will need to work and live harmoniously with members of many diverse groups. Teachers will need to develop the knowledge, skills, and attitudes necessary to prepare a diverse population of students for success in the mainstream, while also respecting their cultures and languages of origin. The preparation of teachers for diverse students will be discussed in Chapter 2.

Geographic variations exist in the diversity of the school-aged population among states, as well as among urban, suburban, and rural areas of the country. For example, comparisons between California and South Dakota show that California has many students in each of the racial or ethnic groups identified, while South Dakota has relatively few (Table 1.3). Language diversity may also be a challenge because in some locations there will be more English language learners than in others. The need for translators and interpreters will vary accordingly.

TABLE 1.3 *Public School Membership, by Race/Ethnicity and State: School Year 2001–02*

State	Students reported[1]	American Indian/Alaska Native	Asian/Pacific Islander	Hispanic	Black non-Hispanic
United States	47,440,514	561,799	2,010,685	8,103,281	8,152,385
Alabama	725,349[1]	5,357	5,869	11,108	264,506
Alaska	134,358	34,210	7,870	4,812	6,254
Arizona	922,180	60,404	19,361	325,661	43,551
Arkansas	449,805	2,300	4,159	18,672	104,951
California	6,108,071[1]	53,314	686,074	2,717,602	512,996
Colorado	742,145	8,710	22,131	172,940	42,361
Connecticut	570,228	1,677	16,878	77,966	78,826
Delaware	115,555	325	2,807	7,600	35,900
District of Columbia	68,449[1]	32	1,121	6,427	57,751
Florida	2,500,478	6,916	48,079	511,247	621,569
Georgia	1,470,634	2,437	34,812	80,776	561,354
Hawaii	184,546	794	133,408	8,384	4,469

(continued)

TABLE 1.3   *Continued*

State	Students reported[1]	American Indian/Alaska Native	Asian/Pacific Islander	Hispanic	Black non-Hispanic
Idaho	246,521	3,238	3,279	27,633	1,908
Illinois	2,071,391	3,535	71,667	335,535	439,478
Indiana	996,133	2,388	10,212	38,943	117,857
Iowa	485,932	2,638	8,344	19,523	19,955
Kansas	470,205	6,286	10,316	45,929	42,023
Kentucky	621,956[1]	1,312	4,287	6,920	63,808
Louisiana	731,328	4,765	9,311	11,358	349,550
Maine	205,586	1,373	2,279	1,324	2,826
Maryland	860,640	3,111	39,401	46,251	320,489
Massachusetts	973,140	3,165	44,148	105,053	83,642
Michigan	1,730,668	18,014	34,493	62,754	345,575
Minnesota	851,384	17,145	44,273	31,935	59,924
Mississippi	493,507	769	3,566	4,208	251,728
Missouri	909,792	2,948	11,100	18,337	159,059
Montana	151,947	16,121	1,560	2,835	962
Nebraska	285,095	4,452	4,502	23,459	19,594
Nevada	356,814	6,158	21,648	97,782	36,737
New Hampshire	206,847	505	3,016	4,255	2,539
New Jersey	1,341,656	2,390	88,558	214,546	239,554
New Mexico	320,260	36,137	3,413	163,378	7,534
New York	2,872,132	12,461	178,495	534,527	571,850
North Carolina	1,315,363	19,336	25,245	68,957	412,192
North Dakota	106,047	8,587	872	1,431	1,138
Ohio	1,804,123[1]	2,382	21,429	33,447	301,480
Oklahoma	622,139	108,800	9,051	40,373	67,334
Oregon	540,813[1]	11,707	22,641	62,392	16,061
Pennsylvania	1,821,627	2,386	37,945	87,219	279,256
Rhode Island	158,046	897	5,098	23,336	12,782
South Carolina	688,258[1]	1,674	6,879	16,187	286,819
South Dakota	127,542	13,004	1,256	1,744	1,635
Tennessee	909,856[1]	1,487	10,575	18,940	225,717
Texas	4,163,447	12,776	116,229	1,735,040	598,223
Utah	484,677	7,456	13,646	47,940	4,934
Vermont	101,179	556	1,524	1,013	1,166
Virginia	1,163,091	3,261	50,094	63,950	315,105
Washington	1,009,200	26,452	75,916	110,468	54,589
West Virginia	282,885	297	1,567	1,173	12,386
Wisconsin	879,361	12,520	29,488	43,621	89,293
Wyoming	88,128	2,834	793	6,370	1,195

State	Students reported[1]	American Indian/Alaska Native	Asian/Pacific Islander	Hispanic	Black non-Hispanic
Outlying Areas, DoD Dependents Schools, and Bureau of Indian Affairs					
Bureau of Indian Affairs[2]	46,476	46,476	0	0	0
DoDDS: DoDs Overseas	56,571[1]	547	5,131	5,262	10,809
DDESS: DoDs Domestic	27,741[1]	170	965	5,137	7,158
American Samoa[2]	15,897	0	15,897	0	0
Guam	31,992	20	31,310	75	104
Northern Marianas	10,479	0	10,429	0	6
Puerto Rico[2]	604,177	0	0	604,177	0
Virgin Islands	18,780	—	—	—	—

— Not available.

[1]Totals exclude students for whom race/ethnicity was not reported.

[2]American Samoa, Puerto Rico, and the BIA reported all of their students in one category of race/ethnicity.

Source: U.S. Department of Education, National Center for Education Statistics, Common Core of Data, "State Nonfiscal Survey Public Elementary/Secondary Education."

References

Bouvier, L. (2007). *Population growth and immigration.* Washington, DC: Center for Immigration Studies.

Casas, M. J., & Pytluk, S.D. (1995). Hispanic identity development: Implications for research and practice. In J.G. Ponterotto, J. Manuel Casas, L.A. Suzuki, & C.M. Alexander (Eds.), *Handbook of multicultural counseling* (pp. 155–180). Thousand Oaks, CA: Sage.

Center for Immigration Studies. (2006). Immigration from Mexico: Costs and benefits for the United States. Washington, DC: Author.

Characteristics of elementary school principals. (2006) *Principal, 86*(1), 42–47.

Frey, W., & Devol, R. (2000). *America's demography in the new century: Aging baby boomers and new immi-grants as major players.* Milliken Institute Policy Brief. Santa Monica, CA: Milken Institute.

Gould, W. T. S., & Findlay, A. M. (1994). *Population and the changing world order.* New York: Wiley.

Harris, N. (1995). *The new untouchables: Immigration and the new world order.* London: J.B. Taurus Publishers.

International Organization for Migration (1999). Retrieved December, 2001, from: http://www.iom.int/

Jacobson, D. (1996). *Rights across the borders: Immigration and the decline of citizenship.* Baltimore: Johns Hopkins University Press.

Juang, L. (2003). Understanding culture and adolescents. *Campus Memo, 5*(15). San Francisco: San Francisco State University.

Kane, L. (2007 April/May). Falfurrias, Texas—a "star" border control checkpoint. Washington, DC: U.S. Customs and Border Protection. In *Today* newsletter.

Katel, P. (2005). Illegal immigration. *CQ Researcher*, 15, 393–420. Retrieved August 6, 2007, from *CQ Researcher Online*, http://library.cqpress.com/ cqresearcher/cqresrre2005050600.

Korzenny, F. (1998). *Acculturation: Conceptualization and measurement*. Retrieved July 2007, from: http:// www.cheskin.com/assets/hispanicacculturation/ measurement.pdf.

Larsen, L. J. (2004). *Foreign born population in the United States, 2003*. Washington, DC: U.S. Department of Commerce, Economics, and Statistics Administration, U.S. Census Bureau.

Mexican American Legal Defense and Education Fund (2007). The rights of immigrant children. Retrieved July 2007, from http://isbe.state.il.us/ bilingual/pdfs/rights.

Marin, G. (1992). Extreme response style and acquiescence among Hispanics: The role of acculturation and education. *Journal of Cross-Cultural Psychology*, 23(4), 498–509.

Meissner, D., Homats, R., Walker, A.G., & Ogata, S. (1993). *International migration challenges in a new era*. New York: The Trilateral Commission.

Merriam-Webster Online dictionary. Retrieved December 2006, from http:www.M-W.com

National Education Association. (1993). *The status of the American public school teacher 1961–1991*. Washington, DC: Author.

Passel, J. (2005). Estimates of the size and characteristics of the undocumented population. Pew Hispanic Center, March 21, 2005. Retrieved July 20, 2007 from http://www.Pew Hispanic Center. org.

Pastor, R. (1983). Migration in the Caribbean Basin: The need for an approach as dynamic as the phenomenon. In M.M. Kritz (Ed.), *U.S. immigration and refugee policy: Global and domestic issues*. Washington, DC: Georgetown University Press.

Renshon, S.A. (2005). *The 50% American: Immigration and national identity in an age of terror*. Washington, DC: Georgetown University Press.

Republican National Hispanic Assembly (2007). *Immigration Reform Now*. A project of the Republican National Hispanic Assembly. Retrieved May 4, 2007 from http://www .immigrationreformnow.org/Bills.htm.

Salins, P. D. (1997). *Assimilation American style: An impassioned defense of immigration and assimilation as the foundation of American greatness and the American dream*. New York: Basic Books.

Sassen, S. (1996). *Losing control: Sovereignty in an age of globalization*. New York: Columbia University Press.

Takaki, R. (1989). *Strangers from a different shore*. Boston: Little Brown.

United Nations. (1997). *International migration and development: The concise report*. New York: Author.

United Nations. (1998). *International migration policies*. New York: United Nations, Department of Economic and Social Affairs Population Division.

United Nations. (1999). *Review and appraisal of the progress made in achieving the goals and Objectives of the Programme of Action of the International Conference on Population and Development*.

U.S. Census Bureau (2000, October). *Current population survey*.

U.S. Commission on Immigration Reform. (1997). Immigration Act of 1990. Washington, DC: General Accounting Office.

U.S. Department of Education (2001–2002). National Center for Educational Statistics. Common Core of Data. "State Nonfiscal Survey Public Elementary/Secondary Education."

U.S. Department of Homeland Security (2004). Yearbook of immigration statistics, 2003. Washington, DC: U.S. Government Printing Office. Retrieved November 17, 2007 from: http:// xlibraryassets/statistics/yearbook/ 2003/2003imm.pdf.

U.S. Department of Justice. (1994). *Statistical yearbook of the Immigration and Naturalization Service*. Washington, DC: Author.

U.S. Office of Homeland security.

Walley, J. Z. (2007). Arab terrorists crossing border: Middle Eastern illegals find easy entrance into U.S. from Mexico. Retrieved July 2007, from http://worldnetdaily.com.

The White House (2007). Retrieved August 31, 2007 from http://www.whitehouse.gov/infocus/immigration.

Yasin, S. (1999). The supply and demand of elementary school teachers in the United States. Washington, DC: ERIC Clearinghouse on Teaching and Teacher Education (ERIC Document Reproduction Services No. ED436529).

2

The Current State of Education for Diverse Students in the United States

The increasing diversity among school-aged children in the United States raises several important questions. First, how is the education establishment responding to the diversity? What is the current progress of diverse students in our public schools? Second, how can multicultural education help us to address the needs of culturally diverse students and their peers and teachers? What have we learned from research in multicultural education about approaches to curriculum reform and effective pedagogy for diverse students? Finally, how can teachers be prepared to ensure the success of the diverse population?

The Educational Progress of Diverse Learners

The progress of diverse students in our schools can be determined from assessment data provided by the National Assessment of Educational Progress (NAEP). The NAEP, which is conducted by the National Center for Education Statistics, regularly reports on the educational progress of students in grades 4, 8, and 12 in public and private schools. Both short-term data and long-term trends are included in the report. Data include average scale scores and achievement levels. Basic, proficient, and advanced levels of students' achievement have been developed by the National Assessment Governing Board in consultation with experts in the respective academic areas. Although eight academic areas are assessed—mathematics, science, reading, writing, U.S. history, geography, civics, and the arts—we will consider only four areas: reading, writing, mathematics, and science. The summaries and interpretations have been provided by the NAEP.

Reading

Average scores for White, Black, Hispanic, and Asian/Pacific Islander students increased between 1992 and 2005. Black and Hispanic students each scored higher in 2005 than in 2003. In 2005 at both grades 4 and 8, White and Asian/Pacific Islander students scored higher, on average, than Black, Hispanic, and American Indian/Alaska Native students. Hispanic and American Indian/Alaska Native students scored higher, on average, than Black students (NAEP, 2007). Scores available in reading are shown in Table 2.1.

At grade 12, scores for both White and Black students declined since 1992. The percentages of students performing at or above Proficient have decreased for White students, but showed no significant change for other racial/ethnic groups (NAEP, 2005).

Writing

At grades 4 and 8, Black and Hispanic students had higher average writing scores in 2002 than in 1998. In 2002, Asian/Pacific Islander students and White students outperformed Black and Hispanic students at all three grade levels (Table 2.2). The most recent assessment was administered from January to March 2007. Results are not yet available.

TABLE 2.1   *Average Performance in Reading (Scale Scores)*

Year	2000	2002	2003	2005
Grade 4				
White	225	229	229	229
Black	190	199	198	200
Hispanic	190	201	202	203
Asian/Pacific Islander	224	224	226	229
Grade 8				
White	270	272	272	271
Black	243	245	244	243
Hispanic	244	247	245	246
Asian/Pacific Islander	264	267	270	271
Grade 12				
White	Not	297	292	293
Black	available	269	267	267
Hispanic		275	273	272
Asian/Pacific Islander		287	286	287

Source: National Assessment of Educational Progress, National Center for Education Statistics, 2007.

TABLE 2.2 *Average Performance in Writing (Scale Scores)*

Year	1998	2002	2005
Grade 4			
White	156	161	
Black	130	140	
Hispanic	134	141	
Asian/Pacific Islander	159	167	
Grade 8			
White	154	157	
Black	130	131	
Hispanic	134	131	
Asian/Pacific Islander	156	154	
Grade 12			
White	155	154	
Black	134	130	
Hispanic	136	136	
Asian/Pacific Islander	150	151	

Source: National Assessment of Educational Progress: The Nation's Report Card, and National Center for Education Statistics, Washington, D.C., U.S. Department of Education 2007.

Mathematics

In 2005 at both grades 4 and 8, Asian/Pacific Islander students scored higher than White, Black, Hispanic, and American Indian/Alaska Native students. Hispanic and American Indian/Alaska Native students scored higher, on average, than Black students. White, Black, and Hispanic students at both grades 4 and 8 had higher average scores and percentages of students scoring at or above Basic in 2005 than in 1990 (NAEP, 2007) (Table 2.3).

Science

At grade 4, White, Black, Hispanic, and Asian/Pacific Islander students had higher average science scores and higher percentages of students at or above Basic than in previous assessment years (NAEP, 2007). The White–Black gap was smaller than in previous assessment, and the White–Hispanic gap was smaller than in 2000 (NAEP, 2007). See Table 2.4.

At grade 8, Black students had higher average science scores and higher percentages of students at or above Basic in 2005 than in 1996. The score gaps between White students and their Black and Hispanic peers remain unchanged from previous assessment.

At grade 12, average science scores for each of the racial/ethnic groups have not increased significantly over the period of the assessments. Significant gaps persist

TABLE 2.3   *Average Performance in Mathematics (Scale Scores)*

Year	2003	2005
Grade 4		
White	243	246
Black	216	220
Hispanic	222	226
Asian/Pacific Islander	246	251
Grade 8		
White	288	289
Black	252	255
Hispanic	259	262
Asian/Pacific Islander	291	295
Grade 12		
White	153	156
Black	122	120
Hispanic	128	128
Asian/Pacific Islander	151	153

Source: National Assessment of Educational Progress, The Nation's Report Card, and National Center for Education Statistics, Washington, D.C., U.S. Department of Education.

TABLE 2.4   *Average Performance in Science (Scale Scores)*

Year	2005
Grade 4	
White	162
Black	129
Hispanic	133
Asian/Pacific Islander	158
Grade 8	
White	160
Black	124
Hispanic	129
Asian/Pacific Islander	158
Grade 12	
White	156
Black	120
Hispanic	128
Asian/Pacific Islander	153

Source: National Assessment of Educational Progress, The Nation's Report Card, and National Center for Education Statistics, Washington, D.C., U.S. Department of Education.

between White students and their Black and Hispanic peers. The White–Black student gap widened between 2000 and 2005. The White–Hispanic gap was not significantly different from either previous assessment (NAEP, 2007).

Achievement Levels Summary

Table 2.5 shows the NAEP scores required for the Basic, Proficient, and Advanced Levels for reading, writing, mathematics, and science. In reading, none of the diverse groups reached the Proficient level from 2000–2005 in grades 4, 8, or 12. White and Asian/Pacific Islander groups were closest to that level and received the highest scores among the groups at the three grade levels.

Based upon the scores in writing for 1998 and 2002, no group reached the score for the Proficiency level in grades 4, 8, or 12, although most groups scored higher in 2002 than in 1998.

In mathematics, White and Asian/Pacific Islander groups were closest to the level of proficiency in 2003, and Asian/Pacific Islander groups scored slightly above the cut-off score (251) for the Proficiency level in 2005 at grade 4. At grade 8, no group reached the Proficiency level in 2003 or 2005. However, White and Asian/Pacific Islander groups were again closest and had the highest scores. At grade 12, no group reached the Proficiency level in 2003 or 2005. Scores were very similar for all groups at this level on the two assessments.

TABLE 2.5   *NAEP Achievement Levels*

	Grade 4	*Grade 8*	*Grade 12*
Reading			
Basic	208	243	265
Proficient	238	281	302
Advanced	268	323	346
Writing			
Basic	115	114	122
Proficient	176	173	178
Advanced	225	224	230
Mathematics			
Basic	214	262	141
Proficient	249	299	176
Advanced	282	333	216
Science			
Basic	138	143	146
Proficient	170	170	178
Advanced	205	208	210

Source: National Assessment of Educational Progress, Department of Educational Statistics, Washington, D.C., U.S. Department of Education.

In science, scores for only 2005 are shown. No group score reached the Proficiency level at grades 4, 8, or 12. White students scored highest at grade 8, Asian/Pacific Islander students scored next highest, followed by Hispanic and Black. Scores for all groups showed little change at grade 12.

Conditions in high poverty schools such as inequality of the teaching staff in comparison with low poverty schools, tracking practices, and deteriorating school buildings all contribute to the discouraging levels of academic achievement among diverse students.

High-Poverty Schools

In 2006, for the very first time, every state was required to submit a plan to the Secretary of Education that would ensure that low-income and minority students in their state were not taught disproportionately by inexperienced, out-of-field, or uncertified teachers (Peske & Haycock, 2006). Despite the intent of the law, inequality in the teachers assigned to high-minority and high poverty schools versus low-minority and low-income schools persists (Peske & Haycock, 2006). In an interesting and valuable study conducted by The Education Trust in 2006, the three largest school systems in Ohio, Illinois, and Wisconsin were included. Large differences were found between teachers in the highest poverty and highest minority schools versus those in low-minority and low-poverty schools (Peske & Haycock, 2006).

Among their findings were the following: Nearly half of the math classes in the high-poverty and high-minority secondary schools were taught by teachers without even a minor in the subject. In grades 5 through 8 about 70 percent of the teachers in math classes were without even a minor in math or a math-related field (Peske & Haycock, 2006). Recently, nine major civil rights organizations called on Congress to make reforming U.S. high schools and improving graduation rates for minority students the most urgent priority as it moves on renewing the No Child Left Behind Act (Maxwell, 2007).

With respect to certification, Justice, Greiner, and Anderson (2003) found that those teachers in Texas with "emergency teaching certification" who have followed an alternate route to preparation were less confident, less likely to find satisfaction in their work, and less likely to continue teaching than those who had completed a full program. They concluded that a correlation was found between teacher preparation, teacher satisfaction, and continuation in teaching. In view of the high turnover in some urban, high-minority, high-poverty schools, the type of preparation can contribute to the problem.

Finally, the physical plant or buildings in high poverty schools are likely to be in disrepair.

The Facilities Gap

Schools that are unhealthy can contribute to the increase of asthma among students ("Facilities Gap," 2007). "Nearly 1 in 13 school-age children has asthma, and the percentage is rising more rapidly among preschool children than other age groups" ("Facilities Gap," 2007, p. 43).

Asthma is the leading cause of absence among students ages 5 to 17; the death rate from asthma for children in the 5 to 14 age group doubled from 1980 to 1998 with African American children and young adults four to six times more likely than White children and young adults to die from asthma ("Facilities Gap," 2007).

In an earlier study, the General Accounting Office (GAO) in 1995 found that "schools in need of repairs were concentrated in central cities and tended to have very high percentages of students from low-income families." (GAO, 1996). Despite improvement projects and considerable funds expended for repairs, problems continue to exist—especially in urban areas. According to the AFT study, the money has not been distributed and spent equitably. Middle and high school students in Washington, DC, and Baltimore, MD, took photos to document the poor conditions in their schools. Such problems as broken water fountains, holes in the walls, missing tiles in the floor, and broken windows were photographed.

Tracking

The arguments for tracking have become more subtle than in the past. Proponents now express their arguments more sensitively. They repeat the fact that it's easier to teach a relatively homogeneous class and unrealistic to assume that every student can master the same curriculum (Education Week, 2007). In addition, they insist that students feel more comfortable and learn better when they are grouped with peers of the same ability levels. Tracking also enables teachers to develop their instruction to address the specific needs of their students (Education Week, 2007).

In an encouraging report by (Grayson, 2005), a group of seven high schools that serve high concentrations of either low-income or minority children were able to accelerate learning for students who entered high school below grade level. In contrast to those schools that assign students below grade level to a lower track curriculum and classes, these schools demonstrated that improvement can occur at the secondary level. Among the practices at the "high-impact" schools were early warning systems. Students were "caught" before they failed. Counselors for the high school analyzed test scores for seventh- and eighth-grade students before they entered the high school. Students identified were assigned to a variety of supports: mandatory summer school and afterschool tutoring, for example. Students were assigned to teachers based upon the teacher's area of study. Extra instructional time in English and math are provided in order to keep students "on track" (Grayson, 2005). One of the high schools was able to raise state test results from 20 percent who met state standards in reading and 4 percent in math to 60 percent in reading and 31 percent in math four years later (Grayson, 2005).

Hallinan (2004) has described a detracking movement that has replaced the old tracking system. Referring to it as the modern form of tracking, she points to a system in which students in each subject are assigned to advanced, regular, or basic courses depending on their past performance. While Hallinan (2004) notes that educators broadly support the practice of tracking in its modern form, and parents of high-performing students also favor tracking, students recognize the tracks for what they are—a separation of students according to ability levels. The students in basic courses are described by their peers as not as smart as others. In addition, students sometimes refer to a peer with comments such as, "He's a 'basic' in math."

In other curricular tracking systems, levels may be labeled academic, general, and vocational (National Science Foundation Report, 2003). The report also noted that grouping students according to ability level is more prevalent in mathematics than science and more prevalent in grades 9 to 12 than in lower grades. In both math and science, according to the report, classes with a high proportion of minority students are more likely to be labeled "low-ability" classes than those with a low proportion of minority students (National Science Foundation Report, 2003). The labels or divisions do not appear to remove the stigma for those students who are performing below average.

High School Completion

The rate of high school completion based upon enrollment in postsecondary institutions is also an indicator of diverse students' educational progress. Accordingly, high school completion rates between 1967 and 1995 increased for Black as well as Hispanic and Asian/Pacific Islander students (U.S. Department of Education, 1999). The following figures show the percentage of those 18 to 24 years of age who completed high school in 2000, the most recent figures available: White, 91.8 percent; Black, 83.7 percent; Hispanic, 64.1 percent; and Asian, 94.6 percent.

No Child Left Behind (NCLB)

In 2001 President George Bush signed into law No Child Left Behind (NCLB). The intent of the NCLB was accountability for the education of all children by the public school system throughout the country. The principles on which the law is based would appear to benefit children from diverse cultures who have been academically lagging behind their peers. In fact, the principles on which the law is based are impossible to criticize: high standards, greater accountability, and a focus on long-overlooked student populations (Stover, 2007).

While many school districts that were previously unsuccessful have enjoyed historic increases in test scores, the law has received much criticism around the country (Stover, 2007). It is due for reauthorization in 2007. A debate by Congress is anticipated as well as by major education organizations. The calls for reform of NCLB have been widely made by the states and "every major education association, civil rights group, state education department, and policy think tank" (Stover, 2007, p. 2).

Problems with the law have been widely identified as overreliance on testing; heavy-handed approach to sanctions; problems related to provisions on teacher quality, school choice, tutoring, the testing of children with special needs, rules concerning adequate yearly progress (AYP), and inadequate funding for implementation of the law by the school districts (Keller, 2007). In addition, "two of the Law's most controversial components include school choice and inclusion of faith-based organizations for services" (Stover, 2007, p. 4).

One of the most important components of the law addresses teacher quality. Leaders in every state must deliver to the Secretary of Education their plans for ensuring that low-income and minority students in their state are not taught disproportionately by inexperienced, out-of-field or uncertified teachers (Peske & Haycock, 2006).

Multicultural Education

The lagging educational achievement of diverse students in the United States has been a major concern of researchers in multicultural education. As noted by Banks (1997), "Multicultural education incorporates the idea that all students regardless of their gender and social class and their ethnic, racial, or cultural characteristics, should have an equal opportunity to learn in school . . . It is a total school reform effort designed to increase educational equity for a range of cultural, ethnic, and economic groups" (pp. 3, 7).

In fact, the dimensions of multicultural education encompass content integration, the knowledge construction process, prejudice reduction, an equity pedagogy, an empowering school culture, and a view of the school as a social system (Banks, 2006). Thus, researchers in the field seek to address important issues involved in curriculum reform, teacher education and pedagogy, and changes in the schools as a system. For proponents, the ultimate purpose is a more just and equitable society (Banks, 2006). See Table 2.6.

For example, Nieto (1996), has defined multicultural education in a sociopolitical context. In her words,

> Multicultural education is a process of comprehensive school reform and basic education for all students. It challenges and rejects racism and other forms of discrimination in schools and society and accepts and affirms the pluralism (ethnic, racial, linguistic, religious, economic, and gender, among others) that students, their communities, and teachers represent. Multicultural education permeates the curriculum and instructional strategies used in schools, as well as the interactions among teachers, students, and parents and the very way that schools conceptualize teaching and learning (p. 307).

The underachievement of diverse students has been attributed, in part, to a traditional school curriculum that has failed to meet the needs of too many students from culturally and linguistically diverse groups. Historically, the traditional curriculum has neglected the participation and contributions of minorities to the history of the United States. U.S. history and social studies, in particular, have been criticized; however, the exclusion of minority groups has occurred, until recently, in all content areas, thereby contributing to the incongruity between the worlds of home–community and school for many students (Phelan, Davidson, & Cao Yu, 1996).

The multiple worlds of students' home, school, and community and the extent to which these worlds are congruent can facilitate the transition among them and students' engagement in school learning (Phelan, Davidson, & Cao Yu, 1996) (see Figure 2.1). A curriculum that integrates the worlds of diverse students becomes relevant to their lives and enables them to engage successfully in the world of the school. As Delpit

TABLE 2.6   *Dimensions and Examples of Multicultural Education*

Category	Definition	Examples
Content Integration	Content integration deals with the extent to which teachers use examples and content from a variety of cultures and groups to illustrate key concepts, principles, generalizations, and theories in their subject area or discipline.	• Biographies of women or persons of color who are scientists and mathematicians • Learning about demographics of diverse groups in mathematics • Using primary documents about the history of non-Anglo-European peoples • Reading and creating multicultural literature • Including images of many kinds of families in the curriculum
The Knowledge Construction Process	The knowledge construction process relates to the extent to which teachers help students to understand, investigate, and determine how the implicit cultural assumptions, frames of references, perspectives, and biases within a discipline influence the ways in which knowledge is constructed within it.	• Examining the degree to which authors who are female or people of color are included in the curriculum • Including the perspectives of both the dominant and non-dominant cultures in any description of historical conflict • Examining labels applied to persons with disabilities from the perspective of the person • Validating the importance of languages other than English • Discussing the difference between Western and nonwestern views on science • Interviewing community elders about their immigration experiences
An Equity Pedagogy	An equity pedagogy exists when teachers modify their teaching in ways that will facilitate the academic achievement of students from diverse racial, cultural and social-class groups. This includes using a variety of teaching styles that are consistent with the wide range of learning styles within various cultural and ethnic groups.	• Knowing the cultural background of students and incorporating them into classroom instruction and procedures • Using cooperative learning or group experiences with students who learn best collaboratively • Placing students in pairs to encourage question and answer exchanges

(continued)

TABLE 2.6   *Continued*

Category	Definition	Examples
Prejudice Reduction	This dimension focuses on the characteristics of students' racial attitudes and how they can be modified by teaching methods and materials.	• Using heterogeneous groups by gender, race and language in cooperative learning groups • Developing racial identity (e.g., through a family tree) • Teaching the concept of race as a social, not biological, construct • Studying various religions in the context of a winter holiday season or historical event
An Empowering School Culture and Social Structure	Grouping and labeling practices, sports participation, disproportionality in achievement, and the interaction of the staff and the students across ethnic and racial lines are among the components of the school culture that must be examined to create a school culture that empowers students from diverse racial, ethnic, and cultural groups.	• Including students in determining classroom rules or allowing them choice of assignment • Including students with disabilities or all students who try out for a performance • Actively recruiting and hiring teachers of color • Reducing the numbers of African Americans and Hispanics who are inappropriately placed in special education programs • Working with community groups to provide mentoring and tutoring programs • Involving families in school decision making bodies

Source: Banks (2006); van Garderen & Whittaker (2006).

(1995) has pointed out, "When a significant difference exists between the student's culture and the school's culture, teachers can easily misread students' aptitudes, intent, or abilities as a result of differences in styles of language use and interactional patterns" (p. 167).

Related to the issue of inappropriate curriculum as a barrier to learning for diverse students is the question of preferred learning styles. Nieto (2000) defines learning style as "the way in which individuals receive and process information" (p. 142). Teachers of students from different cultures may use instructional approaches that confuse both teacher and students concerning the students' ability to comprehend and learn. However, despite intuitive appeal for many educators, little support has been found for matching learning styles according to one's culture, and past attempts to match a culture with a particular learning style have been strongly criticized (Irvine & York, 1995; McDermott & Glutting, 1997). As Irvine and York (1995) in their review of the literature on learning styles and culturally diverse students have indicated, "The assumption that diverse students can learn only if they use their preferred style also ignores what developmental psychologists call the malleability and plasticity of children" (p. 493). In other words, children can master various learning styles with the appropriate instructional and psychological support. Furthermore, differences in the content to be learned often require different approaches to learning.

   Rather than assume that a particular cultural group learns best in a particular way, it is helpful to all students when the teacher employs various approaches that require

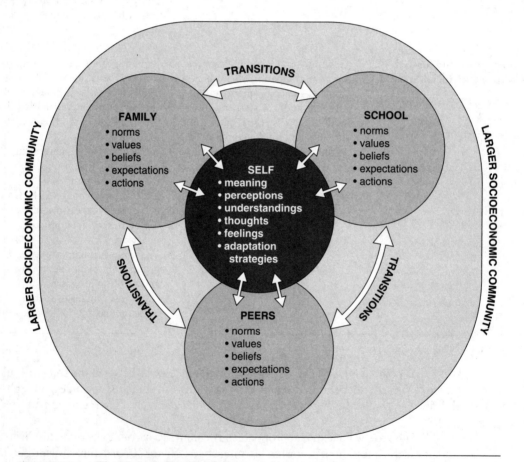

FIGURE 2.1   *The Multiple Worlds Model*
Reprinted by permission of the publisher from Phelan and Davidson, *Renegotiating Cultural Diversity in American Schools*, (New York: Teachers College Press, © 1993 by Teachers College, Columbia University. All rights reserved.), p. 56.

different learning styles and observes how individual students respond. Although there is limited support for matching learning styles with cultures as a basis for planning instruction (the approach does consider the cultural background of students), different students may certainly have different approaches to learning that the teacher must recognize.

Closely related to issues involving learning style is the concept of multiple intelligences. Howard Gardner's (1993) work on multiple intelligences has important implications for learning and teaching diverse students. Gardner has helped educators to understand the narrow focus of most assessments of intelligence and the fact that we shortchange students when we address only verbal–linguistic or logical–mathematical intelligence. He had originally identified seven types of intelligence: linguistic, logical–mathematical, spatial, musical, body-kinesthetic, interpersonal, and intrapersonal. He later added environmental intelligence which has been linked to survival. According to Gardner, "the purpose of school should be to develop intelligences and to help people reach vocational and avocational goals that are appropriate to their particular spectrum of intelligences" (p. 9). These intelligences are related to particular styles of learning, and teachers need to recognize the multiple ways in which students learn in planning and implementing instruction. Traditionally, schools have focused on linguistic and logical–mathematical learning to the exclusion of all others. Gardner's work has broadened our understanding of intelligence and the need for more comprehensive assessment of students' abilities, interests, and approaches to learning.

Alternative Viewpoints

Educational anthropologists have made extensive contributions to the research literature in multicultural education through their studies on the influence of culture on educational progress and the underachievement of diverse students in the schools. In a very enlightening discussion, Erickson (1996) notes that "as educational anthropology became a distinct field in the mid-60s, its members were generally appalled by the ethnocentrism of the cultural deficit explanation" (p. 27).

Sociolinguistically oriented anthropologists identified cultural differences in communication style between teachers and students as the explanation for underachievement, while others pointed to the inequity in access to employment over many generations as the basic explanation (Erickson, 1996). Erickson (1996) labels these two major positions of anthropologists as the "communication process explanation" and the "perceived labor market explanation" (p. 28).

Thus, the culturally learned patterns of verbal and nonverbal communication can explain, for some, the high rates of school failure among some minority students. When the teacher and students have different styles of speaking and listening, miscommunication in the classroom can result (Au and Mason, 1981; Barnhardt, 1982; Erickson & Mohatt, 1982; Heath, 1983; Michaels & Collins, 1984; Phillips, 1983).

John Ogbu (1995), the main proponent of the labor market explanation described by Erickson (1996), has pointed out that it is important to recognize that all culturally diverse students do not underachieve in school. In fact, he notes the difference in achievement between domestic minority students and immigrant minorities, labeling the former "castelike" minorities. Castelike minorities are involuntary immigrant groups characterized by secondary cultural differences developed largely in opposition to the dominant culture. In addition, the phenomenon of cultural inversion exists, which involves the identification of certain forms of behavior, events, symbols, and meanings as inappropriate for the group because they are white American characteristics. Therefore, according to Ogbu, some minority students resist engagement in school learning activities because that means "acting White" (Ogbu, 1995). One example of Ogbu's theory is seen in the positive school engagement among refugees from Southeast Asia when compared with that of African Americans as "domestic or castelike minorities."

However, D'Amato (1996) strongly opposes Ogbu's position, arguing that "resistance to school is not a phenomenon restricted to minority children but occurs among all school children for whom we have close ethnographic accounts" (p. 186). He points out that resistance occurs even among some Japanese schoolchildren and even among "decidedly upper-middle-class Jewish American school children under certain conditions" (p. 186). D'Amato concludes with other examples to show that "the castelike minority position is unable to explain why the children of castelike minorities do not always reject their teachers" (p. 186). D'Amato also rejects the cultural differences or communication process explanation, pointing out that certain immigrant children excel in school despite incongruities between the school and home cultures.

Noting that both Ogbu's position and the communications process explanation have received empirical support as well as "theoretical force," Erickson (1996) finds a synthesis of the two positions held by educational anthropologists as the most acceptable. He concludes, "As an educator I cannot accept the premise that there is nothing we can do to improve the educational situation of domestic minority students in the United States. The task is not only to analyze the structural conditions by which inequity is reproduced in society but to search out every possible site in which the struggle for progressive transformation can take place" (p. 45).

In fact, Erickson argues for "culturally responsive pedagogy" as part of the total solution. This pedagogy will "reduce miscommunication by teachers and students, foster trust, and prevent the genesis of conflict that moves quickly beyond intercultural misunderstanding to bitter struggles of negative identity exchange between some students and their teachers" (p. 48). Teachers' increased attention to communication in the classroom is obviously needed.

Approaches to Curriculum Reform

Geneva Gay (1995) has commented that multicultural education "teaches content about culturally pluralistic contributions to humankind and U.S. society; engages students actively and interactively with their own cultural identity and the cultural identity of others; and develops the kind of social consciousness, civic responsibility, and political activism needed to reconstruct society for greater pluralistic equality, truth, inclusion and justice" (p. 27).

In fact, the importance of integrating the content described by Gay into the curriculum has been stressed by Banks (1997). Banks (1995) has identified four approaches used to integrate ethnic content into the elementary and secondary curriculum: teaching about the contributions of diverse groups, adding content about diverse groups to the curriculum, transforming the curriculum, and social action. Heroes, heroines, holidays, foods, and discrete cultural elements are the focus of the contributions approach. In the additive approach, content, concepts, lessons, and units are added to the curriculum, leaving its basic structure unchanged. At the next level, the transformation approach, the structure of the curriculum is actually changed, enabling students to "view concepts, issues, events, and themes from diverse ethnic/cultural perspectives" (Banks, 1995, p. 13). The action approach provides opportunities for students to make decisions on personal, social, and civic problems and take action to find solutions. Some would insist that only the action approach is acceptable, while others view the four approaches as a continuum through which teachers often move. Ladson-Billings (1994) expresses the essence of the action approach in her discussion of culturally relevant teaching.

> Culturally relevant teaching is about questioning (and preparing students to question) the structural inequality, the racism, and the injustice that exist in society. The teachers I studied work in opposition to the system that employs them. They are critical of the way that the school system treats employees, students, parents, and activists in the community. However, they cannot let their critique reside solely in words. They must turn it into action by challenging the system. What they do is both their lives and their livelihoods. In their classrooms, they practice a subversive pedagogy. Even in the face of the most mundane curricular decisions these teachers make a stand (p. 128).

Sleeter and Grant (1994) have also identified approaches to multicultural education. These include (1) teaching the exceptional and culturally different, (2) the human relations approach, (3) single-group studies, (4) multicultural education, and (5) education that is multicultural and social reconstructionist. In view of the limitations inherent in each approach, Sleeter and Grant (1994) favor the multicultural and social reconstructionist approach, which incorporates the strengths of all the other approaches. In their view, it "goes the furthest toward providing better schooling as well as creating a better society" (p. 243). We have summarized the approaches in Table 2.7.

The aim of curriculum reform has been to teach students to understand different racial, ethnic, and religious groups, which will ultimately improve relationships among all participants in the U.S. society, and to help students to build an ethnoracial identity (Heath, 1995). In her discussion of curriculum theory and multicultural education, Gay has explained that multicultural education has encompassed

> descriptive analyses of educational systems and conditions that ignore or deny the importance of cultural diversity; critical explanations are used to determine why those systems should be changed to be more representative of and responsive to cultural pluralism; and prescriptive recommendations suggest what the changes should embody in order for education to be maximally beneficial to an ever-increasing variety of culturally, ethnically, and socially pluralistic individuals, institutions and communities (Gay, 1995, p. 27).

Curriculum reform has been especially focused on social studies and history. Before the 1960s, American history was white America's history, and students learned nothing of the participation of other groups in the building of this country (Heath,

TABLE 2.7   *Approaches to Multicultural Education*

1. ***Teaching the exceptional and culturally different:*** The aim of those who favor this approach is assimilation of young people into the mainstream. The mainstream society is viewed as basically good and just by proponents of this approach. Sleeter and Grant point out that two orientations to difference exist within this group: a deficiency orientation and a difference orientation toward the exceptional and culturally different. Sleeter and Grant criticize this approach for its assimilationist orientation and the fact that it ignores structural and institutional racism as factors in the lack of progress for many families of color and poor families.
2. ***The human relations approach:*** The emphasis in this approach is on promotion of positive feelings among students and reduction of stereotyping, thereby promoting unity and tolerance in the diverse U.S. population. This approach focuses mainly on affective skills for students, for example, feeling good about themselves and the group to which they belong, and accepting and getting along with those who are different from themselves.
3. ***Single-group studies:*** The focus in this approach is on a single group. Examples include African Americans, Native Americans, Asian Americans, women, and children with disabilities. The goal of this approach is to empower the single group and promote their social equality and recognition.
4. ***Multicultural education:*** Sleeter and Grant describe this approach as promoting social structural equality and cultural pluralism. Within the school, the goals are equal opportunity, cultural pluralism and alternative lifestyles, respect for those who differ, and support for power equity among groups. This approach is broader than the first three. Everyone is included in its goals since the aim is to reform schooling for all children.
5. ***Education that is multicultural and social reconstructionist:*** This is the most extensive approach. The goals include the promotion of social structural equality and cultural pluralism within the society. Within the schools the goals are to prepare students to work actively toward social structural equality and to promote cultural pluralism, alternative lifestyles, and equal opportunity. Sleeter and Grant favor this approach. They point out that the approach has much in common with the multicultural education approach, and it also borrows from the others. However, the approach adds the preparation of students to take social action—to "change the rules of the game." Thus, it offers greater hope for the future. As Sleeter and Grant have noted, "Our thinking is based largely on social conditions that persist and that limit and often damage or destroy the lives of many people" (p. 243).

This is a very brief outline of the approaches and we strongly advise readers to consult the text by Sleeter and Grant for in-depth discussion of their analyses.

Source: Sleeter & Grant (1994).

1995). However, the ethnic studies movement in the 1970s resulted in the publication of textbooks and instructional materials that recognized the contributions of other groups (Banks, 1995). Private religious and racial—ethnic schools have also contributed to the development of new curricula and instructional materials.

Content Integration

In other approaches, literature has been used to enrich social studies and address multicultural goals (Davis & Palmer, 1992; Savage & Savage, 1993). For example, children can vicariously experience others' lives and develop empathy for people of diverse cultures through carefully selected literature (Savage & Savage, 1993). A list of suggested children's and adolescent literature connected to the cases in this text is provided in Table 2.8.

Teachers can also create multicultural units using children's literature, thus helping students to learn about their multicultural world. Davis and Palmer (1992) have developed a model for supplementing textbook material in social studies with children's literature. Their model provides a series of steps that teachers can follow with a central focus on the concepts, facts, generalizations, values, and skills to be taught in social studies (Davis & Palmer, 1992).

Insisting that the best books for or about African American children must be both well written and sensitive to cultural and social realities, Sims Bishop (1997) provides

TABLE 2.8 *Children's and Young Adult Multicultural Literature Related to the Cases in Bridging Multiple Worlds*

Book and Author	Copyright Date	Publisher	Topic and Grade Level
I Love Islam	2005	Islamic Services Foundation	Introduces Islam to young Muslims in the elementary grades.
Learning Islam	2007	Islamic Services Foundation	Series provides an Islamic studies course for grades 6, 7 and 8.
Living Islam	Pending	Islamic Services Foundation	Explores the practical application of Islam into everyday life, for the high school grades.
The Children Stories Series by Uthman Hutchinson	Recent	Amana Publications	Centers on an American Muslim family living in a small American city, and their friends and relatives from America, Afghanistan, Pakistan, and Malaysia.
			Collection of 36 short stories grouped by grade level, one through six.
Si Se Puede! Yes We Can!: Janitor Strike in L.A. by Diana Cohn	2005	Cinco Puntos Press	Through the eyes of one female worker's son, this bilingual story chronicles the 2000 Justice for Janitors Campaign. Grades 2–6
Friends from the Other Side by Gloria Anzaldúa	1997	Children's Book Press	Bilingual story presents the variety of responses to Mexican "illegals" by Chicanos already living in Texas. Grades K–3

Book and Author	Copyright Date	Publisher	Topic and Grade Level
Journey to Ellis Island by Carol Bierman	2005	Hyperion	Depicts a Russian family's immigration challenges of an ocean voyage and arrival at Ellis Island in 1922. Grades 4–8
The Red Comb by Fernando Picó	1998	Troll Communications	An original story set in Puerto Rico about a young girl and her older neighbor who help a runaway slave. Grades 2–4
A Place at the Table edited by Maria Fleming	2001	Oxford University Press	Profiles lesser-known Americans who have fought for human rights — including the disabled, gays and lesbians, Asian and Mexican Americans. Grades 7 up
Who Belongs Here? An American Story by Margy Burns Knight	1996	Tilbury House Publishers	Introduces the question, "Who is an American?" through the story of a Cambodian boy who encounters racism at school. Grades 2–5
Am I Blue? Coming Out from the Silence edited by Marion Dane Bauer	1994	Harper Trophy	Collection of short stories about growing up gay or lesbian, or with gay or lesbian family or friends. Grades 6–8
The Tequila Worm by Viola Canales	2004	Wendy Lamb	Series of stories that show how a Latin girl maintains her cultural integrity while connecting with the culture where she lives. Grades 6–8
Lights for Gita by Rachna Gilmore	2003	Tilbury House	Newly arrived in the U.S. Gita is homesick for India. Grades K–5
The Curious Incident of the Dog in the Nighttime by Mark Hadon	2004	Vintage	Autistic Christopher tells the story of how he solved the mystery of a dead dog. Grades 6–8
Amazing Grace by Mary Hoffman	1991	Dial	Grace is told she cannot play Peter Pan in the school play because she is a girl and African American. Grades K–3

(continued)

TABLE 2.8 *Continued*

Book and Author	Copyright Date	Publisher	Topic and Grade Level
What Are You? Voices of Mixed-race Young People by Pearl Fuyo Gaskins	1999	Henry Holt	Multiracial Grades 5 and up
The Kingfisher Book of Religions by Trevor Barnes	2001	Diane	Religion Grades 3 and up
Joey Pigza Loses Control by Jack Gantos	2000	Farrar, Straus and Giroux	Attention Deficit Hyperactivity Disorder Grades 5–8
From the Notebooks of Melanin Sun by Jackqueline Woodson			Homosexuality Grades 6 and up
Remix: Conversations with Immigrant Teenagers by Marina Tamar Budhos	1999	Henry Holt	Recent immigrants Grades 9 and up
Esperanza Rising by Pam Muñoz Ryan	2000	Scholastic	Migrant workers Grades 5–8
My Heroes, My People by Ruth Katcher	1999	Farrar, Straus & Giroux	African Americans and Native Americans in the West Grades 2 and up
Arab American Encyclopedia by Anan Ameri and Dawn Ramey (Eds.)	2000	Gale Group	Arab Americans Grades 5 and up
Fly Away Home by Eve Bunting	1991	Clarion Books	Grades K–3

useful guidelines for the selection of books. Noting that selection can be complicated, she points out that the sociopolitical premises of multicultural education make it important for us to reject some books. Those in which verbal or visual stereotyping exist or authenticity and authority, perspective, and world view or underlying ideology are unacceptable should be challenged and rejected.

Sims's earlier (1982) categories of books written for and about African American children include realistic fiction with a social conscience, melting pot fiction, and culturally conscious fiction. Realistic fiction attempts to "create a social conscience, mainly in non-African American readers, to encourage them to develop empathy, sympathy and tolerance for African American children and their problems" (p. 17). Melting pot books communicate that all people are the same, ignoring all differences except physical characteristics (Sims, 1982, 1997). According to Sims, without illustrations, one would never know that one of these books was about an African American child. This type of book is positive, however, in that images are usually positive and the grim social problems facing many minority children are omitted. In contrast, culturally conscious fiction comes closest to "constituting a body of literature about African American children and their lives" (p. 49).

In her later work, Sims Bishop (1997) refers to three areas of concerns about the selection of multicultural books: literary, sociopolitical, and educational. The literary includes the need for excellent visual artistry and the quality of the writing. Another concern is what the political message or viewpoint of the work is expressing. Is the book authentically based on cultural mores? Does the author have the authority to write the book? Her educational concern centers on what the book can contribute to the child's education.

Sims Bishop's categories or types of books can provide teachers with a guide for selecting books for their students according to the intended audience and intent of the author. Since teachers need to provide literature for and about diverse children, the definitions can aid the teacher in the selection process.

Oral history can also be utilized to modify the social studies curriculum. Olmedo (1993) presents steps for using oral history with bilingual and English as a second language (ESL) students who may lack the knowledge base or cultural background necessary to engage in social studies instruction. This approach "helps students understand that history is filled with stories" (Olmedo, 1993, p. 7). Steps begin with the identification of concepts, followed by preparation of an interview guide. The guide is then translated by students into their own native languages. Next, students practice by interviewing each other, even role playing various adult members of families. A guest speaker from the community is then interviewed by the class, providing a practice opportunity for the class to tape the speaker and transcribe or summarize the taped interview. Students then identify persons to be interviewed and conduct interviews individually or in small groups. Review, transcriptions, or summaries are then individually completed, followed by students' comparing and contrasting their experiences.

Other models of curriculum reform or content integration include programs such as Robert Moses' Algebra Project. The underlying premise of the project developers is that "all children can learn algebra" and "virtually all middle school students can learn algebra given the proper context" (Silva & Moses, 1990, p. 375). However, the project is especially concerned with the needs of inner-city minority students. The Algebra Project tries to change the way mathematics teachers construct their learning environment by producing teachers who are able to facilitate a math learning environment grounded in real-life experiences and to support students in the social construction of mathematics. Additional goals of the project include the development of

> mathematically literate, self-competent, and motivated middle school learners who are able to master the college preparatory high school mathematics and science curriculum and the mathematics necessary for mathematics- and science-related careers; and to build a broader community of individuals including parents, community volunteers, and school administrators who understand the problem of mathematics education as a problem of mathematics literacy and who understand the question of students' capability as learners as a matter of effective effort (Silva & Moses, 1990, p. 379).

Success for All (Slavin & Madden, 2000) also focuses on mathematics, in addition to reading, and is currently used in many large, metropolitan school districts around the country. Aspects of this program are designed to allow increased movement, call and response strategies, and positive reinforcement in order to appeal to diverse minority groups, particularly African Americans. Observations by one of the authors in a classroom where the program had been implemented confirmed that African American students were enthusiastically engaged in learning. However, the program has been highly criticized in recent publications (Pogrow, 2000).

Publishers are also producing increasing quantities of new materials to address the needs of students to learn about and appreciate diverse groups in the society (see Table 2.8). Increasingly, curriculum materials are also available that address diversity in the school-aged population.

An important note of caution is provided by Delpit in her book *Other People's Children* (1995), in which she writes of the cultural differences that must be understood in selecting instructional approaches and materials for teaching diverse students. She comments that "Appropriate education for poor children and children of color can only be devised in consultation with adults who share their culture. Black parents, teachers of color, and members of poor communities must be allowed to participate fully in the discussion of what kind of instruction is in their children's best interest" (p. 45). Delpit continues,

> [s]tudents must also be taught the codes needed to participate fully in the mainstream of American life, not by being forced to attend to hollow, inane, decontextualized sub-skills, but rather within the context of meaningful communicative endeavors; . . . even while students are assisted in learning the culture of power, they must also be helped to learn about the arbitrariness of those codes and about the power relationships they represent (p. 45).

However, the impetus for curriculum reform has come not only from social scientists and educators who seek a more equitable education for all students and an accurate portrayal of U.S. history that represents all groups in the society, but also from national, state, and local initiatives to raise academic standards and achievement for all students. The requirement to align the curriculum with the new state standards creates additional pressure on teachers, and the tendency to "teach to the tests" may well be counterproductive in teachers' efforts to improve the curriculum for diverse students. Nevertheless, time to plan, discuss, observe, and share ideas with colleagues, money to support the change process, support from colleagues and administrators, and information about assessment strategies and whole-class instructional strategies have been indicated by teachers as important needs in the curriculum change process (Teberg, 1999).

While support from colleagues and administrators is certainly required, a positive relationship between parents and educators is also critical (Konzal, 1997). In fact, to make major changes in curriculum, it is best to enlist the support of all stakeholders, and this includes the community served by the school. For example, an Iowa school district introducing a new middle school mathematics curriculum addressed the anticipated misgivings of parents early and made parents allies in the process (Meyer,

Delagardelle, & Middleton, 1996). In another study of curriculum reform, Anderson (1996) found that the technical, political, and cultural dimensions of curricular reform efforts required even broader consideration: a sufficient provision of time for teachers, changed values and beliefs about the school's goals of instruction and the means of fostering them, collaborative teacher learning, parent learning, new student roles and work, and a systemic view of reform by the entire school staff.

Culturally Responsive and Relevant Teaching

Culturally responsive teaching, also referred to as culturally relevant teaching, has been defined by researchers in multicultural education in a variety of ways. The definition of Ladson-Billings (1994), provided earlier, focuses on questioning, critical thinking, and challenging the system. In his discussion of "situated teaching," Shor's (1992) definition reflects the same elements as that of Ladson-Billings. He notes that the teacher begins with what students bring to class—their knowledge, themes, cultures, conditions, and idioms. According to Shor, situated teaching "avoids teacher-centered syllabi and locates itself in the students' cultures" (p. 44). Describing a problem-posing pedagogy as empowering for students, the subject matter and learning process are adapted for the students so that they can develop critical thinking. Since all education is political, in Shor's view, "critical thought is married to everyday life by examining daily themes, social issues, and academic lore" (p. 44). In Shor's view, this pedagogy will "increase the chance that students will feel ownership in their education and reduces the conditions that produce their alienation" (p. 51).

Shor contributes further to our understanding of critical thinking through his definitions. For example, he notes, "To think critically in this framework means to examine the deep meanings, personal implications, and social consequences of any knowledge, theme, technique, text, or material" (p. 169).

Geneva Gay (2000) describes culturally responsive teaching as "using the cultural knowledge, prior experiences, frames of reference, and performance styles of ethnically diverse students to make learning encounters more relevant to and effective for them" (p. 29). An expanded list of characteristics reflects the teacher's recognition of the students' multiple worlds and the need to bridge these worlds to make the transitions easier for students (see Table 2.9).

Paulo Freire (1998) has also contributed to our understanding of culturally relevant or responsive teaching. In his discussion of "respect for what students know," Freire asks,

> "Why not take advantage of the students' experience of life in those parts of the city neglected by authorities to discuss the problem of pollution in the rivers and the question of poverty and the risks to health from the rubbish heaps in such areas? . . . Why not discuss with the students the concrete reality of their lives and that aggressive reality in which violence is permanent and where people are much more familiar with death than life?" (Friere, 1998, p. 6).

However, the essence of culturally relevant teaching is found in the following question: "Why not establish an intimate connection between knowledge considered

TABLE 2.9 *Characteristics of Culturally Responsive Teaching*

1. Curriculum content and teaching strategies are "filtered through students' cultural frames of refer ence to make the content more personally meaningful and easier to master" (p. 24).
2. Culturally responsive teaching "acknowledges the legitimacy of the cultural heritages of different ethnic groups as worthy content to be taught in the formal curriculum" (p. 29). Students' cultural her itages influence their attitudes, dispositions, and approaches to learning.
3. Culturally responsive teaching "builds bridges of meaningfulness between home and school experiences as well as between academic abstractions and lived socio-cultural realities" (p. 29).
4. Culturally responsive teaching uses a wide variety of teaching strategies that address different learning styles.
5. Culturally responsive teaching helps students to know and affirm their cultures.
6. Multicultural information, resources, and materials are incorporated throughout the curriculum.

Source: From Gay (2000).

basic to any school curriculum and knowledge that is the fruit of the lived experience of these students as individuals?" (Friere, 1998, p. 36).

The work of Ladson-Billings (1994) and others in multicultural education has shown that what Ladson-Billings refers to as "culturally relevant teaching" can facilitate the engagement of diverse learners in classroom learning activities. In a school described by Ladson-Billings, one fourth-grade class studied how cities develop, took trips into the community to learn about branches of city government, and worked on solutions to specific problems in their city. They also wrote letters to the editor of a city newspaper about conditions in their neighborhood. Students participated in a community service program, and parents participated in 20 hours of volunteer service to the school. This school also demonstrated some of the elements of culturally relevant schools defined by Ladson-Billings: providing educational self-determination, honoring and respecting the students' culture, helping African American students understand the world as it is, and equipping them to change it for the better (Ladson-Billings, 1994, pp. 137–139).

Another approach to culturally relevant teaching is available in the use of Mathematics Trails, a collection of activities that demonstrates how the study of math can be extended beyond the classroom and can involve teachers and students in investigative, problem-based experiences in the real world (Ampadu & Rosenthal, 1999; E. Hofstetter, personal communication, December 2000; Lancaster & Delisi, 1997). In this approach the teacher begins with a decision on the sites to be used, which may be found in the students' community or broader environment. Problems can be identified within the students' communities. Thus, students are involved not only in relating math to their real world, but also in tackling meaningful problems in their communities. Another rich example of relating the students' community to classroom instruction has been described by Moll, Velez-Ibanez, and Greenberg (1989). The teacher incorporated information about construction in the community (the barrio) in his reading instruction (see Table 2.10).

TABLE 2.10   *An Example of Culturally Relevant Teaching*

A sixth-grade teacher conducted the following reading activity, incorporating the construction project in progress in a local barrio.

1. Students read library books on constructing houses and other types of buildings.
2. The teacher invited members of the community to speak to the class about building (several were parents of students in the class). A mason talked about how to mix mortar, measure straight lines, and stack bricks neatly. A carpenter talked about sawing and nailing and compared the strength of brick to wood.
3. Students then applied what they had learned to building a model in the classroom.
4. They wrote about the learning experience. In their writing they used new vocabulary they had learned, described the skills used in building, and expressed appreciation for their parents' knowledge.

Source: Adapted from Moll et al. (1989).

In her study on Amy, "a white, middle class teacher who consistently demonstrated culturally sensitive strategies," Powell (1997) described aspects of culturally relevant teaching as "acquiring cultural sensitivity, reshaping the classroom curriculum, and inviting students to learn" (p. 471).

> [Amy] sought ways to acquire a sensitivity for students' lives outside of school and for how their lives influenced her classroom curriculum. Specifically, she continuously explored students' cultural backgrounds and families, linked students' backgrounds to school culture, and assumed various leadership roles at school that were related to racial minority students. Although Amy viewed her classroom as an extension of students' cultural and family backgrounds when she began teaching, this kind of sensitivity became a preoccupation for her, and ultimately became a prevailing theme in her decision making about her classroom curriculum and instruction (p. 473).

Classroom Discourse Patterns

Culturally relevant teaching may require modification of the classroom discourse patterns and participation structure as discussed earlier. Classroom discourse patterns can help or hinder a student's ability to respond to questions and participate in discussions. The teacher's manner of speaking to students and asking questions also contributes to students' successful communication and participation (Mehan, Lintz, Okamoto, & Wills, 1995). Many teachers, perhaps a majority in the United States, use what has been referred to as a "recitation script" (Tharp & Gallimore, 1988). This script involves the initiation of a communication by the teacher, the student's response, and the teacher's evaluation, or an Initiation Response Evaluation (IRE) sequence. Most often, the sequence is directed to an individual student whose response is publicly evaluated. However, studies have shown that this pattern may not be appropriate for some diverse students and may represent discontinuity between the language patterns of the home and those of the school (Mehan et al., 1995). While patterns in Anglo families may be compatible with the recitation script, those in minority group families may not. The discontinuity in patterns could lead to lower achievement and higher dropout rates among minority students (Mehan et al., 1995).

For example, in a study reported by Phillips (1983), Native American children gave more effective performances in classrooms that minimized the public performances of individual students. In this study, the Native American teacher, who focused on groups to maintain classroom control, gave praise in public and criticism in private, and allocated turns so that students did not have to participate as individuals, demonstrated an effective classroom (Erickson & Mohatt, 1982).

Earlier studies reported in the 1980s include that of Puerto Rican students who also demonstrated more positive responses to group-oriented, turn-allocation strategies in which students volunteered their answers (McCullum, 1989). McCullum suggested that the instructional, "conversation-like" approach was more congruent with the conversational patterns in daily Puerto Rican life. Heath (1983) reported that white, middle-income teachers talked to low-income black elementary school students in the typical IRE pattern in contrast to the patterns used in the homes of these students. Parents at home did not ask known-information types of questions; rather, their questions requested nonspecific comparisons or analogies as answers (Mehan et al., 1995). In fact, while the IRE pattern as used in the homes of white students appears to prepare them for the classroom discourse pattern, it is not congruent with patterns used in the homes of low-income black children (Heath, 1983).

Modification of classroom discourse patterns to make the patterns congruent with those of the home has been found to improve academic performance (Mehan et al., 1995). This includes rhythmic language, call and response, repetition, and deliberate body motions (Foster, 1989).

Traditional teaching not only uses the IRE script, but also frequently represents what Freire (1985) refers to as "banking education." This is the view of teaching and learning in which students represent vessels or depositories to be filled by teachers. The teacher is the expert or authority who knows everything, and the student knows nothing. This practice is contrary to the process of knowledge construction, one of the important dimensions of multicultural education (Banks, 1997). In the words of Freire (1998), "to teach is not to transfer knowledge but to create the possibilities for the production or construction of knowledge" (p. 30).

Teacher Preparation

The increasing diversity in our society has been convincing for most school districts throughout the country. Many schools have recognized and accepted the realities of a diverse student population and are struggling to learn how to accommodate the new cultures and languages, while meeting the mandates of national laws such as No Child Left Behind and the annual testing used by the state to ensure accountability.

Thus, the teacher education programs which prepare teachers to educate a diverse population of students must provide effective multicultural education and verify that pre-service teachers acquire the skills necessary to help all children achieve to a high level.

Most programs have developed one of two models to help teachers manage the cultural differences that exist between them and their students. The program tries to (1) recruit more teachers from culturally diverse backgrounds; or (2) develop the multicultural knowledge base and attitudes of predominantly White students. In some cases the attitudes reflect fear of unknown or unfamiliar races, ethnicities, cultures, languages, and religions and teacher education programs try to identify experiences and activities within course requirements that can alleviate the students' fears.

Many programs have found that it is most difficult to prepare teachers who will succeed in urban schools. Preservice teachers often fear the unfamiliar culture of the urban school as well as the discipline challenges. Interestingly, some researchers have suggested that the best type of student to recruit is an older student (30 to 50 years of age) of color, from an urban area, who has raised children, held other jobs, and learned to live in a somewhat violent environment (Haberman, 1996, cited in Sleeter, 2001).

Contradictory experiences have been had by white students (of the author) who participated in a partnership between a university's teacher education program and public schools of one of the largest urban school districts in the U.S. Students began their experience with a semester's placement in diverse classrooms with experienced teachers. This was followed by student teaching in that school in different classrooms. Many students have become eager to remain in the schools and have decided to apply for positions in the urban schools after student teaching. They commented that they had learned so much and had experienced many of the rich resources of a large, urban environment which could enrich their teaching.

Since the teaching force in the U.S. remains predominantly White, we will continue to need effective programs to prepare many White students with the knowledge, skills and attitudes needed to educate the country's population of diverse children. Many White students who enter teacher education programs have grown up in an entirely White, segregated world without meaningful contact or intercultural experiences with other groups. In many cases their knowledge base of other cultures is based upon myths and stereotypes which must be countered with real knowledge, understanding and appreciation of the rich diversity in this country.

In some programs students have lived in culturally different communities; in others, course assignments have included attendance or participation at community events, meetings with parents in their communities, and interviews of community leaders in diverse communities. For those White students who are fearful of differentness, these assignments can help them to be more comfortable and to learn how much alike we all are. They can also learn to appreciate the rich cultural differences that children bring to the classroom. That knowledge can contribute to the development of a culturally responsive and relevant curriculum.

The evaluation of different approaches to preparing teachers for a diverse population of students has not yet received the rigorous testing required. Our multicultural education courses which some programs require, the field experiences now included in many programs, partnerships with urban schools, and other efforts in teacher preparation programs await adequate evaluation to determine their effectiveness.

In support of more effective teacher education, Cochran-Smith (1995) has identified five perspectives on race, culture, and language diversity that are essential to preparing teachers "who see themselves as both educators and activists," who work with others to do what (she) calls "teaching against the grain of institutions of schooling that are dysfunctional and inequitable . . . (1) reconsidering personal knowledge and experience; (2) locating teaching within the culture of the school and the community; (3) analyzing children's learning opportunities; (4) understanding children's understanding; and (5) constructing reconstructionist pedagogy" (p. 500). It is the reconsideration of personal knowledge and experience that can be so easily neglected in efforts to prepare teachers for diverse students. Opportunities to examine one's assumptions, stereotypes, and expectations of children from different languages, cultures, races, classes, and gender can help preservice and in-service teachers to begin to question their beliefs concerning the abilities, motivation, and behaviors of children from diverse backgrounds. Cochran-Smith suggests the use of personal narrative essays for that purpose.

Cochran-Smith also argues against the traditional lesson plan as the basis for instructional planning and proposes the inquiry method as a way for teachers to construct meaningful effective pedagogy for their students. She notes that the typical lesson plan "implies that both planning and teaching are linear activities that proceed from a preplanned opening move to a known and predetermined endpoint, suggesting that knowledge, curriculum and instruction are static and unchanging" (p. 496). On the other hand, an inquiry approach creates opportunities for prospective teachers to develop perspectives on teaching, learning, and schooling that are central to what she labels as "an activist's stance" (p. 495). Furthermore, according to Cochran-Smith, experienced teachers plan in ways that are "more recursive, cyclical, more learner-centered, and structured around larger chunks of content than those of a single lesson" (p. 495). Ultimately, she argues for generative ways for student teachers and teacher educators to "reconsider their assumptions, understand the values and practices of families and cultures different from their own, and construct pedagogy that not only takes these into account in locally appropriate ways but also makes issues of diversity an explicit part of the curriculum" (p. 493).

Another answer to the problems in teacher education is advanced by Darling-Hammond (1995), who stresses the need for the "professionalization of teaching" (p. 478). She points out that "the professionalization of an occupation raises the floor below which no entrants will be admitted to practice; and it eliminates the practices of substandard or irregular licensure that allows untrained entrants to practice disproportionately on underserved and poorly protected clients." She adds, it "increases the overall knowledge base for the occupation, thus improving the quality of services for all clients, especially those most in need of high-quality teaching" (p. 478).

Ladson-Billings (1995) has identified key elements from multicultural teacher education research in both mainstream and nonmainstream settings. The "wisdom of practice, the use of autobiography, restructured field experiences, and situated pedagogies" are included in these elements. Her notion of "culturally specific pedagogy" is described as "teachers' attempts to make the school and home cultures of diverse students more congruent" (p. 754).

In a recent practical discussion of the principles for teaching and learning in a multicultural society, Banks et al. (2001) reflect the goals of multicultural education and the work of researchers in this field. The twelve principles that they present include, among others, professional development programs to "help teachers understand the complex characteristics of ethnic groups within U.S. society and the ways in which race, ethnicity, language and social class interact to influence student behavior" (p. 198) and "the use of multiple, culturally sensitive techniques to assess complex cognitive and social skills" (p. 202). Several principles highlight equitable opportunities for students to learn and achieve high standards and curriculum that "helps students to understand that knowledge is socially constructed and reflects researchers' personal experiences as well as the social, political, and economic contexts in which they live and work" (p. 198). Other principles are concerned with the important areas of intergroup relations, students' knowledge of stereotyping and related biases, students' knowledge of values shared by all cultural groups, school governance, and equitable funding for all schools.

Challenges

Researchers in multicultural education continue to offer promising approaches for the challenges involved in educating an increasingly diverse school-aged population. However, critics have challenged the field in several areas. For example, Garcia (1995) argues that the educational research has been directed primarily at the problems encountered by diverse students—discrimination, desegregation, underachievement, low self-esteem, and limited English proficiency—and has lacked "substantive theoretical underpinnings" (p. 381). Furthermore, in his view, the widely used case study approach has resulted in the identification of generalized cultural characteristics that ignore the within-group diversity that exists in all cultural groups (Garcia, 1995). Therefore, from his point of view, much of the research that has identified some groups as field dependent versus field independent or cooperative versus competitive, for example, is problematic at best and bordering on creating stereotypes at worst. He raises two critical questions: What set of knowledge about diverse cultural groups is educationally important? And what overarching conceptualization of culture is useful in understanding the educational framework of culturally diverse groups? (p. 381).

Ogbu (1995), too, has challenged the field, insisting that multicultural education will not significantly affect the school-learning problems of minority students who traditionally underachieve due to the fact that the field is not based on a "good understanding of the nature of the cultural diversity or cultural differences of minority groups" (p. 582). Ogbu describes the emergence of multicultural education as, initially, a response to cultural deprivation theory and points out that many proponents of multicultural education have not studied minority cultures in minority communities. Furthermore, in his view, school success depends not only on what teachers do, but also on what students do. Some students are able to cross cultural and language boundaries and others are not. As discussed earlier in the chapter, it is those who are unable to cross boundaries with whom he is most concerned, those in groups he has classified as involuntary minorities. Ogbu suggests that teachers and interventionists should learn about the students' cultural backgrounds and use that knowledge to organize classrooms and programs. "We can learn about students' cultures through observation of classroom and playground behavior, interviews of students about cultural practices and preferences, doing research on various ethnic groups with children in school, and the study of published works on children's ethnic groups" (Ogbu, 1995, p. 589).

Critics on both the left (McCarthy, 1990; Ogbu, 1995; Olneck, 1995) and right (Renshon, 2005); (Ravitch, 1990a, b; Schlesinger, 1992; Sowell, 1993) have challenged multiculturalism as a philosophy and approach to education. Yet the responsibility of the education system in the United States to serve an increasingly diverse population of school-aged children, the unacceptable educational progress at this time, and the continuing need to create a more just and equitable U.S. society underscore the power of the philosophy, goals, objectives, and pedagogy developed by researchers in multicultural education. Ladson-Billings (1995) insists that scholars in the field must engage in debate to challenge those who have misinterpreted, misperceived, or distorted the definition, goals, and research in multicultural education. Furthermore, she notes that "multicultural teacher education may well be the determiner of the fate of multicultural education" (p. 756).

References

Ampadu, C., & Rosenthal, M. (1999). Making mathematics real: The Boston math trail. *Mathematics Teaching in the Middle School, 5*(3), 140–147.

Anderson, R. (1996). *Study of curriculum reform. Volume I: Findings and conclusions*. Boulder: Colorado University.

Au, K., & Mason, J. (1981). Social organizational factors in learning to read: The balance of rights hypothesis. *Reading Research Quarterly, 17*(1), 115–152.

Banks, J. A. (Ed.) (1996). *Multicultural education, transformative knowledge, and action: Historical and contemporary perspectives*. NY: Teachers College Press.

Banks, J. (1997). *Multicultural education: Issues and Perspectives* (3rd ed.). Boston: Allyn and Bacon.

Banks, J. A. (1995). Multicultural education: Historical development, dimensions, and practice. In J. Banks & C. A. McGee Banks (Eds.), *Handbook of research on multicultural education* (pp. 1–7). New York: Macmillan.

Banks, J., Cookson, P., Gay, G., Hawley, W., Irvine, J., Nieto, S., Schofield, J. W., & Stephan, W. (2001). Diversity within unity: Essential principles for teaching and learning in a multicultural society. *Phi Delta Kappan, 83*(3), 196–201.

Barnhardt, C. (1982). "Tuning in" Athabaskan teachers and Athabaskan students. *Cross-cultural issues in Alaskan education, Vol. 2*. Fairbanks: University of Alaska, Center for Cross-cultural studies.

Cochran-Smith, M. (1995). Color blindness and basket making are not the answers: Confronting the dilemmas of race, culture and language diversity in teacher education. *American Educational Research Journal, 32*(3), 493–522.

D'Amato, J. (1996). Resistance and compliance in minority classrooms. In E. Jacob & C. Jordan (Eds.), *Minority education: Anthropological perspectives* (pp. 181–208). Norwood, NJ: Ablex Publishing.

Darling-Hammond, L. (1995). Inequality and access to knowledge. In J. Banks & C. A. McGee Banks (Eds.), *Handbook of research on multicultural education* (pp. 465–483). New York: Macmillan.

Davis, J., & Palmer, J. (1992). A strategy for using children's literature to extend the social studies curriculum. *The Social Studies, 83*(3), 125–128.

Delpit, L. (1995). *Other people's children: Cultural conflict in the classroom*. New York: The New Press. Education Record, May 2000. *Challenging the status quo: The Education Record 1993–2000*. Washington, DC: U.S. Department of Education.

Education Week (2007). Tracking. Retrieved June, 2007 from http://www2.edweek.org/rc/issues/tracking.

Erickson, F. (1996). Transformation and school success: The politics and culture of educational achievement. In E. Jacob & C. Jordan (Eds.), *Minority education: Anthropological perspectives* (pp. 27–52). Norwood, NJ: Ablex Publishing.

Erickson, F., & Mohatt, G. (1982). Cultural organization of participation structures in two classrooms of Indian students. In G. D. Spindler (Ed.), *Doing the ethnography of schooling: Educational anthropology in action* (pp. 132–175). New York: Holt, Rinehart & Winston.

The facilities gap. (2007). *American Educator 31*(3), 43–51.

Foster, M. (1989). "It's cookin now": A performance analysis of the speech events in an urban community college. *Language in Society, 18*, 1–29.

Freire, P. (1985). *The politics of education: Culture, power, and liberation*. South Hadley, MA: Bergin & Garvey.

Freire, P. (1998). *Pedagogy of freedom: Ethics, democracy and civic courage*. Lanham, MD: Rowman & Littlefield.

GAO (1996). "School facilities, America's schools report differing conditions." Washington, D.C: U.S. General Accounting Office.

Garcia, E. (1995). Educating Mexican American students: Past treatment and recent developments in theory, research, policy, and practice. In J. Banks & C. A. McGee Banks (Eds.), *Handbook of research on multicultural education* (pp. 372–387). New York: Macmillan.

Gardner, H. (1993). *Multiple intelligences: The theory in practice*. New York: Basic Books.

Gay, G. (1995). Curriculum theory and multicultural education. In J. A. Banks & C. A. McGee Banks (Eds.), *Handbook of research on multicultural education* (pp. 25–43). New York: Macmillan.

Gay, G. (2000). *Culturally responsive teaching: Theory, research and practice*. New York: Teachers College Press.

Grayson, N. (2005). Getting the job done: How some high schools are boosting student achievement. Washington, D.C: The Education Trust. Retrieved July 19, 2007 from http://www2.edtrustorg/EdTrust/Press+Room/High+School2005.htm

Hallinan, M. (2004). The detracking movement. *Education Next*, *4*(4), Retrieved January 24, 2008, from http:www.hoover.org/publications/ednext/3260116.html.

Heath, S. B. (1983). *Ways with words: Language, life and work in communities and classrooms*. New York: Cambridge University Press.

Irvine, J. J., & York, D. E. (1995). Learning styles and culturally diverse students: A literature review. In J. A. Banks & C. A. McGee Banks (Eds.), *Handbook of research on multicultural education*. New York: Macmillan.

Justice, M., Greiner, C., & Anderson, S. (2003, Winter). Determining the influences of traditional Texas teachers vs. teachers in emergency teaching certification program. *Education*, *124*(2), 376–389.

Keller, B. (2007). *NCLB rules on quality fall short*. Retrieved July 11, 2007, from http://www.edweek.org/ew/articles.

Konzal, J. (1997). *Teachers and parents working together for curriculum reform: Possibility or pipe dream?* Paper presented at the annual meeting of the American Education Research Association, Chicago, March 24–28.

Ladson-Billings, G. (1994). *The dreamkeepers*. San Francisco: Jossey-Bass.

Ladson-Billings, G. (1995). Multicultural teacher education: Research, practice and policy. In J. A. Banks & C. A. McGee Banks (Eds.), *Handbook of research on multicultural education* (pp. 747–762). New York: Macmillan.

Lancaster, R., & Delisi, V. (1997). A mathematics trail at Exeter Academy. *Mathematics Teacher*, *90*(3), 234–237.

Maxwell, L. A. (2007). *Civil rights groups press for NCLB to focus on high schools*. Retrieved July 14, 2007, from Education Week @ epe.org.

McCarthy, C. (1990). Race and education in the United States: The multicultural solution. *Interchange*, *21*(3), 45–55.

McCullum, P. (1989). Turn-allocation in lessons with North American and Puerto Rican students. *Anthropology and Education Quarterly*, *20*, 133–156.

McDermott, P., & Glutting, J. (1997). Informing stylistic learning behavior, disposition and achievement through ability subtests—or more illusions of meaning? *School Psychology Review*, *26*(2), 163–175.

Mehan, H., Lintz, A., Okamoto, D., & Wills, J. (1995). Ethnographic studies of multicultural education in classrooms and schools. In J. A. Banks & C. A. McGee Banks (Eds.), *Handbook of research on multicultural education* (pp. 129–144). New York: Macmillan.

Meyer, M., Delagardelle, M. L., & Middleton, J. A. (1996). Addressing parents' concerns over curriculum reform. *Educational Leadership*. *53*(7), 54–57.

Michaels, S., & Collins, J. (1984). Oral discourse styles: Classroom interaction and the acquisition of literacy. In D. Tannen (Ed.), *Coherence in spoken and written discourse*. Norwood, NJ: Ablex.

Moll, L. C., Velez-Ihanez, C., & Greenberg, J. (1989). *Fieldwork summary: Community knowledge and classroom practice: Combining resources for literacy instruction*. Tucson: University of Arizona.

National Assessment of Educational Progress. The Nation's Report Card (2005) and (2007). Reading, Writing, Math and Science scores. National Center for Educational Statistics, Institute of Education Sciences, U.S. Department of Education.

Nieto, S. (2000). *Affirming diversity: The sociopolitical context of multicultural education* (3rd ed.). New York: Longman.

Ogbu, J. (1995). Understanding cultural diversity and learning. In J. A. Banks & C. A. McGee Banks (Eds.), *Handbook of research on multicultural education* (pp. 582–596). New York: Macmillan.

Olmedo, I. (1993). Junior historians: Doing oral history with ESL and bilingual students. *TESOL Journal, Summer*, 7–10.

Olneck, M. (1995). Immigrants and education. In J. A. Banks & C. A. McGee Banks (Eds.), *Handbook of research on multicultural education* (pp. 310–330). New York: Macmillan.

Peske, G., & Haycock, K. (2006). *Teaching inequality: How poor and minority students are shortchanged on teacher quality.* Washington, DC: The Education Trust.

Phelan, P., Davidson, A. L., & Cao Yu, H. (1996). *Students' multiple worlds: Navigating the borders of family, peer, and school cultures: Renegotiating cultural diversity in American schools.* New York: Teachers College Press.

Phillips, S. (1983). *The invisible culture: Communication in classroom and community on the Warm Springs Indian Reservation.* New York: Longman.

Pogrow, S. (2000). Success for all does not produce success for students. *Phi Delta Kappan, 82*(1), 67–80.

Powell, R. (1997). Then the beauty emerges: A longitudinal case study of culturally relevant teaching. *Teaching and Teacher Education, 13*(5), 467–484.

Ravitch, D. (1990a). Diversity and democracy: Multicultural education in America. *American Educator, 14*(1), 16–20, 46–48.

Ravitch, D. (1990b). Multiculturalism: E pluribus plures. *American Scholar, 59*(3), 337–354.

Savage, M., & Savage, T. (1993). Children's literature in middle school social studies. *The Social Studies, 84*(1), 32–36.

Schlessinger, A. M., Jr. (1992). *The disuniting of America.* New York: Norton.

Shor, I. (1992). *Empowering education: Critical teaching for social change.* Chicago: University of Chicago Press.

Silva, C., & Moses, R. (1990). The Algebra Project: Making middle school mathematics count. *Journal of Negro Education, 59*(3), 375–391.

Sims Bishop, R. (1997). Selecting literature for a multicultural curriculum. In V. J. Harris & C. A. Grant (Eds.), *Using multicultural literature in the K–8 classroom* (pp. 1–19). Norwood, MA: Christopher-Gordon.

Sims, R. (1982). *Shadow and substance: Afro-American experience in contemporary children's fiction.* Urbana, IL: National Council of Teachers of English.

Slavin, R. E., & Madden, N. A. (2000). Research on achievement outcomes of Success for All: A summary and response to critics. *Phi Delta Kappan, 82*(1), 38–40, 59–66.

Sleeter, C., & Grant, C. (1994). *Making choices for multicultural education: Five approaches to race, class, and gender.* Upper Saddle River, NJ: Merrill/Prentice Hall.

Sowell, T. (1993). *Inside American education.* New York: The Free Press.

Stover, D. (2007). The big fixes now needed for "No Child Left Behind." *Education Digest, 72*(7), 4–11.

Teberg, A. S. (1999). *Identified professional development needs of teachers in curriculum reform.* Paper presented at the Annual meeting of the American Educational Research Association, Montreal, Quebec, April 19–23.

Tharp, R. G., & Gallimore, R. (1988). *Rousing minds to life: Teaching, learning and schooling in social context.* New York: Cambridge University Press.

U.S. Department of Education. (1999). *The condition of education report.* Washington, DC: Government Printing Office.

van Garderen, D., & Whittaker, C. R. (2006). Planning differentiated, multicultural instruction for secondary inclusive classrooms. *Teaching Exceptional Children, 38*(3), 12–21.

3

Building Partnerships with Diverse Families and Communities

The way schools care about children is reflected in the way schools care about the children's families. If educators view children simply as students, they are likely to see the family as separate from the school. That is, the family is expected to do its job and leave the education of children to the schools. If educators view students as children, they are likely to see both the family and the community as partners with the school in children's education and development. Partners recognize their shared interests in and responsibilities for children, and they work together to create better programs and opportunities for students.

(Epstein, 1995, p. 701)

Proponents of multicultural education agree that family and community participation in the schools is of critical importance (Comer, 2005; Heath, 1995; Ladson-Billings, 1994). Epstein (1995) believes that "with frequent interactions between schools, families, and communities more students are more likely to receive common messages from various people about the importance of school, of working hard, of thinking creatively, of helping one another, and of staying in school" (p. 702).

School–family–community partnerships can improve school programs and climate, create a familylike school, provide support and family services, increase parent and family skills and leadership, serve as school–community liaisons, and help teachers (Sheldon & Epstein, 2005). Within the families and community, educators can also find support for school reform, curriculum reform, assistance in learning about the cultures of students, relevant content for instruction, volunteers as mentors for students, and support for immigrant families and students. Six types of parent involvement have been described by Epstein as parenting, communicating, volunteering, learning at home, decision making, and collaborating with the community (Epstein & Salinas, 2004). The list has been developed as a guide for schools since each type of practice listed has certain limitations or problems to be resolved (see Box 3.1).

BOX 3.1 • *Epstein's Framework of Six Types of Parental Involvement*

1. Parenting: Help all families establish home environments to support children as students.
2. Communicating: Design effective forms of school-to-home and home-to-school communications about school programs and children's progress.
3. Volunteering: Recruit and organize parent help and support.
4. Learning at Home: Provide information and ideas to families about how to help students at home with homework and other curriculum-related activities, decisions, and planning.
5. Decision making: Include parents in school decisions, developing parent leaders and representatives.
6. Collaborating with community: Identify and integrate resources and services from the community to strengthen school programs, family practices, and student learning and development.

Source: Epstein, J. L., & Salinas, K. C. (2004). Partnering with families and communities. *Educational Leadership, 1*(8), 12–18.

Family Involvement in the Schools

The Goals 2000 Educate America Act (U.S. Department of Education, 1994) also encourages building partnerships with families and communities in an effort toward providing quality education for every child. Family involvement can benefit not only the child, but also the school, the family, and the community as well. As stated by Jeffie Frazier, "Community support also does wonders for the learning environment. Our school has extremely beneficial relationships with several community groups. There's a church right on the corner. The church adopted us many years ago. When we want to have a bake sale, they donate all of the ingredients, and all we have to do is bake and sell them. They also send people over to buy, and they advertise for us" (Comer, Ben-Avie, Haynes, & Joyner, 1999, p. 59).

Student Achievement

Furthermore, the positive impact of parental involvement on student achievement and attitudes toward school has been well established (Griffiths, 1996; Jeynes, 2005; Patrikakou, 2004; Riley, 1999).

In fact, according to Funkhouser & Gonzalez (1997), "When children's families are involved in school, the children earn higher grades, attend school more regularly, complete more homework, demonstrate more positive attitudes and behaviors, graduate from high school at higher rates, and are more likely to enroll in higher education than students with less involved families" (n. p.).

This is also a goal for Title 1 which is designed to enable schools to provide opportunities for low-income and low-achieving students. In fact, literacy achievement increased for low-income and low-achieving students grades 1 to 5 when parents' involvement in the school increased (Dearing, Kreider, Simpkins, & Weiss, 2006).

Although parent involvement declines dramatically as children progress in school (Zill & Nord, 1994, cited in Patrikakou, 2004), Patrikakou found that parent involvement had long-lasting effects on the academic achievement of adolescents and young adults. They continue to need support and encouragement and they benefit from the involvement of parents and family although the type of involvement will change as students become older (Patrikakou, 2004). Parental expectations also impacted achievement; the further in school parents believed their adolescents would go, the higher the adolescents' achievement (Patrikakou, 2004).

However, parent involvement has been problematic in many schools across the country, particularly in the case of low-income and culturally diverse families (Comer, Haynes, Joyner, & Ben-Avie, 1996; Ingram, Wolfe, & Lieberman, 2007). Yet, like all other families, most low-income and culturally diverse parents see education as a means to a better life for their children (McGee Banks, 1997). While teachers of children from low-income and culturally diverse families may often conclude that the parents are uninterested in participation in their children's education, researchers have found that diverse families can be deterred by the school's climate and personnel (Quiocho & Daoud, 2006).

Finders and Lewis (1994) found that parents' social, economic, linguistic, and cultural practices are often viewed as problems by the school rather than assets. In addition, communication, especially without an interpreter, is affected by the linguistic patterns of teachers and families when English cannot be mutually understood.

In a two-way bilingual school, where both English-speaking and Spanish-speaking parents were interviewed, Zelazo (1995) concluded that (1) parents' comfort with the staff was critical in their becoming involved; (2) language played a major role in the nature of involvement; and (3) parents' view of their role in relationship to the school, their own level of schooling, and their present economic situation were critical factors in their involvement. We should add, also, their immigration status.

Furthermore, in the past, schools have used strategies to encourage involvement that were based upon assumed deficits in diverse cultures and families. Families and children in poor and low-income households, parents of children with disabilities, and parents and familes of children with low achievement have been looked upon as lacking the knowledge and skills to rear them.

Alternative approaches to promoting the involvement of families focus on their empowerment so that they can become decision makers. Recognition of the family as a system, the family's strengths, the cultural beliefs and expectations, as well as the economic constraints, can help the school facilitate the family's involvement (Table 3.1).

Families and communities of diverse groups who may frequently encounter prejudice and hostility in the society especially need to be met by school personnel who value their strengths and knowledge of their children. In a study of groups of Puerto Rican, African American, Chinese American, and Irish American families, all had experienced prejudice and discrimination in the United States because of their race, culture, or language (Hildago, Bright, Siu, Swap, & Epstein, 1995).

Epstein's typologies of (1) parenting and (2) learning at home were most beneficial in a study involving low-income, at-risk students in Chicago, Illinois (Ingram, Wolf, & Lieberman, 2007). African American males showed improved average to above-average

TABLE 3.1   *Alternative Approaches for Parent–Family Involvement*

1. Consider meetings in community facilities rather than the school.
2. Have parents and families collaborate with the school in setting the agenda for a meeting.
3. Invite members of the extended family who have an important role in the lives of the children.
4. Arrange meetings at times convenient for both the family and school personnel.
5. Consider assisting with transportation, childcare, or other special challenges faced by the family.
6. Consider language differences and the possible need for a community liaison.
7. Facilitate the building of supportive networks for parents.
8. Become aware of families' strengths and the need for structures or opportunities for them to share their strengths with other families and school personnel.
9. Consider creative, nontraditional ways to bring parents into the life of the school.
10. Respect families' preferences for time and place of meetings.
11. Make opportunities for meaningful participation in the education of their children.
12. Know the community and its resources. Consider meetings at churches, neighborhood centers, and recreational facilities.
13. Consider occasional meetings conducted by parents–families.
14. Work to make families feel welcome, respected, and valued for their knowledge and experience.
15. Aim for collaboration with equal partners.

grade point averages as result of their perception of parent–adolescent interactions as positive (Shearin, 2002).

If schools want families to become more involved, they must make schools more family-friendly, more welcoming, and more respectful of the contributions parents can make to the education of their children. One of the helpful publications available from the federal government offices is the "Idea Book," which was designed to assist educators, parents, and policymakers to develop and nurture school–family partnerships (Funkhouser & Gonzalez, 1997). Guidelines for effective partnerships and strategies provided for overcoming barriers to partnerships are shown in Boxes 3.2, 3.3.

The Comer School Development Program (Comer et al., 1999) is one example of a widely used model for family involvement and school–community partnerships. A principal describes Comer's program as "encouraging the collaboration of the home,

BOX 3.2 • *Guidelines for Effective Partnerships*

- There is no "one size fits all" approach to partnerships.
- Training and staff development is an essential investment.
- Communication is the foundation of effective partnerships.

- Flexibility and diversity are key.
- Projects need to take advantage of the training, assistance, and funding offered by sources external to schools.

Source: Funkhouser, J. E., & Gonzalez, M. R. (1997). *Family involvement in children's education: Successful local approaches.* Washington, DC: Office of Educational Research and Improvement, U.S. Department of Education. Retrieved December 12, 2007, from http://www.ed.gov/pubs/FamInvolve/execsumm.html.

BOX 3.3 • *Strategies for Overcoming Common Barriers to Family Involvement in Schools*

- *Overcoming time and resource constraints:* Successful programs find the time and resources for both teachers and parents to develop school–family partnerships.
- *Providing information and training to parents and school staff:* Through workshops and a variety of outreach items such as informative newsletters, handbooks, and home visits, parents and school staff can learn how to trust each other
- *Restructuring schools to support family involvement:* Schools need to create a welcoming environment for parents, to make changes that make the school more personal and inviting
- *Bridging school–family differences:* Strategies are needed to address differences in language and culture:

- Reach out to parents with little formal education.
- Address language differences through bilingual services for communicating both orally and in writing.
- Promote cultural understanding to build trust between home and school.
- *Tapping external supports for partnerships:* Develop partnerships with local businesses, healthcare, and other community service agencies.
- *Allowing sufficient time for change:* A successful partnership requires involvement of many stakeholders.
- *Regularly assessing the effects of the partnership using multiple indicators.*

Source: Funkhouser, J. E., & Gonzales, M. R. (1997). *Family involvement in children's education: Successful local approaches.* Washington, DC: Office of Educational Research and Improvement, U.S. Department of Education. Retrieved December 12, 2007, from http://www.ed.gov/pubs/FamInvolve/execsumm.html.

the school, places of worship and the community to support the life of the school" (Comer et al., 1999, p. 53). The Comer School Development Program (SDP) involves parents and the community through a Parent Team and Comprehensive School Plan (see Figure 3.1 on page 54). The parent team provides meaningful input and support for the School Planning and Management Team, which develops the Comprehensive School Plan, among other responsibilities. The SDP approach is described as having "parents and families at the center of change," a link that is often missing in efforts toward school reform (p. 9). Most important are the guiding principles of the SDP, which are consensus, collaboration, and no-fault. These principles help to sustain the learning and caring community, a positive environment in which "all adults feel respected and all children feel valued and motivated to learn and achieve" (Comer et al., 1996, p. 9).

However, in many situations, school personnel and community members will need to learn how to collaborate. As noted by Weast, Jones, and Howley (1999),

> Everyone says that collaboration is a good idea, so why does SDP (School Development Program) invest so much time and effort training people in this guiding principle? The reason is that in our fragmented educational system, people don't actually know how

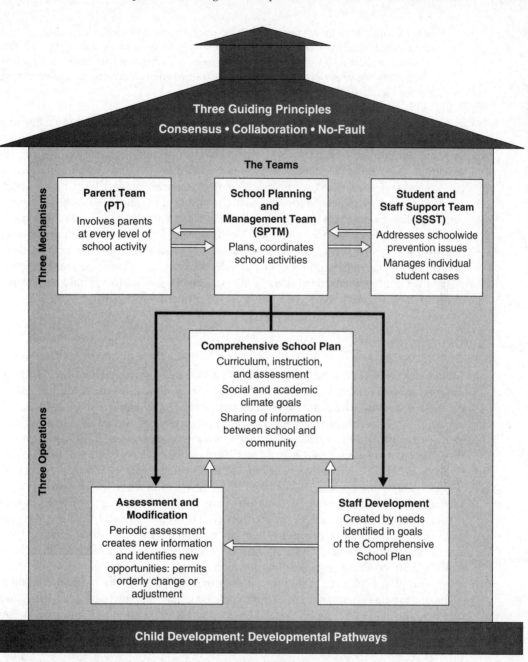

FIGURE 3.1 *The Comer School Development Program*
Source: Reprinted by permission of the publisher from Comer, J., Haynes, N., Joyner, E., Ben-Avie, M., *Rallying the Whole Village: The Comer Process for Reforming Education*, (New York: Teachers College Press, © 1996 by Teachers College, Columbia University. All rights reserved.), p. 48.

to work together as a team because they haven't had opportunities to learn through trial and error. Elementary, middle and high school principals rarely even talk with one another, let alone plan together for the long term. At each school district's central office, staff members are usually too busy to take the time to build a team and change their work routines (p. 256).

Yet, it is critical to build collaborative teams in order to bring about change in a school. School reform requires the collaboration of all stakeholders—families, schools, and communities. However, families need a variety of meaningful opportunities for participation in the life of the school and the educational activities of their children. Diverse parents and families may have different views of school involvement. The Comer model, for example, provides possibilities for participation at different levels of intensity and responsibility. Even so, many families will be unable to enter into the type of ideal partnership so desired by school personnel. There are simply too many constraints due to changing family structures and economic pressures. In addition, researchers have found that family participation in the school takes different forms at different age levels and gender of the children involved (Muller, 1998). Nevertheless, educators should make every effort to develop collaborative relationships with students' families.

The Family System

All families are best understood as systems in which each individual member affects all other members (Bowen, 2000–2004). Although changing family structures in the society make it difficult to assume a dominant family profile, all families share basic needs, values, and dreams. Some face greater challenges than others; some function more efficiently than others. Nevertheless, the view of families as systems helps us to understand the dynamics involved in students' problems in school (Bowen, 2000–2004; Gilbert, 2004). The system has been defined as "a whole made up of interacting parts" (Gilbert, 2004) and a social and/or biological construction made up of a set of people related by blood or intention. A change in one person's functioning is followed by reciprocal changes in the functioning of others (Bowen, 2000–2004). According to Whitechurch and Constantine (1993), modern systems theories about families have been derived from General Systems Theory, which is both a transdisciplinary field of study and a theoretical framework with which theorists attempt to explain the behavior of complex, organized systems such as families. However, the particular components of a family system are viewed differently by family therapists, psychologists, and others in the field of family services. We are using components and design based upon the work of Turnbull and Turnbull (1997).

As we enter the twenty-first century, there are many relationships that can be considered a family. Although a family might consist of mother, father, and children, single parents and children, other roles are also possible. These include single parents, stepparents, same-sex parents, and grandparents as primary caretakers. Three major components of the family system are its group and individual characteristics, its functions, and life cycle.

Family Characteristics

Size and form, cultural background, socioeconomic status, and geographic location are examples of family characteristics. Individual characteristics of each member of the family may include educational level, employment, language proficiency, abilities, talents, and disabilities. In addition, families may be faced by special challenges such as poverty, substance abuse, and HIV-AIDs.

The family system is further composed of parental, marital, sibling, and extended family subsystems. The extended family subsystem is a critical component in many culturally diverse families where economic, physical and social support are provided by the extended family members. In some cases, extended family members may perform roles usually held by parents. Table 3.2 presents an outline of a family system and its subsystems. Subsystems are separated by boundaries created by interactions within the family itself and with outsiders. When boundaries are very open, roles may be flexible, and collaboration between the school and home will be easily accepted. On the other hand, boundaries may be closed to those outside, and collaboration will be difficult to impossible (Turnbull & Turnbull, 1997). Boundaries also serve to define bonding relationships within the family. Bonding is referred to as cohesion, and it is a characteristic that exists on a continuum. When families have a very high degree of cohesion, they are extremely close and may risk the loss of individual autonomy. On the other hand, a family with low cohesion may be unable to provide adequate support and nurturance for its members. Assistance may be required in order to help this family more adequately meet these needs.

Adaptability, a term that refers to the family's ability to change in response to situational and developmental stress, also exists on a continuum. High control and structure are at one end and low control and structure at the other. Families in which control and struc-

TABLE 3.2 *The Family System*

Characteristics		Functions	Life Cycle
Group	*Individual*		
Size	Education	Share affection	Birth
Form	Employment	and love	Early childhood
Culture	Language proficiency	Develop self-esteem	Childhood
SES	Abilities	Meet economic needs	Adolescence
Geography	Talents	Meet physical and	Adulthood
	Disabilities	health needs	
		Address need for	
		recreation, socialization	
		Meet educational needs	

ture are very low may live in chaotic conditions where no one is dependable, rules are nonexistent, leadership is absent, and roles and responsibilities are uncertain and constantly changing (Turnbull & Turnbull, 1997). School social workers or nurse educators may be called upon to assist in efforts to obtain counseling for these families. Obviously, extreme degrees of family control and structure may inhibit individual initiative and independence and can result in immature children unable to function socially. Teachers can consult with other professionals with respect to making referrals, or families can be directed to the school social worker or counselor. In more complex situations, referrals to mental health profesionals may be necessary. An action plan developed according to the Decision-Making Scaffold, which we will introduce in Chapter 4, would include such referrals.

Family Functions

The ease with which children can be engaged in school learning will depend on the family's ability to carry out its functions and meet the needs of all its members. A family struggling to carry out its basic functions may be unable to meet the expectations of the school for participation in children's education. In some of the cases to follow, families are engaged in extreme efforts to meet economic, physical, and health needs; consequently, the children involved are having difficulty progressing in school. A partnership in which the school and community provide services within the school can assist such families and children.

Functions of the family include (1) sharing verbal and physical affection and unconditional love, (2) developing self-esteem in its members, (3) meeting the family's economic needs, (4) meeting physical and health needs, (5) addressing the need for recreation and socialization, and (6) meeting members' educational needs (Turnbull & Turnbull, 1997). Although educators will be most concerned about the educational needs of children, other unmet needs will impact the family's ability to meet educational needs. Without intervention, for example, children without warm winter clothing or adequate medical care will lack the health, freedom, energy, and motivation to engage in school learning. The care of children and their education cannot be separated (Kagan, 1989). In developing a realistic plan of action to assist children, educators need to recognize the family as a system and recommend intervention accordingly.

Diverse families who are learning English may need assistance in identifying and accessing services in the community. Other families who face problems of living in poverty will also need to access services critical to the educational progress and success of their children. Citing the ecological relationship among schools, families, and communities, Crowson and Boyd (1993) point to the lack of concerted efforts to link human services into an "ecosystem for youth" (Timpane & Reich, 1997). Difficulties such as issues associated with "turf, client confidentiality, team-building, financial and budgetary agreements" will challenge professionals who attempt to develop a model of coordinated, collaborative services for children (Lugg, 1994), Nevertheless, an "ecosystem—a total environment supporting the healthy growth and development of America's youth and contributing to their resilience," is needed for every student at this time of great stress in the society for all families, especially for those with fewest resources (Timpane & Reich, 1997, p. 465). An example of a student's ecosystem is shown in Figure 3.2.

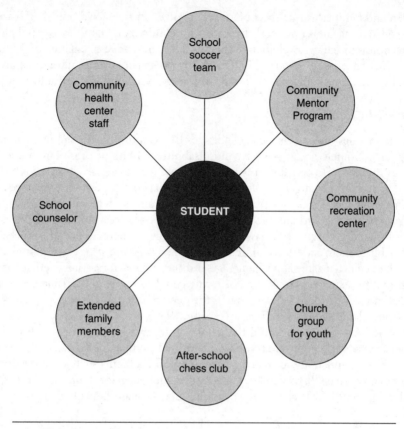

FIGURE 3.2   *A Student's Ecosystem*

The Family Life Cycle

Family functions are directly impacted by the family life cycle, the third component of the family system. The life cycle refers to the changes in a family over time as it goes through certain predictable and stable stages with the accompanying transition periods (Turnbull & Turnbull, 1997). Families generally experience birth, early childhood, childhood, adolescence, and adulthood with related tasks and responsibilities. Thus, a family with young children at the preschool age faces different responsibilities and challenges than the family whose children have reached adolescence. Although theorists vary on the number of stages identified, most agree on at least three stages (Turnbull & Turnbull, 1997). Family life, in general, and family functions and priorities change according to the life cycle stage of its children and adult members. Birth and early childhood bring intense absorption of the family in adapting to and meeting the needs of growing children. During the elementary years, the horizons broaden for both children and families as they become more involved in the world outside. However, adolescence brings new tasks and challenges for children and families as rapid physical and psychological changes challenge the family's cohesiveness, balance of authority, and midlife concerns of parents. Finally, adulthood usually brings autonomy, involvement in the community, and the challenge of change (Turnbull & Turnbull, 1997).

Special Challenges

Some families may face special challenges that can impact the family system and subsystems. Homelessness, poverty, and disabilities of one or more family members can place undue stress on the family system. These challenges are discussed in Chapters 8 and 9. However, refugee families also face special challenges. Refugees face numerous, complex challenges as they try to maintain the family system within a new cultural context. They must negotiate the employment and educational systems, understand immigration and naturalization laws, and try to access whatever social services might be available to them and their children (Huang, 1989). At the same time they are challenged by the need to master a new language and social behaviors. Many refugee families are without the extended family members who could comprise a social and economic source of support. An additional challenge is the need to integrate their experiences—the loss of home, land, family, and friends (Huang, 1989).

Researchers have found that those children who have fled with their families appear to adapt better than those who were unaccompanied (Huang, 1989). The latter group are at much higher risk for psychological problems such as depression, somatic complaints, sleep disturbances, violent antisocial behavior, tantrums, and withdrawals (Huang, 1989). Culturally diverse families may face all these challenges.

Culturally Diverse Families

Culturally diverse families share a great deal in common with all families. Yet, diverse cultural groups in the United States differ as much within groups as they do between groups. Thus, generalizations are very risky. Although a great deal of research exists regarding diverse groups, we prefer to alert teachers to possible differences among parents and families in many areas of their lives and to encourage teachers to become familiar with the particular cultural groups in their schools and classrooms. Even then, it will be important to rely on community persons and families who can act as "cultural informants" to help the teacher understand and appreciate the cultural differences among members of that community and to recognize that it is essential to know each family as individuals.

In fact, cultural differences among families may impact their responses to the changes and challenges involved at each stage of the life cycle. Families will differ in characteristics such as structure, child-rearing, and discipline practices, behavioral and developmental expectations for their children, verbal and nonverbal communication patterns, English proficiency, and knowledge of the schools and how they work (Salend & Taylor, 1993). Teachers will need to recognize these differences in order to build trust and establish positive relationships.

Discipline Practices

Gary Howard (2007) has provided a very practical plan for professional development of educators to meet the changing population in our schools. He describes five phases of a training plan: (1) building trust, (2) engaging personal culture, (3) confronting issues of social dominance and social justice, (4) transforming instructional practices, and (5) engaging the entire school community. As the director of a successful charter school to be described in Chapter 12 recently commented, "The staff of the school and I realized that we must change. The responsibility is on us." (Bill Wilson, Higher Ground Academy, 2007, personal communication, 2007).

Cultural background may explain differences in a family's discipline practices or the extent to which they are concerned about developmental milestones (LaFramboise & Graff-Low, 1989; Ramirez, 1989). Differences in behavioral expectations may cause conflict between the home and school in some instances. When teachers are willing to collaborate with families to develop culturally appropriate and relevant programs that include mutually selected bicultural behaviors and cross-cultural criteria for measuring progress, the partnership is enhanced. Many families want their children to have bicultural competence so that children will show respect and behave appropriately in the mainstream and in their particular cultural group as well.

Teachers may be especially concerned about discipline. The level of noise and movement permitted in the child's home and community may differ from that in the school. Students who continue this practice at school may be viewed as "behavior problems" by uninformed teachers. A nonjudgmental approach will work best as teachers interview students and family members to learn about cultural practices. Students will need to learn that expectations for behavior may change across settings. The home-school differences in behavioral expectations should be considered to explain behavior that the teacher finds unacceptable before negative judgments or a referral for special education is decided.

Home–School Communication

Although differences in discipline methods between home and school can be problematic, effective home–school relationships will strongly depend upon communication. Teachers will need to interpret parental verbal and nonverbal communication within diverse cultural contexts (Salend, 1990). Personal space, eye contact, wait time, voice quality, vocabulary, facial expressions, and touching are forms of nonverbal communication that are likely to vary among cultures (Anderson & Fenichel, 1989). In addition, families from some cultural backgrounds may refrain from talking about their problems or concerns because this may be considered self-centered or "losing face" (Nagata, 1989). Similarly, other families may avoid discussion of the future of their children because they believe that negative or limiting comments about an individual's future can cause it to happen (Locust, 1988).

Culturally competent interpreters, community members who understand the family's culture, can help to minimize potential barriers to communication between culturally diverse families and educators. In fact, Brandenburg-Ayres (1990) suggests that schools employ such "cultural informants" to serve as liaisons among schools, families, and communities; to inform school personnel about relevant cultural variables; to help orient new families to the school; and to prepare culturally sensitive and relevant written documents.

Moreover, families whose cultures emphasize interpersonal relationships over personal expertise will respond best to meetings in which school personnel are warm, friendly, and nonjudgmental. With these families, effective communication will also require sufficient time for family members to express themselves and a seating pattern that is informal and closer together. However, we have learned that many families, especially fathers in diverse families, may rearrange their chairs to a seating pattern that they prefer.

Some demonstration of self-disclosure, respect, and humor by the teacher will be helpful (Anderson & Fenichel, 1989; LaFramboise & Graff-Low, 1989). Some families may prefer to be greeted with a handshake and to sit in close proximity to each other (Ramirez, 1989). Other families may emphasize professional expertise in their relations with professionals and view school personnel more impersonally. These families will prefer an environment that is structured and goal-oriented to help participants accomplish their goals (Nagata, 1989).

Parents from non-English backgrounds may be reluctant to communicate with the school because they believe that they lack the proficiency in English that is expected or required. Furthermore, many schools lack bilingual professionals who could communicate with parents in their own language. Interpreters or translators, preferably from the community, are needed to facilitate oral and written communication between the home and school. Interpreters can assist with oral language, while translators are essential for written communications. Where many languages are represented in the school district, the use of parent and community volunteers can be explored. In some school districts, a regional survey for potential translators has led to a pool of translators and interpreters of various languages (Whittington-Couse, 1998 personal communication) However, the selection of interpreters and translators should be done with care and concern. (See Table 3.3.)

One of the most effective ways to facilitate the involvement of recent immigrant families is to make home visits (Ginsberg, 2007). Teachers, in pairs, can benefit from the visit in that culturally relevant teaching is easier to develop from the "funds of knowledge" that can be obtained (Gonzalez, Moll, & Amanti, 1995). "Funds of knowledge are strengths and talents—academic, civic, or technical—that are characteristic of families" (Ginsberg, 2007 pp. 57–58). Teachers can hear the personal stories of families, demonstrate sincere interest in the educational progress of the children, learn from the family about its culture, and begin to establish a relationship that can make positive contributions to the child's educational progress (Ginsberg, 2007).

After a home visit, a "Funds of Knowledge" chart can be developed where the knowledge, strengths, and talents of a family are displayed. A particular family might have information or skills in the area of immigration policies, faith organizations, family cooperation or household management that would be valuable to other children and their families. Special preparation and practice are needed to conduct a successful home visit with immigrant families.

TABLE 3.3 *Translators and Interpreters*

1. Translators are needed for school–home communications, parent training activities, and family participation in school governance and decision making.
2. Examples of successful programs for parents–families of diverse groups include:
   - School–community councils, organized groups where bilingual teachers or volunteers attend the meetings
   - Parent handbooks published in the languages of the students
   - Home visits by parent volunteers or aides who can translate messages from teachers to parents
   - All school–home communications are published in the students' home languages.
   - All parent meetings and workshops are conducted in English and the other majority languages.
   - Technology (translation equipment) is available for parent meetings.
   - Local radio stations are used to announce coming events or meetings, broadcast educational programs for adults and children, make health-related public service announcements, and conduct interviews of school and community members about current issues or events. Announcements are mainly in the language of the majority of listeners.
   - Home–school liaisons who are fluent in the languages of most families conduct home visits monthly to address discipline, academic, and attendance problems and to help families with paperwork.

Source: National Parent Information Network (1997, October).

School Involvement

Flexible times for conferences, babysitting services, procedures for acknowledging and communicating with noncustodial parents, and using the correct surname for parents (which may differ from that of the student) will also be helpful in increasing their involvement (Mcgee Banks, 1997). Low-income families are generally interested in the education of their children but may face serious obstacles in their efforts to become involved. Migrant families, for example, face poor economic conditions at home and the need to travel to remain employed (Bressler, 1996). Migrant women work in the fields with the men, "doing nearly every kind of farm labor, including harvesting crops and sorting and packing produce" (Bressler, 1996, p. 313). They also handle all the domestic responsibilities (Bressler, 1996).

In the words of one Latina woman, "You work all day in the fields, and then in the afternoon, at night, you have to take care of the children, take them to the clinic, to the hospital when they get sick . . ." (Bressler, 1996, p. 314). It is easy to appreciate the difficulties these families have with involvement in their children's education and the support they need in order to become involved. Furthermore, working in the fields brings income and creates an ambivalent situation regarding allowing the children to remain in school. In fact, students from migrant families who are motivated to continue their education beyond high school may be denied that opportunity by a family who needs the child's labor in the fields (Personal communication, Stevens 1998).

Acknowledgment of the low-income families' interest and concern for their children's education is the first step in building a positive school–home relationship. The adoption of Comer's School Development Program (Figure 3.1) or similar model, which provides many ways in which families can be involved, can also encourage, facilitate, and support families' involvement in the school. In addition, meetings in a neighborhood or community facility or provisions for transportation can be helpful. Even the time for meetings must be flexible since there is no such thing as "personal days" with pay for migrant workers.

The School–Family–Community Partnership

Kampwirth's (1999) definition captures this essential meaning of the partnership in the words "mutual problem-solving by equal partners" (p. 72). Thus, in working with families and community members, educators should reflect their belief in Kampwirth's definition. The strong partnership that can be formed on that basis can help every child to progress. See Guidelines for Effective Partnerships, Box 3.2, p. 52.)

The idea of community as a "web of relationships connecting individuals and institutions whose focus is ensuring that every child has a substantial opportunity to grow up successfully" is appealing (Timpane & Reich, 1997, p. 466). It makes a strong statement for the position of the school as a member of a network, working with other institutions to contribute to successful growth for the children and, often, revitalization of the neighborhood (Prager, 1993). As noted by Dryfoos (1994), "Schools in which quality education and comprehensive social services are offered under one roof (i.e., full service schools) have the potential to become neighborhood hubs, where children and their families want to be" (p. 18). Thus, the most appealing answer to the problems faced by many families and their children is the provision of coordinated services for children, through which the school works in collaboration with other community agencies and institutions to have services available in the school (Crowson & Boyd, 1993).

Models for the coordination of children's services include a school-based approach in which the school is the dominant institution, a school-linked model in which the school is a partner, and a community-based model with the school as a less dominant member (Behrman, 1992; Dryfoos, 1994). Lugg (1994) has differentiated among the models according to the degree of interdependence involved. Collaboration involves a high level of interagency participation, interdependence, and effort, whereas coordination implies moderate levels, and cooperation represents the lowest level of interdependence and interorganizational participation and high degrees of agency and school independence. In the community-based model, the school provides coordination with and referral to community agencies (Dryfoos, 1994). The school-linked approach involves a tighter relationship of the school with various social service agencies, but services remain outside the school. In the school-based model, a true full service school, a variety of social service agencies work together to provide integrated services within the school. Although Behrman (1992) notes that the school-linked model appears to be the most effective, there is no consensus at this time on the best model. From a practical point of view, the school-based model appears most practical because "that's where the children are."

It is important to note that families should be allowed to request assistance, rather than having it forced on them. Some may find community agencies and institutions intimidating and may need advocates to accompany them. Others will be inhibited due to previous negative experiences with mainstream personnel. Teachers can develop referral files to have quick, easy access to the information needed and also be prepared with names, phone numbers, and descriptions of the services offered. In many communities, directories may be available that provide this information. In any case, an investment in knowing the community and its resources can only serve to enhance the teacher–student–family relationship. While communities vary in the quantity and quality of services available, most will provide at least some examples of the following categories of agencies, organizations, and institutions: educational, employment, childcare, legal, healthcare, recreational, government, emergency food, clothing and shelter, and a variety of support groups. Table 3.3 presents a listing of community services frequently available.

TABLE 3.3 *Community Resources for Family Referrals*

Need	Type of Service	Examples: Public and Private Agencies
Food	Soup kitchens Food baskets Food stamps Food banks	Churches, Salvation Army, Goodwill, social services departments Community programs
Clothing	Clothing banks Thrift shops Consignment shops	Churches, Salvation Army, Goodwill Community centers Social service agencies
Shelter	Homeless shelter Battered women shelter Low-cost housing	Neighborhood agencies Churches Social services departments Habitat for Humanity
Furniture, household items	Flea markets Used furniture stores Yard, garage sales Donations	Churches Private agencies Publications
Healthcare	Vision, hearing, medical, dental problems Counseling, family therapy, crisis intervention	Lions Club Neighborhood clinics Hospital emergency rooms University and hospital clinics Local mental health agencies

(continued)

TABLE 3.3   *Continued*

Need	Type of Service	Examples: Public and Private Agencies
Employment	Temporary employment Vocational assessment and training Work permits	Private agencies State department of labor Local businesses and industry Publications
Extended family substitutes	Role models, tutors, advisors, counselors, companions, childcare	Big Brothers Church groups Community organizations Support groups
Recreation	After school programs and activities, summer camps and programs, family recreation activities	Public parks Schools YMCA, YWCA Local library Churches Some bookstores Neighborhood organizations
Support groups	Advocacy, support	Local chapters of national organizations for various disabilities Parent organizations
Legal assistance advocacy	Services for children with disabilities Housing disputes Miscellaneous infractions Minor problems involving individuals with limited proficiency in English	Parent organizations Tenants rights groups Rural poor and migrant advocacy agencies Neighborhood agencies
Education	Basic literacy English language instruction GED Technical and vocational training Parenting skills Early intervention Preschool programs Postsecondary programs	Public libraries Community colleges Vocational and technical schools High schools Literacy Volunteers of America Head Start Private preschools

TABLE 3.3 *Continued*

Need	Type of Service	Examples: Public and Private Agencies
	Adult basic education	
	Citizenship training	
Child care	Day care	Licensed private households
	Special summer programs for children	Job-related programs
	Respite care	

In some schools, social workers, nurses, and psychologists are expected to provide counseling and emergency assistance. Other schools may collaborate with the mental health system or a private agency to provide services in the school. The social services system may collaborate with the school to provide staff and other support that can allow the school social worker to work with a larger number of families and meet emergency needs for food, shelter, or clothing. In some instances, schools have developed their own clothing banks and food pantries. Families can be included in such activities as managers of clothing banks and food pantries. In a Chicago school, Principal Carol Edwards described this type of collaboration.

> We have a parent room on the first floor in the middle of the corridor. In the parent room are tables, chairs, bulletin boards, and some clothes in the back. If we have clothing to give away, we do it in that room. Parent meetings and parent training are held in that room. Specific parent activities, such as distributing books to children as part of the Reading Is Fundamental initiative, are done in that room. Parents eat with the teachers in the lunchroom (Comer et al. 1999, p. 31).

In summary, students benefit when schools, families, and communities develop partnerships. Communities can provide support and resources to help schools to perform their missions, and communities can benefit from the availability of school facilities and programs. In addition, the real-life problems in the community may be resolved as students work with these problems in a context of learning. Families and communities also benefit from the educational progress of their members, who can contribute stability and richness to the community. Students must function in the world of the home, school, and community. A strong partnership can enhance the congruence among these worlds for students and facilitate their transitions among them.

References

Anderson, P., & Fenichel, E. S. (1989). *Serving culturally diverse families of infants and toddlers with disabilities.* Retrieved June 1991, from http://www.eric.ed.gov.

Behrman, R. E. (Ed.). (1992). School-linked services. [Electronic version]. *Future of Children, 2*(1).

Bowen, M. (2000–2004). *Bowen theory.* Bowen Center for the Study of the Family. Retrieved August 11, 2007 from: http://www.theboencenter.org/pages/theory.html.

Brandenburg-Ayres, S. (1990). *Working with parents. Bilingual/TESOL Special Education Collaboration and Reform Project.* Gainsville: University of Florida.

Bressler, S. (1996). Voices of Latina mothers in rural Pennsylvania. In J. LeBlanc Flores (Ed.), *Children of La Frontera.* (pp. 311–324). Charleston, West VA: Clearringhouse on rural education and small schools. Appalachia Education Laboratories.

Casambis, S., & Gartland, J. (1997). *Parental involvement in students' education during middle school and high school.* Report No. 181. Baltimore, MD: Johns Hopkins University; Washington, DC: Howard University, Center for Research on the Education of Students Placed At risk.

Comer, J. (2005). The rewards of parent participation. *Educational Leadership, 62*(6), 38–42.

Comer, J. P., Ben-Avie, M., Haynes, N., & Joyner, E. T. (Eds.). (1999). *Child by child: The Comer process for change.* New York: Teachers College Press.

Comer, J. P., Haynes, N., Joyner, E., & Ben-Avie, M. (Eds.). (1996). *Rallying the whole village: The Comer process for reforming education.* New York: Teachers College Press.

Cooksey, E., & Fondell, M. (1996). Spending time with his kids: Effects of family structure on fathers' and children's lives. *Journal of Marriage and the Family, 58*(3), 693–707.

Crowson, R., & Boyd, W. L. (1993). Coordinated services for children: Designing arks for storms and seas unknown. *American Journal of Education, 101*(2), 140–179.

Dearing, E., Kreider, H., Simpkins, S., & Weiss, H. (2006). *Family involvement in school and low-income children's literacy performance.* Cambridge, MA: Harvard Family Research Project. Retrieved July 19, 2007, from http://www.gse.harvard.edu/hfrp/projects/fine/resources/digest/perf.

Dryfoos, J. G. (1994). *Full-service schools: A revolution in health and social services for children, youth, and families.* San Francisco: Jossey-Bass.

Epstein, J. (1995). School/family/community partnerships: Caring for the children we share. *Phi Delta Kappan, 76*(9), 701–711.

Epstein, J. L., & Salinas, K. C. (2004). Partnering with families and communities. *Educational Leadership, 1*(8), 12–18.

Finders, M., & Lewis, C. (1994). Why some parents don't come to school. *Educational Leadership, 51*(8), 50–54.

Funkhouser, J. E., & Gonzales, M. R. (1997). *Family involvement in children's education: Successful local approaches.* Washington, DC: Office of Educational Research and Improvement, U.S. Department of Education. Retrieved December 12, 2007, from http://www.ed.gov/pubs/FamInvolve/execsumm.html.

Gilbert, K. (2004). *Understanding the family as a system and other theories.* Retrieved September 5, 2007 from http:www.indiana.edu~hyperf258/lectures/system.ppt.

Ginsberg, M.B. (2007). Lessons at the kitchen table. *Educational Leadership, 64*(6), 56–62.

Gonzalez, N., Moll, L. C., & Amanti, C. (1995). *Funds of knowledge: Theorizing practices in households, communities, and classrooms.* Mahwah, NJ: Erlbaum.

Griffiths, J. (1996). Relation of parental involvement, empowerment, and school traits to student academic performance. *Journal of Educational Research, 90*(1), 33–41.

Heath, S. B. (1995). Ethnography in communities: Learning the everyday life of America's subordinated youth. In J. A. Banks & C. A. McGee Banks (Eds.), *Handbook of research on multicultural education* (pp. 114–128). New York: Macmillan.

Hildago, N., Bright, J., Siu, S. F., Swap, S., & Epstein, J. (1995). Research on families, schools, and communities: A multicultural perspective. In J. A. Banks & C. A. McGee Banks (Eds.), *Handbook of research on multicultural education* (pp. 498–524). New York: Macmillan.

Howard, G. (2007). As diversity grows, so must we. *Educational Leadership, 64*(6). 16–22.

Huang, L. N. (1989). *Children of color: Psychological interventions with minority youth.* San Francisco: Jossey-Bass.

Ingram, M., Wolfe, R. B., & Lieberman, J. (2007). The role of parents in high-achieving schools serving low-income, at-risk populations. *Education & Urban Society, 39*(4), 479–497.

Jeynes, W. H. (2007). The relationship between parental involvement and urban secondary student academic achievement. *Urban Education, 42*(1), 82–110.

Kagan, S. (1989). Early care and education: Beyond the school house doors. *Phi Delta Kappan, 71*(2), 107–112.

Kampwirth, T. (1999). *Collaborative consultation in the schools: Effective practices for students with learning and behavior problems.* Upper Saddle River, NJ: Merrill/Prentice Hall.

Ladson-Billings, G. (1994). *The dreamkeepers.* San Francisco: Jossey-Bass.

LaFramboise, T. D., & Graff-Low, K. (1989). American Indian children and adolescents (pp. 114–147). In J. Taylor-Gibbs & L. Nahme-Huang (Eds.), *Children of color: Psychological interventions with minority youth.* San Francisco: Jossey-Bass.

Locust, C. (1988). Wounding the spirit: Discrimination and traditional American Indian belief systems. *Harvard Educational Review, 58*(3), 315–330.

Lugg, C. A. (1994). *Schools and achieving integrated services: Facilitating utilization of the knowledge base.* Paper presented at the Annual Meeting of the University Council for Educational Administration, Philadelphia, October 28–30.

McGee Banks, C. A. (1997). Parents and teachers: Partners in school reform. In J. A. Banks & C. A. McGee Banks (eds). *Multicultural education: Issues and perspectives* (3rd ed.) (pp. 408–426). Boston: Allyn and Bacon.

Muller, C. (1998). Gender differences in parental involvement and adolescents' mathematics achievement. *Sociology of Education, 71*(4), 336–356.

Nagata, D. K. (1989). Japanese American children and adolescents. In J. Taylor-Gibbs & L. Nahme-Huang (Eds.), *Children of color: Psychological interventions with minority youth* (pp. 67–113). San Francisco: Jossey-Bass.

National Parent Information Network (1997, October). Family involvement in children's education: Successful local approaches. Retrieved January 28, 2008 from http://www.ed.gov/pubs/FamInvolve/execsumm.html.

Patrikakou, E. N. (2004). Adolescence: Are parents relevant to students' high school achievement and post-secondary attainment? Retrieved July 18, 2007, from http://gse.harvard.edu/hfrp/projects/gine/resources/digest/adole

Prager, K. (1993). Social capital: The foundation for education. *Issues in Restructuring Schools, 5,* 1–19.

Quicho, A., & Daoud, A. (2006). Dispelling myths about Latino participation in schools. *Educational Forum, 70*(3), 255–267.

Ramirez, O. (1989). Mexican American children and adolescents. In J. Taylor-Gibbs & L. Nahme Huang (Eds.), *Children of color: Psychological interventions with minority youth* (pp. 224–250). San Francisco: Jossey-Bass.

Riley, R. (1999). *Condition of Education Report.* Washington, DC: U.S. Department of Education.

Salend, S. J. (1990). Migrant education guide for special educators. *Teaching Exceptional Children, 22*(2), 18–21.

Salend, S. J., & Taylor, L. S. (1993). Working with families across cultural perspectives. *Remedial and Special Education, 14*(5), 25–31, 39.

Shearin, S. A. (2002). Parent-adolescent interaction: Influence on the academic achievement of African American adolescent males. *Journal of Health & Social Policy, 18*(1/2), 125–137.

Sheldon, S., & Epstein, J. (2005). Involvement counts: Family and community partnerships and mathematics achievement. *The Journal of Educational Research, 98*(4), 196–207.

Timpane, M., & Reich, R. (1997). Revitalizing the ecosystem for youth: A new perspective for school reform. *Phi Delta Kappan, 78,* 464–470.

Turnbull, A. P., & Turnbull, H. R. (1997). *Families, professionals, and exceptionality: A special partnership.* Upper Saddle River, NJ: Prentice Hall.

U.S. Department of Education (1994). Goals 2000 Educate America Act. Washington, DC: Author.

Weast, J. D., Jones, L. M., & Howley, J. P. (1999). A culture of collaboration. In J. P. Comer, M. Ben-Avie, N. Haynes, & E. T. Joyner (Eds.), *Child by child: The Comer process for change in education* (pp. 255–275). New York: Teachers College Press.

Zelazo, J. (1995). *Parent involvement in a two-way bilingual school.* Paper presented at the Annual Meeting of AERA, San Francisco, April 18–22. (ERIC Document Reproduction Number ED 383219).

4

The Development and Use of Cases in Teacher Education

The use of cases as teaching and learning tools is frequently associated with the fields of medicine and law. The visual media have facilitated this phenomenon. Many people can remember nervousness in the voice of a medical student who must present her first patient's case to the attending physician and peers on the clinical rotation in any number of television medical dramas. Television series such as *Law and Order* create cases in which the fate of an individual depends on the knowledge, logic, and dramatic skills of the dueling attorneys. In these situations, cases are depicted as a vehicle for examining precedent and learning through deductive logic.

In medicine and law, the use of teaching cases as an effective pedagogy has its roots in the late 1800s (Doyle, 1990). More recently, the pedagogical approach that has provided the broadest platform is the one developed by the Harvard Business School MBA Program (Christensen, 1987). Faculty and graduate students have developed an extensive series of complex business cases that report the workings of actual companies and serve as the core of the MBA curriculum. The business faculty also has worked with other programs and universities to study and encourage the case study method in a variety of fields (Christensen, Garvin, & Sweet, 1991).

The field of education has recently reawakened to the tremendous benefits that cases can offer to preservice and in-service teachers (Miller & Kantrov, 1998; J. Shulman, 1996; L. Shulman, 1987; Silverman & Welty, 1996; Sudzina, 1999). Although there is evidence that instructors used cases in teacher education as far back as 1864 (Doyle, 1990), most casebooks and discussions of how to teach using cases have been published in the last two decades. There are several reasons for this renewed interest. First, many of the reports that have called for the reform of teacher education have advocated the use of cases to build skills in decision making and collaboration (Goodlad, 1990; Holmes Group, 1995; National Commission on Teaching & America's Future, 1996). Second, researchers are interested in discovering how experienced teachers develop their practical knowledge about teaching and learning by studying and analyzing their actions in the classroom. This type of case study research is based on a belief that we can learn about teaching by observing in classrooms, interviewing teachers about their beliefs, and reviewing relevant documents, rather than by trying to control and manipulate the classroom environment (Clandinin & Connelly, 1995, 2000; Lincoln & Guba, 1985). Finally, cases are essentially stories of teachers, students, parents, and other relevant individuals. Narrative is the means by which people interpret the world by thinking about experience (Clandinin, Pushor, & Orr, 2007). Some would say that narrative is the best, if not only way, to really know how teachers think and learn (Doyle, 1997).

What Is a Teaching Case?

The idea of what constitutes a case varies depending on the field of study. Cases can encompass a wide variety of problematic choice situations. A case can be the story of a family that is confronted with selling its commercial fishing operation (Wassermann, 1994). A case also can be a video of a master teacher implementing an innovative teaching strategy in his classroom (Leinhardt, 1990). Another example of a case is the report of a researcher who has observed, and sometimes participated in, a situation (e.g., school, business, or hospital) for the purpose of understanding how a professional thinks about problems (Schön, 1987, 1991).

The cases in this text are *teaching cases*. That is, we have written them to be read by and discussed primarily with preservice and in-service teachers and other professionals in schools in order to facilitate connections between theory and practice. Furthermore, the content of these cases focuses on the challenges that school staff face in educating students who come from increasingly diverse cultural, linguistic, geographic, economic, religious, and educational backgrounds. We define a *teaching case* as a narrative that describes a specific, complex predicament that is written as an educational tool for exploring critical issues and developing a response. In the pages that follow we will use the terms *teaching case* and *case* interchangeably.

The cases in this book share a similarity in four features: authenticity, concrete detail, narrative form, and open-endedness (Hutchings, 1993). First, all the cases in this book are based on real events in real schools and classrooms. Names and roles have been changed, but the narratives are true for those who have lived them. A case is not intended to be representative of an entire group of people. It is *one* example of a reality faced by teachers in one school setting that may not be generalizable to other locations. However, certain aspects of the case may provide valuable learning for those who face similar situations.

Because these cases are authentic, the perceptions of one individual may conflict with those of another in the case. Although the cases include the voices of students, teachers, administrators, and community members, there are always other characters whose stories or actions related to the case may not be represented at all. Each character has certain beliefs, assumptions, and biases, and it is up to you to recognize these presuppositions.

Our purpose is to transport you outside the university classroom into the school and community. Therefore, we have attempted to include many concrete details that portray the situation physically, emotionally, and mentally. It is important that you hear the dialogue that unfolds between individuals and that you visualize the characters and the settings in which they live on a daily basis. We want you to experience the emotional impact of these situations as well as understand the "facts," since the joys and stress of teaching are as much a part of the decisions that individuals make as are the results of test scores and other more normative information. Therefore, these cases are more than short vignettes about teachers and students. They include individuals both in the school and the community who have a part in shaping a school's program and culture and whose opinions must be considered when making any decision.

Cases are written as narratives and therefore constitute a different way of learning than is common in university classrooms. Much of what you read and hear in teacher preparation has been described by Bruner (1986) as a *paradigmatic* mode of knowing. That is, it is information that leads to theory, analysis, proofs, arguments, principles, and empirical discovery. This type of learning is generalized knowledge; it is useful as a guide, but not as a specific prescription. Bruner also encourages teachers to investigate a *narrative* mode of knowing, because narratives are sensitive to the unique contexts in which teachers work and are most helpful in connecting understanding with action.

Narratives have a form or syntax, such as beginning–middle–end or situation–transformation, that is related by time. They are written specifically to communicate to someone else what the narrator believes happened. It is this social aspect of narratives that is particularly important to teaching cases. Their value is the analysis and response that cases evoke when discussed in a social setting (Whittaker & van Garderen, 2007). This uniqueness of each participant's experiences, understandings, values, and beliefs adds to the richness of the discussion and leads to differences in opinion regarding the issues at stake and the course of action that should be followed. Simply put, cases don't have one answer, and there is no presumption on the part of the authors that there is a "best" answer. The response that a group will make depends on the individuals making the decision and the particular context described in the narrative. However, there *is* such a thing as a bad answer. Knowledge of theory and research should guide the class's deliberations.

These cases are open-ended; the class must tell the rest of the story. Teaching cases are a slice of a problem, question, or concern that individuals in a school are encountering. There may be hints about the options that a character is considering and suggestions of the uncertainties that she feels, but the cases do not come to a resolution. The participants must decide if a narrator's view is adequate or if a character has been fully developed. It is often necessary to step back from the immediate picture and try to get a more comprehensive view. These activities, as well as the enhanced perspective provided by the class dynamic, will contribute significantly to the learning experience. Ultimately, the class will decide on a plan of action.

Cases, then, tell at least part of the story of several individuals' actions, words, and reflections concerning the challenge of a particular student or school situation. It is up to you to create a resolution. As we discuss next, we believe that the creativity and engagement that case discussion demands will help you be better teachers, not just better storytellers.

Why Are Case Discussions Valuable?

How many times have you heard the maxim "experience is the best teacher"? Is "getting out there and trying it" the best way to learn to teach? Or is there a certain body of knowledge related to subject matter, curriculum, instruction, educational contexts, learners, and the purposes and ends of education that must be mastered before starting to teach (Shulman, 1987)?

This dichotomy between theory and practice is the separation that has challenged teacher education throughout history. As teacher educators, we strongly endorse the need for teachers to be grounded in a professional knowledge base. The critical question becomes how this grounding takes place. We believe that school observations, home visits, field experiences, practica, and other school-related assignments can be an invaluable part of teacher education when carefully integrated with coursework. Cases provide another way to experience the real world of teaching, with the additional benefit of inviting the whole class to observe, discuss, and learn from the events that transpire. They are a middle ground in which the sometimes dizzying pace of a classroom can be viewed as a video: slowed down, replayed, and analyzed frame by frame.

Another rationale for case discussions can be drawn from what we know about expert teachers. Researchers have found that expert teachers have practical knowledge, a "complex practically oriented set of understandings which teachers actively use to shape and direct the work of teaching" (Connelly & Clandinin, 1988, p. 19). Teachers cannot always describe this knowledge in terms of theories or beliefs, yet they seem to know intuitively how to proceed in the midst of very complicated and ambiguous situations. When asked to describe the rationale for their actions, they are more likely to tell a story to explain what they know and believe about their teaching.

Practical knowledge is that intuitive, artistic, experiential knowledge that often seems most essential yet elusive to beginning teachers. However, much evidence suggests that expert teachers are not simply those who have taught for many years. Rather, expert teachers are those who are "reflective practitioners" (Schön, 1987). By this, Schön means that expert teachers think about their teaching in one of two ways. When a teacher is surprised by an unexpected result in the classroom, he may look back at a later time to understand what factors in that complex situation, or "swampy lowland," led to this result. Schön terms this "reflection-on-action." Or a teacher may think through the surprise without interruption so that she can reshape the situation while in the midst of it. Schön calls this more immediate response "reflection-in-action." This reshaping of a situation is also referred to as *framing* the problem or bringing all of one's educational and experiential background, values, and understandings to configure the issues in a certain pattern. More recent critiques of Schön's work by social reconstructionists have emphasized the need to reflect on the societal conditions that affect schooling as well as the teacher's inner repertoires (Genor, 2005; Zeichner & Liston, 1996). These theorists would include issues of equity, democratic education, and social action as vital components of the reflection process.

Case discussions allow the readers to reflect on the action of other professionals who are mucking through the swampy lowlands of an ambiguous and multifaceted situation. These cases are unique and therefore will not replicate readers' exact experience. However, we have chosen them because they point toward and illustrate larger theoretical, conceptual, or descriptive categories. Lee Shulman (1996) reminds us that one question we should continually ask ourselves when reading and discussing a case is this: "What is this a case of?" Furthermore, he concedes that cases are so complex and rich that we can create an entire network of associations between theory and practice. While we know that you will not encounter the specific circumstances described in these cases, we are confident that the principles that you extract from them will be applicable in today's diverse schools. Cases allow teachers to develop skills of critical thinking and problem solving that extend beyond the classroom and instructional decision making to include the institutional, cultural, and political aspects of teaching (Harrington, 1995; Kleinfeld, 1998; Lundeberg, Levin, & Harrington, 1999; Silverman & Welty, 1996).

Case discussions allow participants to practice the communication skills and cultural competence needed by effective teachers. Progressive school districts are implementing programs that involve team teaching, collaborative planning, peer coaching, and cross-grade or subject teaming. A case is "nonego invested" because participants are discussing the uncertainty and frustration of someone else's teaching (Hutchings, 1993). Once trust and a culture that supports reflection have been established, it is easier to reveal concerns about one's own teaching or the challenging situations that shape students' lives.

As described above, cases are also an excellent vehicle for reflecting on issues of professionalism and social justice (Moje & Wade, 1997). Teaching is far more than a technical act; it is a moral endeavor. Teachers are constantly modeling what they believe to be important and good for their students and the many individuals with whom they interact each day. What they teach, and how they teach, and how they relate to students and others are testimony to these values and beliefs. We hope that as you discuss these cases you will rethink your own assumptions about teaching and learning. It is one thing to write a philosophy of education on paper and quite another to enact that personal ethic in the classroom and community. Cases will not provide a standard of ethical conduct, but they will allow participants to test out the horizons of their beliefs and the cost that they may entail.

Cases force individuals and groups to think somewhat differently than they have before. Theories, concepts, and techniques are examined in the light of the real challenges that teachers meet in schools. By reflecting on these situations with peers and choosing viable alternatives, teachers broaden their own practical knowledge and test their beliefs.

How Do Participants Analyze a Case?

We have established that one of the marks of an expert teacher is the ability to reflect on practice (Schön, 1987, 1991). Furthermore, we believe that reflection-on-action can occur in a vicarious way through the reading and discussion of teaching cases. But what do we mean by reflection? Is it simply a moment to stop and think in the midst of the ongoing stream of events and dialogue? If teaching is indeed an art, does that mean we must simply wait for inspiration? Is there a scaffold that can support our decision-making process that will promote a well-considered response? We would suggest several decision points that constitute a framework or scaffold for reflecting on a case. This scaffold that we have developed is not meant to be a step-by-step process that you must systematically follow in order to "crack the case." We recognize that thinking rarely occurs in such a linear fashion and, frequently, our thinking processes consider several ideas simultaneously and revisit others recursively. Similarly, there are considerations in the scaffold that participants will omit altogether in some cases and spend a great deal of deliberation on in others, depending on experience and familiarity with similar problems.

The Case Decision-Making Scaffold has five components (see Table 4.1). The following is a description of each aspect of this reflective process.

TABLE 4.1   *A Case Decision-Making Scaffold*

Recognize the Problem

Is there a trigger event that causes an individual to recognize a problem?

What facts do we know about the individuals, the school, the family, and the community?

What discrepancies exist between the individuals' expectations and actual events?

What are the major problems in the case?

Reframe the Problem

What underlying assumptions, values, or beliefs do individuals involved hold about each of the problems?

Which major problems are most important to the various individuals or groups involved?

What values or beliefs regarding the major problems do individuals or groups hold in common?

Search for Alternatives

What can we learn about the major problems from those who have experience and expertise?

What alternatives might address the major problems involved in the case?

What short- and long-term consequences will each alternative have for the student, school, family, and community?

Which alternatives best address the important problems?

Develop and Implement a Plan of Action

How can we prioritize the goals to facilitate implementation?

What activities, referrals, resources, and strategies must be included in the plan of action to address the goals?

Who is responsible for performing the various components of the plan of action?

What criteria will we use to evaluate progress?

Evaluate Progress

What progress has been made based on established criteria?

Are all individuals and groups satisfied with the progress?

What new problems have developed?

What revisions to the plan of action need to be made?

Recognize the Problem

As simplistic as it may sound, a reflective practitioner must first recognize that there is a problem, or a discrepancy between what he expects and what is actually occurring. We have found that it is helpful to identify the primary characters or groups within the case and determine, for each, if they perceive a discrepancy between their expectations and real occurrences. At this stage of decision making, it is important to stick to facts that the case presents without making interpretations regarding beliefs, motivation, and actions. Sometimes there is a trigger event that points to the problems involved. Participants should make statements regarding the major problems involved based on evidence within the case. For example, if Mr. Levitt states that he expects Emanuel to complete all homework to get a passing grade, and Emanuel's parents tell him he must work 20 hours a week to support the family, there is a real discrepancy in expectations. The first time you read a case you will probably uncover a list of problems embedded in the case. This list should then be categorized into a few major problems. We define major problems as those that:

- Have a long term negative effect on a student's educational progress.
- Are multifaceted.
- Stem from differences in attitudes, values, and beliefs that are longstanding.
- Have implications beyond the classroom to the district, community, and organizational levels.
- Are recognized in the educational literature.
- Require a comprehensive plan of action that includes both short- and long-term solutions.

In the example above, a major problem would be differences in expectations between the family and school regarding the importance of completing academic work. Unless changes are made on many levels, Emanuel and students like him will not make educational progress. Once problems are identified, it is possible to better understand these issues by examining the beliefs that each individual utilizes to view the problem.

Reframe the Problem

As discussed in previous chapters, people frame problems based on their own values, culture, experiences, and assumptions. While there may be agreement that there is a problem, there may not be agreement on the issues involved or how to resolve them in an ethical and equitable manner. When a teacher modifies an assignment for Emanuel, who has a severe learning disability, Greg may feel that the teacher is "letting him off" too easily or showing favoritism. The teacher may see the issue as Greg's inability to understand the need for individualized instruction. Similarly, we may make assumptions about the aims of education that simply aren't workable or valued in a particular setting or context. Emanuel's teacher may believe that all students should complete their academic work at home each evening, but this may not be realistic for some families in which staying warm, clothed, and fed is a daily struggle. In this stage of the Decision-Making

Scaffold, you often will describe what characters or groups "believe" or "feel" as shown by what they say, what they actually do, and where they expend their resources.

This reframing stage of decision making is often ignored. Values and beliefs strongly influence the actions of individuals and groups. They are often accompanied by strong emotion. While knowledge and logic must inform decision making, we must also carefully consider the individual's past experience and the emotions involved in this experience. Decision making that ignores these aspects may, at best, receive tacit agreement from those involved, but may ultimately enact little change.

Schön (1987) suggests that part of reflection-on-action is reframing the problem. To institute meaningful change, one must see a problem from multiple perspectives. An important part of the reframing process is considering the values and beliefs that govern action. When we inquire into important issues, they "have at their core fundamental beliefs, values, and human interests at stake" (Sirotnik, 1991, p. 244). This need for examining varying perspectives does not imply that we can or should attempt to alter basic values. Rather, it suggests that by understanding the core beliefs that teachers, students, and families can mutually adhere to we are better able to find common ground and seek viable and acceptable alternatives. Emanuel, his teacher, and his family may find common ground by agreeing that they all value the importance of education for future success.

Search for Alternatives

We have found it to be helpful to take major problem statements established in the first stage of the Decision-Making Scaffold and convert them to goal statements. Returning to Emanuel, the goal might be to establish a system for academic work completion that is agreeable to the school and family. Once the goal is clearly established, it is possible to search for alternatives.

The experience and expertise of others from different backgrounds (students, parents, or school staff) are particularly valuable when you are searching for an alternative plan of action. Furthermore, as educators, it is incumbent on us to be knowledgeable about the research in the field of education that addresses the situations that we face. Therefore, part of our task in searching for alternatives is reading the professional literature, attending educational conferences, consulting experts in the field, and conducting action research in the classroom. Although each situation is unique, the issues involved in these situations are accessible in the professional literature. We enhance our understanding and multiply our options when we use these rich resources to our advantage. In the first three chapters we described some of the important issues and research that will help to guide your problem solving. Furthermore, each succeeding chapter starts with pertinent background information that will supply you with specific information and research regarding the teaching cases.

The expertise of parents, other school staff, and community members is also valuable when we are searching for alternatives. Each person's ability to see the situation through a different lens strengthens the outcome. There must be an agreement on the general goals that are to be accomplished and an understanding that all ideas are welcome and respected. While some in the group may have expertise in a particular area, all members have practical knowledge of their own roles and must be treated with respect. This type of collaborative approach provides a broad repertoire of alternatives and ensures commitment to the goals eventually established.

When a problem is newly encountered or very complex, a thorough search for alternatives may be necessary. However, once individuals have gone through an extended problem-solving process, they tend to make related decisions automatically. This may be part of what is occurring when teachers are said to reflect-in-action. They see a discrepancy between what they expected and what is happening, but can quickly reframe the problem and seemingly choose a viable alternative in seconds. This may be because they have encountered many similar situations in the past and have a rich repertoire of workable alternatives from which to choose. However, most of these cases involve many participants and will require more than a single teacher making a decision.

Once an individual or a group has generated a list of alternatives, choices must be made. This requires examining the short- and long-term consequences of each decision for all the stakeholders. Often, complex ethical issues are involved. For example, Ms. Simmons may believe that it is unconscionable to allow Jesus to be promoted to second grade when he is still reading in English on a preprimer level. However, knowing that Spanish is the primary language in Jesus's home and that holding students back rarely improves their academic skills in the long run (Silberglitt, Jimerson, Burns, & Appleton, 2006), the consequences of retaining Jesus in the same grade the next year must be carefully considered.

When several alternatives seem acceptable within a shared ethical and cultural vision, some criteria for prioritization must be established based on the needs of the child and other stakeholders, the philosophy and legal mandates that govern the school, the constraints of the setting, and the abilities and style of the teacher. Criteria such as excellence, equity, feasibility, cost effectiveness, and legality all must be considered as possible criteria in the decision-making process.

Due to the complexity of the cases in this text, it is likely that you will identify more than one problem and accompanying goal. Once the major goals for implementing a change process have been chosen and prioritized, the steps for achieving these goals must be delineated. This requires a plan of action.

Develop and Implement a Plan of Action

A plan of action may involve specific classroom, school, or community activities, referrals to school personnel or outside agencies; additional resources; or alternative instructional strategies. Each goal will be accomplished through one or more of these activities. Furthermore, tasks must be clearly assigned to one or more individuals who are capable of following through. A plan of action will fail without such built-in accountability. Furthermore, criteria should be established to determine whether the plan has been successfully executed. How will you know if your goals have been accomplished? What changes do you expect to see in individuals? What changes in attitude and actions are reasonable?

Activities and criteria for achievement must be carefully determined and, in many cases, recorded in some fashion. This may take the form of an entry in a teacher's journal, a revised lesson plan, a contract with a student and parent, an agreement among professionals, an addition to the student handbook, or a mission statement for a district-level task force. Even if the plan of action involves only a teacher and student, writing down the plan still allows both parties to understand the terms to which they are consenting. When multiple people have roles in implementing the plan, it is helpful to have a clear statement of what these responsibilities entail. Admittedly, many alternatives are chosen and successfully implemented without a written document. Likewise, some cases that participants discuss in class will not be carried through to the plan of action. However, we would encourage you to think seriously about possible follow-up activities. We believe that action is an integral part of reflection. If teachers do not take steps to change those situations that cause the problem, they will constantly submit themselves to a substandard professional experience and, eventually, may burn out or leave the profession.

Evaluate Progress

One reward that accrues to a reflective practitioner is the satisfaction that comes from seeing positive change. Once criteria are established for choosing an alternative, these criteria can be used to assess progress. This may be as simple as seeing Emanuel proudly submit all academic work due by the end of the week or as complex as having the final draft of a district policy on completion of academic work after a year's worth of meetings with teachers, administrators, and community members.

Of course, the outcome of this process of reflection is actually a continuation of the process. Even successful plans must be modified when the context inevitably changes and new variables are introduced into the equation. It is a mistake to institute a plan that does not allow for ongoing evaluation and modification.

In conclusion, this Case Decision-Making Scaffold is a tool to use while reading, discussing, and responding to the cases in this text. We have no desire to squelch intuition or reduce an art to a skill. Others have contributed valuable ideas for discussing cases, conducting critical inquiry, and developing teacher leadership, and we commend them to you (Shulman, 1996; Silverman & Welty, 1996; Sirotnik, 1991; Sudzina, 1999). The scaffold may be most helpful initially when case discussion is unfamiliar and there is a tendency to devise solutions before thoroughly considering aspects of the issues involved. Later, it may be less necessary to refer to the scaffold as the process of reflection becomes more internalized. We offer it as a scaffold for thinking that should be removed once you have determined your own decision-making process.

How Do Participants Discuss a Case?

Often your instructors will ask you to read a case before meeting together and be ready to discuss the study questions at the end of the case or other questions that he or she has provided. In using these cases with in-service and preservice teachers, we have observed that it is important to read the cases carefully, highlighting important facts or taking notes as you proceed. Facts should be separated from opinions. If characters seem to hold certain assumptions, determine if these beliefs are based on reality. You should analyze your own interpretations and see if you can support them from data in the case. The Case Decision-Making Scaffold may be a good reference to help you to organize thoughts and feelings while thinking through this process.

Some of our students have formed informal study groups that would meet before class to discuss study questions and get a general sense of each individual's reaction to the case. In doing so, they have a better sense of the various perspectives that the case can evoke. By spending time on the initial analysis (that is, recognizing and reframing the problem) outside class, they increase the possibility that class discussion will include all aspects of the decision-making process. In class, your instructor may first ask you to examine the case in small groups. Research on the case study method has demonstrated that individual preparation combined with small group discussion enhanced participants' analysis of cases (Flynn & Klein, 2001). This is another opportunity to learn how others have framed the case and is an excellent chance to practice those communication skills that are so critical to collaborative teaming in schools.

A benefit to discussing cases is that the process can encourage the development of a community of learners. People will frame the issues of the case differently based on their own background and beliefs. This diversity of ideas will provide for an interesting exploration of assumptions and feelings that you may not have considered. Undoubtedly, differences of opinion will surface. You must address all these perspectives before the group can progress and formulate a plan of action.

It can be exhilarating to observe the breadth of ideas that a group of reflective individuals can generate, but there is hard work involved in fleshing out these sometimes disparate notions into a workable plan. People will respond with their intellect and their emotions; both the cognitive and affective aspects of decision making must be considered. However, research suggests that when discussions allow for conflicting views and values, there is a social construction of knowledge and a change in thinking (Lundeberg, 1999). We agree with Kleinfeld (1998) that it is preferable to discuss the potentially emotionally unsettling situations that relate to diverse student populations through case studies before encountering similar events through direct experience. Confrontations in the school can harden teacher's prejudices, rather than create empathy. Within a community of learners, the passion that often accompanies debate can be channeled into mutual understanding and reasoned response.

During both small- and large-group discussions, it is important to establish an atmosphere of cooperation and mutual trust. As previously discussed, many issues will arise on which participants will have very different views, and emotions will inevitably surface. However, the point of case discussion is not to generate a debate and see who can win. The purpose of these cases is to come to some mutual understanding of the complex issues involved and to develop an informed and promising plan for addressing them. For example, once a school planning team has analyzed a problem that they are confronting through divergent thinking, the focus must switch to those alternatives around which stakeholders can reach some degree of consensus. Without agreement on an action plan, nothing is likely to change.

One of the most important skills needed in group discussions is empathetic listening (Cramer & Stivers, 2007). We must understand other's feelings and views of the world. Everyone has had the experience of having the person who follows them in a discussion repeat almost exactly the same ideas unnecessarily. This is probably because the person who followed was too focused on his or her own ideas to listen to the speaker. It is difficult to truly understand what someone is saying (and what he or she may mean but is not saying) while simultaneously constructing a response. More deliberate displays of poor listening are apparent when individuals keep their hand up the entire time that someone is speaking or simply interrupt the speaker. When people feel strongly about something, they are tempted to block out what others are saying and concentrate on getting their own point across. All members must develop the skills of encouragement, clarification, and summarization, which can facilitate an acceptable solution.

It is true that a listener's thoughts are constantly racing in front of the speaker. People simply can't speak as quickly as they can think. However, this allows the astute discussion group member to accomplish several things. She can check the notes from her reading for facts or interpretations, listen carefully and take notes on significant points of agreement or disagreement, and write down ideas that she would like to contribute. When recognized by the discussion leader, she is able to first check with the previous speaker about the accuracy of her own perceptions by reflecting or paraphrasing that person's contribution or asking a clarifying question. Then she can go on to expand on the topic or offer an alternative idea. This is a complicated skill, yet one worth cultivating, since it will also determine the success of your class discussions as a teacher and a member of a collaborative team. There are many extended treatments of the skills needed to develop the art of collaboration (Christensen, Garvin, & Sweet, 1991; Cramer, 2006; Friend & Cook, 2007; Miller & Kantrov, 1998) and we would highly recommend them.

One caveat we would offer is that there are many reasons why individuals modulate the amount and intensity of their contributions to the group. One factor can be a person's own racial or cultural identity. Our experience is that individuals who are not part of the racial or culturally dominant group in the class are not always comfortable with sharing their opinions and experiences. This may be because they are still forming their own racial identity or because they do not feel it is appropriate to speak for others. For example, an individual from an upper-class family in Puerto Rico may have very different experiences and opinions from the child of an undocumented Mexican farm worker. While all class members must be made to feel that their contributions are welcome, those who prefer to remain quiet should be allowed to pass. On the other hand, some individuals have repeatedly experienced racial injustice and may want to make others aware that there is not always equal treatment under the law. However, voicing such inequities in a public forum is always a risk for the speaker. Within the first few classes, all participants should agree on discussion ground rules. For example, we would suggest that all discussion be kept within the group unless permission is granted otherwise. Furthermore, revealing difficult personal experiences can evoke strong emotions of anger or sorrow. All participants must be willing to support each other when emotions overflow and understand that the listeners are not the objects of that emotion.

The cases in this text portray the questions and quandaries that perplex both novice and experienced teachers. The characters represent diverse cultural, linguistic, economic, educational, and religious backgrounds, and the events of these narratives extend beyond the classroom and include the community. You are now familiar with the Case Decision-Making Scaffold and can use it to think through these complex cases. Furthermore, you can utilize the guidelines for discussing the cases to improve the quality of your class interactions. Chapter 5 presents a case and discusses how using the Case Decision-Making Scaffold enables the class to conduct a comprehensive analysis of the case and determine an action plan.

References

Bruner, J. (1986). *Actual minds, possible worlds.* Cambridge, MA: Harvard University Press.

Christensen, C. R. (1987). *Teaching and the case method: Text, cases, and readings.* Cambridge, MA: Harvard Business School Press.

Christensen, C. R., Garvin, D. A., & Sweet, A. (1991). *Education for judgment: The artistry of discussion leadership.* Cambridge, MA: Harvard Business School Press.

Clandinin, D. J., & Connelly, F. M. (Eds.). (1995). *Teachers' professional knowledge landscapes.* New York: Teachers College Press.

Clandinin, D. J., & Connelly, F. M. (2000). *Narrative and inquiry: Experience and story in qualitative research.* San Francisco: Jossey Bass.

Clandinin, D. J., Pushor, D., & Orr, A. M. (2007). Navigating sites for narrative inquiry. *Journal of Teacher Education, 58*(1), 21–35.

Connelly, F. M., & Clandinin, D. J. (1988). *Teachers as curriculum planners.* New York: Teachers College Press.

Cramer, S. F. (2006). *The special educator's guide to collaboration.* Thousand Oaks, CA: Corwin Press.

Cramer, S., & Stivers, J. (2007). Don't give up! Practical strategies for challenging collaborations. *Teaching Exceptional Children, 39*(6), 6–11.

Doyle, W. (1990). Case methods in the education of teachers. *Teacher Education Quarterly, 1*(1), 7–15.

Doyle, W. (1997). Heard any really good stories lately? A critique of the critics of narrative in educational research. *Teaching and Teacher Education, 13*(1), 93–99.

Flynn, A. E., & Klein, J. D. (2001). The influence of discussion groups in a case-based learning environment. *Educational Technology Research and Development, 49*(3), 71–86.

Friend, M., & Cook, L. (2007). *Interactions: Collaboration skills for school professionals* (5th ed.). Boston: Allyn and Bacon.

Genor, M. (2005). A social reconstructionist framework for reflection: The "problematizing" of teaching. *Issues in Teacher Education, 14*(2), 45–62.

Goodlad, J. I. (1990). *Teachers for our nation's schools.* San Francisco: Jossey-Bass.

Harrington, J. (1995). Fostering reasoned decisions: Case-based pedagogy and the professional development of teachers. *Teaching & Teacher Education, 11*, 203–214.

Holmes Group. (1995). *Tomorrow's schools of education.* East Lansing: Michigan State University School of Education.

Hutchings, P. (1993). *Using cases to improve college teaching.* Washington, DC: American Association for Higher Education.

Kleinfeld, J. S. (1998). The use of case studies in preparing teachers for cultural diversity. *Theory into Practice, 37*(2), 140–147.

Leinhardt, G. (1990). Situated knowledge and expertise in teaching. In J. Calderhead (Ed.), *Teachers' professional knowledge* (pp. 146–168). London: Falmer.

Lincoln, Y. S., & Guba, E. G. (1985). *Naturalistic inquiry.* Newbury Park, CA: Sage.

Lundeberg, M. A. (1999). Discovering teaching and learning through cases. In M. A. Lundeberg, B. B. Levin, & H. L. Harrington (Eds.), *Who learns what from cases and how? The research base for teaching and learning with cases* (pp. 3–23). Mahwah, NJ: Lawrence Erlbaum.

Lundeberg, M. A., Levin, B. B., & Harrington, H. L. (Eds.) (1999). *Who learns what from cases and how? The research base for teaching and learning with cases.* Mahwah, NJ: Lawrence Erlbaum.

Miller, B., & Kantrov, I. (1998). *A guide to facilitating cases in education.* Portsmouth, NH: Heinemann.

Moje, E. B., & Wade, S. E. (1997). What case discussions reveal about teacher thinking. *Teaching and Teacher Education, 13*, 691–712.

National Commission on Teaching & America's Future. (1996). *What matters most: Teaching for America's future.* New York: Author.

Schön, D. (1987). *Educating the reflective practitioner.* San Francisco: Jossey-Bass.

Schön, D. (1991). *The reflective turn: Case studies in and on educational practice.* New York: Teachers College Press.

Shulman, J. H. (1996). Tender feelings, hidden thoughts: Confronting bias, innocence, and racism through case discussion. In A. Colbert, P. Desberg, & K. Trimble (Eds.), *The case for education: Contemporary approaches for using case methods* (pp. 137–158). Boston: Allyn and Bacon.

Shulman, L. S. (1987). Knowledge and teaching: Foundations of the new reform. *Harvard Educational Review, 57,* 114–135.

Shulman, L. S. (1996). Just in case: Reflections on learning from experience. In J. A. Colbert, P. Desberg, & K. Trimble (Eds.), *The case for education: Contemporary approaches for using case methods* (pp. 197–217). Boston: Allyn and Bacon.

Silberglitt, B., Jimerson, S. R., Burns, M. K., & Appleton, J. J. (2006). Does the timing of grade retention make a difference? Examining the effects of early versus later retention. *School Psychology Review, 35*(1), 134–141.

Silverman, R., & Welty, W. M. (1996). Teaching without a net: Using cases in teacher education. In J. A. Colbert, P. Desberg, & K. Trimble (Eds.), *The case for education: Contemporary approaches for using case methods* (pp. 159–172). Boston: Allyn and Bacon.

Sirotnik, K. A. (1991). Critical inquiry: A paradigm for praxis. In E. C. Short (Ed.), *Forms of curriculum inquiry* (pp. 243–258). Albany: State University of New York Press.

Sudzina, M. R. (Ed.) (1999). *Case study applications for teacher education: Cases of teaching and learning in the content areas.* Boston: Allyn & Bacon.

Wasserman, S. (1994). *Introduction to case method teaching: A guide to the galaxy.* New York: Teachers College Press.

Whittaker, C. R., & vanGarderen, D. (2007). *Enhancing teacher development using a metacognitive problem solving approach with case-based instruction.* Manuscript submitted for publication.

Zeichner, K. M., & Liston, D. P. (1996). *Reflective teaching: An introduction.* Mahwah, NJ: Lawrence Erlbaum.

5

Putting It All Together: Analyzing and Discussing a Case

The case studies in subsequent chapters are organized under seven issues of diversity: race and ethnicity, culture and language, poverty and socioeconomic status, exceptionalities, gender, sexual orientation, and religion. Each chapter begins with an overview of the issue, with background information and research that we believe to be important to a thorough discussion of the case. The primary issues involved in the cases are clearly related to the chapter title. Other issues will inevitably be relevant. Life, teaching, and these cases are complex.

This chapter is illustrative. It presents the case of Jesus Gonzalez and demonstrates how the authors would employ the Case Decision-Making Scaffold (see Table 4.1 on page 75). We provide relevant background information about migrant farmworkers before the case. We also encourage you to read the overview material in Chapter 7, since the primary focus of this case is culture and language.

Issues Regarding Migrant Farmworkers and Their Families

Migrant farmworkers are individuals who travel to work in agricultural, dairy, or fishing industries. Although they often live in camps or apartments near their work and are relatively invisible to the surrounding community, their labor is essential to the quality and low cost of fruits, vegetables, and other food products in the United States (Whittaker, Salend, & Gutierrez, 1997). Many of these individuals transition to other physically demanding jobs involving construction, landscaping, and ranching.

Migrant farmworkers usually fall into one of two groups based on their movement patterns (Martin, 1996). The largest group consists of workers who usually work in one location in the United States and then return to their homes in Mexico, Central America, or the Caribbean. Another group travels from state to state within the same *stream* from year to year. The three major streams in the United States are the eastern, mid-continent, and western streams (Triplett, 2004). Many migrants bring their families with them, and family members are often close-knit and take their responsibilities to one another very seriously. At least one-third of migrant students who live in the United States are limited English proficient (Salend, 2008; U.S. Department of Education, 2006). Migrant students come from many cultural backgrounds: Hispanics, 89 percent; white, 6 percent; black, 2 percent; Asian–Pacific Islander, 2 percent; and Native American or Native Alaskan, 1 percent.

Sometimes workers are asked by their employers to stay year round. Understandably, if a job exists, migrant farmworkers who are offered a place to live and a minimum wage for physically demanding work often decide to stay in a community all year. Often these circumstances, while unacceptable to most Americans, are better than those that they encounter in their country of origin. These families are often known as *resettled* migrants by the government agencies that provide services for them.

Migrant families face difficult socioeconomic conditions (Salend, 2008). A Department of Labor survey taken in the late 1990s found their average real hourly wages to be around $6.00 with over 60 percent of migrant farmworkers living below the poverty level (Triplett, 2004). They can work six or seven days per week for ten or more hours a day. Often they face poor sanitation in the fields and work camps, overcrowded or substandard housing, and limited healthcare. Migrants have the highest rate of chemically related illness of any occupational group due to pesticide exposure. Most migrant workers are afraid to report unsafe conditions since many are undocumented and fear deportation. Since the late 1990s, the percentage of migrant workers who are illegal immigrants—primarily from Mexico, Central America and the Caribbean—has grown from 52 percent to around 85 percent (Triplett, 2004). Children are often expected to take over household chores and childcare, and about a third of all migrant children work in the fields to help to support the family (Triplett, 2004). They usually live on the farms or in a nearby town or city with several families in one apartment. Usually they depend on others for transportation.

It is not surprising that children of migrant workers often face educational difficulties. Because of their mobility, they may attend schools that have very different educational requirements, programs, and organizational patterns. Furthermore, they have to adjust to new peers each time that they move. Unfortunately, migrant students report that they are sometimes teased and ostracized because of cultural, linguistic, or economic differences. Depending on when and where crops are harvested, migrant students may enroll in school more than thirty days after school begins. Unfortunately, the most recent data indicates that migrant children scored at levels at least 25 percent below students considered proficient in math and reading on both the third- and tenth-grade state assessments (U. S. Department of Education, 2006). The average migrant worker has about a sixth-grade education, and the dropout rate for migrant children is estimated at 65 percent (Triplett, 2004).

An interesting ethnographic study of migrant children who have succeeded in school points to important factors that have allowed these students to be resilient (Garza, Reyes, & Trueba, 2004). Successful students had personal characteristics of self-confidence, self-discipline, and an internal locus of control. Their families highly valued their children's education and gave strong emotional support. Furthermore, their schools and teachers held positive and high expectations of them. Often a particular teacher or staff member acted as a mentor. Finally, these students faced adversity by developing even greater determination and perseverance. They simply would not give up.

In order to encourage resiliency in migrant children, school staff must be aware of programs available to these students through local and state agencies (Hartman, 2006; Triplett, 2004).

The federal government provides limited funding to assist migrant farmworkers. States in which migrants work have a network of agencies that provide health, legal, and educational services to the families. For example, health clinics are available to provide children and adults with basic dental and health care since families do not have health insurance. Furthermore, Migrant Head Start provides preschool programs and transportation for 3- to 5-year-olds in some areas. In the past, educational centers provided tutoring for migrant children during the school year and a full-day summer program. However, due to federal funding cutbacks, some centers have changed to a family advocacy model. This service model assists families by assigning a caseworker who can help the family to access community resources such as literacy training or accompany them when interfacing with school or government agencies. However, individual tutoring for children is less available and summer programs are shorter and serve fewer children. In general, families who have resettled in an area lose services after three years.

It is incumbent on teachers to be aware of the challenges that the children of migrant and resettled workers face and to help them to feel welcome in their classrooms. Too often these children are ignored because they are expected to leave soon or are viewed as problems due to their linguistic differences. One way to assist migrant children in their adjustment to a new environment is to assign a bilingual peer as a buddy. In addition, teachers can introduce the classes to information about the migrant lifestyle. Shafer (2001) and Whittaker, et al. (1997) offer culturally sensitive instructional approaches and resources for integrating the lives of migrant children into the curriculum and emphasizing their significant contribution to our society.

One program that has been shown to have positive effects on the English language acquisition of young migrant children is family involvement training (St. Clair & Jackson, 2006). Parent educators worked closely with kindergarten teachers to provide migrant parents with weekly sessions that modeled how to support their children in learning the school curriculum. Technology and other resources for literacy learning were available for use at home. By the end of first grade the children in the program scored significantly higher on language measures than those who were not in the program.

Clearly, programs such as the ones described above can create an environment that encourages migrant children to reach their personal goals. However, ultimately it takes supportive families and school and community personnel who are willing to go the extra mile if these young people are to break out of the cycle of poverty. When the children of migrant farmworkers are successful in reaching their goals, they become adults whose contributions to our communities are positive and needed.

The Case of Jesus Gonzalez

My first graders had just returned from gym. I knew from hearing their loud voices coming down the hall and seeing their sweaty foreheads as they careened into the classroom that I needed to read them a story before we began the social studies lesson on community helpers that afternoon. All the children were gathered around me on the rug as I read them *The Very Hungry Caterpillar.*

We had just finished the part where the caterpillar had gorged himself and wasn't feeling so well. I looked up from the story, sensing that someone was at the door. A short, sturdy man in dusty jeans and a John Deere feed cap with a "visitor" button on his sweatshirt was waiting there. Not recognizing his face, I rose and approached him.

"May I help you?" I asked.

"Si. I come to get Jesus," he responded, looking beyond me.

Then I remembered that the office had told me that Jesus had to leave early on family business that day.

"Of course," I replied, being sure to smile. "Jesus, get your backpack and jacket."

The rest of the class stayed in their circle, but strained to see the visitor.

"Hey, Jesus. Is that your dad?" queried the ever-curious Zachery.

Jesus ignored him and quickly went to his desk to collect his things. I turned to Mr. Gonzalez, hoping to make him feel welcome.

"It's nice to meet you. I enjoy having your son in class."

Mr. Gonzalez took a step backward and smiled. Jesus was still reaching into the black hole he had created in his desk.

"Vamanos! Es la hora, Jesus!" his father commanded.

Jesus's surprised face appeared from behind his desktop. Clearly embarrassed, Jesus screamed out, "Stop talking Spanish in here!"

Mr. Gonzalez was speechless. He stepped outside the door and Jesus quickly followed.

Jesus's father was halfway down the hall with Jesus running after him before I realized that I had not even said goodbye. My feeble attempt to do so went unheeded. I was so thrown by this brief interchange that I simply could not respond.

What should I have said? "Adios, senor"? This was about the extent of my Spanish. Should I have told Jesus that all languages were welcome in this classroom? Would I be usurping Mr. Gonzalez's parental role by interfering, not to mention embarrassing him further? What should I say to the other children? This kind of situation had never come up in my four years of teaching first grade.

But then, I told myself, why would it? Jesus was the first culturally and linguistically diverse student I had had in my first-grade class. In fact, there were only a handful of these students in the entire school. In our small midwestern town of 7,500 about 98 percent of the population was white and came from European heritage. We live in an area with many truck farms, so Mexican families come here to pick tomatoes and other vegetables. However, most of them leave before school starts. Those who stay on for a few weeks in September often wait until they return home to enroll the children in school. These families usually live on the farms and, although I might see them at the supermarket on Friday evenings cashing their checks and buying groceries, I had little contact with them.

I knew from several conversations with Jesus's kindergarten teacher from last year, Susan Bigelow, that Jesus had been identified as speech impaired and that was why he went for speech therapy for half an hour three times per week. He had not progressed academically or socially as the teacher had hoped, and there was discussion about having him repeat kindergarten. However, a compromise was reached, and during this school year Jesus is in my first-grade class in the morning and with Carolyn Davis, kindergarten teacher, in the afternoon. It was hoped that he would be able to make the transition to first grade more smoothly if he could experience it more gradually. Of course, we also knew that he might need to stay in first grade for another year after this. After four months of working with Jesus, I have little reason to hope that he will be able to manage second grade in the fall.

Besides being pulled out for speech, Jesus goes to ESL instruction with Ms. Vanderpool for half an hour three times a week during our language arts time. Ms. Vanderpool is not a certified bilingual teacher nor does she speak Spanish. However, I think she has been helping him with vocabulary. Susan Bigelow is the one teacher in the school who can speak basic Spanish, and she could talk with the family if I needed to communicate with Jesus's parents. Truthfully, however, until Mr. Gonzalez's appearance at my door, we had had no contact.

I felt somewhat guilty about this because Jesus was having some problems in my classroom. It seemed that Jesus's oral language was improving, but he was still behind in reading, simple addition, and handwriting skills. He lacked organizational skills and was having difficulty working independently. I also was concerned that he often did not have homework completed. Part of me felt that he should have remained in kindergarten where he could develop socially one more year and learn how to "do school."

I could tell that Jesus desperately wanted to be accepted by his peers. This outburst was just one example of his desire to be just like everyone else. He seemed to get along with Zachery and Jonathan and stayed close to them on the playground. However, he was very quiet and shy around most of the other children. He wasn't disliked by anyone; however, he remained on the fringes of the social scene.

After this encounter with Jesus and his father, I decided that I had better talk with Jim McIntyre, our district social worker. He, in turn, put me in touch with Luis Torres, an outreach worker from the Migrant Center, a state-funded agency that helps migrant farmworkers to connect with social and educational agencies when they work in our area. Luis had visited Jesus's family in their home and knew something of their family history. He was extremely helpful in providing information about Jesus's family, which helped me to better understand the ways in which they valued school and the expectations that they had for their son.

Luis explained that Jesus lives with his father, mother, and 4-year-old brother in a small trailer located behind a large packing house on a farm. His father, who is in his early thirties, is a foreman who does odd jobs on the farm, and Mrs. Gonzalez works in the packing plant. Although they are paid only minimum wage, the family is pleased with the arrangement because they live in the trailer rent free with all utilities paid all year around. Therefore, they are able to save some money and hope to buy their own home someday. Mrs. Gonzalez likes working near home so that she can meet the school bus each day.

Mr. and Mrs. Gonzalez came from Mexico seven years ago in search of a better life. Jesus lived in Mexico with his grandmother for nine months when he was 2, but he has been in the United States the rest of his life. The Gonzalezes wanted their children to be born and raised in the United States so that they could get a good education and not have to rely on farmwork to sustain themselves.

Although the family views the educational opportunities in the United States as a benefit, they are worried about the influence that U.S. culture may have on their children. They have extended family in a town about an hour away, but see them only once every other month. Their social contacts, though few, are primarily with other Mexican and Jamaican farmworkers. Jesus is very close to his younger brother and spends most of his time after school playing Nintendo or watching television with him. Just recently, Jesus has been allowed to invite his best friend over to visit once a week if he behaves and does his schoolwork. When he does not complete his work, his parents remind him that if he fails school they will have to return to Mexico where Jesus will have to tend cows for a living and work in the fields all day long.

It was enlightening to know more about Jesus's family life, but I couldn't help but feel that the child I saw in school was not necessarily the same child his parents saw at home. Behind those dark brown eyes that peered out from under a thick fringe of straight, brown-black hair, was a developing mind that I did not fully understand. Yesterday in class was no exception. I asked Jesus for his completed homework and he simply responded, "I forgot." I rummaged through his desk to find his folder and pulled out all the assignments he had not completed. Hoping that he would make up his work in class, I numbered them in the order in which they should be completed and asked him to get to work. Within 5 minutes, Jesus was wandering around the room. He picked up a fallen art project and walked over to my desk.

"Here, Mrs. Kniffen, someone dropped this."

"Thank you, Jesus. Now please go back to your seat and get to work," I responded without looking up.

"But I didn't do it. I just found it on the floor," he interjected.

"Give it to me and I'll put it away. Thank you," I responded, trying to be patient.

Jesus never made it back to his seat. He sat next to Zachery and played with his ruler for awhile. Then he grabbed a pencil from his desk, sharpened it for 2 minutes, and strolled around the room looking at everyone else's work.

"Jesus, you are already behind. Now get back to your desk and finish your work," I said firmly.

I wish that I could say that he finally responded to me, but, in fact, he was up again, ostensibly looking for math manipulatives, in another 2 minutes. However, he passed them by and continued to wander. Not until Mrs. Adams, my teaching assistant, gave him the box of manipulatives did he sit down and start to work.

Although we had an open house in the fall and I sent home monthly newsletters, I had never met either parent or received any communication from them until Mr. Gonzalez arrived at my door. I finally decided that I must have a parent conference and asked the Gonzalezes to come to school. Mr. Torres agreed to come and translate when they had difficulty understanding my English. Mrs. Gonzalez arrived with Mr. Torres at the scheduled time, but said that her husband had to work. I started by telling her how much I liked her son and how well he seemed to get along with his small circle of friends.

"He is a very friendly boy who loves people," she said, smiling slightly.

"I am afraid, however, that he is not very organized in school and often does not bring in his homework," I added.

Mrs. Gonzalez agreed, but said that they always insist that he do his homework each evening. However, she admitted that more recently he has been leaving the kitchen table before he is done to watch television. She is bothered by this disobedience and insists that he return to his work. Then she reported that one evening last week, when she told him to return to his work, he screamed, "No!" He proceeded to slam the refrigerator door and pouted for two hours. Although she has tried letting him go to bed and complete his work in the morning, this plan is rarely successful. She promised that she would force him to complete his work at the table and tell him his best friend would not be able to come over if he did not.

I wanted to impress on Mrs. Gonzalez that Jesus is becoming more fluent in English, but that he is easily distracted and lacks many skills in reading and mathematics. Once again I stressed that, because of his immaturity, he was better off being in first grade half the day. She seemed unsure of this, but yielded to my expertise.

Mrs. Gonzalez wanted me to understand that she was doing the best that she could with her son, but that her own limited English proficiency made it difficult for her to do more. What she did see as her area of control was Jesus's social life. She said that they have kept Jesus and his brother away from the prejudiced people outside the farm and associate with Jamaicans and African American farmworkers that they work with who share their circumstances. They maintain their culture by speaking only Spanish at home and buying Mexican foods in the city nearby. She said that she did not want her children to be exposed to the bad influences that she observed in some local children, although she didn't elaborate.

Although Mrs. Gonzalez and I had ended our meeting with a considerable amount of good will, I found myself staring out the window as she and Mr. Torres left the parking lot. I could not help but feel that there were many things that she was probably expressing to Luis that she would never say to me.

I could empathize with Jesus's mother, yet I wondered if we had made any real progress. We agreed that I would stay in contact with her regarding Jesus's progress and homework completion. However, I doubted that this would have any effect on his performance in school, particularly when she simply could not help him that much. I was haunted by the few defiant outbursts that came from this usually good-spirited boy. Nor could I understand the quiet defiance he displayed by being a nomad in my classroom.

Using the Case Decision-Making Scaffold

Recognize the Problem

The trigger event that alerts us to a problem is Jesus's demand that his father speak English in school. Although Mrs. Kniffen, Jesus's teacher, has been very aware of the academic and behavioral difficulties, this event prompts her into action. For us to determine the source of the problems involved, it is important to identify the relevant information that the case provides regarding each individual or constituency.

The facts that we can garner from the case regarding Jesus are that he is below first-grade level in reading, math, and handwriting, although his oral language skills in English seem to be improving. He lacks organizational skills, is easily distracted, doesn't work well independently, and often does not complete homework. Furthermore, Mrs. Kniffen believes that he is socially immature and notes that he has only two friends in the class.

The school responded to Jesus's difficulties in kindergarten by placing him part time in first grade and kindergarten during this school year. He also has speech and language services three times a week for half-hour sessions and an equivalent amount of time with the English as a Second Language teacher, who does not speak Spanish. The school has a social worker and has placed a teaching assistant in Mrs. Kniffen's classroom, although we know little of their involvement with Jesus.

The community is a small, midwestern farming town, the population of which is 98 percent white. Most farmworkers come for the summer growing season and harvest and leave in the fall. It appears that they live on the farms and have very little contact with community members.

Mrs. Kniffen is a first-grade teacher who has never before had a student who is culturally and linguistically diverse. She doesn't speak Spanish and is unsure of how to interact with the Gonzalez family, although she does feel guilty about it. She notes that she has had minimal contact with the Mexicans that do come in the summer. She tells Mrs. Gonzalez that it is good for Jesus to be part time in kindergarten and first grade, but also lists the multiple academic and social problems that he is having.

The Gonzalez family is living in the United States because the wages that they earn are better than what is available in Mexico. Both parents work on a local farm, where the grower provides them with a trailer for housing. They speak Spanish and need a translator to communicate with school staff. Jesus has a younger brother who is his primary companion at home, although occasionally another friend is allowed to visit. Their social life is confined to other farmworkers and occasional contact with relatives in another town. Lately, they have been experiencing difficulty getting Jesus to complete his homework.

There are many discrepancies between various individuals' expectations and actual events. Mrs. Kniffen clearly expects that Jesus should pay attention in school, complete his homework, and make academic progress, given the program that the school has provided and the curriculum that she has established. She admits that she has little experience with students from diverse backgrounds and has many unanswered questions about Jesus's behavior, but she believes she is treating Jesus fairly and with concern. At this point, we can only make conjectures about Jesus's lack of academic engagement. However, he obviously wants to please his teacher and make friends. His need for belonging is equated with speaking English. Not wanting to be different, he reacts strongly when his father speaks to him in Spanish in front of his peers.

Like Mrs. Kniffen, Jesus's parents want him to complete his homework and do well in school, especially since this is one of the major reasons they came to the United States. They also want him to be a respectful child and obey their requests. However, they would prefer that his social contacts be limited to families of other farmworkers and relatives.

The school expects that children like Jesus will progress within the standard school curriculum and educational program. Obviously, they view the services performed by the ESL and speech language teacher as appropriate for his needs. The school has decided that it is reasonable and, in fact, beneficial for Jesus to be in kindergarten and first grade half-days.

The school also expects that all parents are receiving adequate communication regarding their children's progress through the traditional methods of open house and letters home. Furthermore, the Migrant Center and Mr. Torres have no regular access to the teachers of the children they serve.

Given this differences in expectations, several major problems emerge from the case. There is inadequate communication between the school and home. Furthermore, Jesus's current educational program is not meeting his academic and social needs. A related problem is that teachers do not seem well prepared in strategies for teaching students from culturally and linguistically diverse backgrounds. Finally, there are no established linkages between the community services available for families and the school.

Reframe the Problem

To frame the problem, we must look beyond the facts to the values and beliefs of the individuals involved, since understanding these perspectives is critical to finding effective solutions. When individuals come from different cultures and must speak through a translator, the chances that their assumptions will differ or not be fully communicated increase. A culturally responsive teacher will be aware that her perspectives are culturally bound and make every attempt to understand those of students and parents who come from other cultures.

Jesus's parents place a high value on education. They see it as the only way to avoid the very poor conditions of their own childhood and the difficult, physically demanding labor that they both perform. At the same time, they are proud of their Mexican roots, language, and culture. Yet they live in a community in which few speak Spanish, and the Mexican culture is not celebrated or even apparent. As is true of most Latino families, one of their highest values is family unity. The Gonzalezes believe that their lifestyle is not acceptable to the community at large, and they have deepened this marginalization by choosing to keep to themselves.

In traditional Latino families, the father is the provider and protector of the family and is to be respected. Therefore, we can assume that Jesus's outburst in response to his father's request in Spanish was very disturbing to Mr. Gonzalez, both because of his place in the family and his high regard for his first language. Perhaps Mr. Gonzalez viewed this as just one more indication that, while school is a place to gain an education, a U.S. school will also expose his son to many bad influences. Mrs. Gonzalez certainly said that she didn't want Jesus to be exposed to the negative behavior that she observed in local children.

The fact that Jesus would dare reprimand his father in public demonstrates the extent to which he is struggling to negotiate the worlds of home and school. For half the day he lives in a white, English-only environment that espouses the values of academic success and individual achievement. He undoubtedly knows that his dual placement is an indication of his academic failure. He, like most children, wants to be accepted by his peers, but is unable to communicate enough to make significant social contacts. He is trying to acculturate, but knows that his parents would rather that he avoid the children who surround him all day. The rest of the day he lives in a Mexican, Spanish-only environment that is quite isolated. His frustration in trying to negotiate these two worlds may explain his refusal to complete homework when asked by both his parents and teachers. Neither parents nor teachers really seem able to help him academically.

Mrs. Kniffen and the other school staff assume that the school is providing for Jesus's needs in a way that exceeds what is provided to the typical student. They view the ESL and speech language pullout services as adequate and therefore don't understand why Jesus is not making greater progress. They see the split-day schedule as a positive approach compared to retention, the first option that they had considered. Mrs. Kniffen views Jesus's nomad behavior as a kind of quiet defiance from an otherwise kind boy. Even after the conference with Mrs. Gonzalez, she doubts that Jesus's performance will improve. While she promises to stay in contact with Mrs. Gonzalez, she does not discuss any concrete methods for communicating with her in the future, despite their language differences. Nor does she ask for further communication with Mr. Torres.

There is no indication that Mrs. Kniffen has included information in the curriculum that explains Mexican culture or history in order to help Jesus feel comfortable with his culture and language and gain recognition from the other children. Furthermore, the school sees no reason to provide more extensive ESL or bilingual services. There is no discussion of what is reasonable to expect in terms of language acquisition when a child's only language prior to entering school was Spanish. The assumption is that the problem lies with Jesus and not with the school.

Although no open hostility is apparent in this case, there is a great deal of misunderstanding and mistrust beneath the surface. It is critical that all the individuals involved have the opportunity to understand and communicate these differences in beliefs and find those things that they can agree on. The promising aspect of the case is that both the parents and the school seem to agree that it is important for Jesus to progress in school and receive an education. Given that common ground, they must attempt to discuss alternatives that will accomplish this goal without compromising their basic beliefs.

Search for Alternatives

The issue of how to work with students who come from culturally and linguistically diverse backgrounds is new to Mrs. Kniffen, but it is an issue with which many schools across the country have dealt, some with great success. Although many of these districts lie in urban areas where there is a more diverse population than described here, most areas of the United States are facing similar challenges today. Therefore, it is critical to be informed about programs, practices, and instructional approaches that improve the educational process for children like Jesus.

In addition, we must understand that there may be immediate, short-term actions that can make a difference for Jesus. However, for students like Jesus to be successful, the district must consider a model to implement comprehensive school reform that will sustain positive educational programs over time (McChesney & Hertling, 2000). Ultimately, changes that assist Jesus must be supported by an entire school program that will promote high standards for all students, including those who are culturally and linguistically diverse. Thus, we must understand those factors that currently impede his progress and design a program that will eliminate these barriers.

Research tells us that Jesus faces multiple barriers to learning. First, while he is acquiring basic interpersonal communication skills (BICS) in English, he has only been exposed to the English language consistently for a little over a year and to ESL instruction for several months. In other words, he can communicate on the playground with friends but does not have cognitive academic learning proficiency (CALP), the extensive vocabulary needed to comprehend academic tasks (Cummins, 1984). We know that children need CALP as well as discrete phonological and grammatical language skills to achieve in school and that this type of language proficiency may take four to seven years to acquire depending upon the child's proficiency in their first language and the amount of uninterrupted schooling in their country of origin (Cummins, 2003; Thomas & Collier, 2002). We also know that second language learners often present academic difficulties that appear to be learning disabilities, but actually result from the normal process of language acquisition, while others actually are delayed in both languages (Wilkinson, Ortiz, Robertson, & Kushner 2006). Furthermore, immigrants go through stages of adjustment and sometimes exhibit a "silent period" during which they listen to a new language, but say little (Igoa, 1995). Proper assessment and comprehensive planning that support Jesus's understanding of Spanish while he acquires English are clearly needed. Several studies have found that when students are taught in their first language it is easier for them to learn a second language as well as keep up with peers in the content of the general education curriculum (Krashen, 2005; Thomas & Collier, 2002). The controversy over whether children learn best in bilingual education programs continues to rage; however, the practical reality is that there are not enough students in Jesus's school and age range to financially support such a program. Therefore, it is critical that all teachers, not just the ESL teacher, differentiate instruction by using effective ESL approaches (Salend, 2008).

"Student academic motivation, commitment to democratic values, and resistance to problem behaviors all depend on their experience of the school as a community" (Schaps & Lewis, 1999, p. 215). It is difficult for students who do not hear their first language in school, do not see their culture and history in their textbooks or classroom walls, and do not see teachers of their racial group to experience a caring community. Yet this Eurocentric experience of school is still the norm in schools today (Bohn & Sleeter, 2000). One way that teachers can create community is by including the languages, traditions, and histories of their students in the curriculum when possible.

We also know that a key component to student success is the support of families and the community. Although Jesus's parents want desperately to see Jesus succeed in school, they face many barriers in their attempt to achieve this. Parents who do not speak English and know little about the culture of American schools are not likely to be involved in their child's education (Mitchell & Bryan, 2007). They are limited in the extent to which they can offer their child academic assistance at home or advocate for their child at school. If they feel uncomfortable in the school or experience prejudice from the community, there is little likelihood that they will be willing to use the regular communication channels (parent–teacher conference, phone calls, notes, parent–teacher organization meetings, volunteering and the like).

Long-term solutions for this situation involve examining the academic subject areas across grade levels, implementing research-based changes, sharing common goals, providing professional development, aligning resources across grade and content areas, and facilitating parent and community involvement (Education Commission of the States, 1998). In particular, the district must determine how it can best design programs for students who do not reach state or local standards and students who are second language learners. Furthermore, it must involve community members, including parents whose first language is not English, and community agencies as it sets goals and determines priorities. Teachers must be provided with in-service education that will assist them in incorporating the principles of multicultural education into their teaching philosophy and introducing research-based instructional strategies for second language learners.

The task of choosing goals that will address the issues in this case must be accomplished collaboratively by the family, school district, and community. This joint effort should be based on the belief held by all stakeholders that it is important for Jesus to gain an education. Based upon the review of research outlined above, stakeholders should be better prepared to set forth a plan of action to accomplish the following goals: (1) improve home and school communication, (2) redesign an educational program for Jesus, (3) prepare school staff to work effectively with students from culturally and linguistically diverse backgrounds, and (4) establish linkages with community services and develop new initiatives.

Develop and Implement Plan of Action

Mrs. Kniffen has already taken the first step toward improving communication by meeting with Mrs. Gonzalez and Mr. Torres. Given the desire by all that Jesus improve academically and the rich research on the positive outcomes of family involvement on school achievement, it makes sense to make the goal of improving home and school communication a priority.

It is essential that a plan of action be developed that clearly defines each goal, establishes methods to implement the goal, assigns responsibility to specific individuals, and determines criteria and time lines for evaluation. The goal of establishing communication might be accomplished by identifying translators for parent–teacher meetings, establishing regular planning meetings, and identifying a bilingual advocate for the Gonzalez family from the community, and determining a method for other communications (see Table 5.1). While accomplishing each of these action steps will undoubtedly require the services of various individuals in the school and community, it is important to assign responsibility for each step to one or two individuals. Similarly, workable criteria and a time line are critical for evaluating progress.

Once an effective communication system is established, it will be possible to determine an action plan that includes both short- and long-term goals for improving the educational program for Jesus and other students like him. As stated previously, cases do not have one answer. Each time we discuss these cases with participants, outcomes vary based on the beliefs of the discussants, access and exposure to research and expertise, individual experience, and time available. However, the goals that discussants establish are frequently similar. In this case, additional goals often include redesigning an educational program for Jesus, professional development for teachers in strategies for teaching students who are culturally and linguistically diverse, and establishing a district task force to examine resources and programs for all students. An example of one plan of action for accomplishing these goals is listed in Table 5.2.

TABLE 5.1   *Goal 1: Improve Home and School Communication*

Activity, Referral, Resource, Strategy	Person(s) Responsible	Criteria for Evaluation	Time Line
1. Identify translators for parent and teacher meetings	School social worker	Translators attend each meeting and parents indicate understanding of conversation	One month
2. Establish regular parent-school meetings to develop and implement a program for Jesus	Mrs. Kniffen School social worker	An educational program that results in academic and social improvement for Jesus	Monthly
3. Identify bilingual advocate for Jesus's family who can attend school meetings	Luis Torres School social worker	Advocate attends all meetings at request of parents and assists with implementation of Jesus's program	As needed
4. Determine method for communication between parents and school beyond regular meetings	Luis Torres School social worker	Parents receive communication from school in Spanish	As needed

TABLE 5.1   *Goals 2–4*

Activity, Referral, Resource, Strategy	Person(s) Responsible	Criteria for Evaluation	Time Line
Goal 2: Redesign an Educational Program for Jesus			
1. Assess Jesus's academic abilities in English and Spanish	Mrs. Kniffen ESL teacher	Written report of standardized and informal assessments	Within two weeks
2. Meet with Child Study Team, Jesus's teacher, and parents to discuss assessment and determine appropriate educational program	Child Study Team coordinator	Plan of action designed at Child Study Team meeting	Within one month
3. Establish collaborative program that utilizes present school staff and community resources to educate Jesus	Mrs. Kniffen School social worker	Meeting of school staff and community agencies to coordinate instructional program for Jesus	Bimonthly
4. Determine Jesus's educational needs that are not met by present school program and program development needs for other students who are culturally and linguistically diverse	Child Study Team coordinator	Written report of program development needs for the principal and Board of Education	Within four months

Goal 3: Prepare School Staff to Work Effectively with Students from Culturally and Linguistically Diverse Backgrounds

1. Assess school staff needs for professional development and curriculum materials and technology for working with diverse students	Building Leadership Team Coordinator	Survey of professional development and curricular materials needs	Within one month
2. Identify inservice approach and qualified professionals to facilitate professional development	Building Leadership Team Coordinator	Evaluation of professional development by school staff	Within three months
3. Determine specific materials needed based upon established school curriculum and student diversity	Curriculum Committee Coordinator	List of materials and technology needed for library and specific grade levels	Within five months

(continued)

TABLE 5.2   *Continued*

Activity, Referral, Resource, Strategy	Person(s) Responsible	Criteria for Evaluation	Time Line
4. Request and approval of materials and technology	Superintendent and Board of Education	Materials and technology supplied	Within seven months
5. School staff enact professional development plans that incorporate inservice training and new materials and technology	Principal and School staff	School staff are evaluated based upon professional development plans	Within one year

Goal 4: Establish Linkages with Community Services and Develop New Initiatives

1. Establish task force to identify community services available to students and families	Superintendent	List of Community Task Force members	Within one month
2. Determine present services available in the community	Community Task Force chair	List of contact information for all community services	Within three months
3. Disseminate listing of contact information to school staff and community members	Community Task Force chair	List is available to all online or in hard copy in English and Spanish	Within six months
4. Determine needed community services for children and families	Community Task Force chair	Focus groups with community members	Within eight months
5. Develop new community services	Appropriate community agency	Funded grant proposal	Within two years

Evaluate Progress

The evaluation of progress is essential to the success of any action plan. The evaluation process is tied to the discussion of teacher reflection in Chapter 4. While we have chosen to display evaluation as the last part of the Case Decision-Making Scaffold, evaluation or reflection is an ongoing process that all individuals concerned must undertake individually and collectively. Regular meetings of stakeholders formalize the reflection process and establish a means for revising the plan of action when needed.

In the cases presented in the following chapters, we have presented one slice of a real teaching situation. We have chosen not to present follow-up information for these cases so that the discussants can analyze the case from their own perspectives. However, occasionally we have been able to follow up on a case. Because we believe that evaluation is a critical component of change, we have chosen to present further information about Jesus so that readers will be able to evaluate the progress of the plan of action that was actually undertaken.

Follow-Up on Jesus Gonzalez

As I thought more about my meeting with Mrs. Gonzalez and Mr. Torres, I decided that I would make an attempt to include more of the Spanish language and Mexican American culture in my classroom. However, I did not have the background in second language acquisition or curriculum resources in my classroom to give Jesus the support and recognition that he needed. Certainly, I could consider getting additional training in working with students like Jesus, but that was a long-term solution. I needed help now. Mrs. Vanderpool was doing what she could three times a week for Jesus, but I wanted to know what I should do the other 28½ hours each week when Jesus was with me.

I called Mr. Torres the next day and asked if he had any ideas. He suggested that I try to encourage Jesus to talk about his family, culture, and language with the rest of the class so that they would understand more about Jesus. I agreed that it would be important for Jesus's self-concept to be able to share these things with the others, but that he resisted any attempts I had made to get him to speak to me privately about his language and culture; I doubted that he would talk to the whole class. Then he had a wonderful suggestion. He said that he knew that there was a graduate program in education at Clearwater State that was designed to encourage students to get their master's in multicultural education. He knew of someone in the program who used to work with him and thought perhaps I could find out more through her.

It wasn't easy making the contacts, but within two weeks Estrella Cortez was on her way to my classroom to observe Jesus. She was enrolled in the graduate program that Mr. Torres had mentioned and was interested in observing and possibly designing a curriculum unit for my class to fulfill a class assignment. The first time Estrella came she just sat in the back of the class, observed, and took copious notes. Jesus was off task at least half of the time she was there. The next week she sat with Jesus as he was trying to complete his reading worksheet and noted the words that he could not read or write. She also spent time just talking with him about his family and told him about her memories of first grade in Puerto Rico. Although she did not try to speak to Jesus in Spanish, I'm sure he realized from her accent that her first language was Spanish, too.

We spent time after school discussing Jesus's areas of strength and weakness. I told Estrella about the incident in class with Mr. Gonzalez, as well as of my conversation with Mr. Torres and Mrs. Gonzalez. She suggested that she come to my class weekly for a month and read children's literature that related to his culture and language to the whole class. Then she would plan activities that related to the books. She wouldn't single him out unless he volunteered. I readily agreed, since I knew the number of books in the school library about Mexican Americans was limited; at least it wouldn't hurt.

The first week Estrella read *Radio Man*, the story of a Mexican American family that travels from Texas to the Pacific Northwest to pick crops. The son always listens to the local radio stations and sends messages in to these stations about his arrival to an area. He hopes that his best friend will hear the message and contact him. It is a bilingual text, so Estrella read both languages to the children and they were spellbound. They wanted to know how to say different words in Spanish, and Estrella was happy to respond and obviously proud of her first language. Afterward she asked if anyone knew a migrant worker or spoke Spanish. Jesus did not say a word and she did not press him.

Fortunately, Estrella wasn't easily discouraged by Jesus's lack of response. She said that she understood what a big risk it is to talk about being different in any way when you want so much to be accepted. The next week she brought in the book *Con Mi Hermano*, a delightful bilingual text about two brothers. She began to read the English and then the Spanish. Then she asked if there was anyone who would like to help her read. I'm still not sure whether it was because the book was on an easy reading level or because it was about two brothers or because Jesus had seen the children enjoy Estrella reading in Spanish last week. But Jesus volunteered to read—in both English and Spanish! The children applauded when he was through, and he was beaming. During snack time, the children crowded around Jesus; they wanted him to talk in Spanish and teach them new words.

Estrella said that she wanted to visit Jesus's family in their home, and I said it was fine with me, if his parents consented. Mrs. Gonzalez agreed to have Estrella visit after school the next week. Estrella talked about the progress she thought Jesus was making both in staying on task and in his willingness to speak Spanish. Of course, Mrs. Gonzalez was very pleased. Estrella took her several books that were in English and Spanish that she could read with her son. Mrs. Gonzalez said that it was hard for her to visit the school—that there were too many Anglos there. However, she was grateful for the help that Jesus was getting and recognized that, to some extent, he was going to be Americanized.

I knew things were changing for Jesus when Estrella read *Amazing Grace* to the class. Grace is a willowy African American girl who wants to be Peter Pan in the school play, but is told that she can't since Peter Pan is white. Ultimately, she gets to star in the show and says, "No one can tell me I can't." Estrella set up a role play in class in which the main character needed to speak Spanish. Jesus immediately volunteered. When asked by the classmate in the role play, "What if someone told you that you couldn't speak Spanish?" Jesus boldly replied, "No one can tell me I can't."

The last week Estrella came to class she asked the students to draw a poster with a picture of themselves on it. They were supposed to write down things that they could do and that they liked about themselves. Jesus had several things written on his poster, but the one that I will always remember is "Yo hablo Espanol" (see Figure 5.1).

Evaluation of Follow-Up to the Case of Jesus Gonzalez

The follow-up to the case portrays a much more hopeful view of Mrs. Kniffen's approach to Jesus's education and his attitude toward school. Mrs. Kniffen recognizes that she is lacking in the professional knowledge and curriculum materials needed to assist Jesus. She acknowledges that she needs additional professional development in instructional approaches for English language learners. However, she also wants immediate assistance and uses contacts through the Migrant Center and the local university to identify

FIGURE 5.1 Jesus's Poster

a graduate student, Estrella, who is able to serve as a role model for Jesus, implement effective instructional approaches, and provide appropriate children's literature that celebrates Jesus's language and culture. Estrella's demonstration of ESL approaches also serves as an excellent model for Mrs. Kniffen to use in planning her future lessons.

When we read Jesus's confident assertion that no one can tell him not to speak Spanish, we must admit that Jesus's attitude toward his first language has undergone significant change. This is a major breakthrough that can fuel motivation toward further academic and social progress. However, if we examine the goals identified in the plan of action, we must also recognize that the short-term solutions enacted so far are only a start. Although Estrella has contacted Mrs. Gonzalez, the communication process between school staff and the family is unchanged. Similarly, while Mrs. Kniffen now sees the academic and social benefits of using multicultural literature with her class, she still needs professional development in strategies for working with culturally and linguistically diverse students. Furthermore, apart from the changes that have occurred due to Estrella's presence in the classroom, Jesus's educational program remains the same. In fact, the goals that are most likely to institute long-term change in the district have not even begun. The entire school staff needs professional development in multicultural education, and the district has no comprehensive plan for establishing linkages to community services.

The cases in the following chapters are equally as complex as that of Jesus and require a comprehensive response. As demonstrated, the Case Decision-Making Scaffold provides participants with a guide for thoroughly discussing and reflecting on each case. Furthermore, we trust that it will provide a helpful support for your deliberations as you face other equally challenging cases in your teaching career.

References

Bohn, A. P., & Sleeter, C. E. (2000). Multicultural education and the standards movement: A report from the field. *Phi Delta Kappan, 82,* 156–159.

Cummins, J. (1984). *Bilingualism and special education: Issues in assessment and pedagogy.* San Diego: College-Hill.

Cummins, J. (2003). Reading and the bilingual students: Fact and friction. In G. Garcia, (Ed.), *English learners: Reaching the highest level of English literacy* (pp. 2–33). Newark, DE: International Reading Association.

Education Commission of the States. (1998). *Comprehensive school reform: Identifying effective models.* Denver, CO: Author.

Garza, E., Reyes, & Trueba, E. R. (2004). *Resiliency and success: Migrant children in the United States.* Boulder, CO: Paradigm Publishers.

Hartman, C. (2006). Students on the move. *Educational Leadership, 63*(5), 20–24.

Igoa, C. (1995). *The inner world of the immigrant child.* New York: St. Martin's Press.

Krashen, S. (2005). Skyrocketing scores: An urban legend. *Educational Leadership, 62*(4), 37–39.

Martin, P. L. (1996). Migrant farmworkers and their children: What recent labor department data show. In J. L. Flores (Ed.), *Children of LaFrontera: Binational efforts to serve Mexican migrant immigrant students* (pp. 19–24). Charleston, WV: Clearinghouse on Rural Education and Small Schools.

McChesney, J., & Hertling, E. (2000). The path to comprehensive school reform. *Educational Leadership, 57*(7), 10–15.

Mitchell, N. A., & Bryan, J. A. (2007). School-family-community partnerships: Strategies for school counselors working with Caribbean immigrant families. *Professional School Counseling, 10*(4), 399–409.

Salend, S. J. (2008) *Creating inclusive classrooms: Effective and reflective practices* (6th ed.). Upper Saddle River, NJ: Merrill/Prentice Hall.

Schaps, E., & Lewis, C. (1999). Perils on an essential journey: Building school community. *Phi Delta Kappan, 81,* 215–218.

Shafer, G. (2001). Standard English and the migrant community. *English Journal, 90*(4), 37–43.

St. Clair, L., & Jackson, B. (2006). Effect of family involvement training on the language skills of young elementary children from migrant families. *School Community Journal, 16*(1), 31–41.

Thomas, W. P., & Collier, V. P. (2002). A national study of school effectiveness for language minority students' long-term academic achievement. Santa Cruz: CA: Center for Research on Education, Diversity and Excellence. (ERIC Document Reproduction Services No. ED475048)

Triplett, W. (2004, October 8). Migrant farmworkers. *CQ Researcher, 14,* 829–852. Retrieved July 4, 2007, from CQ Researcher Online, http://library. cqpress.com/cqresearcher/cqresrre2004100800

U.S. Department of Education. (2006). *Migrant education program annual report: Eligibility, participation, services (2001–2002) and achievement (2002–2003).* Washington, DC: Office of the Planning, Evaluation and Policy Development, Policy and Program Studies Service. (ERIC Document Reproduction Services No. ED494735.

Whittaker, C. R., Salend, S. J., & Gutierrez, M. B. (1997). "Voices from the fields": Including migrant farmworkers in the curriculum. *Reading Teacher, 50*(6), 482–493.

Wilkinson, C. Y., Ortiz, A. A., Robertson, P. M., & Kushner, M. L. (2006). English language learners with reading-related LD: Linking data from multiple sources to make eligibility determinations. *Journal of Learning Disabilities, 39*(2), 129–141.

6

Race and Ethnicity

Race should not be understood as a bundle of genetically determined traits that generate of themselves social differences—a view that has been repudiated by the vast majority of social scientists—but as a kind of social classification used by members of a society.

(Borgatta & Borgatta, 1992, p. 575)

Current Concepts of Race

Although earlier social scientists addressed the contradictions and inherent weaknesses of race as a category for classifying human beings, the recognition of and respect for contributions by social scientists of color who emerged after the 1960s resulted in a more diverse and balanced literature on race in America (Borgatta & Borgatta, 1992). Thus, the concept of race has changed over time, although social scientists continue to differ on its meaning. Noting that the term *race* was used at the beginning of the twentieth century to refer to any "geographical, religious, class-based or color-based grouping," Barkan (1992) believes that a shift in the concept of race from "a part of the natural order based upon real or assumed racial distinctions to that of racism as an oppressive and dogmatic ideology" was due to the scientific discourse on race among a small group of British and American anthropologists and biologists, probably considered "outsiders." The change in the concept of race represented an awareness on the part of some members of the British and American societies that racial terminology was not value free and that social organization based on a racial hierarchy was repugnant (Barkan, 1992). As Michael Omi (2001) has pointed out, "over time, the idea of race as a biological construct was increasingly discredited in academic and scientific circles" (p. 12). In the words of Mukhopadhay & Henze (2003), "The concept of race is a cultural invention, a culturally and historically specific way of thinking about, categorizing, and treating human beings" (p. 673).

Loury (1995) agrees that "racial identity in America is inherently a social and cultural construct, not simply a biological one—it necessarily involves an irreducible element of choice" (Loury, 1995, p. 2). He describes a friend whose pale skin color made him unacceptable as "black" to many African Americans, yet he was also uncomfortable when categorized as "white." Unable to cope with the ambiguity, Loury's friend suffered isolation and alienation.

Interestingly, the U.S. Census continues to use the term "race" and racial categories, (Box 6.1). However in recognition of the fluid, sometimes arbitrary, nature of race and racial identification, census takers were instructed to accept whatever racial classifications were chosen by an individual. For the first time, one could name all the races that describe her, supporting the view that "race" is a personal choice, a social construct (Loury, 1995; Marable, 1995; Webster, 1992). Although it is difficult to determine the actual percentage of Americans who identify themselves as multiracial, the results of the 2000 U.S. Census support the fact that 1.9 percent (excluding Hispanic or Latino) identified themselves as "two or more races"; and of the Hispanic or Latino group, 1.3 percent chose "two or more races." (See Box 6.1.)

Marable (1995) has captured the essence of race as a paradoxical fixture in U.S. society which has changed over time. In his words, "The racial prism creates an illusion that race is permanent and finite, but, in reality, "race" is a complex expression of unequal relations which are dynamic and ever-changing" (p. 9).

BOX 6.1 • *Reproduction of Questions on Race and Hispanic Origin From Census 2000*

→ **NOTE: Please answer BOTH Questions 5 and 6.**

5. **Is this person Spanish/Hispanic/Latino?** *Mark* ⊠ *the "No" box if **not** Spanish/Hispanic/Latino.*

☐ **No**, not Spanish/Hispanic/Latino   ☐ Yes, Puerto Rican
☐ Yes, Mexican, Mexican Am., Chicano   ☐ Yes, Cuban
☐ Yes, other Spanish/Hispanic/Latino — *Print group.* ↗

6. **What is this person's race?** *Mark* ⊠ *one or more races* to indicate what this person considers himself/herself to be.

☐ White
☐ Black, African Am., or Negro
☐ American Indian or Alaska Native — *Print name of enrolled or principal tribe.* ↗

☐ Asian Indian   ☐ Japanese   ☐ Native Hawaiian
☐ Chinese   ☐ Korean   ☐ Guamanian or Chamorro
☐ Filipino   ☐ Vietnamese   ☐ Samoan
☐ Other Asian — *Print race.* ↗   ☐ Other Pacific Islander — *Print race.* ↗

☐ Some other race — *Print race.* ↗

Source: U.S. Census Bureau, Census 2000 questionnaire.

Other social scientists have observed that the significance of race in United States has declined (Wilson, 1987, 1997). Wilson has pointed out that socioeconomic differences among groups in the society are superceding race in importance. Furthermore, Webster (1992) charges that the continuation of racial classifications of social groups in the United States in itself creates a racist society obsessed with race and racial conflicts.

Ethnicity

The concept of ethnicity, like race, appears to be fluid and subject to different perceptions and definitions. Race and ethnicity are frequently interchanged, yet some define race as a special case of ethnicity (van den Berghe, 1981). In this view, ethnic groups share a common ancestry and culture. Language, religion, styles of clothing, and foods would identify persons of a certain ethnic group. According to Borgatta and Borgatta (1992), members of ethnic groups frequently marry within their group, share a sense of solidarity, identify themselves as members of the group, and are so identified by others. On the other hand, Weber (1922, cited in Borgatta & Borgatta, 1992) has provided a classic definition of ethnicity in which he maintains that

> an ethnic group is one whose members entertain a subjective belief in their common descent because of similarities of physical type or customs or both, or because of memories of colonization and migration. It does not matter whether or not an objective blood relationship exists. Those who view race as a form of ethnicity describe an ethnic group as one whose members are believed by others, if not also by themselves, to be physiologically distinctive (Borgatta & Borgatta, 1992, p. 576).

Ethnicity, as with race, has been viewed from different perspectives. D'Alba (1990) favors the view of symbolic ethnicity. This refers to the fact that ethnic identities of many whites are actually a symbol of the emergence on the American scene of a new ethnic group. D'Alba points to the belief among scholars and lay persons that ethnic differences "form a possible permanent substructure in the society" (1990, p. 2). The belief was especially prominent during the 1960s and 1970s when an "ethnic revival" and cultural pluralism emerged, according to D'Alba. In contrast to earlier views that assimilation would decrease group differences, the ethnic revival at that time heightened ethnic assertiveness in the United States (D'Alba, 1990). He noted that an ethnic hierarchy based on staggered arrivals, economic success, and varied backgrounds has occurred. Thus, ethnicity, too, like race, has been a source of unequal progress for some groups. Ethnicity and race also interact, resulting in differential treatment for many. Since race and ethnicity are frequently used synonymously in the literature, we have chosen not to differentiate the terms as we continue to discuss the cases in the text.

Racial and Ethnic Identity

The integration of race into personal identity varies among individuals. For some, it becomes a dominant component of their identity, while for others it is subservient to membership in other groups (Cross, 1995). Tatum (1997) notes that children become aware of physical differences very early in their development. In the early preschool years they notice differences in color and other physical characteristics and may try to account for them with assumptions such as "Eddie says my skin is brown because I drink too much chocolate milk" (Tatum, 1997, p. 70). She recommends that an adult could give the child a simple explanation about melanin in order to correct the misunderstanding. Or a child may attribute a darker skin to dirtiness and, again, according to Tatum, an adult should correct this misperception based on the cognitive ability and developmental stage of the child. A direct response, rather than quieting the child or expressing embarrassment, is preferred in order to prevent the child's development of a negative self-image.

The issue of racial identity becomes more critical in adolescence when important questions such as "Who am I?" and "Who can I be?" occur. Some adolescents must also answer "What does it mean to be black, or Asian, or Latino?" In pointing out that black students may sit together in the school cafeteria in answer to their developmental need to explore the meaning of their identity with others engaged in the same process, Tatum (1997) provides a rationale for that phenomenon. As an alternative, she suggests a daily group meeting for students in the company of a supportive adult where they can discuss identity issues together. The opportunity to get together with others facing the same challenges is needed. As Tatum has suggested, educators need to provide students with "identity affirming experiences and information about their own cultural groups" (Tatum, 1997, p. 71). This perspective can be helpful to all diverse groups.

White Identity

White children will also need to integrate a positive racial identity so that their identity will not be developed at the expense of children of color. A close relationship exists between White racial identity and racism (Helms, 1990). Thus, according to Helms, an important aspect of the development of a positive racial identity for White children is the elimination of racism.

Until the 1990s, in the field of multicultural education, the study of race and politics had most often been the study of White racial attitudes and research on racial identity usually focussed on non-white identity. Yet, Helms (1990), among others, pointed out that a positive White identity is essential if racism is to be avoided. This means that White students must recognize that they are members of the socially constructed White race, and there is a long history of abuse and oppression of peoples of color by White Americans.

Identity development is the major developmental task of adolescence and racial identity is an important part of that process. Positive outcomes of identity development are academic achievement, nonauthoritarian commitments, and successful resolution of the intimacy crisis to come later (Wires & Barocas, 1994). In contrast, negative outcomes result in academic underachievement, low self-esteem, failure to establish intimacy at a later time, and possible drug abuse (Wires & Barocus, 1994).

In our increasingly diverse society, where one must learn to get along with many diverse Americans, the changing answer to the adolescent question of Who am I? must also include coming to terms with what it means to be White in this society and recognition of the historic privileges and power associated with white skin. As expressed by Dalton (1995), "the first step is for Whites to conceive of themselves as members of a race and to recognize the advantages that attach to simply having White skin" (p. 6). Few White people think of themselves in racial terms, often identifying themselves simply as "American." In Dalton's view, that is because "in settings where Whites dominate, being White is not noteworthy" (p. 6). However, their skin color establishes their place in the social pecking order. While Blacks have often been labeled "disadvantaged," Whites are rarely labeled "advantaged" (Dalton, 1995). According to Dalton, the second step for racial progress in our increasingly more diverse society is for Whites to accept partial ownership of the U.S. race problem. Although many Whites will often point out that "I didn't create the race problem," many of us have added to it or helped to perpetuate it in one way or another (Dalton, 1995). For example, when racist practices occur in the school or other familiar settings and the teacher or other individual does not try to stop them or protest, he or she is helping to perpetuate them.

Thus, the major developmental task of adolescence is not only to make decisions and compromises in the areas of occupation, sexuality, politics, religion—and later, intimacy—it also includes understanding the nature of racial conflicts in the country and finding a positive answer to the question "What does it mean to be White?"

In order to be helpful, teachers will want to know how they can contribute to that understanding and development of a positive identity in their White students. Teachers need to understand the dynamics and challenges involved in helping young children and adolescents to become "healthy, hopeful, justice-oriented" members of the society (Eichstedt, 2001, p. 18). Table 6.1 shows literature that can be helpful and most publishers now carry multicultural games and other resources. However, teachers, as well as parents, need to be willing to discuss race at home and in the classroom when the topic arises. Copenhaver-Johnson (2006) points out that our silence affects our children. When we refuse to discuss race, a powerful message is sent that discussion of

TABLE 6.1 *Multicultural Literature*

Title	Author	Publisher	Date
Mama	Lee Bennett Hopkins	Simon and Shuster	2000
You be me, I'll be you	Mandelbaum	Kane/Miller	1990
The table where rich people sit	Byrd Taylor	Scribner	1994
The Maldonado miracle	Theodore Taylor	Avon Books	2003
Coolies	Yin	Philomel	2001
Free to be you and me	Thomas Marlo	McGraw-Hill	2002
Her stories: African American folk tales, fairy tales, and true tales	Virginia Hamilton	Knopf	1993

race is taboo (Copenhaver-Johnson, 2006). She suggests that it is the desire to avoid conflict, the lack of understanding of what race really is, and fear of saying something unexpected or "unseemly" that can explain the silence. In the words of Lieberman and Kirk (2004), "the silence of many Whites about race may make it difficult for children trying to understand and develop a positive White identity" (p. 139).

The authors have learned that students' visits with diverse families, preferably in their community setting, interviewing the families after preparation for the interview, and attending community events in diverse communities can help to alleviate some of the fear of different cultures and communities that students may express. Home visits can also be made when carefully planned and approved by the families. It is usually practical for two students together to make the visit after role-playing the visit beforehand.

In an interesting comment that is applicable to many Americans at this time, Kinchloe (1999) has commented that "In the postmodern condition, individuals must wear several identities as they travel in and out of multiple cultural locales. Gone is the memory of 'genuine cultures' who pass along their mores and folkways unchanged to the next generation" (p. 9).

Children of Mixed Race/Ethnicity

James McBride (1996) has written a moving story about his interracial family with emphasis on his mother as a single parent. The following quote from his book, *The Color of Water: A Black Man's Tribute to His White Mother*, reveals an occasion on which he wants to know, "What am I?"

> One afternoon I came home from school and cornered Mommy while she was cooking dinner.
> "Ma, what's a tragic mulatto?" I asked.
> "Where'd you hear that?" she asked.
> "For God's sake, you're no tragic mul . . . What book is this?"
> "Just a book I read."
> "Don't read that book anymore." She sucked her teeth.
> "Tragic mulatto. What a stupid thing to call somebody. Don't you ever use that term."
> "Am I Black or White?"
> "You're a human being," she snapped. "Educate yourself or you'll be a nobody."
> "Will I be a Black nobody or just a nobody?"
> "If you're a nobody," she said dryly, "it doesn't matter what color you are."
> (McBride, 1996, p. 92).

A question frequently asked of mixed-race children by their peers and others is "What are you?" The question can be received as intrusive, even hostile, focusing on superficial aspects of an individual rather than the "real person." In response, one may hear a variety of answers. The following responses of biracial children are examples.

> "If I'm having a good day, I won't answer in a hostile way. But if I'm having a rough day, it gets annoying. My answer also depends on how they ask the question. If they ask,

'What are you?' I just give them a smart answer. I say, 'I'm a human being. Why, what are you?' " (Derek, age 15, from Fuyo-Gaskins, 1999, p. 21)

"I've had people walk up to me out of the blue and say, 'What are you?' I just think it's rude. I can't imagine walking up to a complete stranger and asking them something really personal like that . . . . My ethnic background is a highly personal thing. There are times when I will just not answer people." (Christy, age 25, Fuyo-Gaskins p. 23)

"I get mad because people are always trying to categorize me. People try to fig-ure me out like I'm some puzzle . . . . Why can't they leave me alone? I am what I am. I really respect people who get to know me first and ask me later." (Nicole, age 17 Fuyo-Gaskins p. 35)

"People tend to want to label me one or the other. To make me say I'm one or the other is like making me deny one of my parents and a part of myself. It's like making me deny what I am because I'm not White and I'm not Black. I'm both." (Amanda, age 16 Fuyo-Gaskins p. 49)

Furthermore, interracial families continue to encounter problems in community acceptance and approval, social isolation, and job discrimination. Although published reports of extreme hostility appear to have diminished, families continue to report the experience of "stares" and refusal by some neighbors to recognize their presence (see Lisa Golden's case on page 116). Biracial or multiracial youth may also suffer differen-tial treatment or rejection by some family members, peers, and communities (Fukuyama, 1999; Gibbs, 1989; McBride, 1996; Wardle, 2000). Again Fukuyama has shared that, "Race did not have personal meaning for me until, as a young child (age 4 or 5) I was mocked by another child for the shape of my eyes" (1999, p. 1). Wardle (2000) has noted that children of mixed heritage "experience harassment from mainstream soci-ety and from members of minority groups" (p. 4). Direct assaults on their identity from students and insensitive, hostile interactions from educators occur (Wardle, 2000).

In fact, even educators who take multicultural education courses do not often learn about multiracial or multiethnic children (Wardle, 2000). Filling out school forms that ask for racial or ethnic identification, for example, is difficult for many of these children. "Students or parents who refuse to designate a single identity, or who select an alternative response may be harassed, accused of being uptight about their racial identity, or denied entrance into a program" (Wardle, 2000). This author makes an important point in noting that, historically, schools have viewed these children as hav-ing the racial or ethnic identity of the parent of color. However, as seen in "Other Voices" (Box 6.2), parents may choose to have the children identified according to all the groups to which they belong. In any case, schools can make these students feel invisible and uncomfortable.

Like all other students, multiracial or multiethnic students need familiar images in textbooks and instructional materials, interracial hands-on activities, posters, and literature, and extracurricular activities such as special clubs that are inclusive.

Referrals may be necessary for adequate counseling to facilitate the development of a positive self-concept and resolution of conflicts. School personnel can assist the chil-dren to lead productive and fulfilling lives. The parents and children's views to be read later in this chapter illustrate their needs.

BOX 6.2 • *Other Voices*

When kids ask, "What are you?" we answer, "Native American, African American, European, and French Canadian. That's the answer that mother gave us when we asked her, "What are we?" Mother is French Canadian and Dad is African American and Native American. We have been learning some things about the Native American culture, although we don't know which tribe we're from. . . . We only know that it is a Southeastern U.S. Native American tribe—probably Seminole." (Andre, age 11, August, 2000)

"One day a classmate saw me with my Dad, and she had already met my mom. . . . She asked me if that was my Dad and said, "Oh, now I understand why you're the color that you are." (Angie, age 12, August, 2000)

Angie's and Andre's mom described their current school experience: "Angie and Andre have attended a magnet school (here in the Midwest) that focuses on community cultures and environmental science. The school is multiage and multiracial, and every student takes a community cultures class. Since they entered when the school was only a year in operation, its reputation was yet unknown, and requests to enter were not excessive. There was no problem in admission. Now there's a long waiting list. The school serves a very diverse population of students where there is no majority. We have all been pleased with it.

"The school has good, empowering leadership by the principal, and standards and testing are not important at the school. However, I'm worried about next year because although Andre will continue at the magnet school, Angie will attend a traditional middle school for seventh grade where 97 percent of the students are White. The school, grades 7 and 8, is located in a White suburb. We expect that there will be some difficulties, including questions like, "What are you?" Hopefully, she can handle them since she has learned good responses in a special program she attended. Kids in that program were taught how to take social action, how to stand up for what they think is right. Angie has had experience with protests, and she participated in the Children's March on Washington, so I hope that she will be able to manage."

(Emily Green, mother of Angie and Andre, August, 2000)

Racism

Although racism has existed throughout history, its modern forms are distinctly different than those during slavery, "Jim Crow," and other periods of legalized segregation and discrimination. However, the attitudes and behaviors underlying racist behaviors have not changed, nor have the forms of racism changed in some regions of the country.

Furthermore, the focus of racism in our diverse society may be on any of the individuals or on the group of color. In fact, our society continues to have a problem with "differentness," whether it be in skin color, clothing, language, disabilities, customs such as the prayers of people who practice the Islamic religion, individuals with disabilities as indicated in incidents involving children with autism, and other behaviors related to diverse cultures or religions. Myths and stereotypes also contribute to racist behavior. In fact, people currently act on myths and stereotypes about migrant workers.

In Kentucky, the Southern Poverty Law Center (2007a) recently sued two klansmen who "savagely beat a teenage boy at a carnival in July, 2006." The boy, who was the son of a Kuna Indian from Panama, was mistaken for Hispanic.

Among the immigrants to the United States, migrant workers, who are all thought to be "illegal," according to racist thinking, now face hostility and abuse in many communities. In fact, hostile responses have occurred in suburban communities to proposals to build decent places where immigrants seeking work could gather. It is ironic that the same community residents who were "up in arms" about the men who gathered on corners and in front of convenience stores to wait for potential employers were also incensed about the possibility of a building in which they could wait "in our neighborhood" (Tomlinson, Personal communications, 2006–2007).

In another recent example, a high school student who wore a burqa for an entire day received many hostile comments and threats. In fact, "The hateful and abusive comments that she endured that day horrified the student, her teachers, and many of her classmates" (Gordon-Fox, 2007). Comments were such as "Hey, we rape your women" and "I hope all of your people die." Another angry observer shouted, "You're probably going to kill us all. Why do they let people like you in this country?" (Gordon-Fox, 2007).

Padilla (2006) reported on a study that investigated the effect of skin color on acculturation among a group of 102 Mexican students at a southwestern university. The findings revealed that students with the darkest skin had significantly lower levels of acculturation (measured on a heritage–mainstream culture continuum) than did those with lighter skin. Other researchers who have studied the impact of skin color on the life chances of Latinos have obtained similar results (Gomez, 2000; Portes & Rumbaut, 2001, cited in Padilla, 2006).

In fact, based upon the research available, Padilla (2006) concluded that "the research findings support the contention of Portes and Rumbaut [2001] that newcomers pay a penalty for being immigrants or later generation ethnics who differ in phenotype from the host society, and they pay an even greater penalty for being darker and more Indian looking (or Asian or African) in phenotype." As Clarence Page has written, "Every White person who is not too caught up in his or her own sense of righteous victimization knows that White skin still affords certain privileges in our color-coded society (Mazel, 1998, p. 97).

Meanwhile, White supremacist groups continue to spread their literature in various communities. A report was made on the news recently about cards with swastikas left at each home in a pleasant East Coast community. Fortunately, neighbors interviewed on the newscast condemned the act (Taylor, Personal observation by author July, 28, 2007).

In an example of recent racism with echoes of the past, in 2003, a mentally disabled Black man was taunted, beaten, and left unconscious beside a road by a group of young White men in Texas (Southern Poverty Law Center, 2007b). The man was left with permanent brain damage and is in a nursing home. The case finally came to trial in 2007, and the juries who heard the cases acquitted the men of felonies. The judge sentenced three of the men to 30 days in the county jail and one man to 60 days (SPLC, 2007).

One of the most important avenues of current research involves the impact of racism on the health of U.S. minorities, particularly Blacks, who suffer more health problems than White Americans. More than 100 studies, most published since 2000, now document the effects of racial discrimination on physical health (Drexler, 2007). In recent studies, subjects have shown a linkage between blood pressure and recollected encounters with bigotry. Researchers have also recorded the cardiovascular reactions of volunteers subjected to racist imagery in a lab. While scientists have cautioned that the findings are as yet preliminary, studies could ultimately establish racism as a public health problem (Drexler, 2007). As Drexler has pointed out, "African Americans today, despite a half century of economic and social progress since the Civil Rights Movement, face a higher risk than any other racial group of dying from heart disease, diabetes, stroke, and hypertension" (p. 2).

Resisting Racism

We can combat racism through more open dialogue on race. The message of Cornel West (1993) is relevant where he speaks of "our truncated public discussions of race, [that] suppress the best of who and what we are as a people because they fail to confront the complexity of the issue in a candid and critical manner" (p. 2). However, West also points out that "To engage in a serious discussion of race in America, we must begin not with the problems of black people, but with the flaws of American society—flaws rooted in historic inequalities and longstanding cultural stereotypes" (p. 3). "To establish a new framework, we need to begin with a frank acknowledgment of the basic humanness and Americanness of each of us" (p. 4).

Gary Howard (1996) has also offered several thoughts on what a new framework for race relations will require. In his words: "A peaceful transition to a new kind of America in which no ethnic or cultural group is in a dominant position will require considerable change in education and deep psychological shifts for many White Americans" (p. 324).

From a somewhat different perspective, Peggy McIntosh (1988) has written of the privilege associated with white skin. In order to eliminate racism, one thing that must take place is the recognition of this privilege. In her words, "It seems to me that obliviousness about white advantage, like obliviousness about male advantage, is kept strongly inculturated in the United States so as to maintain the myth of meritocracy, the myth that democratic choice is equally available to all" (p. 4). In fact, an important aspect of the "inner work" that teachers must do, as counseled by Gary Howard (1999), is to raise their consciousness of white privilege and its effect.

All children and adolescents will need knowledge and understanding of racism in order to resist the myth of meritocracy and other myths and stereotypes associated with racial classifications in the United States. Children will need information about how racial myths and stereotypes operate in order to combat them. They will also need affirming racial identity opportunities as recommended by Tatum (1997). Through multicultural education, an appreciation for diverse races and cultures can be promoted and enhanced by teachers. An abundance of curricular materials and pedagogy is available for schools that aim to help their students to learn to live in a democratic nation in which equality for all is assured. As Marable (1995) has noted, "We must rethink old categories and old ways of perceiving each other. We must define the issue of diversity as a dynamic, changing concept, leading us to explore problems of human relations and social equality in a manner which will expand the principles of fairness and opportunity to all members of society" (Marable, 1995, p. 118).

Educators who understand the evolution of racism, current concepts of race and ethnicity, the development of racial and ethnic identity, and the issues faced by an increasing population of multiracial or multiethnic students will be able to effectively address the issues faced by their students and create a truly inclusive classroom where all students can learn.

The Case of Jim Peterson

Jim had begun student teaching only a week ago, and his enthusiasm was already beginning to wane. Mrs. Fitzgerald, the cooperating teacher, was strict and inflexible with the students, in Jim's opinion, and he felt that she treated him that way, too. Nevertheless, she was the wife of the principal, and Jim wanted to make a very positive impression on her so that she could, hopefully, make positive comments about him to the principal. Jim had waited so long to get a regular teaching job and, as an older student at 35, he was desperate for any hopeful situation.

Jim thought of himself as "laid back," easy to get along with, and usually liked by the adolescents with whom he had previously worked. He believed that when the curriculum addressed students' interests and needs, behavior problems would be minimal. The key to good classroom management, in Jim's opinion, was a relevant curriculum. Furthermore, the profanity used by some students and talking out without permission by many did not really bother Jim as long as the behaviors were not too disruptive. Yet these were the very behaviors that Mrs. Fitzgerald would not tolerate.

Mrs. Fitzgerald explained her inflexibility to Jim as necessary because "These students have serious behavior problems, and you cannot let up or they'll take over." She repeated to Jim many times that "Behavior management is more important than anything else you do." The principal agreed with her in his comments to the teacher and students and in his expectations. Mr. Fitzgerald insisted that all classroom doors remain open at all times. He would patrol the corridors frequently to shout at students out of class without permission or to intervene in a noisy classroom. At close to 7 feet tall, his height and deep voice easily intimidated both students and teachers.

The eight-week summer program served students with disabilities who were eligible for twelve-month educational services. Thirteen classes were located in the bright, cheerful building of U-shaped corridors painted in vibrant colors. However, there was no air conditioning, and life in the building became difficult for students and staff on many sultry afternoons. There was a schoolwide discipline system in which students began each day with 100 points and lost them for various infractions throughout the day, a response cost system. At the end of the week, points were exchanged for rewards. Mr. Fitzgerald expected every classroom to operate accordingly.

Mrs. Fitzgerald's class consisted of seven students, ages 11 to 13, who were classified seriously emotionally disturbed. Six students were African American and one was White. However, the composition of the class did not represent the population throughout the region. In each county of this semirural and small urban region, minority students were only 3 to 5 percent of the school population and in some areas they were less than 1 percent. The largest numbers of students of color came from the older urban areas of the region. Mrs. Fitzgerald's class did represent, however, the disproportionate placement of African American students in classes for students who are emotionally or behaviorally disturbed, which exists throughout the country. Also, because it was a summer program, students came from many schools in several counties, and Mrs. Fitzgerald's students did not know each other, a fact that Mrs. Fitzgerald did not consider important. Nor did she consider important the fact that she was White, as were the majority of teachers in the school.

She preferred to begin academic lessons the first day of school and she used traditional materials and methods. Thus, when Jim began to plan instruction, she told him, "I use basal readers and various easy paperback books. There are teacher editions available for the science, social studies, and mathematics texts that I use, and they will be helpful to you in planning lessons." Jim silently disagreed with her traditional approach, and he looked forward to being more creative.

Jim believed that he had a good understanding of the students' interests and needs. In fact, Mrs. Fitzgerald's students reminded Jim of others whom he had recently tutored at the college he attended. Actually, Jim thought of himself as an experienced teacher, since he had also worked the past summer at a school for adolescents with serious emotional disabilities. He had been a childcare and residential counselor and later a teacher's aide at the school. Many of the students with whom he had worked were African American and Latino, and Jim felt that he had been very successful with them. Although Jim was White, he had worked in many situations in which he was in the minority. He had worked as a sergeant in the military and had no problems with discipline. Jim's other jobs included work in a restaurant and convenience store. He felt quite proud of the experience he had accumulated and his preparation for teaching.

Actually, as the time for student teaching approached, Jim had smiled when his classmates expressed anxiety about beginning student teaching. "I don't feel any nervousness at all," he told one classmate. "I have worked with lots of students like those I will have in my student teaching." In fact, he also expressed his confidence and experience to Mrs. Fitzgerald on the first day. However, he was somewhat disappointed when she responded, "Don't forget that you are a student teacher, after all, with lots to learn, and the students here are very challenging."

Jim searched for some way to remain optimistic, and he found it in the makeup of the class. The majority of the students were African American, and Jim became excited about implementing many of the ideas that he had learned about in his courses on multicultural education. He had learned about materials that he could use immediately.

His first responsibility in Mrs. Fitzgerald's classroom was to take over the reading instruction. Jim believed that stories about African American sports heroes would motivate the students and hold their interest. As required, he met with Mrs. Fitzgerald to discuss his plans. It was obvious to Jim that she was not too pleased when she said, "You can try the material, but you must remain firm and consistent and maintain control. I do not want chaos in my classroom."

On the following Monday morning Jim began reading instruction with the story on Jackie Robinson. All the students were present and curious about the new material. Motivation was not a problem. They were all seated at a rectangular table and, after Jim introduced the story, students took turns reading aloud as he provided cues and prompts. After each chapter of the story, there was a brief discussion, which Jim led using stimulating questions. This procedure was followed each day until Thursday, when the classroom fell into chaos.

The single White student in the group jumped out of his seat, threw his material on the floor, and shouted, "I ain't reading this no more. I'm sick of niggers!"

Two of the African American students immediately responded with, "We'll whip your ass."

The White student ran out of the room with Jim running close behind. Mrs. Fitzgerald remained in the classroom.

As he returned to the room holding the student by the shoulder, Jim could see that Mrs. Fitzgerald was angry. She shouted at him, "Mr. Peterson, put away that material immediately and do not plan to use it again!" Jim found her words really piercing when she added, "You have created chaos in my classroom!"

He was devastated. All he could think of was how well prepared he had been and that he never anticipated this kind of problem. What went wrong? His good intentions, his knowledge of multicultural education, his prior teaching experience, all the training in working with students who have emotional disabilities—all seemed useless. He hated to think about tomorrow and his shaken confidence. Sure, he would ask for a conference with his university supervisor, but Mrs. Fitzgerald was obviously unhappy with him. He did not believe that he could change that.

Besides, he had some questions that he couldn't answer about diversity and multicultural education. What happened in this situation? Was it too risky to use such materials in a group where only one student was different? What should he have done with that student? The practicum was only eight weeks and already two weeks were completed. Would he make it through? He needed a job so badly . . . should he ask to start over in another placement?

Discussion Questions

1. Describe the students' classroom situation and the particular aspects that might prove challenging for any teacher.
2. What discrepancies exist between Jim's expectations for his student teaching and what actually occurred? What discrepancies exist between what Mrs. Fitzgerald expected and what actually occurred?
3. What perceptions did Jim have of himself when he began student teaching? What were the beliefs he held about multicultural education, instructional approaches, and classroom management?
4. How did Jim's beliefs about teaching conflict with Mrs. Fitzgerald's? With the students' views of what and how they were to learn?
5. What do we know about multicultural education and culturally responsive classroom management from experts in the field that would help to guide the decisions that need to be made in this situation?

6. How could the university supervisor reframe the issues in this conflict to help Jim and Mrs. Fitzgerald move forward in the student teaching experience?
7. What goals should Jim and Mrs. Fitzgerald set for themselves and for the class from this point on?

The Case of Lisa Golden

Lisa's mother, Mrs. Golden, expressed her frustration: "When your children are mixed, how do you find the middle? What is the middle? For Lisa's sake, her father and I need to determine the answer. Children at school are constantly asking her, 'What are you?' and we need the best possible answer. Although both Lisa and Tommy asked questions about their skin color and hair very early, our former answer to them doesn't seem sufficient now. Since Lisa is browner and Tommy is whiter, we explained then that they were a mixture of daddy and mommy. The kids at school who keep pestering Lisa obviously want a different answer.

"Lisa is now 12 years old and will begin seventh grade this September at Kennedy Junior High School. In fifth and sixth grade at the elementary school, she appeared to be trying to identify first with a group of white kids and then with a group of African American kids. I believe that she has been trying to find out where she belongs, as well as to find friends with whom she feels comfortable. Earlier this year during sixth grade she became friendly with an African American girl who needed tutoring, and soon they had a small group of four African American girls and Lisa who hung out together. However, Lisa eventually tired of helping the girl, describing her as needing too much tutoring. The other girls became angry with Lisa when she stopped the tutoring. They thought that she should continue and sometimes help them, too. That ended the friendship. It was difficult, but, after all, Lisa is an outstanding student who is so academically driven that her father and I decided to enroll her in a swimming class to provide more balance in her life. Now she's just as driven about excelling in swimming!

"Her teacher, Mrs. Johanssen, has been quite concerned about Lisa's difficulty in developing a racial identity and a sense of belonging. However, Lisa has a nice group of friends now who happen to be all White.

"We really like the diversity in the school district and in the individual schools. Although the district's desegregation plan was initially court mandated, the plan has resulted in diversity throughout the district schools. Furthermore, the magnet school choices appeal to most parents, and the lottery system used to place students according to their choices seems to work fairly. At the beginning of each school year you fill out a form stating your six choices of programs at the various magnet schools (Box 6.3). For example, Lisa wanted the magnet school offering programs in the fine and performing arts as her first choice for seventh grade. We just learned that she will not get the first choice, but her second choice was granted.

"We are very pleased with this system since we are accustomed to diversity in our community and schools. We moved here from a large, metropolitan area where there were all kinds of people. Both children were born there, and Tommy attended kindergarten in that community. When we moved here, Lisa was just ready to begin kindergarten and Tommy was ready for first grade.

BOX 6.3 • *Magnet Schools*

The U.S. Supreme Court mandate in 1954 for school desegregation in *Brown* v. *Board of Education* resulted in a search by many school districts across the country to develop strategies to accomplish integration of schools since "separate but equal" was declared unacceptable. Although avoidance strategies such as the development of private "academies" for White children, refusals to obey the law, and home schooling were some tactics utilized by those who opposed the ruling during the 1970s and 1980s, the focus of desegregation was on the physical integration of African American and white students.

Magnet schools, one of those options, appear to encourage more cooperation than other measures such as busing. It appears that, if a school district can develop programs that are sufficiently appealing to its constituents, white parents will choose to send their children to schools attended by black students as well as other minority groups. Lisa's school district has chosen consolidation of the city and suburban schools into an enlarged school district, as well as magnet schools, to achieve integration of the students and positive responses of all district parents and families.

A magnet school has been defined as "a public school with any grades K–12, that offers 'whole-school' or 'program-within-a-school' programs characterized by the following: special curricular theme or method of instruction designed to attract students district-wide; enrollment on a district-wide basis; and some type of racial/ethnic enrollment goals or controls" (Blank & Archibald, 1992, p. 82). The schools are usually classified according to the curriculum content or instructional approaches. Schools generally try to use methods to determine admission to the schools or programs that will seem most fair to parents and students. The magnet schools are usually created and regulated by the state and public school district.

It is important to add that there is a disturbing trend described by Weiler (1998), who has pointed out that, although many of the above efforts are continuing in school districts across the nation, courts are declaring more and more large urban districts "unitary," thus moving toward resegregation. The term *unitary* refers to the release of school districts from court supervision of their desegregation efforts (Weiler, 1998).

"This is a small city, with many characteristics and problems of older, urban areas. I just read in the paper that the unemployment rate in our city is approximately 8 percent and the population of approximately 26,000 includes about 51 percent Whites. Blacks and Hispanics constitute the largest percentages of the remaining 49 percent. The city population has decreased over the past ten years, while the suburbs have grown. We actually live in a nice fringe area of the city in which most of our neighbors are White. Only one family appears to respond to us negatively, never coming too close when we meet them outside. However, I must say that many times when I attend meetings or community events people look surprised when they learn that I am Mrs. Golden. Many people do not expect a brown-skinned person with that name!

"The school population includes a total of approximately 12,000 students of which about 10 percent are considered English language learners and 43 percent are eligible for free lunch. To be able to achieve racial–ethnic and socioeconomic diversity in the schools, the district decided to enlarge to incorporate the surrounding, newer suburban areas. This provided more White students and more students of middle-income levels for integration of the schools. Yet most of the teachers remain White. Our children have had only two African American teachers and no Hispanic teachers so far. One possible explanation is that, until recently, there were no bilingual programs in their school. It seems that bilingual education programs can provide some culturally diverse teachers who are bilingual.

"Interestingly, Tommy is getting along fine as he begins high school. Tommy is now 14 years old and has a circle of friends who have accepted him. Although the circle of friends happens to be White, Tommy gets along with all types of kids. He moves easily among all the different racial–ethnic groups. His cultural background is not a major concern for him.

"However, the question of our family's racial and ethnic heritage became an issue for us when we first enrolled the children in school here. We had to decide how to identify the children just in case there was an advantage in being Hispanic. Although the lottery was in use, we thought that our racial–ethnic designation just might mean whether we got the kids into the magnet school of our choice. It was painfully difficult to decide on Hispanic–Puerto Rican as opposed to Caucasian, because we thought that the first choice just might give us an advantage. The school officials assured us that only the lottery was used, but it was hard for us to believe that they didn't take some other things into account. Although my husband doesn't feel as strongly about his German–Jewish heritage as I do about my Puerto Rican background, I think it's still important to recognize both sides of the family. Fortunately, we did get our first choice, the magnet school for gifted and talented children.

"Although Lisa's teacher now is concerned about helping her in response to her classmates' questions, I believe that the development of racial or ethnic identity in children is personal and private and mainly the responsibility of the family. My husband agrees that schools and teachers should not try to be guides for the development of racial or ethnic identity in children. It is too easy for teachers to step on parents' toes, since parents will differ in their views and choices. In addition, teachers will vary in their preparation and may be completely unprepared to deal with such issues as racial or ethnic identity.

"Another consideration is the increasing emphasis on testing and standards across the country. Many teachers are overloaded already, teaching to the tests, and dealing with curricula for social skills and violence prevention. They have little time for one more area of responsibility. The district does not have a multicultural education curriculum or program. They do, however, have a culture day when all students get a chance to share aspects of their culture. We think that this is very helpful, but don't see how teachers could find time for a multicultural education curriculum.

"Teachers can be most helpful when they teach children about all the different cultures in the community so that children who do not learn about their culture at home, for example, can gain knowledge of it at school. In addition, all children can learn to appreciate and respect the diversity of cultures represented. Teachers need awareness and knowledge of the diverse cultures in order to teach about them responsibly and accurately (see Box 6.4).

"Since major questions such as 'What will be the family traditions?' and 'Which culture will we practice?' can only be decided by the family, and each family will have its own unique responses, it is obvious that teachers can make no assumptions about children of

BOX 6.4 • *What Teachers Can Do*

Suggestions Made by Angie, 12, and Andre, 11, Multiracial Siblings Who Attend a Midwestern Public School

- Teachers can study the cultural backgrounds of the kids in the school and teach about each culture over the school year.
- Teachers should be trained to understand that "Just because your ancestors were 'like that'—alcoholics, for example—doesn't mean that you will be like that."
- Teachers should expand their knowledge of cultures.

- Teachers can ask their students how they feel about current events.
- Teachers can visit museums, attend cultural events, conduct interviews, and read books to learn about other cultures.
- Teachers should get copies of the book, *How Rude*, and have it available for their students to read. It is published by Free Spirit Publications.
- It's important to have a variety of literature available for students.

---

mixed heritage. In our family, my husband and I agreed early that the Puerto Rican culture would be dominant. Since my husband's German mother taught him very little of that culture, it has been essentially lost. However, since we both practiced the Lutheran religion when we married, we did not have to make a choice of religion for the family.

"My husband and I firmly believe that a family of mixed races and cultures, in which parents' cultures and values are shared and taught to the children, the children learn about tolerance and how to respond to and deal with intolerance, and, above all, the parents really love each other, can cope successfully with all of society's challenges and demands.

"Lisa's teacher, Mrs. Johanssen, called me again this morning to discuss her concern about dealing with the students' questions about Lisa's heritage. She mentioned that positive racial or ethnic identity development in children is very important, and she feels that she cannot ignore such important questions from the students. In her opinion, students need opportunities to discuss race and ethnicity and their concerns about it. We strongly believe that she should ignore their questions, referring them to their families for assistance. We know best how we want Lisa to answer such questions for others and for herself. I only hope that Mrs. Johanssen and I can find a way to resolve this disagreement. I hope that our relationship won't be damaged by this difference in our viewpoints."

Discussion Questions

1. What discrepancies exist between parent and teacher expectations for how racial identity should be addressed in school? What underlying assumptions follow their expectations?
2. Based on expert opinions, should teachers respond to students' questions about racial and ethnic identity?
3. To what extent does Mrs. Johanssen have the responsibility to help her students in their search for racial or ethnic identity?

4. To maintain a positive relationship with this family, how should the teacher respond to Lisa's parents' request to ignore the students' questions about Lisa's heritage?

5. In view of the rapidly increasing diversity in the United States and the rate of intermarriage, how should schools respond to help children to understand and appreciate the nature of this diversity?

References

Barkan, E. (1992). *The retreat of scientific racism.* New York: Cambridge University Press.

Borgatta, E. F., & Borgatta, M. L. (Eds.). (1992). *Encyclopedia of sociology*, Vols. 2, 3. New York: Macmillan.

Copenhaver-Johnson (2006). Talking to children about race: The importance of inviting difficult conversation. *Childhood Education, 83*(1), 12–21.

Cross, W. (1995). The psychology of Nigrescence: Revising the Cross model. In J. Ponterotto, J. M. Casas, L. A. Suzuki, & C. M. Alexander (Eds.), *Handbook of multicultural counseling* (pp. 93–122). Thousand Oaks, CA: Sage.

D'Alba, R. (1990). *Ethnic identity: The transformation of white America.* New Haven: Yale University Press.

Dalton, H. (1995). *Racial healing: Confronting the fear between Blacks and Whites.* New York: Doubleday.

Drexler, M. (2007). How racism hurts—literally. Retrieved July 25, 2007, from: http://www.boston./news/education/higher/articles/2007

Eichstedt, J. 2001. Problematic White identities and a search for racial justice. *Sociological Forum, 16*(3), 445–471.

Fukuyama, M. (1999). Personal narrative: Growing up biracial. *Journal of Counseling and Development, 77*(1), 12–14.

Fuyo-Gaskins (Ed). (1999). *What are you? Voices of mixed race young people.* NY: Herry Holt

Gibbs, J. Taylor. (1989). Black American adolescents. In J. Taylor Gibbs & L. Nahme Huang (Eds.), *Children of color: Psychological interventions with minority youth* (pp. 179–223). San Francisco: Jossey-Bass.

Gomez, C. (2000). The continual significance of skin color: An exploratory study of Latinos in the Northeast. *Hispanic Journal of Behavioral Sciences, 22*(1), 94–103.

Gordon-Fox, T. (2007, March 12). Behind burqa, student gets an education in bigotry. *The Hartford Courant,* p. A1.

Helms, J. (Ed.). (1990). *Black and white racial identity: Theory, research and practice.* Westport, CN: Praeger.

Howard, G. (1999). *We can't teach what we don't know: White teachers, multiracial schools.* NY: Teachers College Press.

Howard, G. (1996). Whites in multicultural education: Rethinking our role. In J. A. Banks (Ed.) Multicultural education: Transformative knowledge and action. Historical and contemporary perspectives (pp. 323–334). NY: Teachers College Press.

Kinchloe, J. 1999. The struggle to define and reinvent whiteness. *College Literature, 26*(3), 162–195.

Lieberman, L., & Kirk, R. C. (2004). Reflections from the field: What should we teach about the concept of race? *Anthropology & Education Quarterly, 35,* 137–145.

Loury, G. (1995). *One by one from the inside out.* New York: The Free Press.

Marable, M. (1995). *Beyond black and white: Transforming African American politics.* London: Verso.

Mazel E. (1998) (Ed.) *And don't call me a racist.* Lexington, MA: Argonaut Press.

McBride, J. (1996). *The color of water: A black man's tribute to his white mother.* New York: Riverhead Books.

McIntosh, P. (1988). *White privilege.* Wellesley, MA: Wellsley Center for Research on Women: Working papers.

Mukhopadhay, C. & Henze, R. C. (2003). How real is race? Using anthropology to make sense of human diversity. *Phi Delta Kappan, 84,* 669–678.

Omi, M. (2001). Counting in the dark. *Color lines,* Spring, 2001, pp. 12–14

Padilla, A. (2006). Bicultural social development. *Hispanic Journal of Behavioral Sciences, 28*(4), 467–497.

Southern Poverty Law Center (2007a). *Close to slavery: Guestworker programs in the United States.* Montgomery, Alabama: Southern Poverty Law Center.

Southern Poverty Law Center (2007b). *Southern Poverty Law Center Reports,* 37(1), Montgomery, AI.: Author.

Tatum, B. (1997). *Why are all the black kids sitting together in the cafeteria? And other conversations about race.* New York: Basic Books.

U.S. Census Bureau (2000). *Census 2000 questionnaire.* Washington, D.C. United States Census Bureau. Retrieved November, 2007 from: http://www.census.gov.

van den Berghe, P. (1981). *The ethnic phenomenon.* New York: Elsevier.

Wardle, F. (2000). Children of mixed race—no longer invisible. *Educational Leadership,* 57(4), 68–72.

Webster, Y. (1992). *The racialization of America.* New York: St. Martin's Press.

Weiler, J. (1998). Recent changes in school desegregation. ERIC/CUE Digest Number 133. (ERIC Document Reproduction Number ED419029).

West, C. (1993). *Race matters.* Boston: Beacon Press.

Wilson, W. J. (1987). *The declining significance of race: Blacks and changing American institutions.* Chicago: University of Chicago Press.

Wilson, W. J. (1997). *When work disappears.* Chicago: University of Chicago Press.

Wires, J. W., & Barocas, R. (1994). Determinants of adolescent identity development: A cross-sequential study of boarding school boys. *Adolescence, 29,* 367–377.

7

Culture and Language

The influence of culture and language on the lives and actions of individuals in many of the cases in this text is prominent. However, we have chosen to include two cases in this section as exemplars of the issues that arise when bridges between the multiple worlds of culturally and linguistically diverse students have not been adequately built. The first is a report of the events that occurred in the Onteora School District in Boiceville, New York, when some community members requested that the board of education re-evaluate the choice of an Indian as a school mascot. The second is an account of the obstacles that Qureshi Fome, an immigrant boy who is Pakistani, faced trying to learn in a U.S. school. While these two cases are prototypes of the barriers that cultural and linguistic differences can present in the schools, you will find similar threads running through many of the cases in this book.

Important issues regarding culture and language are addressed in previous chapters that are relevant to these cases. First, we discuss the processes of acculturation and assimilation. Especially relevant to the second case is the insight that immigrants frequently experience marginalization when they are transplanted from their own language and culture without the educational experience, background, or cultural awareness necessary to manage in the United States. Then we discuss the inequities that many students who are English language learners (ELL) and those from nondominant cultures face and argue for the need for multicultural education. Finally, we describe the cultural divide that can exist between the home and school and suggest bridges across a child's multiple worlds. Our purpose in this chapter is to define culture and language, review perceptions of children who are culturally and linguistically different, and briefly discuss effective educational strategies and programs for these students. In addition, we will provide background information on Native American mascots to better inform your discussion of the cases that follow.

Definition of Culture

There is disagreement among social scientists as to what constitutes a culture. Values and the more abstract aspects of culture are often emphasized. Gollnick and Chinn (2006) characterize culture as that which is learned throughout life by participation in the family and society, is shared by an identifiable group, is developed to accommodate to environmental conditions and available resources, and is dynamic. Because cultures change over time based on complex circumstances, it is difficult if not harmful to determine a fixed view of a culture. At best, such descriptions lead to stereotypes (McDermott, 1997).

Historically, the dominant culture in the United States has been Western European. Our political system and language derive from Great Britain. In general, the dominant culture values individualism, competition, freedom, and industriousness. As with all individuals in a particular culture, those in the dominant society often view their culture as the "only" or "correct" viewpoint. This "inability to view other cultures as equally viable alternatives for organizing reality" is known as ethnocentrism (Gollnick & Chinn, 2006, p. 19). Without an ability to look through other cultural lenses, individuals and cultures will frequently misunderstand each other. Such misunderstandings are often the roots of mental anguish, verbal conflict, and physical harm.

TABLE 7.1 *Components of Culture*

Variables	Description	Example
Values and Behavioral Styles	Abstract, generalized principles of behavior to which members of a group attach a high regard.	Some cultures are socialized to work in groups, whereas others prefer to work independently.
Languages and Dialects	Most nation states have a national language, but people within that state speak a variety of languages and dialects.	English is the first language of most Americans, but many Americans speak Black English.
Nonverbal Communications	People communicate with their physical movements as well as with their words.	Cultures vary in the distance they normally place between the speaker and the listener.
Cultural Cognitiveness	Individuals are aware of and think about their culture as distinct from other cultures.	Some people with hearing impairments strongly identify and participate with the Deaf culture, while others do not.
Perspectives, Worldviews, and Frames of Reference	Particular points of view occur more within a culture or micro-culture than others.	The views of Evangelical Protestants regarding the theory of evolution differ from these of other Christians.
Identification	The degree to which a person feels a part of a group and internalizes its goals and values.	Some Americans identify themselves as Irish, whereas others say they are Americans.

Source: Banks (2006).

The subgroups within cultures vary in significant ways from one another. The national or shared culture of the nation-state or society of the big culture can be referred to as the macroculture, whereas subcultures or microcultures may have distinctive cultural patterns while sharing some traits and values of the macroculture (Banks, 2006; Gollnick & Chinn, 2006). Because culture is defined by primarily intangible values, it is important to understand some of the elements, or components, of culture (see Table 7.1). Furthermore, microcultures defined by gender, ethnicity, race, class, language, religion, ability, and geography exist within the greater macroculture. An individual's cultural identity is formed by the interaction of microcultures in the person's experience and the degree of importance of each microculture at a particular time.

Definition of Language

Language is a vehicle for communication, a means of shaping cultural and personal identity, and a way to socialize an individual into a cultural group (Gollnick & Chinn, 2006). Communication can be verbal or nonverbal. Nonverbal communication may involve the degree of social space between speakers; the body language conveyed by facial expressions, posture, and gestures; vocalizations such as pitch or intensity; or vocal qualities such as rhythm or articulation. Linguists have determined that American Sign Language is a language, although it is not oral (Box 7.1). The term "literacy" encompasses more than verbal or nonverbal language to also include reading, writing, and listening.

Literacy development in one's first language (L1) depends on many complex variables. There is tremendous variation among individuals in terms of mastery of language and literacy (Addison Stone, 2006). Some teachers and researchers focus on the structural aspects of literacy such as phonology, morphology, and syntax. For example, in any kindergarten class there will be a significant range among students of the sounds that they articulate correctly and the number of words in their vocabulary (Bos & Vaughn, 2002; Smith, 2007). Therefore, some teachers and programs focus heavily on

BOX 7.1 • *American Sign Language*

Unlike people with other disabilities, many people with profound hearing loss consider themselves *not* people with disabilities but, rather, people who are members of a minority group . . . They are members of the Deaf community and are united by Deaf culture, a culture rich in heritage and traditions. In the United States their primary language is American Sign Language (ASL)—a language that uses manual communication signs, has all of the elements (grammar, syntax, idioms) of other languages, and is not parallel to English in either structure or word order. ASL is not a mere translation of oral speech or the English language (as is Signed English); it is a fully developed language. (In fact, many states allow ASL as an option to meet the high school foreign language requirement, and the same is true at many colleges and universities). (Smith, 2007, p. 352).

phonemic analysis and grammar. Others focus on the meaning of the communication and use of language in social settings. Here the emphasis is on comprehension of ideas and concepts in the context of the cultural settings. Most experts agree that reading and writing are not learned naturally. Our sign systems are cultural artifacts that must be learned. Therefore, there is an attempt to understand the needs of each child and offer a balanced literacy approach.

The teaching of literacy requires additional expertise when the child is introduced to a second language (L2). The continuing immigration from non-English-speaking countries ensures that all school districts will have students whose first language is not English. In fact, in many major cities in the United States over 100 languages are spoken. For many immigrants in these larger cities, it is possible to survive by understanding a minimal amount of English because their jobs are primarily menial and their first language is commonly spoken in their neighborhood. The degree to which an immigrant family speaks English at home is another influence on a child's language development. Historically, some families have encouraged their children to speak their first language while learning English. Others, primarily for economic and social reasons, have encouraged their children to speak only English. The assimilation vs. acculturation debate in Chapter 1 is relevant here.

Most researchers agree that second language acquisition is positively correlated with the degree of first language acquisition (August & Shanahan, 2006; Cummins, 1981; Snow, 1993; Thomas & Collier, 2002; Zecker, 2006). A child whose family comes to the United States when the child is quite young and discourages use of the primary language may unknowingly retard English acquisition because a threshold of language proficiency in the first language is needed to learn the second language. In addition, if older children come from a strife-ridden country where there is little or no schooling, their chances of competing successfully with middle-class U.S. students may be significantly decreased (Suárez-Orozco & Suárez-Orozco, 2001).

Language and culture are inseparable (Trueba, 1993). To learn a language, one must learn the culture, and vice versa. Both are needed to participate successfully in a society. Furthermore, the process of acquiring a new language and culture will inevitably change the nature of the first. For example, the Spanish spoken by Mexican immigrants varies from that in Mexico, and their lifestyles are typical of neither the White mainstream nor the individuals in their homeland. The extent to which the first language and culture can be preserved is related to the degree of national tolerance for pluralism in the receiving country. For children, this includes the degree to which their language and culture are accepted and respected in schools.

Cultural and Linguistic Difference

Educators and social scientists have proposed three major orientations or theories toward understanding individuals who are outside the dominant culture and/or whose first language is not English. These frameworks have been termed a deficiency orientation, a difference orientation, and a political orientation or stand.

Deficiency Orientation

A deficiency orientation toward those who come from culturally and linguistically diverse backgrounds focuses on what attributes the individual lacks (McDermott, 1997; Sleeter & Grant, 1999). This negative view holds the values of the dominant culture (e.g., time orientation, high English literacy skills, independence) as important for success and classifies those who lack these skills as at risk, disadvantaged, or culturally deprived. Children from poor or ethnic backgrounds have been variously described as deficient in achievement, IQ, social skills, sensory stimulation, rich or elaborated language, and moral stability. The assumption is that something is lacking either within the individual or in the individual's environment.

This was certainly the orientation that Jesus's teacher, Mrs. Kniffen, held in regard to Jesus in Chapter 5. His teacher did not view his bilingualism or biculturalism as strengths, and this ethnocentric bias was communicated to the entire class. Jesus understood this all too well and, enculturated with the middle-class values of school, he responded to his father and his native language with shame and anger.

Difference Orientation

A cultural difference orientation views cultural and linguistic diversity as strengths and builds on the knowledge and skills that students bring with them (Sleeter & Grant, 1999). Multiculturalism and multilingualism are viewed as desirable traits that should be encouraged. Differences in communication and cognitive styles are recognized and accommodated. If children have problems learning, the assumption is that the main limitation is inappropriate teaching. This orientation suggests a celebration of differences, rather than a denigration of them.

Estrella, the graduate student who visited Jesus's classroom at Mrs. Kniffen's invitation, adopted this orientation. As a person from a Latin culture who spoke Spanish, Estrella broke whatever stereotypes Mrs. Kniffen or her students had about the competence of culturally different individuals. Furthermore, Estrella brought a culturally responsive curriculum and pedagogy to the classroom that encouraged Jesus to not only participate, but to excel in the classroom.

Social Reconstructionist Orientation

The social reconstructionist theory grows out of an attempt to understand the reasons behind school failure (Gutman, 1987; McDermott, 1997). School failure is often attributed to those who are defined as poor, culturally or linguistically different, or intellectually subnormal. This theory suggests that we must change the unit of analysis from the individual to the culture. In other words, school failure is a cultural fabrication that must be understood in terms of the battle for access and resources by all groups. Furthermore, the dominant society must question the markers that measure school success: grades, standardized tests, high school completion, college graduation. Rather than look only at the schools for change, one must confront the systemic problems of the society as a whole. This view parallels Banks's (2006) characterization of the social action approach to multicultural education and education that is multicultural and reconstructionist as described by Grant and Sleeter (2003).

Implications for Education

Individuals and systems adopt a social reconstructionist approach to education because it takes into account the power relations within a society (Grant & Gillette, 2006). Those who adopt this view assume that all students should be provided with the opportunity to develop academic and social abilities that will enable them to be full participants in a democracy. To accomplish this, school personnel and community members cannot be politically neutral and, therefore, must challenge the values of the dominant society. The case of the Onteora Indian is an example of the type of conflict that can arise when members of a school district question the status quo. We offer the following background on Native American mascots to assist you in thoroughly analyzing that case.

Native American Mascots

The issue of using Native American names and symbols for school and team mascots is an ongoing national controversy. Many universities and school districts have changed their names over the years. For example, Stanford went from the Indians to the Cardinals, and Miami University of Ohio retired the Redskins for the Red Hawks, and Southeastern Oklahoma State University retired Savages to adopt Savage Storm. Recently, University of Illinois, under pressure from the NCAA, saw their mascot Chief Illiniwek dance his last dance and changed their nickname to the Fighting Illini (Staurowsky, 2007). However, other national sport teams (e.g., Cleveland Indians, Washington Redskins) and universities (e.g., University of North Dakota's Fighting Sioux) persist in having mascots, sometimes with the support of local tribes (National Congress of American Association, 2007). As many as 2,500 schools in the United States still have mascots that employ Native American images (Staurowsky, 1999).

Proponents for maintaining Indian mascots and names usually advance a number of arguments for their position (Molin, 1999). First, the polls of alumni and fans often report that a majority is in favor of keeping the mascot. They view the mascot, along with the logos, nicknames, or rituals that accompany it, with nostalgia and resist the idea of losing a part of their past. Second, supporters say that they are honoring indigenous peoples and have respect for their mascot or they would not continue using it. Sometimes individuals who claim Native American descent put this argument forth. Finally, some maintain that the movement to change mascot names is just another exercise in political correctness by overly sensitive groups.

Those who want to eliminate the use of Native American names and mascots for sports teams and schools argue that those who view a mascot with nostalgia are, at best, exhibiting dysconscious racism (Pewewardy, 1999, 2004). Dysconscious racism is an uncritical habit of mind (i.e., perceptions, attitudes, assumptions, and beliefs) that justifies inequity and exploitation by accepting the existing order of things as given (King, 1991). It is an ethnocentric view that assumes that the values and myths of the dominant society are correct and justifiable. If an individual has grown up with Hollywood images of cowboys and Indians, corporate images of Cherokee Jeeps and Land of Lakes butter, and stereotypical school celebrations of the first Thanksgiving, they assume that such symbolism is acceptable and correct. However, these caricatures assigned to Native Americans become more objectionable when one considers what it would be like to have the "Hispanics" or the "Asians" as a team nickname with an accompanying cartoon-like mascot (Fleming, 2006).

There is real irony in objecting to the loss of a school mascot as an elimination of some part of one's personal history, when so much of the history and culture of indigenous peoples has been ignored or distorted. Deculturalization, the educational process of eliminating cultures, is a common strategy used by one country or group to dominate another (Spring, 2004). Deculturalization is implemented by segregating a people, forcing a change of language, imposing the dominant culture through the curriculum, denying expression of the dominated group's culture, and using teachers from the dominant group.

For example, the federal government's policy toward Indian education from the Revolutionary War until the publication of the Meriam Report in 1928 was one of deculturalization (Spring, 2004). Native Americans were removed to reservations as a result of the Indian Removal Act of 1830 and, thereby, segregated from whites. At first, schools were established primarily on reservations, and the purpose of the curriculum, taught by white teachers, was to promote the "dignity of labor" and the values of "civilization." However, reservation schools were not always viewed as successful in accomplishing these goals, so many nonreservation boarding schools were founded. The philosophy was that children should be removed from their families and tribal customs and learn vocational skills, English, American history, and U.S. government. In the 1920s, investigators were often horrified by the conditions that they found in Indian schools, and finally the publication of the Meriam Report began the process of reversing many of these repressive policies.

The argument that fans show respect by having Indian mascots is viewed by opponents as disingenuous. "Invented behavior like the tomahawk chop and dancing around in stereotypical Hollywood Indian style makes a mockery of Indigenous cultural identity and causes many young Indigenous people to feel shame about who they are as human beings, because racial stereotypes play an important role in shaping a young person's consciousness" (Pewewardy, 1999, p. 178). Furthermore, harm is done to all children when stereotypes go unchallenged, and the sacred or cultural symbols of any group are trivialized. Such ignorance is symptomatic of a public school curriculum that marginalizes or distorts the history, culture, and spirituality of Native Americans and other nondominant groups (Hirschfelder, Molin, & Wakim, 1999; Loewen, 1995).

Therefore, opponents assert, the movement to eliminate Native American mascots cannot be trivialized as simply an attempt at political correctness. Rather, understanding and respecting Native American history and culture are an important part of promoting cultural literacy in our schools. It is hypocritical to include a character education curriculum that emphasizes values of truth, democracy, and justice and simultaneously to omit information about the inequitable treatment our society has meted out to Native Americans. President Clinton's Race Initiative Advisory Board reported that

Native Americans experience more pronounced levels of racism in the form of economic and physical abuse than any other identified group (Staurowsky, 1999). One step toward ameliorating this unacceptable treatment is to own all of U.S. history and include it in our textbooks.

Many governmental, professional, and Native American organizations have criticized the use of Indian names and mascots. The Commission on Civil Rights issued a position on the use of Indian team names at non-Indian schools, saying they could be viewed as disrespectful and offensive and could create a racially hostile environment ("Indian Mascot," 2001). This statement was prompted by the grassroots efforts of thousands of American Indian parents nationwide. The National Education Association, the NAACP, ACLU, and the NCAA have issued statements supporting the elimination of Indian names and mascots (Pewewardy, 2004). Similarly, the National Congress of American Indians, the National Indian Education Association, and the National Coalition for Racism in Sport and Media have opposed what they see as a dehumanizing practice (Staurowsky, 1999).

In spite of these strong statements from so many political and educational groups, the conversation about the use of Indian mascots is far from over in the wider society, as the case study of the Onteora Indian will show. A video docu-memoir of the entire Indian mascot controversy in the Onteora School District, entitled "School Board Blues," vividly portrays the intensity of feelings that erupted in that community (Carey & Carey, 2005). Administrators are facing such divided communities across the country and, often, months and months of controversy (Riede, 2001). While some administrators have slowly and quietly worked toward the elimination of nicknames and logos on stationery, school uniforms, and other paraphernalia, others are facing hundreds of community members at special meetings on the issue and lawsuits. Communication with school groups and the media, well-organized and run meetings, and repeated attempts at mediation are among the recommended process strategies for minimizing conflict. However, the larger issues of including factual information about Native Americans in the curriculum and countering the stereotypes the media and many textbooks perpetuate is still a pressing challenge for all educators (Fleming, 2006; Hawkins, 2005)

English Language Learners

The next case in the chapter, Fome Querishi, highlights the interrelationship between culture and language and the importance of teaching both in the public schools. Experts tell us that using a child's native language does not impede the acquisition of English; rather, it offers many advantages (August & Hakuta, 1997; August & Shanahan, 2006). Businesses today view an individual who speaks two languages and is cross-culturally competent as an asset and will frequently offer a higher salary for these skills (Suárez-Orozco & Suárez-Orozco, 2001). Research suggests that children who are bilingual have advantages over monolinguals of the same socioeconomic background in their linguistic, cognitive, and social development.

In addition, English, as well as other languages, has dialectical differences that vary from the standard language. While no dialect should be considered inferior to another, a child who enters a classroom speaking a different dialect from the rest of the children can experience social isolation. Therefore, a starting point for effecting change in schools for students who are culturally and linguistically diverse is to view biculturalism, bilingualism, and bidialectalism, as strengths.

Given the above, it is clear that it is the political and economic climate in the United States that is dictating the state of bilingual education today, rather than a commitment to educating all learners. Research in the field of bilingual education tells us that the vast majority of programs for students who are ELL fall short of providing exemplary programming. Furthermore, schools must recognize that, even with research-based instruction in place for students who are ELL, most students will need a minimum of four years before they are ready to negotiate the demands of general education without some type of support. Acquiring the proficiency needed in the second language for academic success takes from four to seven years and a threshold proficiency in the first language (Collier, 1987; Cummins, 1981).

As described in Chapter 5, teachers often confuse a student's adequate basic interpersonal communication skills (BICS) with his or her ability to accomplish content area tasks that require cognitive academic learning proficiency (CALP). The distinction between BICS and CALP is particularly important for learners who have been called *Generation 1.5* because they have characteristics of both first- and second-generation immigrants (Horwitz, 2007). Like second-generation individuals, these students seem to be acculturated into U.S. society, but like first-generation immigrants, they are not literate in English. While they may get along orally in the classroom, their written work in English shows difficulties with CALP. Some Generation 1.5 English learners never learned to read and write in their L1 and, therefore, do not have CALP in any language. This can be particularly true for transnationals, individuals whose families move back and forth between the United States and their countries of origin (Horwitz, 2007). Schooling for children in these families is frequently disrupted and inevitably disjointed. Given the multiplicity of factors that influence language acquisition, all teachers must plan instruction that is comprehensible, contextualized, and meaningful in a low-anxiety environment (Rothenberg & Fisher, 2007).

The Bilingual Education Act of 1968 provided financial assistance to local education agencies for the purpose of developing and maintaining new and innovative programs to meet the needs of students who are ELL (Miller-Lachmann & Taylor, 1995). In addition, the 1974 Supreme Court case *Lau v. Nichols* asserted that school districts had to provide special language programs, either English as a second language or bilingual education. However, bilingual education faced political opposition in the late nineties. For example, in California in 1998 Proposition 227 dismantled most bilingual programs so that today only about 30 percent of students who are ELL receive bilingual education and, of those, only 18 percent have a certified bilingual teacher (Bennett, 2007). In 2002 the Bilingual Education Act was replaced by the English Education Act, which is part of NCLB. Debates over the most appropriate and successful models for educating students who are ELL continue (Krashen, 2005).

Given the educational research, it seems clear that the decision being made in some states to dismantle bilingual education is often based on economic, cultural, and political agendas, instead of on what is best for the learners. This is not to say that this is an unequivocal issue. The variety of programs that exists even within the framework of transition, maintenance, total immersion, and English as a Second Language programs makes comparative research difficult. However, educational research continues to show that bilingual education that supports the maintenance of the second language has a positive effect in promoting achievement among bilingual students (Merino, Trueba, & Samaniego, 1993; Thomas & Collier, 2002).

Yet the practical aspects of actual implementation of bilingual education are far from ideal. Even in states where bilingual education is still offered, certified bilingual teachers are in short supply and most are Spanish speakers (Merino et al., 1993; Suárez-Orozco & Suárez-Orozco, 2001). Furthermore, some programs are characterized by poor administrative support, inadequate resources, segregation from English language models, and basic secondary content courses that place students on a separate track from those who are college bound.

There are four basic instructional models for serving students who are ELL (Rothenberg & Fisher, 2007). These approaches vary depending upon the amount of first-language instruction provided and the approach to academic content used. They can be described as those that use (1) the native language in content areas, (2) the native language for support, (3) English as a Second Language (ESL) approaches that do not involve the native language, and (4) sheltered instruction or structured immersion that integrates content area instruction with English language development. One model that uses the native language is a two-way bilingual program that typically includes an equal number of students who speak the L1 and the L2. The goal of two-way programs is to promote proficiency in both languages. Some bilingual programs attempt to move students as quickly as possible to English-only general education classrooms, whereas others last longer and attempt to maintain both languages. Programs that use the L1 for support typically use bilingual teachers or paraprofessionals to translate unfamiliar vocabulary or explain lesson taught in English. This type of model is described more fully in the case on the Higher Ground Academy in Chapter 12.

The later two programs are used most frequently when the ELL population includes multiple native languages. ESL programs typically are pull-out programs that gradually increase the amount of time students are in general education as students learn more of the L2. ESL programs can vary depending upon how much they emphasize grammar, communication or grade level materials to learn English. The schools described in Jesus Gonzalez in Chapter 5 and Fome Querishi in this chapter use an ESL model. Sheltered instruction attempts to teach grade-level content while also promoting English language development. For example, the research-based Sheltered Instruction Observation Protocol Model requires teachers to specify language objectives in every content area lesson (Short & Fitzsimmons, 2007). Sheltered instruction also is defined as a program model in which ELL take sheltered courses (e.g., sheltered earth science, sheltered algebra) in addition to content-based ESL classes. Content-based ESL classes are taught by language educators who are trying to increase English language proficiency, but do so through interdisciplinary units (Short & Fitzsimmons, 2007).

Approximately 70 percent of all students who are ELL are Spanish speakers. However, the diversity of languages spoken in some school districts makes bilingual education impossible, given the lack of bilingual teachers for all those languages.

For example, although New York City began a school to teach Arabic and Arab culture in 2007, it is the first school of its kind (Marks, 2007). Therefore, it is difficult for teachers to know the particular challenges that the transition from the L1 to English may present. For instance, it has been noted that native speakers of Arabic have particular difficulty with reading comprehension in English. Some researchers have suggested that this is because of notable differences in the representation of vowel sounds in written Arabic and English (Hayes-Harb, 2006).

Given the undersupply of certified bilingual educators who are proficient in languages other than Spanish, English as a Second Language instruction and sheltered instruction are the only viable alternatives for many students who are ELL. Nevertheless, many instructional techniques that enhance background knowledge and integrate reading, writing, listening and thinking are available that can enhance their achievement. Approaches such as cooperative learning, role playing, readers' theater, visual representation, total physical response, and graphic organizers offer the contextual support needed (Cummins, 1996; Faltis & Coulter, 2008; Rothenberg & Fisher, 2007).

Perhaps the greatest challenge in educating students who are ELL is at the secondary level since they are simultaneously expected to learn a second language and acquire content area knowledge in order to pass the high stakes tests required by NCLB. A recent report, *Double the Work* by the Center for Applied Linguistics on behalf of the Carnegie Corporation, reports that 31% of ELLs fail to complete high school and outlines the problems inherent in our educational and social systems for adolescents acquiring English (Short & Fitzsimmons, 2007). After an extensive review of the research and visits to model programs, the advisory panel made the following suggestions for educators, researchers, and policymakers regarding policies for this population: (1) set common criteria for identifying these learners and tracking their progress; (2) develop new assessments of their native language abilities, English language developments, and content knowledge; (3) build capacity among preservice and current educators to instruct effectively; (4) design flexible secondary programs that offer time and coursework that account for the process of learning a second language; (5) use research-based practices more widely and consistently; and (6) fund and conduct more research on the long term academic outcomes of programs. A thorough review of this report is recommended for all present and future secondary educators.

The Case of the Onteora Indian

In 1952 the Onteora Central School District was incorporated. The largest district in New York State, Onteora encompasses rural areas in the Catskill Mountains and the town of Woodstock, made famous by the 1960s festival and now a popular home for those in the arts community.

Onteora is a high-performing district. Historically, the percentage of students passing state-mandated exams has exceeded both county and state averages. The high school offers advance placement courses in a considerable number of areas, and 60 to 80 percent of the students attend college after graduation.

During the 2000–2001 school year, the district served 2,277 students. Of that number, 307 received free lunch and 130 received reduced-priced lunch. The racial distribution of the district was American Indian or Alaskan Native (1), Asian or Pacific Islander (53), Black (81), Hispanic (72), White (2070).

The major highway running through the district is Route 28, also known as the Onteora Highway, and it is from this supposed Indian word that the district chose its name and mascot, the Onteora Indians. However, the historical record does not support the existence of Indian settlements in the area. The Esopus and the Mohicans were the nearest Native Americans who settled along the Hudson River.

Dennis Yerry, a parent in the district, questioned the use of an Indian as a school symbol in 1998, but he received no subsequent support from the school board at that time. By the 1999–2000 school year, there was enough public support to raise the issue once again (see Box 7.2 and Figure 7.1).

On January 10, 2000, the Onteora school board revisited the issue of the school name and accompanying images after receiving a letter of discontent from parents and a citizen's group known as Community: One Love One Race (COLOR). The board decided to hold a public hearing on the issue at the January 24 regular meeting of the school board and then vote on whether to retire the name.

The meeting began at 7:00 at the junior–senior high school with a thorough report on the district technology programs and accompanying budgetary needs of the district, but few questions regarding the report were asked. The board then moved to public comment and gave each speaker who had called the district office ahead of time 2 minutes to speak. Over 200 people attended the meeting, and 50 of them were on the list to speak. Throughout the crowd there were people wearing armbands with a red circle and slash crossing out the words "racist stereotypes," which had been distributed by COLOR.

Speakers from outside the district came, as well as community members. Ray Tin-Koshyula, a Lakota Indian from the Pine Ridge reservation in South Dakota, began by presenting the board with several red and blue feathers as a symbol of friendship and showed them an empty liquor bottle with the brand name Crazy Horse to emphasize how names could be demeaning to American Indians. Later, Kay Olan, a teacher in a local district and member of the Mohawk Nation, said that, although she believed that no harm was meant in establishing the symbol originally, human decisions must be reconsidered when people become more enlightened. She emphasized the need for all involved to talk and listen with open minds and include these discussions in the school curriculum.

A coach from the district stated that he felt that the name was not discriminatory and had been chosen out of respect. A community member supported his view saying that the determined, muscular Indian figure painted on the gymnasium wall in 1997 was an inspiration to all school teams and that they had done well under the eye of that figure. Another man from the community stated that it was ridiculous to change the images just because a politically correct group in the community said they were racist or insensitive. He called the wall painting a work of art and said that removing it would be censorship. He called those objecting to the image thin skinned and dysfunctional.

A black man with dreadlocks who wore an armband said that there was no question that the symbols used by the school were racist and were an insult to the First Nation. He received a great deal of applause. Then a woman who was a graduate of

BOX 7.2 • *Indian Mascots Draw Criticism*

Some See Images as 'Derogatory'
In the Onteora school district, the Board of Education is expected to vote Monday on whether to abolish the longtime symbol of its teams.

By Jonathan Ment
Freeman Staff

BOICEVILLE, JANUARY 23, 2000—The Onteora school board is expected to vote Monday on whether to eliminate the American Indian as a school symbol.

The district's athletic teams are nicknamed the Indians, an annual dance and the high school yearbook sport the name "Tomahawk," and a muscular American Indian breaking through a cinder block wall is painted on the wall of the high school gymnasium.

Dennis Yerry, who says he's "part Seneca, part Dutch and part Irish," stepped forward two years ago to protest the use of American Indian images.

"I don't feel it's a sports issue or a popularity issue," said Yerry, a 1977 Onteora graduate who now has an 8-year-old in the school district. "I feel it's an education issue. The term 'Indians,' as the mascot for the sports team and the logos on the wall, have become curriculum for students at the high school."

Yerry said seventh-graders have two weeks of planned study on American Indian life and culture; third-graders have about a month.

"According to the school, there's not much in the curriculum from ninth to 12th grade," Yerry said. "The only thing they get is the mascot and the totem pole in the cafeteria. . . . The bottom line is I don't think any group of people should be used as the mascot for a sports team."

Although Yerry let go of the issue locally when he "felt no support from the (school) board," others have come forward to champion the cause, and in greater numbers. Yerry is now active in the issue nationally.

The issue has received enough attention across New York state to prompt the Education Department to begin evaluating the use of American Indian images in schools.

"There were some concerns communicated to the department from around the state," said Bill Hirschen an Education Department spokesman. "There are no conclusions, but there's a survey (circulating) to determine the extent of this in the state . . . and to gather the opinions of school officials."

Hirschen said there's no time limit for the study and no related state Education Department Policy.

Onteora school board President Marty Millman said the logos in the building and on the playing field "have disturbed a great deal of the local people."

Onteora suggested that it would be a shame to wipe out the tradition of the Indian and that it would be possible to change the images without changing the name. Later, a man who identified himself as 25 percent Indian, stated that his wife had graduated from Onteora and that no one in his family found the mascot objectionable. He felt the Indian promoted spirit and school tradition and wished that people were as concerned about the drug problem as they were about this issue. He said that racism was not a problem in the district and encouraged the board to put the issue up for a public referendum.

A woman who stated that her husband is part Native American and part Latino said that her children had been subjected to demeaning comments about their ethnicity. Another speaker who identified himself as a Jewish American reminded the audience

FIGURE 7.1 *Mural of Onteora Indian*
Source: *Daily Freeman*, Kingston, N.Y.

that symbols could be used to dehumanize people and justify genocide. He stated that a person should not be used as a mascot and also called for better information within the school curriculum regarding the history of native peoples in the United States.

Josh Telson, the vice-president of the Student Affairs Council, said that most students at Onteora didn't care whether the mascot was kept or not. He did point out that the cost of changing school uniforms would be considerable and urged the board to fund the change if they made it.

After over 2 hours of public comment, the board voted to retire the Indian. It was a 4 to 3 vote, with school board president Martin Millman in the minority. The board received a standing ovation from some in the audience. Superintendent Hal Rowe commended the audience for its eloquence and said that if any image disturbs the people that it represents it should be eliminated.

The school board's decision was the beginning, not the end, of a long and often heated debate over the Onteora Indian. Because of the outcry against the decision that surfaced over the ensuing week, the board agreed to hold another hearing at their meeting on February 7 to determine whether voters should decide the question of retiring the symbol by holding a referendum in May. That morning about 200 middle and high school students conducted a 45-minute sit-in in the cafeteria to protest the board's decision. The day after the vote, students had begun to circulate a petition to support a return to the Indian mascot and were continuing to get signatures during the sit-in. A controversy arose when eleven students were given a five-day suspension for refusing to return to class (see Box 7.3).

At least 300 people attended the February 7 meeting, and the overwhelming majority of the forty who spoke, were in favor of keeping the Indian symbol. Trustees were given petitions containing more than 2,000 signatures opposing their decision to retire the Indian. Sadie Finkle, president of the Student Advisory Council, stated that the majority of students wanted to keep the Indian name and perhaps change the images. Josh Telson took a different view: "When people realize the issue here is respect, they'll change their minds and realize it's no big deal. It's time to move on. If students develop a new name themselves, they'll have school spirit over that" (Twine, 2000). Eighth-grader Rachel McCallum wore face paint and a decorated headband, with a sign that read "Proud of My Indian Heritage and My School Emblem." At the end of the meeting the Onteora Board of Education voted 4 to 3 against trustee Joseph Doan's resolution for a public referendum along the same lines as the previous vote.

"A democracy is not always the will of the majority of people who have the right to vote," stated Marino D'Orazio, a trustee. "In our system, bodies of elected officials vote based on the best information they have and ultimately, their conscience. Tough decisions are always unpopular because they go to the heart of what we live by" (Twine, 2000).

After this and other board of education meetings, it was discovered that cars of board members who had voted to rescind the mascot had been damaged. Tires were punctured, among other things. No one was ever caught in connection with these incidents.

In subsequent months the issues raised by these two meetings resurfaced in countless conversations throughout the area in homes, schools, and other community settings. Local editorial pages frequently contained strong words on both sides of the debate, although supporters of the Indian mascot seemed most vocal. Editorials accused the board of catering to special interest groups, ignoring majority opinion, abandoning their educational mission, and modeling poor parliamentary procedures.

Although most teachers agreed with the board's decision to change the mascot, some were upset by the process. They, like the students, felt that a democratic process was not followed and that teachers should have been polled or consulted more thoroughly regarding the issue, since they were the ones who had to live with implementing any changes. However, few teachers attended school board meetings or voiced their opinions at those meetings. Teachers on both sides of the issue were reluctant to speak up.

BOX 7.3 • *Students Who Cut Classes for Petition Drive Are Suspended*

Onteora officials discipline 11 youngsters who were collecting signatures in support of keeping the school's Indian symbol.

by Cynthia Werthamer
Freeman Staff

BOICEVILLE, FEBRUARY 9, 2000 — Eleven Onteora High School students received five-day out-of-school suspensions Tuesday for cutting classes while they circulated petitions asking the school district to keep the school's Indian mascot.

Tommy Clare of Boiceville, one of those suspended, called the punishments disrespectful of the students' rights. His mother said the students were promised school time to circulate the petitions but didn't get it.

School authorities said the students were told three of them could continue circulating the petitions but that any others refusing to return to class would be suspended.

The students began asking for petition signatures Tuesday, the morning after the Onteora school board, by a 4–3 vote, stood by its earlier decision to stop using the Indian as the district's symbol. About 200 students protested the retirement of the symbol Monday morning by staging a 45-minutes sit-in in the school cafeteria.

Three of the eleven suspended students had spoken at the board meeting's public comment session, supporting retention of the mascot, Clare said.

The students were promised a longer homeroom period than usual so they could seek signatures, but the period wasn't extended, said Barbara Clare, mother of the 15-year-old freshman.

The group moved to the cafeteria, then into the hallway, effectively spending most of their school day soliciting names, Tommy Clare said.

"The principal (Thomas Jackson) saw us in the morning and said, 'Just make sure you spell everything right' on our posters. He was pretty sarcastic," he said. "Then he tried to split us up, suggesting three representatives stay out. But it was important that we stick together. It was like a sit-down strike.

"I think we were treated very unfairly," Clare said. "I know I cut (class), but we were standing up for our rights. We have the right to speak our minds, and we weren't getting respect from the principal and the higher authorities."

He added that the group did not encourage others to cut class, warning those who choses to join that they risked being suspended.

Assistant Principal Vincent Bruck said the students were not singled out because of their speeches the night before. "In fact, this morning on the PA (public address system), we complimented the students who attended the board meeting," he said. "We also said we expect students to be in classes today or face the consequences. We gave them ample opportunity to go back to class, which they didn't do."

He said the administration agreed to requests by students on Monday that they be allowed to meet with members of the school board about the mascot decision and that they be allowed to vote on the mascot in a school referendum, with the results to be given to the board.

Clare said students were upset both by the removal of the Indian, which he said has been the school's symbol for 49 years, and the fact that students weren't consulted before the board's decision.

Source: *Daily Freeman*, Kingston, N.Y.

State and federal governmental groups became involved. For example, in March a representative from the U.S. Community Relations Service, a branch of the U.S. Justice Department, met with Superintendent Hal Rowe and other district leaders to discuss possible solutions. One idea was to bring in trained mediators who would meet with middle and high school students to resolve some of the differences in opinion regarding the board decisions. In April, consultants in conflict resolution affiliated with Rutgers University met with seven middle and high school students to determine the students' perceptions of the issues regarding the Indian mascot. However, this was the only time that mediators met with the students since further meetings would have required board-approved funding.

That same month, Andrian Cooke, acting coordinator of the Native American Education Unit for the New York State Education Department, wrote to the Onteora board commending their courageous stand against racism. He wrote, "Our children must be taught not to demean certain groups of people with who(m) they must coexist in today's society. The images presented by [Onteora yearbook] pictures create negative feelings toward Native American people within the community" (Kemble, 2000a). New York State Department spokesman Tom Dunn indicated that an official position on Indians as school mascots was expected to be released by Commissioner Richard Mills, which would provide school districts with guidance in dealing with these issues.

At the April 3 board meeting, Josh Telson reported on the process for choosing a new mascot. Students would soon be surveyed in homeroom for their top three choices, with the understanding that the symbol cannot be racially derogatory. Then a list would be generated based on frequency, originality, color scheme, and school atmosphere. The top three choices would be voted on. Once chosen, students would be involved in developing the logo and mascot costume. This process never occurred. However, in April a policy was passed to prohibit the use of racial "images and artifacts" in the district.

On May 8 the board held a hearing for the 2000–2001 Onteora Central School District budget scheduled May 16 for a vote. The proposed budget was approximately $35,500,000, a 6.94 percent increase over the previous year. In addition, voters were given the opportunity to vote on three propositions: school buses, maintenance vehicles, and computer equipment. About 30 people attended the meeting, but few comments were made about the actual expenditures. However, community members raised concerns that voters would vote down the budget because of their displeasure with the mascot issue. May 16 was also the evening when district residents would vote for school board trustees. Two of the three individuals running against incumbents were in favor of restoring the Indian mascot.

The predictions about the results of the May 16 election in Onteora were accurate. The budget was voted down, albeit by a vote of 2,099 to 2,057. The only proposition to pass involved technology support. Of the nine school districts in the county, only four school budgets were approved. However, the budgets that were rejected had higher spending increases than Onteora's, and the district that had a comparable budget received approval. Furthermore, the two candidates that had run on a pro-Indian platform were elected to the board. The night of the election there was a physical altercation between one of the successful candidates and the partner of a woman who ran unsuccessfully. Stories were conflicting regarding fault, and both members were required to appear in town court, although the judge eventually determined no penalties or jail time.

On June 5 one of the first actions of the new school board was to rescind the January resolution to eliminate the use of the Indian name and symbols after the 1999–2000 school year with a vote of 5 to 1. In addition, trustees passed the first reading of a policy that would delete language referencing the use of ethnic images and artifacts as district symbols. There was disagreement over whether the board could approve the first reading without discussion of the language. Attorneys with the American Indian Movement, a Minnesota-based organization, later stated that they would file a lawsuit against the district if racially based images were used as district mascots and symbols.

In addition, the new school board decided to put the budget up for another vote. According to New York State law, if a budget is defeated a second time, the district is forced to adopt an austerity spending plan that puts a 2.64 percent limit on increases in nonmandated spending. Mandatory spending includes salaries and expenditures for academic programs. Given the narrow margin of defeat and the belief by many that the mascot controversy influenced voters, the new board decided to put a slightly reduced budget of $35.46 million up for vote on June 20.

At the June 19 school board meeting, attended by about 175 people, members of the community criticized Superintendent Hal Rowe and other district officials on a variety of issues. These included failure to take seriously a female student's charges of sexual assault, overcrowding in school buildings, and creating dissension by openly taking sides in controversial issues and hiding others. Other parents supported the administration, saying Dr. Rowe was caring and cooperative and that the criticisms were unfair. On June 20 the budget was defeated by a 1,438 to 1,348 vote, requiring the board to cut approximately $800,000 from the 2000–2001 budget.

Over the summer a vote on rescinding the policy on racial images and artifacts was delayed based on advice from the New York State attorney general's office and the school board attorney. Likewise, a suggestion to form a three-person committee to study the infusion of Indian history and culture into the curriculum was not enacted. Also during the summer, the board received a lengthy letter from the state attorney general's office outlining the district controversy and similar case decisions across the country (Kemble 2000b). The letter advised the board to review the U.S. Civil Rights Act of 1964 before rescinding the policy enacted by the previous board to prohibit a race of people or its symbols or artifacts from being used as district symbols. The letter outlined relevant legal issues (see Box 7.4).

In the fall of 2000 the school board voted 5 to 2 to rescind the policy banning the use of racial images in the district. This was done despite considerable progress on a compromise policy being negotiated by representatives of the state attorney general's office. The American Indian Movement stated that it would proceed with a lawsuit against the district challenging all federal funding that the district receives.

In February 2001 the Commissioner of the New York State Department of Education, Richard Mills, issued a letter to all public schools that states: "I have concluded that the use of Native American symbols or depictions as mascots can become a barrier to building a safe and nurturing school community and improving academic achievement for all students. I ask the superintendents and presidents of school boards to lead their communities to a new understanding on this matter. I ask the boards to end the use of Native American mascots as soon as practical." (Mills, 2001). Furthermore, in April 2001 the U.S. Commission on Civil Rights urged schools to stop using Indian team names and mascots, saying that the practice may violate antidiscrimination laws

BOX 7.4 • *State Warns of Consequences of Keeping Indian Mascot*

Onteora school officials are advised to carefully consider the legal implications of rescinding the policy banning the use of racial images or artifacts as district symbols.

By William J. Kemble
Correspondent

BOICEVILLE, AUGUST 3, 2000—A five-page letter from the state Attorney General's Office to the Onteora school board outlines the history of the district's mascot controversy and advises trustees to review similar cases where court action has been threatened over the use of Indian symbols.

The letter, written by state Civil Rights Bureau Chief Andrew Celli, was released by state officials Wednesday after school district representatives denied the *Freeman's* request for a copy.

To emphasize how other school districts have adapted to changing sensitivity over the issue, Celli cited a U.S. Department of Justice investigation of a North Carolina school district and the decisions of school systems in Dallas and Los Angeles to cease the use of Indian mascots.

"The degree to which the maintenance of 'Indian' team nicknames, the use of 'Indian' imagery, the use of native religious symbols, gestures or chants in a secular (and potentially demeaning) context and/or the maintenance of an 'Indian' mascot implicate the anti-discrimination laws under these and other relevant statutes can only be determined on a case-by-case basis, with careful attention to the facts," Celli wrote.

Onteora trustees were advised to review the U.S. Civil Rights Act of 1964 carefully before voting to rescind a policy enacted by the previous board to prohibit "a race of people or its symbol or artifact" from being used as district symbols.

Source: Daily Freeman, Kingston, N.Y.

"It is the view of the (Attorney General's Office) that these considerations, as well as others, should be borne in mind when a decision about the Onteora Indian and related imagery is made," Celli wrote.

Investigators for the state attorney general have attended the past two Onteora school board meetings, and Celli said the situation will continue to be monitored. He also offered recommendations for reviewing policy involving the Indian mascot, saying the "relevant legal issues" to consider include:

- The nature of the team nickname and whether it is "patently offensive" in how it uses or refers to American Indians as hostile or warlike.
- Use by athletic teams of Indians items of historical or religious significance, such as a feather headdress, face paint, totem poles or tomahawks, in a non-religious event or in a manner that may have the effect of demeaning American Indian traditions.
- Depictions of American Indians in a comical fashion, as cartoon characters or with aggressive or hostile features or expressions.
- Allowing the language or gestures of American Indian culture to be distorted, including the use of a person dressed as an Indian to lead cheers.
- The extent of efforts by the district to educate students about American Indian history and traditions, with an emphasis on discerning fact from the stereotypical images that have been depicted by schools with Indian mascots.

(Kemble, 2001a). On May 15, 2001, the school board authorized a nonbinding referendum asking residents if the Onteora Indian should remain the title of all sports teams and all other student athletic activities (Kemble, 2001b). Despite statements from the New York State Education Department that ballots for issues such as these were not appropriate, the referendum was held. The results showed that 1,950 individuals were for keeping the Indian mascot and 1,883 were against it. At the writing of this edition, the Onteora Indian remains the school mascot and the depictions in the school cafeteria and gym remain on the walls.

Discussion Questions

1. Regarding the use of the Onteora Indian as a name and symbol, what are the views of each of the following groups: students, teachers, community members, board of education trustees, and administrators? Does there appear to be any consensus within or between groups?
2. What underlying beliefs motivate those who want to eliminate the Indian name and what underlying beliefs motivate those that want to maintain it?
3. To what extent are the views of the student body sought or represented in this case?
4. How has the controversy over the Indian mascot affected other aspects of the school program?
5. If you were teaching in this district, what would be your personal response to the situation?
6. What could teachers and administrators do individually or corporately to work toward resolution of this issue?

The Case of Fome Qureshi

September 6

A new school year, a new teaching position, a new group of students and curriculum, two new school faculties, a new beginning. Not everyone gets to experience this much "newness" in mid-life! After eighteen years of teaching study skills to underprepared community college students and three years of teaching ESL to adults, teaching in the public schools is a welcome but challenging change.

I'm glad that my master's is behind me and I have a teaching position in ESL to show for it, even if I am traveling back and forth between the elementary school in the morning and the middle school in the afternoon each day. The district has chosen to bus all students who are ELL to Lincoln Elementary and Henderson Middle, rather than ask us to travel to eight different elementary schools and two middle schools. We only have an ESL program since none of the grade levels have enough speakers of any one language to warrant bilingual instruction. Yet the number of students who are in the district is increasing month by month. While the largest percentage of students who are ELL is Spanish speakers who come from Mexico, the program includes students from twenty different language groups.

Teaching elementary students is quite a contrast to teaching middle school students! Working with middle schoolers is like taking a roller-coaster ride every day. I have the additional challenge of having students whose primary languages include Spanish, Arabic, Chinese, Gujarati, and Urdu. Half of the teachers in this school have never heard of Urdu, so I have to continually say, "That's what they speak in Pakistan." Fome Qureshi is the first student I've worked with who speaks Urdu, so I want to try to keep a log of his activities.

He's a handsome young man with thick black hair, respectful behavior toward his teachers, and an eagerness to learn. He's only been in the United States since May of last year and, after a month in New York City, his parents and two younger sisters came to Riverton. He dresses like all the other boys, so you wouldn't necessarily know his cultural background without asking. It's clear that the Qureshis are concerned parents since they immediately brought Fome to school and he was given the Language Acquisition Survey (LAS) last June. Fome's oral level was low, and he was on level 1 for reading, which is equivalent to being a nonreader. He has quite a way to go to reach level 3 to be out of ESL, but right now I just want to help him to acclimate to sixth grade in the United States.

September 13

I've had a chance to review the records that Fome's parents gave June Adams, his guidance counselor, when they enrolled him last spring. June said the Qureshis arrived with the district supervisor for ESL and Mrs. Mukherjee, a fifteen-year resident of Riverton who grew up in India and speaks Urdu. She wasn't sure how much they understood of what she said. June believes that Mr. Qureshi understands fairly well because he responds with some English phrases, but Mrs. Qureshi says little in English beyond greetings.

It's time for me to arrange a meeting with Fome's parents, but it's not a simple task to get everyone together. Without a translator, we might as well not meet.

September 23

I'm anxious to meet Fome's parents. I'm concerned about his vision. Fome's big, dark eyes are usually watery, and he often tells me that he must go put drops in them. I hope he's been to a doctor.

His transcript from his last school in Rawalpindi is difficult to interpret; they don't use letter grades and I can only guess at what the numbers mean. I can easily see that he took math, science, Pakistani history, and Urdu. It looks like he took Islamiat (sounds like religion) and scouting. He also had English, but often the study of English in another country is very different from what he'd learn in the United States. What I didn't realize until now is that Fome was born in Libya and actually lived in Tripoli until he was 8 years old.

This year guidance has agreed that Fome should be in science, reading, math, English, physical education, and a quarter each of health, music, and art. However, in order to fit him into the one period when ESL is offered, they're exempting him from social studies. He usually stays ninth period for help with his homework, but that is a voluntary period. His ESL class includes all emerging readers: two students from Mexico, a student from Saudi Arabia, and one from Puerto Rico. He won't be receiving report card grades this quarter since they would all be failing if he were compared (unfairly) to his classmates. Instead, he receives a comment such as "ESL: No grade assigned. Satisfactory effort." However, I think some of his teachers do show him what his grades are on papers and tests and, naturally, they are low.

September 27

I spoke with Mrs. Mukherjee, who has been helping Fome's mother get to know the community. Mrs. Mukherjee says that Fome has always gone to schools where Islam is taught and practiced and, at this age, he would be attending an all-boys school. This kind of separation just doesn't exist in our public schools. Riverton is a city of 25,000 in which there is only a small mosque off the main street and there are probably fewer than seventy families that are Islamic.

October 13

Natalie Vaughn, his science teacher, says that Fome is very quiet in class and doesn't usually know the answer when she asks him a question. I know she tries to use hands-on experiments when she can, but he's still on the BICS level and most of what they are talking about involves CALP. Besides, who knows how much science background he got in Pakistan?

On the other hand, Fome is starting to talk quite a bit in ESL. We're reading a simplified version of *Oliver Twist*, and I've been having them act it out as they read. The students seem to really enjoy this, and it helps us talk through the new vocabulary. Of course, allowing students to act also opens the door for all kinds of interaction, both positive and negative. Fome and Omar aren't friends, and sometimes I have to separate them or they get into a verbal altercation. Omar has a reputation for getting into trouble. Last year he pulled the fire alarm. He's been in the United States for several years and has made little progress academically. I think Fome is actually a little afraid of Omar, but so are a lot of students. Unfortunately, he's going to have to learn to deal with it.

November 5

Linda DeNunzio showed me a story Fome wrote for English class. I guess she asked them to write about a friend. She wondered if I knew why he lines his words up in columns like this.

My	friend	name	is	Michel.
He	was	bron	at	St. Mary
hospital	in	Riverton,	On	14, Oct.86
He	was	named after	a	person
in	a	movie.	He	has lived
in	Riverton	and	Columbia.	
He	has	two	brothers	and
three	sisters.	He	had	a
pet.	His	pet	name	
is	pitbull.	He	likes	
his	dog.	His	easy	subject
is	Math.	His	best	year
is	97	because	He	
like	the	homework.	He	always
do	one	work	in	his
roller	skiting.	His	favorite	station
is	Rap.	His	favorite	sport
team	is	49	ners.	

I know that Urdu is written from right to left, but I'm not sure how that would relate to this. Fome knows how to use simple sentences and his spelling is respectable even if his vocabulary is still limited. He's still confused by verb tenses and the use of possessives. I wonder what he means by "one work" in the sentence about roller "skiting" (skating)? Linda told him he would get a C for content and D for mechanics on this assignment if she were giving him a grade.

Apparently, Fome doesn't let that kind of news bother him. He wrote another paragraph about how much he likes his teachers at Henderson Middle School. I'll have to find out more about what school in Libya and Pakistan is like.

December 2

We just got back from Thanksgiving vacation and Linda asked the students to write something of their own choice for their portfolio. This is what Fome contributed:

> I like thanksgiving but I forget to check and burn my turkey. I am going to tell my mom. They turkey was ready. Come down and check it. Before my mom came down the cat come frist. And then me and the cat try to put the turkey in the oven. Then my friend coming out. And I go play outside to play two hour later I smell burning. And I tell my friend my friend I burned my turkey. And they make fun on me.

I thought he did a nice job of telling the story (although we certainly still need to work on verb tense and not starting sentences with "And"). However, I'd be surprised if he had turkey for Thanksgiving!

Mr. and Mrs. Qureshi didn't come for parent–teacher conferences (a miscommunication). I want them to know that Fome is trying hard, and I have many questions to ask them. Things are too hectic now, but after winter break, I'm going to ask June to call them in so we can talk using Mrs. Mukherjee as the translator.

Natalie Vaughn says that Fome is trying, but he says that she is talking too fast for him to understand. She doesn't feel that she really talks too fast. In fact, she tries to restate things frequently to Fome and others in the class. He is doing his homework and he continues to be respectful and well behaved. He's willing to work in groups, but hasn't seemed to develop that many friendships outside the boys he knows in ESL.

January 10

Finally! The Qureshis met with June, Natalie, Linda, Mrs. G, and me today. They were a little late because they had to take a taxi. Mr. Qureshi has a job at a service station but had off this morning. Mrs. Qureshi had on a beautiful green kameez (shirt) and salwar (pants) and covered her head with a dupatta. He did most of the talking and then Mrs. Mukherjee translated. Sometimes Mrs. Qureshi would add things, especially about Fome's school experience.

We started by asking how they like Riverton. They seemed most pleased that it is not crowded and that the children like school. They were glad to hear that Fome is trying hard in school, but were concerned that he doesn't study more at home. They want him to go to college. We assured them that he is doing most of his homework. We encouraged them to get him a library card so that he can take out books at the public library.

I asked about his eyes, which seem better but are still red. Apparently, Rawalpindi is a huge city and he lived in the commercial section where there are few plants. He has developed asthma and severe allergies here, which are aggravated by the sun. He was riding his bike all over, but they had to take it away from him. Fome, while not overweight, looks like he's gained 20 pounds since he arrived. Perhaps he's not getting enough exercise—or perhaps he's enjoying having food so readily accessible in the United States!

I asked about Fome's school experience in Pakistan. In fifth grade, Fome had 38 students in his class. Pakistan's educational system is essentially the British system, which bases promotion to the next grade on yearly exams. There are both public and private schools, and there is a great difference in the quality of education between the two. The Qureshis have always paid for Fome and his two sisters to go to a private school. He has been taking English for several years. The books are in English, but the teachers often speak in Urdu. Islamiat is an explanation of the holy book Qur'an in Urdu. Boys and girls take this class separately. It's still not clear to me how much Fome was required to write and speak in English before coming here.

When the Qureshis were in Tripoli, Mr. Qureshi worked for an Italian oil company. The children went to a Pakistani school that included children who spoke Arabic, Chinese, English, and Filipino. I can't imagine being an ESL teacher there!

I wondered why the Qureshis came to the United States since they don't have relatives here at all. Apparently, they submitted their names to an emigration lottery. Within six months, their names were called. They answered questions, filled out forms, and they were on their way to the United States. Mr. Qureshi is working double-shifts six days a week and Mrs. Qureshi manages the household.

Another important piece of this lengthy conversation was about Islam. The Qureshis explained that Fome must pray five times a day since this is one of the five pillars of their faith. He must go home and "make up" the afternoon prayer that he didn't offer in school. One of the evening prayers takes about 25 minutes before he goes to bed. Soon he will be fasting for Ramadan. He is not to eat pork, and red meat must be "halal," which is something like kosher from what I could gather. These are things I didn't realize, since Fome does not speak of them in school.

I really was pleased to have Mrs. Mukherjee there as our conversation would have been minimal otherwise. The Qureshis seem like very concerned parents. They say that they like U.S. schools because their children like the teachers and parents can be more involved than in Pakistan.

P.S. The Qureshis said they did *not* have turkey for Thanksgiving since they didn't know about these traditions.

January 27

I decided to sit in on one of Linda's English classes so that I could see how Fome and the other ESL students in that class respond. She's right—they are quiet in the regular classroom! The period started with sustained silent reading. Fome has listed about twelve books that he has read since September, including *The Matchlock Gun*, *Super Hoops*, *Dragons Don't Cook Pizza*, and two Nancy Drew stories. Fome got up from his seat to ask Linda what the word "grave" meant (the burial place). After 10 minutes,

Linda asked the students to take out their language arts book and reminded them they were reviewing nouns, verbs, adjectives, and adverbs. The definition of each of these terms was on the board, and they discussed them. Then they went over the homework, which was on forming comparative and superlative adjectives. Here are some of the types of errors Fome made on fill-in-the-blank items:

early	*earlyer*	*earlyest*
bravely	*more bravelyer*	*most bravelyest*

On the sentences, these are samples of his responses:

> Of these two, I like pea soup *well.* (Then he corrected it to "best.")
> Joe drives *more recklessly* of all the race car drivers.

He did get some right, but I'm not sure that he wasn't just benefiting from the law of averages. It's obvious that Fome doesn't understand all the rules that are operating here, and it's not easy to teach them all when he still is working on a basic understanding of vocabulary. It would also help if English didn't have so many exceptions. I guess I'll try to work on some of this in ESL. Forty-two minutes just aren't enough. Fortunately, he often stays after school for extra help (and also to socialize). Linda does make an extra effort to look over Fome's shoulder as he's working and to help him when he asks.

At the end of class, Linda asked them to write a response to one of the following two writing prompts in the book for homework:

1. A wizard has just cast a spell. You and your best friend will be fish for the next 24 hours. You will be a shark and your friend will be a goldfish. Write a brief paragraph telling who has the better time and why. Use several adverbs in the comparative form in your paragraph.
2. In old television westerns, the good cowboys wore white hats and rode white horses. The bad cowboys wore black hats and rode black horses. In movies about King Arthur and Sir Lancelot, good knights wore white armor and bad knights wore black armor. Write a short story about the cowboys or the knights. Compare the good guys and the bad guys. Use both adjectives and adverbs.

This should be interesting!

February 3

Today Linda showed me the story that Fome wrote for that homework assignment. He said he didn't want to write on the topics assigned, and Linda said that was fine. This is what he produced:

Fome Qureshi	English
2/28/98	Period 1

Life is hard without school & collage

Without school and Collage the life

is bad. You cannot do nothing. You don't go

school then you have to work in Pizza hut, Plaza

Pizza e.t.c. You do robbery and said bad word to
other people. If you want to go to school. You don't do your home. Its not
teacher responsibility Example you have 5 subject homework. You just do 1. If she
told you to stay 9th you don't stay. You don't go school. then you pay.

I guess that's why Fome always stays for ninth period to get extra help. He does-n't want to work at Pizza Hut! I think the only adjective he used correctly is "bad." However, I would love it if I could transfer this work ethic to several other students. It's clear that Fome has heard admonitions like these at home. Mrs. Mukherjee told me that the Qureshis came here primarily because they want their children to get a good education. Yet it seems like they have left so much behind—culture, language, and family. I believe that the Qureshis used to live with almost their whole family. Mrs. Mukherjee said they had a three-story house where Mr. Qureshi's four brothers and their families live. They shared one kitchen and ate together, watched TV together, and shared the household work. There were twelve children in the house, so they never needed to find playmates. They could even play tennis on the large roof of the house, so they didn't go out of the house that frequently.

February 24

June came in this afternoon to tell me that Fome and his family may be leaving to go back to Pakistan for a while! Apparently, Mr. Qureshi's father is quite ill and they are concerned about him. The family feels that they should all return to Pakistan. It seems so pointless to take the children out of school after just six months and then possibly return six months later. What should I do? I certainly hope that the family will return, and I believe they will. However, Fome's English skills may regress while he is gone. Our district will never have enough Urdu speakers to have a bilingual class at the middle school. In fact, I'm not sure that I can even advocate for more than one period of ESL instruction, although Fome needs it. As students get older, they tend to come for help after school less and less so I can't depend on that. Next year the district will expect his teachers to grade him, and he'll have to take the high stakes test toward the end of the year. There are so few teachers who even understand the challenges that students that are ELL face, much less try to differentiate their instruction for them. Fome and his family came here for the educational opportunities, but sometimes it seems the obstacles are insurmountable.

Discussion Questions
1. What problems does Fome face in gaining an education in the United States?
2. What are the family's priorities regarding their children's education?
3. What do we know about second-language acquisition that should affect school programming?
4. What goals for educating Fome will Fome, his parents, and the school be able to agree on?
5. As Fome tries to acculturate, what conflicts does he face in school and at home?
6. What long-term goals must the district implement to enable students that are ELL to develop academically and socially?

References

Addison Stone, C. (2004). Contemporary approaches to the study of language and literacy development. In C. Addison Stone, E. R. Sillman, B. J. Heren, & K. Apel (Eds.), *Handbook of language and literacy: Development and disorders* (pp. 3–24). New York: Guilford Press.

August, D., & Hakuta, K. (1997). *Improving schooling for language minority children: A research agenda.* Washington, DC: National Academy Press.

August, D., & Shanahan, T. (Eds.). (2006). *Developing literacy in second-language learners: Report of the National Literacy Panel on Language-Minority Children and Youth*: Mahwah, NJ: Lawrence Erlbaum Associates.

Banks, J. A. (2006). *Cultural diversity and education: Foundations, curriculum, and teaching* (5th ed.) Boston: Allyn and Bacon.

Bennett, C. I. (2007). *Comprehensive multicultural education: Theory and practice* (6th ed.). Boston: Allyn and Bacon.

Bos, C. S., & Vaughn, S. (2002). *Strategies for teaching students with learning and behavior problems.* Boston: Allyn and Bacon.

Carey, T., & Carey, M. (Co-Producers). (2005). School board blues [motion picture]. (Available from Tobe and Meg Carey, P.O. Box 194, Glenford, NY 12433)

Collier, V. P. (1987). Age and rate of acquisition of second language acquisition for academic purposes. *TESOL Quarterly, 21,* 617–641.

Cummins, J. (1981). The role of primary language development in promoting education success for language minority students. In California State Department of Education (Ed.), *Schooling and language minority students: A theoretical framework* (pp. 3–50). Los Angeles: Evaluation, Dissemination and Assessment Center, California State University.

Cummins, J. (1996). *Negotiating identities: Education for empowerment in a diverse society.* Ontario, CA: California Association for Bilingual Education.

Faltis, C. J., & Coulter, C. A. (2008). Teaching English learners and immigrant students in secondary schools. Upper Saddle River, NJ: Pearson.

Fleming, W. C. (2006). Myths and stereotypes about Native Americans. *Phi Delta Kappan, 88* (3), 213–217.

Gollnick, D. M., & Chinn, P. C. (2006). *Multicultural education in a pluralistic society* (7th ed.). Upper Saddle River, NJ: Pearson.

Grant, C., & Gillette, M. (2006). *Learning to teach everyone's children: Equity, empowerment, and education that is multicultural.* Belmont, CA: Thomson Wadsworth.

Grant, C. A., & Sleeter, C. E. (2003). Turning on learning: *Five approaches to multicultural plans for race, class, gender, and disability* (3rd ed.). New York: Wiley.

Gutman, A. (1987). *Democratic education.* Princeton, NJ: Princeton University Press.

Hawkins, J. (2005). Smoke signals, sitting bulls, and slot machines: A new stereotype of Native Americans? *Multicultural Perspectives, 7*(3), 51–54.

Hayes-Harb, R. (2006). Native speaker of Arabic and ESL texts: Evidence for the transfer of written word identification processes. *TESOL Quarterly, 40*(2), 321–339.

Hirschfelder, A. P., Molin, F., & Wakim, Y. (1999). *American Indian stereotypes in the world of children: A reader and bibliography.* Lantham, MD: Scarecrow Press.

Horwitz, E. K. (2007). *Becoming a language teacher: A practical guide to second language learning and teaching.* Boston: Allyn and Bacon.

Indian mascot opponents pleased. (2001, April 15). *New York Times,* Sports Section, p. 6.

Kemble, W. J. (2000a, April 26). State education official praises Onteora's Indian mascot vote. *Daily Freeman,* p. A3.

Kemble, W. J. (2000b, August 3). State warns of consequence of keeping Indian mascot. *Daily Freeman,* pp. A1, A4.

Kemble, W. J. (2001a, April 14). No more Indian names, civil rights panel urges. *Daily Freeman,* pp. A1, A8.

Kemble, W. J. (2001b, April 25). Onteora duo wants "Indian" off May ballot. *Daily Freeman,* pp. A1, A6.

King, J. E. (1991). Dysconscious racism: Ideology, identity, and miseducation of teachers. *Journal of Negro Education, 60*(2), 133–146.

Krashen, S. (2005). Skyrocketing scores: An urban legend. *Educational Leadership, 62*(4), 37–39.

Lau v. Nichols 414 U.S. 563 (1974).

Loewen, J. W. (1995). *Lies my teacher told me: Everything your American history textbook got wrong.* New York: Simon & Schuster.

Marks, A. (2007, June 1). Arabic school in N.Y.C. creates stir. *Christian Science Monitor.* Retrieved July 12, 2007, from http://www.csmonitor.com

Ment, J. (2000, January 23). Indian mascots draw criticism. *Daily Freeman,* pp. A1, A8.

McDermott, R. (1997). Achieving school failure: 1972–1997. In G. D. Spindler (Ed.), *Education* and cultural process: Anthropological approaches (3rd ed, pp. 110–135). Prospect Heights, IL: Waveland Press.

Merino, B. J., Trueba, J. T., & Samaniego, F. A. (1993). Toward a framework for the study of the maintenance of the home language in language minority students. In B. J. Merino, H. T. Trueba, & F. A. Samaniego (Eds.), *Language and culture in learning: Teaching Spanish to native speakers of Spanish* (pp. 5–25). Washington, DC: Falmer Press.

Miller-Lachmann, L., & Taylor, L. (1995). *Schools for all: Educating children in a diverse society:* Albany, NY: Delmar.

Mills, R. P. (2001, February 5). *Public school use of Native American names, symbols, and mascots.* Albany: New York State Education Department. Retrieved July 16, 2007, from http://www.emsc.nysed.gov/deputy/Documents/schoolmascots.htm

Molin, P. F. (1999). American Indian mascots in sports. In A. Hirschfelder, P. F. Molin, & Y. Wakim (Eds.), *American Indian stereotypes in the world of children: A reader and bibliography* (2nd ed., pp. 175–184). Lantham, MD: Scarecrow Press.

National Collegiate Athlete Association (2007, February 16). *Native American mascot policy-status list.* Retrieved July 19, 2007, from http:www.ncaa.org

Pewewardy, C. D. (1999). From enemy to mascot: The deculturation of Indian mascots in sports culture. *Canadian Journal of Native Education, 23,* 176–189.

Pewewardy, C. D. (2004). Playing Indian at halftime: The controversy over American Indian mascots, logos, and nicknames in school-related events. *Clearing House, 77*(5), 80–185.

Riede, P. (2001). More than a mascot. *School Administrator, 58*(8), 27–33.

Rothenberg, C., & Fisher, D. (2007). *Teaching English language learners.* Upper Saddle River, NJ: Pearson.

Short, D., & Fitzsimmons, S. (2007). *Double the work: Challenges and solutions to acquiring language and academic literacy for adolescent English language learners—A report to the Carnegie Corporation of New York.* Washington, DC: Alliance for Excellent Education.

Sleeter, C. E., & Grant, C. A. (1999). *Making choices for multicultural education: Five approaches to race, class,* and gender (3rd ed.). Upper Saddle River, NJ: Prentice Hall.

Smith, D. D. (2007). *Introduction to special education: Making a difference* (7th ed.). Boston: Allyn and Bacon.

Snow, C. (1993). Bilingualism and second language acquisition. In J. B. Gleason & N. Ratner (Eds.), *Psycholinguistics* (pp. 392–416). Fort Worth, TX: Harcourt Brace.

Spring, J. (2004). *Deculturalization and the struggle for equality: A brief history of the education of dominated cultures in the United States* (4th ed.). New York: McGraw-Hill.

Staurowsky, E. J. (1999). American Indian imagery and the miseducation of America. *Quest, 51,* 382–392.

Staurowsky, E. J. (2007). "You know, we are all Indian": Exploring White power and privilege in reactions to the NCAA Native American mascot policy. *Journal of Sport and Social Issues, 31*(1), 61–76.

Suárez-Orozco, C., & Suárez-Orozco, M. M. (2001). *Children of immigration.* Cambridge, MA: Harvard University Press.

Thomas, W. P., & Collier, V. P. (2002). *A national study of school effectiveness for language minority students' long-term academic achievement.* Santa Cruz: CA: Center for Research on Education, Diversity and Excellence. (ERIC Document Reproduction Services No. ED475048)

Trueba, H. T. (1993). Culture and language: The ethnographic approach to the study of learning environments. In B. J. Merino, H. T. Trueba, & F. A. Samaniego (Eds.), *Language and culture in learning: Teaching Spanish to native speakers of Spanish* (pp. 26–44). Washington, DC: Falmer Press.

Twine, R. (2000, February 8). "Indian" fans lose bid for referendum. *Daily Freeman,* pp. A1, A6.

Werthamer, C. (2000, February 9). Students who cut classes for petition drive are suspended. *Daily Freeman,* pp. A1–A2.

Zecker, L. B. (2006). Learning to read and write in two langauges. In C. Addison Stone, E. R. Sillman, B. J. Heren, & K. Apel (Eds.), *Handbook of language and literacy: Development and disorders* (pp. 248–265). New York: Guilford Press.

8

Poverty and Socioeconomic Class

Socioeconomic diversity among the school-aged population affects the overall quality of students' lives as well as their educational outcomes. Children in families who are poor or low-income are more likely to live in the central cities of large, metropolitan areas or poor rural areas where segregated, high poverty schools with the shameful characteristics described earlier, substandard housing, inadequate health care, and poor nutrition all contribute to unequal outcomes for these students. Yet, education is most often their only way out of poverty.

In addition, attitudes of the school staff may reflect negative, lower expectations of the students and their families. In effect, the children who are most in need of a highly trained and experienced teaching staff to provide enriched learning experiences are least likely to receive them.

Expectations and Realities

The following quote from a boy who was homeless expresses his sense of instability and sadness:

> David, age 10: For a while we were sleeping in our car. That was scary. And it was cold, too. My dad had to wake up and start the car and turn on the heater so we wouldn't freeze. I slept on the floor in the back seat but it was hard to get comfortable and we were hungry all the time. There was nowhere to cook or go to the bathroom. It was real awful. I don't want to make friends here at school because my dad says we will probably leave soon. Maybe we are going to Alaska or California or someplace. Then I can make friends because we are going to stay there and not move anymore. I don't know what's going to happen. (From Mann, 1995).

146

Imagine David trying to concentrate on learning in school. Imagine, as his teacher, wondering why he never smiles or tries to make friends with his classmates. Children who are homeless are not alone in their difficulties. Migrant children, refugees, children of diverse races or ethnicities, and new immigrants are also among the poor.

As can be seen in Box 8.1, diverse children, with the exception of Asian children, are disproportionately represented among those who live in families meeting the poverty level in income. In fact, it is disturbing to find that the same groups who show the lowest rates of academic progress also have the highest rates of poverty. Children who are Black or Hispanic show more than twice the rates for White children. The interaction of poverty and poor academic achievement can exert powerful barriers to successful lives. Since large numbers of diverse children live in families who are of low-income or poor, one must raise the issue of discrimination as a possible explanation. Although poverty and poor academic achievement are complex issues, one must question why the same groups are predominant in both situations.

The U.S. Department of Health and Human Services has published the 2007 poverty guidelines (Table 8.1). Two groups of the poor are classified as (1) the poor—those whose income is $20,650 for a family of four and (2) low-income—those in families whose income is $43,000 for a family of four.

The federal government does provide programs to assist those families. Programs that use the HHS guidelines to determine eligibility for assistance include: Head Start. The Food Stamp Program, the National School Lunch Program, the Low-Income Home Energy Assistance Program, and the Children's Health Insurance Program. In general, cash public assistance programs (Temporary Assistance for Needy Families and Supplemental Security Income) do not use the poverty guidelines to determine eligibility (U.S. Department of Health and Human Services, 2007).

Teachers need to realize that the realities of the children's lives may easily conflict with the expectations of the schools. This is particularly true when we consider that the orientations of the majority of schools and teachers in the United States can be best described as either middle income–middle class or aspiring to belong to the middle

BOX 8.1 • *Child Poverty Nationwide by Race (2005)*

35% of Black children live in poor families. Poverty rates among Black children range from 20% in New Jersey to 43% in Ohio.

28% of Latino children live in poor families. In the ten most populated states, rates range from 20% in New Jersey, Florida, and Illinois to 35% in Texas.

29% of American Indian and 11% of Asian children live in poor families.

10% of White children live in poor families.

Nationwide, 18% of children live in families officially considered poor. Child poverty rates range from 7% in New Hampshire to 27% in Mississippi.

Source: Fass & Cauthen, 2006.

class. Not only will teachers need to recognize that all children will not be able to meet the school's demands for appropriate clothing, school supplies, family involvement, good health-care, extracurricular expenses, and outside experiences; they will also need the attitudes, knowledge, and skills required when they must address these difficulties with the children and their families. Furthermore, all members of the family system are affected by such conditions. The school's expectations for parents and families can be totally unrealistic when families in poverty are without telephones, transportation, access to health care and funds for medication, child care, and jobs that grant time off for personal business or sickness.

Current Facts

More than 17 percent of children under 18 lived in poverty in 2005, and that was greater than the figure for 18- to 64-year-olds (11.1 percent) and people 65 and older (10.1 percent) (U.S. Census Bureau, 2006). Families and children are defined as poor if family income was below $20,650 in 2007, the federal poverty threshold (one of the measures of poverty used by the federal government). However, research has shown that, on average, families need approximately twice the income defined as the poverty level to make ends meet (Fass & Cauthen, 2006).

Families and children are defined as low income if the family income is less than twice the federal poverty threshold, or $42,400 in 2008 (National Center for Children in Poverty, n.d.). Thirty-nine percent of children lived in low-income families in 2006. Among diverse children, 26 percent of White children, 60 percent of Black children, 61 percent of Latino children, 27 percent of Asian children, and 63 percent of Native American children lived in low-income families in 2006 (NCCP, n.d.).

It is obvious that diverse children are disproportionately living in families considered poor or low income. Three critical questions arise from these data:

1. What is the explanation for the difference?
2. What is the impact of poverty and low income on school-aged children?
3. How can the schools help so that children from these families can come to school ready to learn?

Poverty guidelines for 2007 have been provided by the United States Department of Health and Human Services (see Table 8.1). Programs that use the guidelines for eligibility include Head Start, the Food Stamp Program, the National School Lunch Program, the Low-Income Home Energy Assistance Program, and the Children's Health Insurance Program (U.S. Department of Health and Human Services, 2007). In general, cash public assistance programs such as Temporary Assistance for Needy Families (TANF) and Supplemental Security Income (SSI) do not use the poverty guidelines to determine eligibility (U.S. Department of Health and Human Services, 2007).

However, broader perceptions of poverty also consider the lack of resources other than income that can enable individuals to climb out of poverty. Emotional

TABLE 8.1   *2007 Health and Human Services Poverty Guidelines*

Persons in Family	Guideline Amount 48 States and DC	Alaska	Hawaii
1	$10,210	$12,770	$11,750
2	$13,690	$17,120	$15,750
3	$17,170	$21,470	$19,750
4	$20,650	$25,820	$23,750
5	$24,130	$30,170	$27,750
6	$27,610	$34,520	$31,750
7	$31,090	$38,870	$35,750
8	$34,570	$43,220	$39,750
For each additional person, add	$3,480	$4,350	$4,000

Source: U.S. Department of Health and Human Services (2007).

resources such as stamina and perseverance, mental resources required to deal with the challenges of daily life, and physical, spiritual, and supportive resources or systems can be equally important (Payne, 1998). Payne describes emotional resources as the stamina to withstand difficult and uncomfortable emotional situations and feelings. Mental resources are needed to access and use information from many different sources. A support system can provide individuals to whom one can turn for help in a crisis or emergency. All the resources identified by Payne and others can contribute to an individual's resilience. Resilient families and children are able to bounce back from crises and hardships. Payne (1998) also refers to hidden rules that exist in all socioeconomic classes in the United States. In her view, an individual's knowledge of these hidden rules can also be considered a resource. She describes these rules as the "salient, unspoken understandings that cue the members of the group that this individual does or does not fit" (Payne, 1998, p. 18). Suggesting that people in poverty comprise a socioeconomic class or group, she identifies hidden rules among those living in poverty, such as acceptance of high noise levels, the importance placed on nonverbal information, and the value placed on an individual's ability to entertain.

The danger in this author's viewpoint on hidden rules among classes is her implied acceptance of the outdated and highly debatable concept of a "culture of poverty." People living in poverty are as diverse as members of any other group in society. Nevertheless, the behaviors described by Payne may be confused with a behavior disorder or emotional disturbance when exhibited by children in school.

Furthermore, earlier research has shown that the length of time spent in poverty varies among individuals and families. While some families and children may be in and out of poverty for brief periods, others may be trapped for long periods of time. A 1998 report by the U.S. Census Bureau pointed out that over a three year span, 30.3 percent of the population lived below the poverty level for at least two months. But just 5.3 percent of them stayed poor for two full years ("Report: U.S. Poverty," 1998). The information described poverty as a trap door for a few and a revolving door for many. On average, people were poor for 4.5 months. However, the most likely to be poor at that time were families headed by single mothers who lived in poverty for at least two months in a row, more than three times the rate for married couples. Among the chronically poor, single mothers were eight times as likely as married couples to live in poverty for at least two years. In fact, according to Cheal (1996), "No type of poverty is more characteristic of discussions of postmodern family life than that of the female-headed, sole-parent family" (p. 2).

Poverty rates also continue to differ dramatically by race (Chinyavong & Leonard, 1997). Blacks, Hispanics, and children are among the poorest groups in the nation. As Cheal (1996) has noted, "The entrenched nature of poverty today has become a major political issue and a major topic for social research, especially in the U.S. Inevitably, it has also become linked to, and confounded with, prominent issues in the U.S. policy discourse concerning race, crime and urban decay" (p. 2).

Cheal (1996), in fact, refers to a "new poverty," which seems to be economically and politically intractable. In his words, this "new poverty appears to be a curious conjunction of increased family instability and increased employment instability" (p. 180). This view is also supported by Bauman (1998), who notes that "the present day economy does not need a massive labor force, having learned how to increase not just profits, but the volume of products while cutting down on labor and its costs" (p. 90).

Bauman describes the poor as "such people as are not fed, shod and clad as the standards of their time and place define as right and proper; but they are above all people who do not live 'up to the norm,' that norm being the ability to meet such standards" (Bauman, 1998, p. 86). The words of Bauman reflect the influence of society's norms and standards, particularly in the United States, which relegate those who are unable to consume at adequate levels to the ranks of the poor. Norms and standards in the United States are based on high levels of consumption or consumerism, and those who are unable to display the signs of acceptable levels of consumption may be considered poor. Bauman expands his view in this comment: "Contemporary society engages its members primarily as consumers; only secondarily, and partly, as producers. To meet the social norm, to be a fully fledged member of society, one needs to respond promptly and efficiently to the temptations of the consumer market" (p. 90). In fact, Bauman's discussion is helpful in our understanding of the stigma, sense of alienation, and rage that can result from living in conditions of poverty. Again, in Bauman's words,

> The phenomenon of poverty is also a social and psychological condition; as the propriety of human existence is measured by such standards of decent life practiced by any given society, inability to abide by such standards is itself a cause of distress, agony and self-mortification. . . . Poverty means being excluded from whatever passes for a "normal life." It means being "not up to the mark." This results in a fall of self-esteem,

feelings of shame or feelings of guilt. Poverty also means being cut off from the chances of whatever passes in a given society for a "happy life." . . . This results in resentment and aggravation, which spill out in the form of violent acts, self-deprecation, or both (Bauman, 1998, p. 37).

In one of the cases to follow, the parents of Maria and her sisters become targets for charges of child abuse and neglect because the children have come to school in the winter wearing clothes described as flimsy, the medication for Maria has not been purchased as prescribed, and the family is without an automobile for transportation. Although they lack things that are considered essential in the United States, the lack of these things may not be considered abusive or neglectful of children in many other parts of the world.

Who Are the Poor?

Female householders, no husband present, (28.7 percent) and related children under 6 in families (20%) are among the largest groups of the poor without consideration of race or ethnicity (U.S. Census, 2006). Children living in families with low-income also face the cruelties of poverty. In 2005, for example, 39 percent of children lived in low-income families. Among children age 6 and lower, 42 percent lived in low-income families in 2005. Forty-nine percent of children in urban areas and 47 percent of children in rural areas lived in low-income families in 2005 (NCCP, 2006).

As shown in Box 8.1, poverty rates for Black children vary among the states with a range from 20% in New Jersey to 43% in Ohio. The rates for Latino children range from 20% in New Jersey, Florida and Illinois to 35% in Texas. Nationwide, child poverty rates range from 7% in New Hampshire to 27% in Mississippi (Fass & Cauthen, 2006). However, diverse groups who face special challenges also suffer a high level of poverty. These include, among others, migrant workers and the homeless.

In addition to residence, factors such as single parenthood, low education level of parents, and part-time or no employment also contribute to the risk of poverty for young children. Children who lived with a single parent in 2005 were five times as likely to be poor as those living with two parents. Fifty-one percent of children in low-income families live with a single parent, while 17 percent of children above low-income levels do so. While children under age 6 with two unemployed parents or a single parent who was unemployed faced extremely high rates of poverty, part-time employment of a single parent was not sufficient to change the poverty status of most young children (National Center for Children in Poverty, 2006). Furthermore, the facts that wages have not kept pace with inflation, the number of families headed by single parents has increased, and the level of government assistance for poor families with children has decreased provide additional explanations (Ohlson, 1998).

Despite the fact that 65 percent of poor young children had at least one employed parent, a figure that is higher than at any time in more than 20 years, the high poverty rate continues (National Center for Children in Poverty, 2006). Nevertheless, parental education does make a difference. As the parental level of education increases, the poverty rate for young children in the family decreases. The poverty rate in 1997 among children under 6 whose better educated parent had earned a college degree was only three percent (National Center for Children in Poverty, 2006). In contrast, the rate among children whose parent or parents lacked a college degree increased by 31 percent. The powerful combination of single motherhood, relatively low educational attainment, and less than full-time employment results in extremely high poverty rates (National Center for Children in Poverty, 2001).

Fathers, too, are increasingly assuming the role of single householder with children and are confronted by the same issues of poverty and low-income as their female counterparts (Blair, n.d.). One in seven single-parent families is now headed by a father (NCCP, 2007).

Migrant Families

One group that suffers a high level of poverty is migrant families. As they move from location to location, these families and children suffer "poor sanitation in the fields and work camp facilities, overcrowded, substandard housing and poor diets, exposure to pesticides and other hazards of agricultural work (particularly hazardous to pregnant women and young children), limited health care and low wages" (Salend, 2008). In the case of Maria to follow, the family can be described as "resettled migrants" who no longer travel constantly to seek work. Nevertheless, their living conditions and income meet the definitions of poverty.

The educational progress of children who are migrants may be negatively affected. Migrant workers, their families, and children are frequently provided substandard housing where conditions do not allow for areas of privacy, independent activities, homework and studying, or recreation. Children sometimes help in the fields while they try to attend school. Fortunately, advocacy groups in various areas of the country where migrant labor is utilized often protest the conditions in which migrant families and children must live (R. Witt, personal communication, 2001).

Jose Martinez tells his story in *With These Hands: The Hidden World of Migrant Farmworkers Today* by Daniel Rothenberg (1998):

> I was in second grade the first time I stepped into a field to work. . . . It was difficult to work and go to school at the same time. Since we'd come up to Michigan before the end of the regular school year, I had to complete two months of extra school work before we left Texas. Then, when school started again, we'd enroll here in Michigan, stay until early November, and then go back to Texas. Sometimes, the school in Texas wouldn't accept Michigan's work or vice versa. (p. 273)

Rothenberg (1998) notes that the Martinez family of ten members has picked asparagus, strawberries, cherries, blueberries, grapes, and apples at a family income of about $15,000 a year.

Homeless Families and Children

Homeless families and children are also included among the poor. In fact, over 2 million men, women, and children were homeless in 2000. Within the diverse homeless population, 37 percent were families with children and 25 percent were children. Other groups included veterans (30 percent), drug- or alcohol-dependent persons (40 percent), persons with mental disabilities (25 to 30 percent) and workers (25 to 40 percent) (National Law Center on Homelessness and Poverty, 2001). Many homeless persons belong to more than one subgroup, which accounts for the fact that the numbers cannot be added to 100 percent.

High levels of absenteeism and tardiness are common among homeless children, who are constantly moving, often without dependable transportation and knowledgeable advocates for their needs. Nevertheless, homeless children do have rights that must be recognized by the schools (see Box 8.2).

In view of the numerous factors involved in a family's socioeconomic condition, it is essential for the school to consider a variety of important explanations for the fact that children are unable to meet the school's expectations for preparedness to learn. Full-service schools, as described in Chapter 3, where the educational and support needs of families and children can be met, are sorely needed.

BOX 8.2 • *McKinney-Vento Homeless Education Assistance Act of 2001*

Who is protected? Children who live:

1. In a shelter, motel, vehicle, or campground
2. On the street
3. In an abandoned building, trailer, or other inadequate accommodations
4. Doubled up with friends or relatives because they cannot find housing or afford housing

Rights or protections under the Act:

1. You must be given access to the same public education provided for other students.
2. You can continue in the school you attended before you became homeless or the school you last attended, if that is your choice and feasible.
3. You can receive transportation to the school you last attended before becoming homeless or school last attended.
4. You can attend a school and participate in school programs with students who are not homeless.
5. You can enroll in school without giving a permanent address. Schools cannot require proof of residency that might prevent or delay school enrollment.
6. You can enroll and attend classes in the school of your choice even while the school and you seek to resolve a dispute over enrollment.
7. You can receive the same special programs and services, if needed, as provided to all other students served in these programs.
8. You can receive transportation to school and to school programs.

Source: National Law Center on Homelessness and Poverty (2007).

Impact of Poverty on School-Aged Children

Children are expected to enter school being able to learn in groups; to cope with public evaluation of their academic and social behaviors, which may be culturally different from those expected by the school; to learn to compete with other students, which may also be culturally alien; to respond as expected to the authority of teachers and other school personnel; and to socialize with their peers. In addition, they are expected to be adequately and appropriately clothed, fed, and sheltered so that they can attend school regularly and be punctual, be able to engage in learning activities at school, have the necessary space and tools with which to complete school tasks at home, and have parents who are free to help their children at home and participate in necessary activities and conferences with teachers at the school. As we consider the limitations on families living at the poverty level, it is easy to anticipate the conflicts between the conditions of their lives and the expectations of the school.

Although some may view the federal definition of poverty as too narrowly based on income, money does buy essential things for children. Good food, appropriate clothing, safe and decent shelter, opportunities to learn, reduced family stress and conflict, a decent neighborhood, healthcare, health supplies and safety devices, healthy recreation, transportation, communication, and economic opportunity are essential resources that depend on income (Fass & Cauthen, 2006). One might also add a sense of stability and predictability in one's life that contributes to the freedom to learn.

Poverty increases the risks that children must face and threatens their determination, self-discipline, and resilience. Children in poverty are more likely to suffer health problems and learning problems, attend inferior schools, live in substandard housing, move more often, and even face earlier deaths than those whose families have sufficient economic resources. Health problems and the risk of disabilities are particularly critical. As cited by Ohlson (1998), many researchers have found that "children in low-income families are more likely to experience chronic illness and disability" (p. 192).

Impact on Brain Development

Since school-aged children are primarily engaged in learning experiences, it is important to consider the potential impact of poverty on brain development. Inadequate nutrition, substance abuse, maternal depression, exposure to environmental toxins, trauma and abuse, and quality of daycare may negatively affect brain development in young children (National Center for Children in Poverty, 2006).

Thus, children in poverty may begin their school years with impaired development. As noted by Shore (1997), "Researchers have gathered new evidence on the importance of the first years of life for children's emotional and intellectual development" (p. 4). Despite the resilience found in many children, impaired brain development may be unavoidable. During the period when the brain is most sensitive to environmental stimulation, children in poverty may be exposed to risk factors affecting brain development (Shore, 1997).

Low and middle SES children differ on most tests of cognitive performance. For example, in a group of healthy low SES 6 year olds, average I.Q. was 81 and only 20 percent scored in the normal range (Farah, Kimberly & Hurt, (2006). Furthermore, a $10,000 increment in family income was associated with a 600% increase in high school graduation for low-income and poor children (Duncan et al. cited in Farah et al., 2006). Thus, a significant question, which some current researchers pursue, becomes "Is there any direct relationship between socioeconomic status and brain development?"

In order to answer this question, Farah et al. (2006) conducted studies of the functioning of five key neurocognitive systems: (prefrontal) executive, (left perisylvian) language, (medial/temporal) memory, (parietal/spatial) cognition, and the (occipitotemporal/visual) cognition. These researchers found that the middle income children performed better than the low SES children on the battery of tests overall. However, the difference in the results for the two groups was large and significant only on the executive and language systems while differences in other systems were not. Follow-up studies supported those findings.

Farah et al. summarized the results as: "The most robust neurocognitive correlates of SES appear to involve the left perisylvian/language system; the medial temporal/memory system, and the prefrontal/executive system" (p. 9). They continue with the comment that the low SES children show the greatest disparities in systems needed for language, memory, working memory and cognitive control. These systems "would be expected to affect children's life trajectories" (p. 9).

The researchers note that a recent study of twins showed that IQ variation was far less genetic than environmental in origin (Turkheimer et al. (2003) cited in Farah et al., 2006). Studies have also shown that the period in a child's life when poverty is experienced is important. Effects are greater on young children (Duncan et al., 1994, cited in Farah et al., 2006). Some aspects of a child's environment can directly affect brain development by direct effects on the body while other aspects may do so through less direct psychological mechanisms. The Center for Children and Poverty has identified 3 significant risk factors for low cognitive achievement as: inadequate nutrition, substance abuse, and lead exposure. This list is obviously incomplete.

Lack of stimulation and stress are examples of psychological factors. Stress, in particular, causes the secretion of stress hormones that affect the brain (McEwen, 2000, cited in Farah et al., 2006). The brain of young children is especially sensitive to those effects.

Farah et al. have shown that "the concomitants of poverty have negative effects on children's neurological development. As researchers in neuroscience continue to study the effects of poverty on children, the "disadvantages of childhood poverty may become a bioethical issue rather than merely one of economic opportunity in the society" (p. 22). This research supports the critical need for high quality early childhood education delivery to children in poverty.

State and Federal Provisions

Welfare Changes

The tenth anniversary of the welfare reform law occurred in 2006. That law helped to remove many single mothers from welfare into the workforce, although they were still left in poverty (Eckholm, 2006). There is a sizable group that has not made the transition. Some mothers are so overwhelmed by their problems that they have been unable to keep jobs. Others have simply given up and are neither working nor receiving benefits (Eckholm, 2006). Meanwhile, their children will continue to suffer the impact of poverty in their lives. The number of problems faced by a poor family can be overwhelming. Examples presented by Eckholm include the following.

> Ms. Autry, 25, with a tenth grade education, was finally overwhelmed by the demands of work and family, and early in the year she showed up at the People's Emergency Center, a social service agency, with her three children, a fourth on the way, no job, and no place to live. She, five brothers, and a sister grew up with a mother who was on welfare after the split from her father. Mrs. Autry became pregnant in tenth grade, dropped out of school, and worked, moving from job to job. Mrs. Autry is currently living in a one room "transitional apartment" at the emergency center. (p. A13).

As we enter the twenty-first century, families in poverty also suffer the impact of welfare reform. President Bill Clinton, who promised to "end welfare as we know it," signed the Personal Responsibility and Work Opportunity Reconciliation Action (PRWORA) in August 1996. According to Ohlson (1998), "The intent of the legislation is to remove incentives to remain on welfare that many believe were inherent in the Aid to Families with Dependent Children (AFDC) program, and to encourage the personal responsibility of welfare recipients by mandating work" (p. 191). Federal funds for AFDC, food stamps, and Supplemental Security Income have been reduced. Actually, AFDC has been replaced by the Temporary Assistance to Needy Families (TANF) program, through which the federal government provides states a block grant that is capped with a fixed level of funding (Ohlson, 1998). TANF includes a work requirement provision in which "states may require individuals who have received TANF for 2 months to participate in community service or risk loss of benefits." Unfortunately, "allowable work" does not include attending school, so parents who have limited education cannot improve their employment situation through additional education (Ohlson, 1998).

The law does allow a "hardship" provision, which permits states to waive work requirements for up to 20 percent of its TANF recipients. However, there is a lifetime limit of 5 years of assistance. Other provisions of the PRWORA that are especially harsh include the fact that, under the new Supplemental Security Income (SSI) changes, many children with disabilities will lose their SSI benefits. Ohlson (1998) points out that SSI has "historically assisted many impoverished parents to manage additional expenses related to their child's disability" (p. 194). Another provision for those in poverty, Medicaid, has not been changed under PRWORA. However, childcare assistance for all families participating in welfare-to-work provisions is limited by the Child Care and Development Block Grant, which uses a fixed funding formula that limits the amount of funding available to the states.

Major cuts have been made in the food stamps program and the Federal Child Nutrition Program, which, in part, reduce the amount of funds for daycare providers operating in low-income areas. Funds are also cut under the Social Services Block Grant, which supports several programs for families who are homeless, among others. In addition, the immigrant provisions of PRWORA denies many legal immigrants TANF and SSI and restricts the provision of "means tested federal benefits to legal immigrants who arrived in the U.S. after August 22, 1996" (Ohlson, 1998).

Becker (2001) has reported that private food charities are trying to fill the gaps created by reduced federal aid to the poor. In fact, more people are getting food from private charities over the course of the year than are participating in the federal food stamp program (Becker, 2001). There has been a decrease from 21.9 million people using federal food stamps in 1997 to 17.7 million in 2001. "Emergency feeding sites around the country serve more than 7 million people in a given week. Both the U.S. Senate and House are recommending increases in the food stamp program" (Becker, 2001, p. A14). Religious groups, who run most of the private programs, are also supporting an increase in money for food stamps. Results of a survey by the Mathematica Policy Research group showed that nearly one-half the households receiving aid included children, working families made up 40 percent of those seeking aid, women accounted for nearly two-thirds of adults who sought emergency food aid, and nearly one-third of those seeking emergency food assistance also received food stamps (Becker, 2001).

Ohlson (1998) points out that families already in poverty who are struggling to raise children will be under additional stress due to the changes in welfare. Increased levels of stress in the families will affect parents' ability to care for their children and to meet the demands of the schools. An expansion of the cost-effective prevention programs is needed.

What Can Schools Do?

In low-performing high schools, the Manpower Demonstration Research Corporation (MDRC, 2006), suggests that

1. It may not be realistic to expect teachers to create their own curriculum reflecting the themes of small learning communities; they are more likely to benefit from well-designed curricula and lesson plans that have already been developed.
2. Good advance training and ongoing coaching can help teachers make use of well-designed curricula.
3. Student achievement may be enhanced by professional development activities that involve teachers working together to align curricula with standards, review assignments and discuss ways of making classroom activities more engaging.
4. Both academic departments and small learning communities should be regarded as key venues for instructional improvement.
5. Administrators must provide guidance for teachers to focus on instructional improvement and follow up to ensure that meeting time is used productively.

In some schools, a homeless coordinator addresses the needs of homeless children, funded by a grant from the McKinney-Vento Act. In order to receive funds, the school must have at least fifty homeless students.

In most schools, the social worker has the responsibility to address the needs of children in distress. Clothes banks, food pantries, and other resources available in a full-service school can benefit all children in need.

The full-service schools described in Chapter 3 can answer the needs of many children whose families are caught in the harsh circumstances of poverty with only reduced state and federal assistance available. For example, in several New York City schools where dental services are now available, principals have found that dental health has led to improved academic performance (Bahrampour, 2001). In Maria's case, which follows, the health services, eye test, and medication that she needed and the lack of eyeglasses that prevented her progress in school could have been obtained in a school where community agencies, in collaboration with the school, provide critical services to children. In view of the limited assistance available to families and children in poverty, it is urgent to remember Kagan's comment that "the education of children cannot be separated from their care" (1989, p. 189).

Mayeroff (1998) has argued for the importance of connectedness, a support system or network that most students need "to succeed in education" (p. 426). He notes that "when students gain a sense of connectedness to the people and institutions whose guidance and assistance will help them to advance themselves, their social capital increases" (p. 426). (See Figure 3.2, Student's Ecosystem, Chapter 3.) In his view, the school is perceived as part of the ecosystem that includes all parts of a student's life. Thus, the school's linkages with the home and community is essential. In Chapter 3, we have discussed the critical importance of building a strong school–home–community relationship. Mayeroff (1998) reinforces this view in his comment that social capital, "the whole system of networks, values, norms and trust may count for as much as book learning and have as much to do with finding a place in the mainstream" (p. 432). Ultimately, we want every child to find a place in the mainstream.

The Case of Maria Ramirez

As she dressed for school on Monday morning, Mrs. Corea felt energetic for the first time in many weeks. Finally, the multidisciplinary team at Washington Elementary School was meeting to consider Maria Ramirez's eligibility for special education. It was now February, and Mrs. Corea had been frustrated with Maria since the school year began. It seemed as if nothing that she tried made a difference for Maria, and it had been impossible to communicate with the parents who did not speak English.

Mrs. Corea took her usual route to Washington Elementary School, a lovely drive along the river that avoided the poorest area of the city where the Ramirez family lived. Mrs. Corea thought about the contrast of Maria's neighborhood with that of the majority of students at Washington and wondered how the Ramirez children could find friends. The Ramirez's neighborhood had the appearance of a war-torn city where abandoned houses, small businesses, and factories were boarded up, windows broken, and structures gutted. The street on which Maria's family lived was typical of many. Broken sidewalks and potholed streets were littered with broken glass, rocks, and other debris. Signs of neglect were everywhere. At one end of the street there were eight small houses of two stories, several with occupants who sat on the front steps, their faces expressing sadness or boredom as they watched the passing cars or the children who sometimes played in the street.

The Ramirez building was sandwiched between two abandoned factories. Directly facing their house, on the other side of the street, another empty factory stood as a reminder of the jobs lost to the community. Neither grass nor trees enlivened the surroundings. However, in a vacant lot a pile of branches lay waiting to be removed. In the tiny basement apartment where the Ramirez family lived, two small front windows with curtains flapping in the wind allowed the only air to enter.

Miss Anacasta, the school social worker, had said to Mrs. Corea earlier that even among the small group of poor families at their school the Ramirez children lived in a most desperate situation. Roaches and mice ran about freely in the old building, and sometimes the girls' clothing had a roach on the sleeve of a coat or sweater. In the cold winter weather the girls often wore clothing that was too small and inappropriately flimsy. It was no wonder that they were often sick. The tiny apartment of three rooms had no bedroom for the girls. Their bed was placed in the small foyer at the front door, which could be very cold when the temperature dropped well below freezing. Nevertheless, Mrs. Ramirez worked hard to keep the place neat and even decorated for the holidays.

The school's multidisciplinary team was finally meeting today to consider Mrs. Corea's referral. It had been difficult to get at least one of Maria's parents to attend any meeting, and everyone was relieved to see Mrs. Ramirez. Mr. Ramirez, as usual, was looking for work, interviewing whenever and wherever possible, and could not attend the meeting. Mrs. Ramirez, on the other hand, had a job at a private school laundry where she had to report at 6:30 A.M. and was not allowed to take time off without losing pay. Thus, she was never home early enough to attend school meetings. However, Miss Anacasta had convinced her of the importance of today's meeting, and Mrs. Ramirez would lose the day's pay.

In addition to Mrs. Corea, the multidisciplinary team included the chairperson, Miss Burns; the school psychologist, Mr. Bowen; Mrs. Ramirez; Miss Houghton, the district's translator; and Miss Anacasta, the social worker. They met in a large conference room at a rectangular table. Miss Burns sat at one end and other members of the team sat together on one side. Mrs. Ramirez and Miss Anacasta sat together on the other side, facing the other committee members. The facial expressions of the committee reflected the serious nature of the meeting.

As the meeting began, Miss Burns welcomed everyone and explained, "We will deviate a little from our usual procedure in order to allow Mrs. Ramirez to share her view of Maria's problems. This is the very first time that Mrs. Corea and Mrs. Ramirez have met and had an opportunity to exchange information." She then turned to Mrs. Ramirez and asked her to describe what she believed to be her daughter's strengths and also what difficulties she thought Maria might be having.

Mrs. Ramirez spoke through the translator. "I am very worried about Maria. She doesn't like school and she wants to stay at home whenever possible. She never talks about school and doesn't seem to have much interest in it. She's having lots of trouble learning, and the school officials recently held a meeting that we were asked to attend, but I am not allowed to leave work early or I lose the pay and my husband had a job interview that day. When I arrived at the school, everyone had left."

Miss Burns then asked, "What was school like for Maria before she came here?" Mrs. Ramirez replied, "Maria has had lots of problems since she started school. Although she was born in the United States, she attended kindergarten in Mexico and first grade in Texas. When she started school in New York, she began second grade, and because she did not learn to speak or read English, the teacher decided that Maria should repeat second grade here at Washington Elementary. Even now, in third grade, Maria's English isn't very good. I wish I could help her more, but I don't know English and my husband, Manuel, doesn't either. We speak only Spanish at home, so it's difficult to practice English. Recently, I started a night class to learn English so that I will be able to help Maria and the other children with their schoolwork."

"Tell us about how Maria gets along with other children," Miss Burns remarked. Mrs. Ramirez continued, "Maria is a sociable, friendly girl who has friends around her age with whom she gets along well. She likes to please people, is very affectionate, expressive, and sentimental. Like all other children, she's very active and energetic and she enjoys sharing her favorite activities—riding a bicycle, playing, and watching television. Maria doesn't have many chores at home; she's not asked to do much. She tries to clean up sometimes when she feels like it, but she doesn't do a good job. So she has lots of time for playing."

"What about Maria's medical history?" Miss Burns asked. "We know that she has recently had some problems."

Mrs. Ramirez responded, "Maria has sure been sickly. She weighed only 3 pounds when she was born and she needed oxygen because the cord was wrapped around her neck. She was in an oxygen machine for 24 hours. Maybe that's why she's always sick now. She always has colds and sore throats, and now she has urinary infections, too. I know the school nurse is very concerned about these infections, but sometimes our old car won't run and many times we have no money for the medicine. I wish that Maria could get an ultrasound test to find the cause of the urinary infections."

As Mrs. Corea tried hard to maintain her attention, she thought how difficult it was to wait for the translation of whatever Mrs. Ramirez had to say. Nevertheless, she was impressed by the problems that Mrs. Ramirez had described.

Mrs. Correa looked around the table and tried to catch Miss Burn's eye. She and Miss Burns had had conversations in the past about the immigration status of Mr. and Mrs. Ramirez. While she knew that she had no legal right to question Mrs. Ramirez in this regard, she also wondered if the parents avoided asking for assistance from governmental agencies because they were undocumented immigrants and feared deportation.

Mrs. Corea then turned to Maria's mother and said, "Is there anything else that might help us to understand Maria's problems in school?"

Mrs. Ramirez answered with obvious sadness in her voice, as Miss Houghton translated, "It has been almost four years since we came to America to find a better life and we have had many troubles. We have five girls, ages 16, 12, 10, 9, and 8, and I worry about all of them. I am now 38 years old and Manuel, my husband, is 48. I know that we have not been stable parents for the girls. We've moved a lot and it has been hard to find work. There have been times when either my husband or I had to work far away from home and could see the children only one weekend every other month or two. Maria always asks me, 'Do you love me?' She doesn't believe that we love her as much as we love her sisters. Now, with my job at the laundry and my night class, I am away from home until 9:30 many evenings, but I want to learn English so that I can help the girls with their schoolwork."

Mrs. Corea, thinking about the personal feelings shared by Mrs. Ramirez, turned to express appreciation to her, "Mrs. Ramirez, I know that it must have been difficult to share that information. It really helps me to understand the circumstances in which Maria has lived that could have affected her educational progress. I would like to share my observations now and my experiences with Maria as her teacher.

"At the beginning of the school year Maria's second-grade teacher told me that Maria's strength was in mathematics and that she would need help with work habits, completing her work, and organizational skills. But, in my opinion, Maria's areas of excellence are her manners and respect for authority. She did learn some sight words in second grade because she received daily help in the ESL class."

After the translation, Mrs. Corea continued, "Maria doesn't seem to have a clue about what's going on in the classroom. She often wastes time and is limited in all academic areas, as well as in oral expression. Even when I modify work for her, she only occasionally completes it. Maria is at the preprimer level in reading according to the Botel Reading Test that I recently gave her. I believe that she has a disability and needs a special education program. I would really like to see her needs addressed so that she can begin to make some progress in school."

Miss Burns smiled and inquired, "How would you describe Maria's social development, Mrs. Corea?"

The teacher responded, "I must say that Maria is basically well behaved, but recently she has been periodically nasty, hits other students, and sometimes cries in class. Nevertheless, her behavior continues to be manageable since she does respond to authority. Then, too, she seems to like being here and she blends easily into the room. But, I really think that Maria needs special education."

The chairperson nodded and said, "Thank you, Mrs. Corea, it seems that you and Mrs. Ramirez agree on the fact that Maria needs help now, and I hope that we can help her. Perhaps Miss Anacasta can also shed some light on Maria's difficulties."

Miss Anacasta, the school's social worker, had been to the Ramirez home several times to try to help the family obtain winter clothing, food, and transportation. She had also sought answers to questions concerning the girls' health problems. She began her comments with a heavy sigh, "Well, I certainly don't think that Maria should be placed in special education. When I talk to her in Spanish, she seems really intelligent. My experience with Maria has been very positive. She has a very pleasant and friendly manner and she smiles and laughs a lot. When I tutor her sometimes, she tries hard to complete the tasks involved. She appears to want to learn and to succeed in her schoolwork."

Miss Anacasta continued, after the translation, "The Ramirez family is very close and supportive, which helps Maria and the other children. However, it is difficult for the parents to help their children with schoolwork because neither speaks English. In addition, Mr. Ramirez only completed ninth grade in Mexico, and Mrs. Ramirez completed eighth grade there. When you consider, also, the long hours that Mrs. Ramirez works and the difficulties with employment for Mr. Ramirez, it is obvious that assistance for the children is not often possible. Nevertheless, Mr. Ramirez insists that the girls go to the library more often so that they will improve in reading.

"When I first met the family at home, only Mrs. Ramirez seemed friendly. Mr. Ramirez was not very enthusiastic about my visit and asked several times why I had come. He appeared to be very authoritative and to make all the family decisions. For example, he decided that the girls must do the laundry every Saturday and they must walk with the laundry to the nearest laundromat, which is far from the home. In fact, the entire day is occupied in this way on Saturday. Mr. Ramirez is currently doing factory work off and on; his employment has been unstable for the past eight months, and the family has had difficulties obtaining food, clothing, and transportation. They have a very old car that runs far less than it does run. I must say, however, that gradually Mr. Ramirez has become friendlier and now, in hesitant English, he likes to talk with me about the difficulty in learning a second language.

"The family's only place for community involvement and socialization is their church, which does give them such assistance as Thanksgiving and Christmas food baskets. However, the children continue to have many needs that are unmet, primarily health—vision and hearing tests, for example. While Maria's difficulties are most critical, all the children have problems. Some of their health needs have been met through collaboration of the school and community health center. However, the most recent problem faced by the family involves an investigation of child neglect and abuse by the State's Child Protective Services. This was prompted by a series of problems observed by the school: Maria's recurring urinary infections; the fact that often she receives no medication because the family has no money or transportation; the inappropriate clothing worn by the children—flimsy and too small during the winter; and the frequent crying in school by some of the girls.

"In my opinion, Mr. and Mrs. Ramirez appear to be sincerely concerned about their children; however, the dire poverty in which they live, in addition to their limited English proficiency, interferes with their best intentions. The family needs decent housing and the opportunity to earn adequate income. Perhaps the poverty contributes to the children's' difficulties with their peers. Sometimes the girls have reported to me that children on the bus have turned up their noses when they sit beside them, as if the Ramirez children smell bad. They have also been called negative names by their classmates on the bus."

Miss Anacasta turned to Mrs. Ramirez to say, "I know that you would certainly like to live in a better place." On hearing the translation, Mrs. Ramirez smiled and nodded her head in agreement.

Miss Burns thanked the social worker and turned to Mr. Bowen, the school psychologist. "What have you determined to be Maria's major problems, Mr. Bowen, and what did your testing show?"

Mr. Bowen responded. "I believe that Maria's health problems are interfering with her ability to learn. Even now, she needs testing for lead. Her eye exam was finally completed a few days ago after a long delay and now we know that she cannot function without glasses. This means that her earlier test scores are probably unreliable. On testing she showed problems in memory and information processing in both Spanish and English. Her expressive vocabulary is very limited in both languages. Maria has a considerable delay in reading, but is on grade level in mathematics. She scored in the slow learner range on the intelligence test, but we must consider that her language, vision, and physical problems probably interfered. Socioeconomic difficulties and culture could also influence the test results.

"I did observe Maria in the classroom several times during the language arts period. The 28 students sat in a random pattern; however, Maria sat behind a bookshelf, like a room divider, which did not allow for good visibility of Maria from the teacher's desk. On one occasion, students were completing a worksheet. Maria was **able** to follow directions and volunteered the correct answers to several questions. **Sometimes** she seemed distracted, talking to a student nearby or tying her shoe. Eventually, Mrs. Corea directed Maria to move her desk where it could be seen.

"The class was then told to write a paragraph with at least six words in each sentence and Maria appeared puzzled. The teacher then directed them to finish the paragraph for homework and read it to someone at home. I think that Maria probably wasted a little time during the lesson, but she was involved."

"Yes," interjected Miss Burns, "your observations are helpful. The test results are somewhat unreliable since Maria did not have glasses." The chairperson then began to summarize all the evaluation data that had been collected. She continued, "The following tests were completed: physical examination, reading assessment, language assessment, intelligence testing, and home visits. The team is ready to make a decision and recommendation. However, Maria does not fit any of the thirteen disability categories. She is not eligible for a learning disability classification due to her IQ test score, and since she has 20/40 vision with glasses, she cannot be considered visually impaired. We are unable to verify a specific disability. Another point to consider is that Maria cannot be retained another year. Furthermore, there is really no resource room program that will help her."

The team determined that Maria was not eligible for special education services. However, they also agreed that Maria needed assistance that she currently was not receiving.

Miss Burns suggested, "I believe we need to call another meeting in the next two weeks to discuss what services the school can provide for Maria. I would ask each of you think this over and make suggestions to me about other professionals who should be present at the meeting. Mrs. Ramirez, I will let you know when that meeting is scheduled."

As the meeting ended, they all felt as if they had gone around in circles. "What's next," Mrs. Corea sadly reflected as she left the room, angry and disappointed. "What in the world will happen to Maria? Is there anything I can really do to help her? How will I manage?"

Discussion Questions
1. What are the effects of poverty on the Ramirez family?
2. What differences in beliefs and priorities are evident around the table as Maria's situation is discussed?
3. To what extent does Mrs. Corea's ignorance of Maria's culture and language contribute to Maria's lack of progress?

4. How would you explain Maria's ineligibility for special education?
5. Describe the change in Mrs. Corea's attitude before and after the meeting.
6. Identify the options now available to Maria and her family that could improve Maria's academic achievement.

The Case of Sue Wilson

"Ann Oliver. There's a phone call for you in your office," announced our school secretary over the loudspeaker.

I opened my office door and dropped my bag. It was 8:00 a.m. and Sue Wilson was on the phone. While I was used to her almost daily phone calls, there was a special urgency in her voice.

"Ann, I'm so sorry to bother you. I hate to call all the time, but I had to call the police at 10:00 last night to come get Michael. He threw a ball through a window at the shelter and wouldn't listen to anyone. He was swearin', swingin' a bat at me and refused to come inside. They took him to the hospital . . ." she choked out and then dissolved into tears. "I'm really scared and I don't know what to do."

I talked to her until she was able to calm down a bit and promised to get over to the hospital as soon as I could. I went across the hall to talk with Steve Baker, Michael's teacher. Steve started his teaching career at the middle school last year, but we're fortunate to have him at Rosa Parks Elementary this year. He just completed his master's degree and is energetic but firm with the kids. I am the therapeutic social worker for his classroom.

"Steve, I just got a call from Sue Wilson. Michael won't be in school today. He had a meltdown at the shelter last night and they put him in the hospital. I think I should go over to see him."

"Oh, man . . . I'm sorry. I had hoped that Michael would be better once he and his family were living in the shelter," Steve Baker said. "We had a honeymoon period with Michael the first two weeks of September, but since then the 'real Michael' has been coming out," said Steve shaking his head. "Michael has to learn to control his anger."

We could hear the kids coming down the hall from breakfast and there was no time to talk.

"You go to the hospital," said Steve. "I've got to get to class. We'll talk this over during our afternoon planning period."

It was an unusually cold March day as I drove through the city to the hospital. As I passed through the working class neighborhood surrounding the school, I tried to piece together the events of Michael's life to try to understand what this was all about. The last 5 of his 11 years had been filled with turmoil. Five years ago his mom and dad had split up. Sue moved to another state and wasn't able to take her 3 sons with her as planned. His dad got custody and, at the beginning of this school year, was living with his sons in a two bedroom apartment that qualified for Section 8 reimbursement. Many of the students at Rosa Parks Elementary lived in that crowded complex and it was rumored that the boy's dad was involved with drugs. Apparently, when Sue found out that their dad had been drinking a lot and her sons were living in an abusive environment, she came back to try to get custody. I remember my first conversation with Sue.

"When I came back to the city, all I had was a backpack with a few changes of clothes, shampoo and deodorant. That was it," said Sue in her forthright manner. "When I lived out of state I used to talk to my kids on the phone; they said they were fine. Then a friend called me and let me know what was really happening. I knew I had to come back. If it weren't for my pastor in Carolina, listening to me and praying with me, I don't know if I would have had the courage to come back.

"It's expensive to live in this city. A two bedroom apartment in the tough part of town costs $900. So I lived in the shelter for women until the judge gave me custody. It was a miracle I ever got them, but they were really living in an awful situation with their dad. Then they wanted me to just take one boy at a time. How do you do that? How do you pick? So beginning in February I took Billy and we moved to the Family Inn. One week later I got Michael, then Joseph. It was the first time in 5 years that we had all been together. I was scared to death. I just didn't know if I could do it."

The one thing that has typified Michael's behavior all year is his inability to control his temper. At various times he's been angry with everyone. He's been angry with his dad but never really wants to talk about it. If he admits to his dad is abusing him one day, he retracts it the next. Michael told the judge he wanted to be with his mom, but he's angry at her, too. I remembered another conversation with Sue.

"You should hear what Michael says to me sometimes. He'll say, 'F. . . you, mom. Why should I listen to you?' I know he's angry that I left them. I just couldn't afford to keep coming back for the custody hearings. I didn't have any money. So he deserves to be angry, but it's tough to listen to. I'm trying, but there's a lot to deal with when you have three boys and no money.

"And the boys just don't like it at the Family Inn. You have one room for the whole family to sleep in. That's the only place you have to yourself. But you can't eat in your room. There's a nice playroom for the kids, but it closed at 4:00. So by the time the kids come home from school, there isn't much time for them to go there. And boys are always hungry. Michael is a big kid. He wants snacks when he gets back from school and there are none. Michael will just take off. I can't keep him here. It's hell living here."

Sue isn't always negative about the Family Inn. She is grateful to have a place to stay that is heated and food for the boys, but there were plenty of problems living with other single moms and their kids. Sue has gotten to be good friends with some of the moms in the shelter, but has learned to stay away from others.

I remember talking about the Family Inn with our district homeless coordinator, Pat Mitchell, about Billy's adjustment issues. She's a social worker like I am and is in charge of assisting the 188 students in the district who qualify for services. She makes sure they get transportation to the school they were going to before they entered temporary housing, gets the families vouchers for clothes at Wal-Mart, and coordinates community services and school meetings.

Pat reminded me that the shelter is really just a place for families to stay no more than three months at a time. Communal living is tough and, in some ways, it takes away the authority that most parents typically have. The meals are brought in by someone else. Paid staff run the shelter and enforce rules that everyone is supposed to follow. While Sue's kids are trying to reattach to their mom, they know all too well that she isn't running the show. When they were living with dad, his parenting skills were erratic at best. So Joseph really became the dad and had to take care of his younger brothers the best he could. It was a bad situation, but it was what they knew. Suddenly, everything is different and, Michael, in particular, is not dealing with the changes.

Steve and I try to get together every day during our planning period to discuss the various students in the class. We agree that, despite all the hardships, the shelter was one of the best things that has happened to Michael. He doesn't come to school in dirty clothes anymore. He has a good dinner every night. When we send home a communication sheet to mom to let her know how Michael is doing, he brings it back the next day. He is healthier, if not always happier.

The family also has access to community services that they would not have connected with otherwise. The boys can attend Boys and Girls Club in their neighborhood after school. Because the family has been in a longstanding cycle of domestic violence, they need mental health services. At the shelter they receive counseling and education from a counselor that most people would be on a waiting list for months to get.

At school we really provide Michael with a lot of support. He's in a self-contained special education class of eight students in his local elementary school. Last school year he was falling behind academically and exhibiting a lot of inappropriate behavior, so he was classified as emotionally disturbed. Steve and I have two full-time teaching assistant working with us and each week Michael receives individual and group counseling. I have a separate office where I can take kids for crisis counseling when their behavior is inappropriate. My goal is to have them calm down, talk through the problem and return to class.

My most recent encounter with Michael was just a few days ago. He was sitting in class, refusing to do his academic work. The teaching assistant had tried to redirect him several times, but Michael just sat there. When she asked him once more, he threw his book on the floor and stormed out of the room.

When I asked Michael what was going on he shouted, "I'm pissed off because I have to do this work!"

I took him to my office to see if I could get him to settle down and talk through his feelings. We have a social skills session each week and Michael has had lots of exposure to our problem solving process. He knows the steps.

"Michael, tell me what the problem is," I began again.

He didn't respond.

"Michael, you're not listening to me. How can I tell that?"

"Because I'm not looking at you," he replied, still looking down.

We went through all the steps of naming the problem, talking through a better alternative than walking out of class, saying he was sorry.

I reminded him once again that, "Tomorrow is another day."

Once Michael calms down he can talk the whole situation out. But he just doesn't seem to be able to carry through. If he has a good day three days in a row, he can have lunch with me—the goal he chose when we wrote up his behavior contract. Unfortunately, Michael rarely makes it three days without a blow up.

Believe me, we've tried everything. Over the course of this school year Michael's behavior contract has involved teachers, the principal, the cafeteria aides, and the maintenance staff. I wish I had a dollar for every time I've told him, "Positive behavior leads to positive consequences. Negative behavior leads to negative consequences." I just keep emphasizing that change takes time. It's a slow process, but I believe he can make it.

Michael has great potential. He can be very kind, gentle and inquisitive. Michael actually is a leader in the class, but he doesn't always lead in the right direction. He's had so few positive role models in his life. He still looks up to his dad, but is confused by all the conflicting messages dad has sent when his words didn't match his actions.

Words not matching actions. I guess that's a lot of what Michael has experienced in life. Sue is trying to give him reason to trust her words now. She's been calling me on a regular basis and, although she doesn't always like some of the consequences we've had to give Michael, ultimately she's been very cooperative, supportive and models our techniques at home. It's hard to be patient and look at the big picture.

I know exactly what Steve will say this afternoon. He's said it many times.

"Michael doesn't have any investment in improving academically. He thinks he'll be in special education forever. I've told him his behavior has to improve if he wants to graduate from elementary school this June, go to middle school and be in regular classes."

He's right. Steve's emphasis is on academic improvement, as it should be. Michael will have to pass state tests, just like everyone else. But we've got to keep helping Michael with his volatile emotions and behavior. We have to remember that he's going through a lot of changes living in the shelter. He's trying to find something he can control in his life.

Steve will look at me and say, "So what's the plan for when Michael comes back to school? What can we do that we haven't already done?"

That's a good question.

Discussion Questions

1. What are the effects of poverty on Michael's academic progress and emotional health?
2. What are the values that the school district personnel and Sue Wilson hold in common?
3. What short and long term goals should be established to create a school and home environment in which Michael can flourish?
4. What types of programs and support should the educational community provide for Michael and other students like him?
5. What changes must occur on the local, state and national levels to improve outcomes for families that experience homelessness?

References

Bahrampour T. (2001, January 3). *Getting homework checked (and teeth as well)*. *New York Times*, Metro Section, p. B8.

Bauman, Z. (1998). *Work, consumerism, and the new poor*. Buckingham, PA: Philadelphia Open University.

Becker, E. (2001). Shift from food stamps to private aid widens. *New York Times*, Nov. 14, 2001, National Section, p. A14.

Bloir, K. (n.d.). *Single, custodial fathers, fact sheet*. Columbus, OH: Ohio State University, Family and Consumer Sciences. Retrieved February 2, 2008 from http://ohioline.osu.edu/hyg-Fact/5000/5310.html

Cheal, D. (1996). *New poverty: Families in postmodern society*. Westport, Ct: Praeger.

Chinyavong, A., & Leonard, J. (1997). *Poverty matters: The cost of child poverty in America*. Washington, DC: Children's Defense Fund.

Eckholm, E. (2006, August 18), A Welfare law milestone finds many left behind, *The New York Times*, A13.

Farah, M., Noble, K. & Hurt, H. (2006). Poverty, privilege, and brain development: Empirical findings and ethical implications. In J. Illes (Ed.) *Neuroethics in the 21st century*. New York: Oxford University Press.

Farah, M. J., Noble, K. G., & Hurt, H. (2006). Poverty, privilege, and brain development: Empirical findings and ethical implications. In J. Illes (Ed.), *Neuroethics: Defining the issues in theory, practice, and policy* (pp. 277-288). New York: Oxford University Press.

Fass, S., & Cauthen, N. K. (2007). *Who are America's poor children? The official story*. New York: National Center for Children in Poverty, Columbia University.

Kagan, S. (1989). Early care and education: Beyond the school house doors. *Phi Delta Kappan, 71*(2), 107–112.

Mann, R. (1995). *Learning about homeless children, youth and families: A teaching guide* (2nd ed.). Seattle, WA: Atlantic Street Center.

Manpower Demonstration Research Corporation (MDRC). (2007). Improving instructional content and practice in low-performing high schools. Retrieved August 18, 2007, from http://www.mdrc.org/area-issue17.html

Mayeroff, G. (1998). Altered destinies: Making life better for school children in need. *Phi Delta Kappan 79*(6), 425–432.

National Center for Children in Poverty. (2006). *Basic facts about low-income children*. Retrieved March, 2007 from: http://www.nccp.org/publications/pub

National Center for Children in Poverty. (2007). *A rapidly changing portrait of fatherhood in America and how the states are responding to it*. Retrieved July 28, 2007 from http://Fatherfamilylink.gse.upenn.edu/

National Center for Children in Poverty. (2007). *A rapidly changing portrait of fatherhood in America and how the states are responding to it*. Retrieved August 18, 2007 from http://fatherfamilylink.gse.upenn.edu/org/nccp/portrait.htm

National Center for Children in Poverty (n.d.). United States: Demographics of low-income children. Retrieved February, 2008, from: http://www.nccp.org/profiles/US_profile_6.html

National Law Center on Homelessness and Poverty. (2001). *What you need to know about the education of homeless children*. Retrieved November 28, 2001, from http://www.nlchp.org.

National Law Center on Homelessness and Poverty (2007). *Educating homeless children and youth: The guide to their rights*. Washington, DC: Author.

Ohlson, C. (1998). Welfare reform: Implications for young children with disabilities, their families, and service providers. *Journal of Early Intervention, 21*(3), 191–206.

Payne, R. K. (1998). *A framework for understanding poverty*. Highlands, TX: RFT Publishing.

Report: U.S. poverty temporary. (1998, August 10). *Poughkeepsie Journal*, p. B4.

Rothenberg, (1998). *With these hands: The hidden world of migrant farmworkers today*. New York: Harcourt Brace.

Salend, S. J. (2008). *Creating inclusive classrooms: Effective and reflective practices* (6th ed.). Upper Saddle River, NJ: Merrill/Prentice Hall.

Shore, R. (1997). *Rethinking the brain. New insights into early development*. New York: The National Health/Education Consortium.

U.S. Census Bureau. (2006). *Current population survey, 2005 and 2006 annual social and economic supplements*. Retrieved February 11, 2008, from http://www.census.gov/hhes/www/poverty/poverty05/table4.pdf

U.S. Department of Health and Human Services (2007, January 24). The 2007 Health and Human Services poverty guidelines. *Federal Register, 72*(15), 3147-3148. Retrieved February 8, 2008, from http//:aspe.hhs.gov/poverty/07poverty.shtml

9

Exceptionality

The term *exceptionality* has been used in the education field to refer to students who are recognized as disabled or gifted and are eligible for services under the Individuals with Disabilities Improvement Education Act (IDEIA), 2004, or the 1988 Gifted and Talented Students Education Act (P.L. 100-297). IDEIA defines a student with a disability as one who meets the criteria specified by at least one of the following classification areas: specific learning disabilities, speech or language impairments, mental retardation, serious emotional disturbance, autism, hearing impairments, multiple disabilities, orthopedic impairments, other health impairments, visual impairments, deaf-blindness, or traumatic brain injury (Salend, 2008). P.L. 100-297, on the other hand, applies to students who are described as gifted and talented. These are students who possess demonstrated or potential high-performance capability in intellectual, creative, specific academic, and leadership areas or in the performing and visual arts and require services or activities not ordinarily provided by the school to develop such capabilities (Smith, 2007).

IDEIA, because of its specificity, is a more powerful piece of legislation than P.L. 100-297. It mandates that all students that meet the definitions are entitled to a free, appropriate public education regardless of the nature and severity of the disability. Each student has an individual education program (IEP) based on a multifactored assessment of his or her strengths and weaknesses. In contrast, P.L. 100-297 does not mandate specific services for gifted and talented students; therefore, programs depend more on the legislation and allocations made by individual states and the types of programs developed by school districts.

Issues of Definition, Identification, and Appropriate Programs

Many have questioned the system that these laws have created (Dunn, 1968; Sailor & Blair, 2005; Wang & Reynolds, 1997). IDEIA requires that students be assessed using multiple standardized or criterion-referenced assessments and that a team of individuals

169

determine whether the child is eligible for services. Of course, there is a fair amount of controversy about the criteria and scope of the definitions stated in the laws for a number of reasons. These include the stigma that a label can engender, the varying interpretations of the definitions, the reliability and validity of the assessments used to determine eligibility, and the lengthy process involved in referral, assessment, and program determinations. Yet the law provides services that are available only to those students who go through this process. Prior to the enactment of the law in 1975, many students were not receiving an appropriate education, and some were not being educated at all. This law has changed that situation dramatically, but some or all of the previously mentioned problems can affect its participants.

Another serious issue regarding identification is the disproportionate representation of minority students in special education. Disproportionate representation involves a higher or lower representation of individuals in a specific group than you would expect based upon their representation in the general population (Salend, 2008). Examination of data for specific disability classifications shows that students from various racial groups are both overrepresented and underrepresented in special education programs (see Table 9.1). Another way to determine disproportionality is to calculate a risk index by dividing the number of students with the disability in the racial group by the total number of students in that group in the school population. When you compare the risk index of one racial group to all other groups, you get a risk ratio (see Table 9.2). This means that nationally, Black students are three times more likely to be identified as having mental retardation and over two times more likely to be classified as emotionally disturbed when compared to their peers. Furthermore, these students are overrepresented in more restrictive special education settings (Skiba, Poloni-Staudinger,

TABLE 9.1   *Disability Distribution, by Race/Ethnicity, of Students Ages 6 through 21 Receiving Special Education and Related Services: Fall 2002*

Disability	Students Ages 6–21 (%)	American Indian/Alaska Native (%)	Asian/ Pacific Islander (%)	Black (not Hispanic) (%)	Hispanic (%)	White (not Hispanic) (%)
Specific learning disabilities	48.3	55.3	40.8	45.1	58.3	46.8
Speech/ language impairments	18.7	16.2	25.6	14.4	18.1	20.1
Mental retardation	9.9	7.8	9.1	16.8	7.8	8.3
Serious emotional disturbance	8.1	7.9	4.7	11.3	4.9	7.9

Source: U.S. Department of Education, Office of Special Education and Rehabilitative Services, Office of Special Education Programs. (2005). *26th Annual (2004) Report to Congress on the Implementation of the Individuals with Disabilities Education Act.* These data are for the 50 states, DC, Puerto Rico, BIA schools, and the four outlying areas.

TABLE 9.2   *Risk Ratios for Students Ages 6 Through 21 with Disabilities, by Race/Ethnicity and Disability Category: Fall 2002*

Disability	American Indian/Alaska Native	Asian/Pacific Islander	Black (not Hispanic)	Hispanic	White (not Hispanic)
Specific learning disabilities	1.53	0.39	1.34	1.10	0.86
Speech/language impairments	1.18	0.67	1.06	0.86	1.11
Mental retardation	1.10	0.45	3.04	0.60	0.61
Serious emotional disturbance	1.30	0.28	2.25	0.52	0.86
All disabilities	1.35	0.48	1.46	0.87	0.92

Source: U.S. Department of Education, Office of Special Education and Rehabilitative Services, Office of Special Education Programs (2005). *26th Annual* (2004) *Report to Congress on the Implementation of the Individuals with Disabilities Education Act*. These data are for the 50 states, DC, Puerto Rico, BIA schools, and the four outlying areas.

Gallini, Simmons, & Feggins-Azziz, 2006). Considerable debate surrounds this issue given the multiple factors involved (Artiles & Kozleski, 2007; Hosp & Reschley, 2004; O'Connor & Fernandez, 2006). As discussed in Chapter 2, the achievement of African American students and Hispanic students falls behind that of their peers. Although disproportionality must be placed in the context of the relatively low income of many of these students and the higher incidence of disabilities associated with poverty due to poor healthcare and environmental factors, issues of personal or institutional racism and underfunded schools also are involved.

Some groups are underrepresented in special education. For example, Asian–Pacific Islanders are underrepresented in the categories of learning disabilities, mental retardation, and emotional disturbance, and Hispanics are underrepresented in the categories of mental retardation and emotional disturbance (see Table 9.2). Given the data on disproportionate representation, the U.S. Office of Special Education Programs and the U.S. Office for Civil Rights are concerned that students may be unserved, receive inappropriate services, or be misclassified and that their placement in special education may be a form of discrimination.

To address these problems, it is critical that schools offer early intervention programs, promote family involvement, employ culturally responsive teaching, implement effective prereferral services, increase the accuracy of referral and evaluation, provide and monitor appropriate services, and include the community in policymaking bodies (Burnette, 1998; Sailor & Blair, 2005; Salend & Garrick Duhaney, 2005).

As with students with disabilities, students who are gifted also face problematic situations. Presently, about two-thirds of the states are mandating either identification of or services for students who are gifted (Smith, 2007). Individual districts determine an identification system for students who are gifted, and such assessments may include

IQ tests, standardized achievement test scores, creativity assessments, checklists, and evaluation of students' work or performance (Turnbull, Turnbull, & Wehmeyer, 2007). Researchers are concerned that assessments do not always take into account the effects of language, culture, and socioeconomic status, so the reliability and validity of the assessment instruments are questioned. Presently, African Americans and Hispanics are underrepresented in gifted education (Milner & Ford, 2007).

Another issue associated with defining exceptionality is the question of whether such a concept exists at all. Some view exceptionality as a social construct based on a determination by the dominant members of society of what is normal or acceptable behavior (Dudley-Marling, 2004). By determining that some individuals are exceptional, it is possible to place differing values on them as people and consequently limit or enhance their access to educational programs. Rather than view the individual as abnormal, it is argued that society can change its physical, financial, governmental, and educational structures to accommodate the needs of all within the society. Such an approach would be based on a system that would provide services based on educational need, rather than on the numbers of individuals that fit into a definition category.

The Inclusion Controversy

One manifestation of this controversy regarding definitions and appropriate educational services is the inclusion movement. Descriptions of inclusion range from the operational to the philosophical. Idol (2006) defines an inclusive school as one in which all students are educated full-time in age-appropriate general education programs. Others believe that the hallmark of inclusive schools is the belief that everyone belongs and is accepted by peers and other members of the school community (Sapon-Shevin, 2003; Stainback, Stainback, & Stefanich, 1996). The debate over where students should be educated and with what types of instructional approaches and groupings continues (Kauffman, Landrum, Mock, Sayeski, & Sayeski, 2005; Zigmond, 2003). To understand this debate, it is important to understand the law and legal precedents, the research on inclusive schooling, and the dynamics of school change.

IDEIA shows a preference for integration of students with disabilities by mandating that they be placed in the least restrictive environment with proper supplementary aids and services (Etscheidt & Bartlett, 1999). States must assure that, to the maximum extent appropriate, students with disabilities are educated with children who do not have disabilities, and that removal from the general education classroom occurs only when the disability is so severe that the curriculum and instruction of the general education classroom cannot be adapted to achieve satisfactory results (McLeskey, Henry, & Axelrod, 1999). Nevertheless, recent case rulings have found that students whose behavior interferes with their own learning or that of others were correctly removed from general education, underscoring the law's emphasis on individualization and appropriateness (Yell & Drasgow, 1999).

Those who have examined the rapidly accumulating body of research related to inclusive schooling have generally concluded that the effect of inclusion on the academic and social performance of students with disabilities is mixed (Salend, 2008; Salend & Duhaney, 1999). When inclusion is properly implemented, rather than seen as a way to cut costs by eliminating special education personnel, the majority of studies yield positive results in a variety of areas (Burstein, Sears, Wilcoxen, Cabello, & Spagna, 2004; Moore, Gilbreath, & Maiuri, 1998). Placing students with disabilities in general education and providing structures that promote positive peer interactions result in improved social competence and communication skills (McGregor & Vogelsberg, 2000). However, the degree of social acceptance experienced by students with disabilities often varies depending on the degree of severity of the disability, the age of the student, and the teacher's ability to promote positive social interaction.

The effects on typical peers in inclusive classrooms have been positive in that their academic performance has not been compromised. They improve in social cognition, and they benefit from the instructional strategies and organizational approaches that teachers initiate in inclusive classrooms (Manset & Semmel, 1997; McGregor & Vogelsberg, 2000).

Similarly, studies on the academic performance of students with disabilities show varied results. Research indicates that students with mild disabilities can show positive achievement gains in the general education classroom (Moore et al., 1998; Rea, McLaughlin, & Walther-Thomas, 2002). These gains are apparent on standardized test scores, reading performance, mastery of IEP goals, and grades (Salend, 2008). There continue to be reservations by teachers, researchers, and professional organizations about the suitability of providing services in the regular classroom for various student groups. Much of this concern is related to the degree to which general education teachers have the knowledge, time for planning and collaboration, administrative support, and willingness to differentiate instruction for students of all abilities. While there is a concern that students with disabilities may not receive "specially designed instruction" as required by the IEP, many are receiving content area instruction in general education and performing as well as their typical peers (Cawley, Hayden, Cade, & Baker-Kroczynski, 2002; Manset & Semmel, 1997).

A concern that both law and practice have begun to address is the need for early intervention. IDEIA supports funding for two potentially complementary approaches that are designed to assist students earlier in their schooling: prereferral or problem solving teams and Response to Intervention. Prereferral teams are composed of a variety of school professionals that meet to define, analyze, and address an academic or behavioral problem that an individual student is experiencing. Research shows that these teams can assist teachers in using evidence-based practices as well as reduce referrals to special education (Bahr & Koveleski, 2006). If a prereferral team includes one or more individuals who are expert in issues of bilingualism, teachers will receive better support in teaching these students, and fewer children from culturally diverse groups will be inappropriately placed in special education (Ortiz, Wilkinson, Robertson-Courtney, & Kushner, 2006).

Another initiative that holds promise for intervening earlier when students struggle and reducing the number of referrals to special education is Responsiveness to Intervention (RTI) (Bradley, Danielson, & Doolittle, 2007). RTI has been endorsed as an alternative to the current system for identifying students with learning disabilities, which waits for students to fail before they receive services. Instead, students are referred for assistance at the first sign of nonresponse to traditional classroom instruction. IDEIA gives states the option of developing their own system for RTI, although current models usually involve a prevention program with at least three tiers that gradually increase the intensity of research-based intervention. Movement between tiers is based on ongoing assessment and progress monitoring. The limited research on the effectiveness of RTI usually focuses on literacy instruction. Some predict that RTI can reduce the overrepresentation of students of color in disability categories such as emotional disturbance (Harris-Murri, King, & Rostenberg, 2006). However, we know little about how effective it will be once implemented on a large scale with multiple content areas and all grade levels. Whatever the model adopted, RTI will require the training and involvement of all school personnel, not just special educators.

Creating Inclusive Schools for Students with Disabilities

Perhaps the greatest challenge to any initiative, whether it is inclusive education, standards-based assessment, prereferral teams, or RTI, is creating a unified educational system that is effective and sustainable. There are conditions and policies that must be in place if restructuring efforts are to result in positive outcomes for children. One framework for standards-based reform involves six policy goals:

1. A curriculum that establishes high standards for achieving individual potential.
2. Measurable results for teaching and learning.
3. Responsibilities among all stakeholders.
4. Necessary training for all personnel.
5. Maximum use of all funding sources.
6. Central leadership and support with local control and responsibility (Roach, Salisbury, & McGregor, 2002).

Districts that are serious about improvement must evaluate those policy areas that are weak to plan and enact long-term change that unites the mandates of NCLB and IDEIA.

NCLB has required all states to establish curriculum goals and high stakes tests that purportedly measure those goals. Whether a district can offer a full range of content area, arts, physical education, and vocational courses necessary to educate students who are gifted as well as students with disabilities is still debatable. Many are concerned that high stakes testing has narrowed the curriculum since so many teachers feel they must teach to the test (Lewis, 2007). While some students with disabilities are making adequate yearly progress, it appears to be unrealistic to expect students who grew up in underresourced communities to reach the same benchmarks, even with the implementation of research-based practices (Shippen, Houchins, Calhoon, Furlow, & Sartor, 2006). Questions abound regarding the types of assessments used and the criteria for establishing adequate yearly progress.

Furthermore, research has shown that all teachers must have input in planning and decision making during reform (Burstein et al., 2004). For example, the implementation and maintenance of the RTI model will flounder unless both general and special educators are involved. All teachers need intensive and training in effective practices to confidently and competently enact such changes. The commitment of teachers increases as they have time to collaborate with others who are enthusiastic and knowledgeable about inclusive practices. If new organizational structures such as alternative scheduling, multiage classrooms, or schools within schools are indicated, teachers should have input regarding implementation.

Obviously, funding for change must be available to all, not just to districts with families of higher socioeconomic status (Biddle & Berliner, 2002). Unfortunately, the federal government contributes less that 50 percent of the funding level authorized by IDEIA and less than 20 percent of the total cost (National Education Association, 2007), leaving local districts to raise the majority of the funding. Schools that are underfunded will not be able to attract and retain administrators and teachers who can establish and sustain a shared vision of change. Administrators must work with staff to integrate the accountability demands of NCLB and the inclusive, individualized emphasis of IDEIA (Sindelar, Shearer, Yendol-Hoppey, & Liebert, 2006).

Certainly, student differences in learning preference and cognition necessitate differentiation of approach. The concept of Universal Design for Learning (UDL) is a framework for ensuring that curriculum, instructional strategies, technology, and assessment for a variety of learners are chosen during the planning process (Rose & Meyer, 2002). Based upon brain research, UDL holds that barriers to learning can occur on one of three levels: recognition (the "what" of learning), strategic (the "how" of learning), and affect (the "why" of learning). Recognition barriers may be overcome by providing flexible options for learning, such as the use of digital media rather than fixed media such as print. Strategic barriers might be addressed by teaching learning strategies that assist students in everyday academic tasks, such as comprehending text, writing narrative and expository text, taking notes, solving a mathematical word problem, or taking a test (Lenz & Deshler, 2004). Affective or motivational barriers often are hurdled when teachers give students some choice in what and when they learn or employ technology. One example of a universally designed curriculum is "Thinking Reader," which integrates the strategy of reciprocal teaching into digital version of award-winning children's literature (Palincsar & Brown, 1984; Rose & Meyer, 2002).

While UDL may appear to involve a high degree of individualization, it is less so if special education and general education teachers work together on initial planning so that lessons incorporate some of these approaches up front and require fewer adjustments after the fact. Teachers can use a unit planning template that incorporates the tenants of UDL, differentiated instruction, and multicultural education to plan integrated, standards-based instructional units for the general education classroom (van Garderen & Whittaker, 2006).

Another group of students that must be provided with differentiated instruction are the gifted and talented, who often are stuck in the inflexible age–grade classrooms of most public schools. While schools must provide intellectual access for gifted students to the full range of the curriculum, multiple issues related to identification, assessment, and programming must be recognized by those planning inclusive school programs.

Issues in the Education of Students Who are Gifted and Talented

School programs for students who are gifted and talented have increasingly come under attack for failing to identify, include, and appropriately serve an expanding list of students. In fact, because many gifted programs have been havens for upper-middle-class white students, some would suggest that this may be a subtle form of racial and ethnic discrimination (Gallagher, 1995). There are adequate data to confirm that many students of color are underrepresented in programs for gifted learners. Black, Hispanic and Native American students are underrepresented in programs for gifted students, whereas Asian/Pacific Islander vary greatly in their participation rates (Ford, 2006; Smith, 2007). Likewise, students who are bilingual or limited English proficient often are not included in such programs (Barkan & Bernal, 1991; Shaunessy, McHatton, Hughes, Brice, & Ratliff, 2007). Not all inequities relate to race or language. For example, low socioeconomic status also is a factor in the exclusion of children from programs for the gifted (Frasier, 1991).

Causes of Underrepresentation

There are multiple reasons for these discrepancies: limiting definitions of giftedness, negative stereotypes and inaccurate perceptions of the abilities of children of color, inequitable program referrals, assessment measures and techniques that are not culturally sensitive, and inadequate preparation of teachers in issues and practices appropriate for the multicultural school population (Maker, 1996; McBee, 2006; Patton, 1997; Tomlinson, Callahan, & Lelli, 1997).

The issue of identification and assessment is particularly thorny. There has been a paradigm shift in gifted education, which views intelligence as having multiple forms and as being developmental and process-oriented, rather than stable and unchangeable. For example, in many districts Howard Gardner's concept of multiple intelligences continues to influence identification of and programming for students who are gifted (Gardner, 2006). Alternatively, Sternberg (2007) views intelligence as having analytical, creative and practical components.

While there probably will never be one test that is a valid and reliable measure of the abilities found in a all cultural and linguistic groups, work is being done in this area (Maker, 1996; Naglieri & Ford, 2005; Pfeiffer et al., 2007; Rueda, 1997; Scott & Delgado, 2005; Sternberg, 2007; Tomlinson et al., 1997). The still common reliance on IQ scores and teacher nomination has effectively precluded the classification of many students, and even the use of checklists designed for diverse and disadvantaged populations, quota systems, and a matrix to weigh data from multiple sources has not changed disproportionate representation.

The identification process must be guided by a knowledge of culture, language, values, and the world view of culturally and linguistically diverse learners and their families (Sternberg, 2007). Problem-solving ability and recognition of leadership skills have been effective predictors of later academic performance (Clasen, 2006). Evaluators need sensitivity to intragroup differences as well. It is becoming increasingly evident that intelligence must be studied by observing how individuals recognize and solve problems in their own environment from a young age.

Teacher Attitudes and Family Involvement

Even with improved identification procedures, children from culturally and linguistically diverse groups have not always been successful in programs because their behavior did not fit with the teacher's beliefs about giftedness (Barkan & Bernal, 1991; Ishii-Jordan, 1997; Maker, 1996). For example, it is assumed that a child must have attained a certain level of English proficiency before he or she can be considered for gifted education. The same framework that guides new assessments must guide program development or students who are not high achievers in the traditional curriculum will receive inappropriate instruction, become frustrated, and fail or drop out.

Family involvement is a definite factor in the achievement of gifted students of color. Clark (1983) found that Black students from low socioeconomic groups who were achieving had parents who were assertive in parent involvement efforts, kept track of their children's progress, and perceived themselves as having effective coping mechanisms. These parents set high and realistic expectations for their children, held achievement-oriented norms and role boundaries, engaged in experiences that promoted achievement, and had positive parent–child relations. However, parent educational level does not appear to be a predictor of gifted student's academic performance (Ford & Thomas, 1997). Successful programs for gifted students who come from underrepresented groups frequently include a family involvement component in which parents learn English, act a cultural informants, learn parenting skills, participate in school activities with their children, or attend family meetings (Cropper, 1998; Tomlinson et al., 1997).

Programming for Gifted and Talented Students

Differentiated instruction has become one of the most frequently recommended pedagogical approaches for gifted learners as well as for all learners in the general education classroom (Tomlinson, 2004; Tomlinson, Brighton, Hertberg, Callahan, Moon, Brimijoin, Conover, & Reynolds, 2003). One way of defining differentiation is the modification of teaching and learning routines to address a broad range of learners' readiness levels, interests, and learning preferences by considering the content, process, products, affect, and learning environment possible in any classroom (Tomlinson & Eidson, 2003). Gifted learners will spend the great majority of the day in general education, so it is incumbent upon all teachers to design their instruction taking all learners' abilities into consideration. Unfortunately, while some teachers enthusiastically embrace the concept of differentiated instruction, in many classrooms the practice of differentiation is minimal or nonexistent. Other practices to enhance the academic and social needs of children who are gifted include acceleration and enrichment and use of technology (Smith, 2007).

Academic acceleration is one alternative for precocious youth that has been supported in the research literature as positive (Van Tassel-Baska, 2004). Many educational practitioners appear to be unaware of this research and, relying on common sense and little personal experience, report being opposed to acceleration (Southern & Jones, 1991). Their concerns center on hurrying the child through school and risks to social and emotional development. With careful screening for social and emotional maturity, as well as academic aptitude, early kindergarten entrance or acceleration in the primary grades can provide appropriate challenge and promote positive attitudes toward school while participating in general education (Colangleo, Assouline, & Gross, 2004).

Another type of acceleration is providing younger children who show potential giftedness with special programming on weekends and in the summer. Several model programs have been developed for students of color and those from low economic backgrounds who are gifted (Clasen, 2006; Ford & Thomas, 1997). One such program in Ohio identifies students from urban areas who show promise in math and science by presenting real-life problems in the environment on Saturdays, followed by a ten-day residential program at a university campus in the summer (Coleman & Southern, 2006). Teachers can develop multiple opportunities for advanced content and critical thinking by providing enrichment. Learning centers, field trips, bibliotherapy, mentorships, service learning, and internships are all excellent examples of enrichment activities in and beyond the classroom that can engage an advanced learner cognitively and also promote affective and gender development (Hebert, Long, & Neumeister, 2001; Higgins & Boone, 2003). In addition, some approaches suggest that students experience success when curricula and instruction are designed to be culturally and linguistically compatible (Tharp, 1989; Tharp & Gallimore, 1988).

A final area of concern is a dearth of programming for young students who are gifted and little research on programs that do exist (Sankar-DeLeeuw, 2004). When programs are nonexistent, concerned parents can only request that teachers provide changes in curriculum and approach for their child. Unfortunately, teachers are not always receptive to parental requests that their gifted child receive curriculum modifications, especially when the child may present challenging social behaviors (Mooij, 1999). When a more engaging curriculum for the gifted learner is absent, young children can react with negative emotions toward teachers and school as well as become underachievers. However, children who show precocity even in kindergarten can be encouraged by allowing them to pursue their academic interests, work with one or more other gifted students on projects or alone, and accomplish tasks that promote independence and responsibility. If students are reading, writing, or pursuing other learning experiences that typically are introduced in later grades, they should be provided access to advanced materials and have opportunity to discuss what they are learning with someone (Rotigel, 2003). Other recommendations for encouraging young gifted children are listed in Box 9.1.

While there continues to be a need for research on how best to identify and serve children who are identified as disabled or gifted and talented, much that is already known is not being applied in districts across the country. School districts can take advantage of an array of free resources developed by the National Research Center on the Gifted and Talented at the University of Connecticut (www.gifted.uconn.edu), which provides free information about research, exemplary curriculum, how to reverse underachievement in gifted students, and resources for families (Reis, 2007). As described above, the challenge is one of integrating these ideas into a unified district program.

BOX 9.1 • *Ways to Nurture Young Children Who Are Gifted*

- Make clear assessments of the child's social, emotional, physical, and educational strengths and needs.
- Talk with children to discover their level of understanding regarding their giftedness.
- Remember that some children are gifted and disabled.
- Recognize that giftedness may be associated with children who are socially sought after by peers or who are bragging, impatient, and prefer solitude.
- Remember that although children may interact with adults in a mature way, their emotional development may more closely match age peers.

- Use flexible grouping strategies to encourage the child to discover appropriate intellectual, social, and emotional peers.
- Ensure that the gifted child has intellectual peers who are also agemates.
- Do not expect the gifted child to spend too much time tutoring classmates.
- Encourage creative aesthetics, play, hobbies, second language acquisition, and interactions with mentors.
- Gradually increase on-task behavior.
- Address children's philosophical questions about meaning and spirituality.
- Establish preschool and kindergarten programs that nurture giftedness.

Source: Adapted from Gould, Thorpe, & Weeks, 2001; Rotigel, 2003; Sankar-DeLeeuw, 2004.

Issues in the Education of Students with Attention Deficit Hyperactivity Disorder

Another area of the field of special education that has engendered great controversy for decades is the assessment and treatment of attention-deficit hyperactivity disorder (ADHD). ADHD is the most commonly diagnosed childhood psychiatric disorder in the United States (Turnbull et al., 2007). ADHD is defined as "a persistent pattern of inattention and/or hyperactivity–impulsivity that is more frequent and severe than is typically observed in individuals at a comparable level of development" (American Psychiatric Association, 2000, p. 92). The symptoms must have been present before the age of 7, be present in at least two settings, and show clear interference with developmentally appropriate functioning.

There are three subtypes of ADHD. The predominantly inattentive type describes children who have difficulty paying attention, appear apathetic, seem internally occupied, are socially neglected, may be anxious or depressed, and are often underachievers (Barkley, 1990; Lahey & Carlson, 1991). The predominantly hyperactive–impulsive type includes children who often talk excessively, have difficulty sitting still, often challenge boundaries, interrupt and blurt out answers, and can be accident prone (Turnbull et al., 2007). Children who are described as having the combined type may be inattentive as well as hyperactive and impulsive.

The identification and treatment of children with ADHD has been particularly controversial. Children and Adults with Attention Deficit Disorders (Ch.A.D.D), an organization that provides advocacy and education about ADHD, estimates that 3 to 5 percent of the school-aged population has ADHD, but in some areas of the country, particularly urban areas, the percentages are much higher (Turnbull et al., 2007). While some argue that this increase is due to an awareness of the condition, others believe stimulant drugs are overprescribed and are concerned about possible side effects, such as insomnia, headaches, irritability, moodiness, nausea, and weight loss. They also wonder if the fact that two to four times as many boys as girls are diagnosed is related to teacher perception of acceptable behavior.

Some students with ADHD will be identified as needing special education services under IDEIA as "other health impaired," some may receive reasonable accommodations under Section 504 of the Rehabilitation Act, and others will not receive any support through federally mandated laws. Nevertheless, general education teachers will need to determine how to assist these students in learning. At present, researchers believe that children who take stimulants such as Ritalin or Dexedrine for ADHD should show signs of improvement relatively quickly, or the regiment or diagnosis should be reevaluated (Schlozman & Schlozman, 2000). Although it appears that medications are more effective than behavior therapy alone in controlling the characteristics of ADHD (Smith, 2007), changes in academic achievement result only when medication and behavior interventions are combined. Therefore, educators should strongly consider interventions such as behavior management, organizational training, counseling, peer tutoring, and instruction in self-regulation (DuPaul & Eckert, 1998; Prater & Pancheri, 1999; Salend, 2008; Schlozman & Schlozman, 2000). Finally, it is essential that parents, physicians, teachers, school nurse, and counselors collaborate to evaluate the effectiveness of all interventions.

ADHD frequently coexists with other exceptionalities such as learning disabilities, emotional disturbance and giftedness. As many as 70% of students with ADHD are also classified as having a learning disability (Smith, 2007). Similarly, there is quite a bit of overlap between students with ADHD and those who exhibit conduct disorders and these students often display antisocial and criminal behavior in adolescence (Gresham, Lane, & Beebe-Frankenberger, 2005). Such a student can be identified fairly early and should receive interventions that include social skills training and individualized behavior intervention plan. Finally, researchers are only beginning to study students who have characteristics of ADHD and giftedness. One study suggests that nine-year-old boys who were both gifted and ADHD were underachievers, had difficulty sustaining long term projects and homework completion and were unorganized (Zentall, Moon, Hall, & Grskovic, 2001). These boys seemed to enjoy hands-on activities, particularly in science, and group activities. While they needed assistance to learn to monitor their own work habits, it was counterproductive to simplify their work or isolate them from other children.

Special education and gifted education have undergone dramatic changes in the past 40 years. Understanding the research and issues that influence educators, parents, and communities today as they attempt to provide services for students who are exceptional will be critical for designing successful outcomes for individuals such as those in the case studies that follow.

The Case of Selina James

It was 8:34 A.M. and Carol, the social worker; Yvonne, the art teacher; Lillian, the reading specialist; and Sharon, the computer lab teacher, were gathered around a table with me. We were making small talk.

Carol began, "I think we should start. Ann Elliott has asked me to call this Student Review Team meeting to discuss Selina James. As all of you know, Selina is a very bright kindergartner whose reading skills far surpass most of the students in Ann's class. I thought we should start by having Ann explain her concerns about Selina."

"Selina doesn't present the typical scenario for calling a meeting, but I think it's important that we address her needs as well as those who struggle academically. Selina is a gifted student; there's no doubt about that. She can read books that are on a second- or third-grade level independently. With help, she has been reading even more complex texts. Once she learns to read and spell a word, she doesn't forget it. And her comprehension is exceptional. She can retell a story with all the important events in sequence. It's even more impressive when you realize she was born in August and, although she doesn't look it, is one of the youngest 5-year-olds in the class."

"I am concerned that I am not challenging Selina enough. She thrives on adult attention, but I just don't have the time to devote to her exclusively very often, and none of the other children are close to her reading level. I have given her permission to read whatever books she chooses from the library, and she reads voraciously. I've also asked her to tutor some of the children who need assistance, but I don't want to take advantage of her in that way. I try to listen to her read when I have a few spare minutes, and she loves the attention. In fact, she loves being able to read to any adult who will listen.

"But I'm not sure that these things are enough, and it's starting to show up in her relationships with other children. For example, last week Bridgett was showing me a wonderful picture of a lion in the cage that she had drawn, and I complimented her saying, 'You're a good artist, Bridgett!' Immediately, Selina chimed in and said, 'But I'm a GREAT artist!' I'm glad she's proud of her own accomplishments, but she needs to learn how to interact with the other children appropriately."

This is how I presented Selina's case to the team last Friday. I'm still unsure about which of their recommendations I can live with. We have a policy at Lincoln Elementary that the team can make any suggestions that they may think of, but the teacher directly involved ultimately decides whether the ideas are workable. Possible suggestions included involving Selina in circle time in a first-grade classroom two days a week, teaching her to be a peer tutor, including her in the afterschool book group sponsored by the librarian, having an older child or adult carry on an e-mail conversation with her weekly, contacting community youth theater or music programs to see if Selina could receive a scholarship, and promoting her to second grade next year.

The latter suggestion was the most extreme option, and I'm uncomfortable with the ramifications of such a move. The long-term social implications of promotions are serious: Selina would be a senior at 16. However, I did like the idea of her becoming involved in the first-grade circle activity if Norma and I can coordinate it. The afterschool book discussion is a great idea if Selina's parents will allow her to stay. The e-mail idea is a good one, but takes coordination. I wonder if Selina has the social skills to be a peer tutor. The theater group may not have scholarships; they are struggling to stay afloat.

These are the alternatives that have been swimming through my head over the last few days. We're having a follow-up meeting next Monday and I have to decide which of these options we should pursue. More importantly, none of them seem to address the long-term needs of kindergarten children who are gifted and placed full-time in an inclusive classroom.

This is my twenty-fourth year of teaching in Howard City Schools, with fourteen of them spent in kindergarten. Although I have many years of instructional ideas to draw on and adequate materials and supplies, it seems that I never have enough human resources to call on. I am fortunate to have had Donna, my teaching assistant, with me full time for four years now, and can count on her to reinforce the instruction that I deliver. Isabella Myers, the consultant teacher, comes in for 45 minutes every day during language arts time, so we can do some small-group work then. I'm thankful for her help, but that's a small part of the day.

As I look at the diverse needs of the class I have this year, sometimes I feel like I should have a Student Review Team meeting each week on a different child.

A teacher and a teaching assistant just can't get around to twenty-three students adequately when their social and cognitive skills range from 3 to 8 or 9 years old. Two children were retained last year and now are in kindergarten again since we don't have a "transition" class. Right now there are ten students who have IEPs in my classroom, with labels including learning disabled, emotionally disturbed, and mentally retarded. Four students had been in preschool special education programs before they entered kindergarten, but since two had received those services and then were removed from special education, I didn't see their files and didn't know until I asked the parents directly. Two children aren't in special education, but do receive speech services. I'm hoping that the IEP team will agree that at least three students no longer need services this spring at the annual review since they've made considerable progress. Eighteen of my children receive free lunch. There are ten white, eight African American, one Hispanic, and four biracial children in the class. Thirteen are boys, and ten are girls.

I love my students, but some of them can really be a challenge. Take Shakeem, for example. His dark brown eyes are beguiling, yet he sometimes has tears running down his chocolate cheeks. He came to me at the beginning of the year with behaviors that were typical of a 3-year-old. He would crawl around the room, scream, and have tantrums. Initially, we had to remove him several times a day from the classroom. He had been in a special education preschool and still is receiving services in my classroom. In September he knew none of his letters and sounds and now, in March, he knows about half of them. During journal time, he still prefers to draw. He'll try writing the alphabet independently if he's in a good mood, but he needs one-on-one assistance to write a word, much less a sentence. The one thing that keeps him on task for long periods of time is the computer. However, he's come a long way in the area of social skills, and tantrums are rare.

Then there is Larry. He also received special education services during his preschool years and still has an IEP. At the beginning of the year he seemed like just a small, pale face hiding behind his glasses; he wouldn't talk at all. Then there would be days when he would kick or pinch Donna. He's talking now, but he's made minimal improvement on reading skills. He only knows about five letter sounds consistently. He'll still bite or pinch when there's more change in the classroom than he can manage.

I could go on and on. Each child has special needs regardless of whether they are in special education. And they range from the ridiculous to the serious. Last week Lamont's dad asked if I would get the snot out of Lamont's nose since he can't manage it himself. I told him to talk to the nurse. Over the weekend Patrick's dad died of a heart attack at age 40, leaving four children to survive on their mother's minimum wage job. In one day my emotions can flip-flop between joy and depression with one phone call or one child's remark.

These are some of the concerns that cross my consciousness while I'm trying to teach this morning. My twenty-three kindergarten students sit cross-legged in a semicircle around the easel. I have put a morning message on newsprint in a cloze format for the children to read. Next to the message there are letters and numbers on individual sticky notes. The children can choose one of these to fill in the blanks.

To_ay is Tues_ay, _arch, 20__. _ix baby ch_cks have
_atched from the e_gs. We _ave _rt class t_day.

As I wait for all the children to direct their eyes toward me, I am reminded of what an impossible expectation such undivided attention might have been back in September. Six months ago Larry might have been climbing under his table trying to avoid circle time completely. Shakeem might have still been in the cafeteria finishing his breakfast. Today I knew that if I simply praised those who were attending to me, the rest would quickly follow suit. I was pleased with the considerable progress that they had made in socialization skills.

Donna is sitting between Selina and Shakeem, the two extremes of my class's ability spectrum. Selina's alert, dark eyes are constantly scanning her surroundings. Shakeem is dressed in the finest in kindergarten wear and is playing with the ties on his hightop Nikes. Donna's wonderful skills as a teaching assistant are evident once again. She knows that these two students need her attention and places herself accordingly.

I explain that they should raise their hands if they know what letter or number belongs in the blank. We start with the first word and immediately about two-thirds of the children raise their hands. I choose Larry because he often does not even attempt to raise his hand. He has no immediate response, so I tell him to look around the room to see if he can see the whole word and he finds it. He comes to the board with a slight smile when he sees the answer. He holds his shoulders a bit straighter as he returns to his place in the circle.

We go on to the next word. Selina is waving her hand high into the air and, I know, whispering the answer to Donna. I decide to call on her next, and she confidently places the correct letter in the blank. Her light brown cheeks seem to grow even more rounded with pleasure when I applaud her correct response.

I go on to call on other children and find that I have to give a fair number of prompts to help them to choose the right symbol for the blank. I believe that it is important for them to be successful, so I try to direct them to environmental print and other visuals posted around the room to give them clues. Of course, this takes time. I can tell that Donna has her hands full. Shakeem is bouncing on his knees while making animal sounds. Simultaneously, Selina is waving her hand in the air and whispering answers in Donna's ear.

Several of the children seem to be reaching the outer limits of their attention span, so I try to finish up. I called on another girl to fill in the last blank and notice that Selina pulls down her hand in disgust.

"Mrs. Elliott doesn't call on me because I'm smarter than the other kids," Selina complains to Donna, loud enough for me and several of the other children to hear. Donna leans over to remind Selina that I can't call on her each time she has her hand up.

I ignore Selina's remark and quickly move on to the next activity I had planned, a class read-aloud of the big book *The Little Red Hen*. While some of the students can read along only when we read the repetitive sections, others surprise me by recognizing words that we have not discussed in class before. There is only one child that reads practically every word along with me—Selina.

During our planning time I express my frustration to Donna about Selina's snobbish comment. I certainly had not ignored her.

"The more attention you give her, the more she wants," agreed Donna. "That's not the first time I've heard her say things that are hurtful to the other children. It's not as if everything she does is perfect. Yesterday she rushed through that writing assignment so she could read a book. Her handwriting was sloppy and she only wrote one sentence."

"But look at Selina's reading skills!"

"I know. I know. But Selina's got to learn not to put down the other children. She has to follow the instructions, too. She seems to think that she's special and deserves extra attention. There are too many children who demand my attention now," Donna answered.

"Selina is gifted in some areas, but not all," I agreed. "She certainly needs more help with aspects of her interpersonal intelligence. I told the Student Review Team that, too."

As I drive home, I try to imagine what changes can be made to improve Selina's social interactions and also keep her interested and challenged in school. It is hard to remain positive, however, when I think about all the demands that the children in the class place on me. It is clear that they need this full-day kindergarten program since so many are below developmental norms. At least the school district recognizes that.

This year at Lincoln Elementary we added a third kindergarten because of the large enrollment. In spite of this, my class size is over the twenty-two-student limit "directive" established by the school district. Contractually, I could have thirty in this class. Every classroom in the school is used and, while my classroom is adequate in size,

I could always use more room, especially when Isabella comes in and we divide into small groups. However, there is no room to create additional classrooms or programs.

We are a neighborhood school situated in one of the poorest sections of the city. We try very hard to promote the values of kindness, respect, and responsibility that seem important to most of our parents. To promote respect for our backgrounds, this year our faculty has worked hard each quarter to decorate our school display case with artifacts representing the various cultures from which our children or their families have immigrated. Yet we are faced with the reality that some parents cannot give their children the educational and financial support that they need. Some of them became parents when they were 15 years old.

Recently, we had a citywide vote on two school district issues. The expenses for "noncontingent" items (extracurricular activities, sports, music and art programs, the gifted program) were part of that budget. Second, five places on the school board were up for a vote and there were five members of the local taxpayers group who ran against incumbents on a platform to cut future budget expenditures. The outcome was that the noncontingent budget passed by a narrow margin. However, four of the five candidates from the taxpayers group were elected.

This certainly does not give me much hope that I'll be getting any more resources, human or material, to help with the diversity in my classroom. If anything, I'll be lucky to hang on to what I have now. It's even conceivable that the funding for the gifted program and some of the afterschool enrichment programs at Lincoln Elementary will be reduced or eliminated in the future. Although our gifted program does not extend to the kindergarten level, such a cut would mean that Selina would not be able to be involved in such programs in the future.

Selina's family does not have the financial resources to provide her with the music lessons, theater classes, or other special training that more affluent parents might insist on. She has three older siblings and her mother just had a baby girl one month ago. Her mother is from Puerto Rico and her father is African American. While they seem to be a solid family, with only Mr. James working as a maintenance person in the city recreation program, they certainly can't afford any extras. They live in public housing that is clean and well cared for, but crowded for seven people. Selina's dad often picks her up after school and walks her and her older sister home. He says that she went to a pre-K program for two years and knew her alphabet and could count to 100 before kindergarten. She taught herself to read.

The only thing that I can think of to do at this point is to make sure that at least some of the suggestions of the Student Review Team are implemented. But which ones? And will incremental changes like these really make a difference? Our state has a miserable record for funding gifted education, and we have few resources to rely on. However, I feel strongly that a child like Selina should be challenged to meet her own potential. At the same time, I also believe that many students with disabilities can make tremendous behavioral and academic gains when placed in a general education setting. But one of the many attacks on the idea of including students with disabilities in the regular classroom is that other children will not receive adequate attention. I do not want that to be the case in my classroom, yet I realize how difficult it is to keep a balance.

Discussion Questions

1. Describe Selina's academic and interpersonal abilities as compared to her peers.
2. What options are presently available for Selina for this year and beyond?
3. What does the research indicate regarding the assessment and placement of students of color in programs for the gifted?
4. What does the research indicate about the problems of identifying and serving young children with disabilities?
5. What does Selina's teacher, Ann, believe might be the best program for Selina? For the children who achieve at a much lower level?
6. What assumptions and underlying values does the school district hold regarding the inclusion of students from a broad ability range in the regular classroom?
7. What issues must be addressed to provide an appropriate education for Selina? Who should be involved in determining and providing this program?
8. What type of professional development or support does Ann need to continue to find kindergarten teaching fulfilling and meaningful?
9. What district, state, and national policies affect Selina's education?

The Case of Matthew Simpson

"If I can't leave by the door, I'll leave by the window," Matthew shouted as he ran toward the windows in the classroom. I dashed to the window and slammed it, wondering if Matthew had taken his Ritalin that morning. On his worst days he had usually left home without it. Today, like so many other days, I had kept Matthew in for recess because he had called out all morning. Only today, I had to lock the door when he tried to leave despite my directions to remain seated.

As an African American teacher, I worry about Matthew and many other African American students who should not be in special education. It's so obvious to me that students are often placed in my classroom because of behavior. Sometimes my fifteen years of experience here at Stevens Elementary School and my MS degree in special education seem almost useless in dealing with some of the students. The challenges are greater every year. Yet I refuse to alter my philosophy because I believe that it is my duty to prepare as many as possible to return to general education. Thus, unlike too many special education teachers, I stress academics in my classroom and I use the regular curriculum. Each year, in June, I always feel elated at the end of the school year when I can recommend that several of my students return to regular sixth grade classes when they graduate to middle school.

However, there are times when Matthew really tries my patience and tests my philosophy. He can disrupt the entire class when he insists on calling out, conversing with students seated nearby, asking multiple questions, or giving endless answers to one of my questions. On rare occasions when I lose it, I actually shout, "Shut up, Matthew! That's enough!"

My self-contained special education class consists of fifteen children aged 9 to 11. There are nine African American students (including Matthew), five Latinos, and one white child. Although the grade levels supposedly range from 3 to 5, students are functioning academically from grade 1.0 to 7.7 in reading and math. The highest scores belong to Matthew, who is 11 years old. With so many levels in reading and math in my classroom, how can I possibly individualize work for Matthew? I have five reading groups and, of course, he is in the top group; however, that group is only on the fifth-grade level. Often he has read the story earlier and already knows all the answers. This means that he raises his hand for every question asked, and sometimes he blurts out the answer without raising his hand. When he doesn't take his Ritalin, Matthew shouts out all the answers and the day is usually unbearable.

Matthew really stands out in my classroom, not only because he is the tallest, but also due to his academic ability and behavior. One day I sent him out into the hall to sit in a chair because I had to speak to him too many times that morning. When I looked out to check on him, he was pacing the floor. Then he came to the door, stuck his head in, and asked if he could sharpen his pencil. I shouted "No" before I thought. He needed the pencil in order to do some work! Matthew is often out of the room, in the principal's office, or sent home for the same unacceptable behaviors—calling out, talking back, and not listening. Sometimes he even complains that he's bored and that's the reason he talks so much. I can't totally disagree with Matthew. In school, he's not being challenged. At home and in the community there is little for a bright, active child to do.

The surrounding neighborhood, in which all the children live, suffers the problems of many inner-city communities. There is a lack of decent housing, excessive crime and drug activity, and a scarcity of recreational activities. No playground or park is available in the area. An organized neighborhood group does try to make a difference, but appears to be powerless in dealing with the political structure of the city. For example, the group has tried to fight drug activity through the presence of a community police office. However, the office remained unstaffed for six months and was finally closed despite letters to the mayor and other politicians. Interestingly, there are several large, formerly all-White churches in the neighborhood that are struggling with how to develop better relationships with the community, and progress has been very slow, thus far.

Matthew lives with his mother, Mrs. Simpson, who has a full-time job. She has no phone at home, but did call me once when I sent a note home with Matthew that I wanted to speak with her. After expressing some of my concerns about Matthew's behavior and above-average intelligence, she told me that she, too, had had problems in school.

"But I was a fighter," she said. "I fought with everyone and got put in a special school. It was one of the teachers there that was good to me and helped me graduate," she insisted.

She continued to tell me that most of the time Matthew is left in the care of his grandmother. He has a sister aged 23, a brother who is 19, and a 5-year-old sister.

Recently, when Matthew was absent for an entire week, I realized how peaceful my classroom could be. The class was working quietly in their reading groups the following Monday when the door opened suddenly and Matthew entered, followed by the guidance counselor, who held the door. Matthew's right leg was bandaged in bright blue from ankle to groin and around the blue bandage were wide white bands. He hobbled on two crutches. Surprised to see him after a week's absence, several students and I asked in unison, "Matthew, what happened to you?"

He responded proudly, "I pulled a ligament in my leg; in fact, I tore two ligaments."

Matthew always loves the class's attention and he appeared to relish their interest in his leg. However, one student muttered, "Uh-oh, the class comedian is back." I told Matthew to get his book for reading, and he joined my reading group who were engaged then in reading *Charlotte's Web*, a story that Matthew seemed to know already. After 5 to 10 minutes, having answered every question that I asked, Matthew announced, "I'm so bored."

Nevertheless, he remained cooperative throughout the remainder of the period. This was admirable, given his frequent distractibility, impulsivity, and endless chatter. In fact, when you ask Matthew a question, it's necessary to plan for a 5-minute answer. He never stops with a simple answer, but is forever elaborating on and expanding his initial response.

Matthew is classified as emotionally disturbed, although his recent test scores indicated that he is very capable of advanced work. Not only is he currently reading at a grade level of 7.7, but his grade-level mathematics score is 7.3. However, on an older WISC intelligence test, which was administered five years ago, his full scale IQ was 82. Matthew seems much brighter than the old IQ score, and his academic abilities are certainly higher than would be expected for a student with those scores.

I had a talk with Matthew one afternoon immediately after our science lesson. During the lesson it had been evident that he already knew much of the material on the earth's composition and had volunteered, as usual, to answer each question that I asked, in his lengthy manner of providing three times the quantity of information expected. He also volunteered to help distribute materials to the class and was very cooperative throughout the lesson. However, he appeared very subdued, almost drugged, and I wondered if the Ritalin was responsible.

The day before Matthew had become impossible in class. I had tried every behavior management technique my fifteen years of teaching had provided and nothing seemed to be working, so I sent him down to the office. Apparently, Mrs. Arnold, the principal, was also at the end of her rope. She called his mother at work to say, "Come and get him. He can't come back until his behavior is manageable."

I wondered if an increase in the Ritalin was responsible for Matthew's sluggish behavior. I decided to talk with him to see what he thought about taking the medication.

"Matthew, do you think taking Ritalin helps you in school?" I asked.

"Now that I take Ritalin, I can concentrate better. Before, the other kids around me would bother me and it was hard to finish my work," insisted Matthew.

I thought it might be helpful to find out more about Matthew's background. Maybe it would help me to stay calm when he was driving me nuts to know some of his history.

"Matthew, have you always lived here in Sagamore City?'

"No, I was born in Vermont. I went to preschool and kindergarten there. I liked kindergarten, 'cause I could play games and make things. But I had to come here to live with my grandmother because my mother had too many fights with my father. I started first grade at Truman School and they put me in special ed.

"After first grade I began to hang out with my cousin, Noah. He taught me how to steal bikes and do other bad things. One time we found a pile of hay and got some matches. What a fire! We ran away 'cause it just kept getting bigger and we were scared. But someone saw me and I ended up in big trouble. I was kicked out of school and placed on probation. I negotiated the probation. The police said to me, 'Take your choice. You either go to jail or go on probation.' I told them, 'I'm only 8 years old. Put me on probation.'"

Matthew was just getting warmed up, so I quickly interjected, "Did you eventually go back to Truman?"

"No, we moved to a different apartment and I went to Collingswood. But the kids beat me up all the time. Then the principal threw me out."

"So when did you come to Stevens Elementary?"

"I was in third grade. All the grown-ups liked me but the kids picked on me because I have a big nose and big head. I got in a lot of fights. My grandmother told me, 'Tell the kids to stop messing with you only twice. The third time, you take care of it.'"

I knew that many fights and trips to the office had followed. I wondered if Matthew had any outlets for his frustrations and boundless energy.

"Matthew, what do you do after school?"

Matthew described his activities after school with a bored facial expression. "I go out to play or go to the YMCA, but there really isn't much for kids to do. I don't stay in the house much, but sometimes when I do I read some of my mom's old books. The Y is the only place to go, but they don't have much—a few games, Ping-Pong and basketball. There's nothing for kids to do after school. I wish we could start a Boys' and Girls' Club."

I knew that Matthew liked to play basketball, but he had many interests, including art and inventing. He certainly did not mention any family travel or visits to museums or special events that would give him the opportunity to develop these aspects. I had a feeling his family was too poor to finance special lessons, trips, or summer camps.

"Matthew, what would you like to do as a career someday?" I asked hoping to find out ways to motivate him.

"Oh, I'd like to be a computer specialist, baby doctor, real doctor, karate teacher, store owner, jet pilot, technology specialist, or creator of suits for people to wear in space. I'd also like to buy a house someday."

Despite Matthew's long history of totally unacceptable behavior, you couldn't help but like Matthew when you talked with him on a one-to-one basis. But it seemed that Matthew needed that kind of adult attention all day long to keep him out of trouble. It bothered me that Matthew was on Ritalin at all, but even more so when I saw him so sluggish. I also recognized that Matthew's complaints about being bored didn't stem from a lack of motivation or low cognitive abilities. In fact, at 11 years old, Matthew was well aware of the problems faced by his community, and he is motivated to help to change things.

We are approaching the end of the school year and Matthew will go to sixth grade at the middle school. I have decided to recommend him for placement in a regular sixth-grade program. I'm very concerned about his placement next year because I want him to succeed. This was my reason for disagreeing with the guidance counselor at our recent meeting when she favored recommending Matthew for the middle school gifted and talented program. I worry that the demands of the gifted and talented program, a new school, and moving between classes may be overwhelming for Matthew. After all, he has been in segregated special education classes since first grade. I prefer the Pace Program, an enriched reading pull-out program available for sixth-grade readers. The annual meeting at which these recommendations will be formally made is only a week away and I must be ready to make and defend my position.

Meanwhile, my students have made a great deal of progress this year, and my poetry unit was a great success. Their behavior has calmed down so much, and they can listen to me attentively during my lessons. However, our big, end-of-year field trip to the museum was disappointing because some of the students did not behave appropriately. Nevertheless, I'm looking forward to the graduation ceremony for the fifth graders, including Matthew.

Discussion Questions
1. What are the major issues in the case?
2. How does this teacher perceive Matthew's problems?
3. What is Matthew's perception of his difficulties in class?
4. What responsibility does the school have for providing an educational program for Matthew?
5. In planning for Matthew's promotion to sixth grade, what are some critical needs?
6. In an action plan, what would several goals and objectives for Matthew include?

References

American Psychiatric Association. (2000). *Diagnostic and statistical manual of mental disorder* (4th ed.). Washington, DC: Author.

Artiles, A. J., & Kozleski, E. B. (2007). Beyond convictions: Interrogating culture, history, and power in inclusive education. *Language Arts, 84,* 357–364.

Bahr, M. W., & Kovaleski, J. F. (2006). The need for problem-solving teams: Introduction to a special issue. *Remedial and Special Education, 27,* 2–5.

Barkan, J. H., & Bernal, E. M. (1991). Gifted education of bilingual and limited English proficient students. *Gifted Child Quarterly, 35,* 144–147.

Barkley, R. A. (1990). *Attention deficit hyperactivity disorder.* New York: Guilford Press.

Biddle, B. J., & Berliner, D. C. (2002). Unequal school funding in the United States. *Educational Leadership, 59,* 48–59.

Bradley, R., Danielson, L., & Doolittle, J. (2007). Responsiveness to intervention: 1997–2007. *Teaching Exceptional Children, 39*(5), 8–12.

Burnette, J. (1998). *Reducing the disproportionate representation of minority students in special education.* Reston, VA. ERIC Clearinghouse on Disabilities and Gifted Education.

Burstein, N. Sears, S., Wilcoxen, A., Cabello, B., & Spagna, M. (2004). Moving toward inclusive practices. *Remedial and Special Education, 25,* 104–116

Cawley, J. F., Hayden, S., Cade, E., & Baker-Kroczynski, S. (2002). Including students with disabilities into the general education science classroom. *Exceptional Children, 68,* 423–435.

Clark, R. (1983). *Family life and school achievement: Why poor black children succeed and fail.* Chicago: University of Chicago Press.

Clasen, D. R. (2006). Project STREAM: A 13-year follow-up of a pre-college program for middle- and high-school underrepresented gifted. *Roeper Review, 29*(1), 55–63.

Colangleo, N., Assouline, S., & Gross, M. (2004). *A nation deceived: How schools hold back America's brightest students (Vol.1).* Iowa City: University of Iowa.

Coleman, L.J., & Southern, W.T. (2006). Bringing the potential of underserved children to the threshold of talent development. *Gifted Child Today, 29*(3), 35–39.

Cropper, C. (1998). Fostering parental involvement in the education of the gifted. *Gifted Child Today, 21,* 20–25.

Dudley-Marling, C. (2004). The social construction of learning disabilities. *Journal of Learning Disabilities, 3,* 482–489.

Dunn, L. M. (1968). Special education for the mildly retarded—is much of it justifiable? *Exceptional Children, 35,* 5–22.

DuPaul, G. J., & Eckert, T. L. (1998). Academic interventions for students with attention-deficit/hyperactivity disorder: A review of the literature. *Reading and Writing Quarterly: Overcoming Learning Difficulties, 14*(1), 59–82.

Etscheidt, S. K., & Bartlett, L. (1999). The IDEA amendments: A four-step approach for determining supplementary aids and services. *Exceptional Children, 65*(2), 163–174.

Ford, D. Y. (2006). Closing the achievement gap: How gifted education can help. *Gifted Child Today, 29*(4), 14–18.

Ford, D. Y., & Thomas, A. (1997). *Underachievement among gifted minority students: Problems and promises.* Reston, VA: ERIC Clearinghouse on Disabilities and Gifted Education (ERIC Document Reproduction Service No. ED 409660).

Frasier, M. M. (1991). Disadvantaged and culturally diverse gifted students. *Journal for the Education of the Gifted, 14,* 235–245.

Gallagher, J. J. (1995). Education of gifted students: A civil rights issue? *Phi Delta Kappan, 79,* 408–410.

Gardner, H. (2006). *Multiple intelligences: New horizons.* New York: Basic Books.

Gould, J., Thorpe, P., & Weeks, V. (2001). An early childhood accelerated program. *Educational Leadership, 59*(3), 47–50.

Gresham, F. M., Lane, K. L., & Beebe-Frankenberger, M. (2005). Predictors of hyperactive–impulsive–inattention and conduct problems: A comparative follow-back investigation. *Psychology in the Schools, 4,* 721–736.

Harris-Murri, N. King, K., & Rostenberg, D. (2006). Reducing disproportionate minority representation in special education programs for students with emotional disturbances: Toward a culturally responsive response to intervention model. *Education & Treatment of Children, 29,* 779–799.

Hebert, T. P., Long, L. A., & Neumeister, K. L. (2001). Using biography to counsel gifted young women. *Journal of Secondary Gifted Education, 12* (2), 62–79.

Higgins, K., & Boone, R. (2003). Beyond the boundaries of school: Transition considerations in gifted education. *Intervention in School and Clinic, 38,* 138–144.

Hosp, J. L., & Reschley, D. J. (2004). Disproportionate representation of minority students in special education: Academic, demographic, and economic predictors. *Exceptional Children, 70,* 185–199.

Idol, L. (2006). Toward inclusion of special education students in general education. *Remedial and Special Education, 27,* 77–94.

Ishii-Jordan, S. R. (1997). When behavior differences are not disorders. In A. J. Artiles & G. Samora-Duran (Eds.), *Reducing disproportionate representation of culturally diverse students in special and gifted education* (pp. 27–46). Reston, VA: Council for Exceptional Children.

Kauffman, J. H., Landrum, T. J., Mock, D. R., Sayeski, B., & Sayeski, K.L. (2005). Diverse knowledge and skills require a diversity of instructional groups: A position statement. *Remedial and Special Education, 26,* 2–6.

Lahey, B. B., & Carlson, C. L. (1991). Validity of the diagnostic category of attention deficit disorder without hyperactivity: A review of the literature. *Journal of Learning Disabilities, 24*(2), 110–120.

Lenz, B. K., & Deshler, D. D. (2004). *Teaching content to all: Evidence-based inclusive practices in middle and secondary schools.* Boston: Pearson.

Lewis, A. (2007). How well has NCLB worked? How do we get the revisions we want? *Phi Delta Kappan, 88,* 353–358.

Maker, C. J. (1996). Identification of gifted minority students: A national problem, needed changes and a promising solution. *Gifted Child Quarterly, 40*(1), 41–50.

Manset, G., & Semmel, M. (1997). Are inclusive programs for students with mild disabilities effective? *Journal of Special Education, 30,* 121–132.

McBee, M. T. (2006). A descriptive analysis of referral sources for gifted identification screening by race and socioeconomic status. *Journal of Secondary Gifted Education, 1,* 103–111.

McGregor, G., & Vogelsberg, R. T. (2000). *Inclusive schooling practices: Pedagogical and research foundations: A synthesis of the literature that informs best practices about inclusive schooling.* Baltimore, MD: Paul H. Brookes.

McLeskey, J., Henry, D., & Axelrod, M. I. (1999). Inclusion of students with learning disabilities: An examination of data from reports to Congress. *Exceptional Children, 66*(1), 55–66.

Milner, H. R., & Ford, D.Y. (2007). Cultural considerations in the underrepresentation of culturally diverse elementary students in gifted education. *Roeper Review, 29,* 166–172.

Mooij, T. (1999). Integrating gifted children into kindergarten by improving educational processes. *Gifted Child Quarterly, 48*(2), 63–74.

Moore, C., Gilbreath, D., & Maiuri, F. (1998). Educating students with disabilities in general education classrooms: A summary of the research. Eugene, OR: Western Regional Resource Center (ERIC Document Reproduction No. ED 419 329).

Naglieri, J. A., & Ford, D.Y. (2005). Increasing minority children's participation in gifted classes using the NNAT: A response to Lohman. *The Gifted Child Quarterly. 49,* 29–36.

National Education Association. (2007). Education funding: The facts. Retrieved June 7, 2007, from http:www.nea.org/lac/funding/thefacts.html

O'Connor, C., & Fernandez, S. D. (2006). Race, class and disproportionality: Reevaluating the relationship between poverty and special education placement. *Educational Researcher, 35*(6), 6–11.

Ortiz, A. A., Wilkinson, C. Y., Robertson-Courtney, P., & Kushner, M. I. (2006). Considerations in implementing intervention assistance teams to support English Language Learners. *Remedial and Special Education, 2,* 53–63

Patton, J. M. (1997). Disproportionate representation in gifted programs: Best practices for meeting this challenge. In A. J. Artiles & G. Samora-Duran (Eds.), *Reducing disproportionate representation of culturally diverse students in special and gifted education* (pp. 59–86). Reston, VA: Council for Exceptional Children.

Palincsar, A. S., & Brown, Al. L. (1984). Reciprocal teaching of comprehension fostering and monitoring activities. *Cognition and Instruction, 1,* 117–175.

Pfeiffer, S I., Petscher, Y, & Jarosewich, T. (2007*).* Sharpening identification tools. *Roeper Review, 29,* 2006-211.

Prater, M. A., & Pancheri, C. (1999). What teachers and parents should know about Ritalin. *Teaching Exceptional Children, 31*(4), 20–26.

Rea, P. J., McLaughlin, V. L., & Walther-Thomas, C. (2002). Outcomes for students with learning disabilities in inclusive and pull-out programs. *Exceptional Children, 68*(2), 203–222.

Reis, S. D. (2007). No child left bored. *School Administrator, 64*(2), 22–26.

Roach, V., Salisbury, C., & McGregor, G. (2002). Applications of a policy framework to evaluate and promote large-scale change. *Exceptional Children, 68,* 451–463.

Rose, D. H., & Meyer, A. (2002). *Teaching every kid in the digital age: Universal design for learning.* Alexandria, VA: ASCD.

Rotigel, J. V. (2003). Understanding the young gifted child: Guidelines for parents, families, and educators. *Early Childhood Educational Journal, 30,* 209–214.

Rueda, R. (1997). Changing the context of assessment: The move to portfolios and authentic assessment. In A. J. Artiles & G. Samora-Duran (Eds.), *Reducing disproportionate representation of culturally diverse students in special and gifted education* (pp. 7–25). Reston, VA: Council for Exceptional Children.

Sailor, W., & Blair, R. (2005). Rethinking inclusion: Schoolwide application. *Phi Delta Kappan, 86,* 503–509.

Salend, S. J. (2008) *Creating inclusive classrooms: Effective and reflective practices* (6th ed.). Upper Saddle River, NJ: Merrill/Prentice Hall.

Salend, S. J., & Duhaney, L. G. (1999). The impact of inclusion on students with and without disabilities and their educators. *Remedial and Special Education 20*(2), 114–126.

Salend, S. J., & Garrick Duhaney, L. M. (2005). Understanding and addressing the disproportionate representation of students of color in special education. *Intervention in School & Clinic, 40,* 213–221.

Sankar-DeLeeuw, N. (2004). Case studies of gifted kindergarten children: Profiles of promise. *Roeper Review, 26,* 192–207.

Sapon-Shevin, M. (2003). Inclusion: A matter of social justice. *Educational Leadership, 61*(2), 25–28.

Schlozman, S. C., & Schlozman, V. R. (2000). Chaos in the classroom: Looking at ADHD. *Educational Leadership, 58*(3), 28–33.

Scott, M. S., & Delgado, C. (2005). Identifying cognitively gifted minority students in preschool. *Gifted Child Quarterly, 49,* 199–210.

Shaunessy, E., McHatton, P., Hughes, C., Brice, A., & Ratliff, M. A. (2007) Understanding the experiences of bilingual, Latino/a adolescents: Voices from gifted and general education. *Roeper Review*, 29, 174–182.

Shippen, M. E., Houchins, D. E., Calhoon, M.B., Furlow, C.F., & Sartor, D. L. (2006). The effects of comprehensive school reform models in reading for urban middle school students with disabilities. *Remedial and Special Education*, 2, 322–328

Sindelar, P.T., Shearer, D. K., Yendol-Hoppey, D., & Liebert, T.W. (2006). The sustainability of inclusive school reform. *Exceptional Children*, 72, 317–331.

Skiba, R. J., Poloni-Staudinger, L., Gallini, S., Simmons, A. B., & Feggins-Azziz, R. (2006). Disparate access: The disproportionality of African American students with disabilities across educational environments. *Exceptional Children*, 72, 411–424.

Smith, D. D. (2007). *Introduction to special education: Making a difference* (6th ed.). Boston: Allyn and Bacon.

Southern, W.T., & Jones, E.D. (Eds.). (1991). *The academic acceleration of gifted children.* New York: Teachers College Press.

Stainback, W., Stainback, S., & Stefanich, G. (1996). Learning together in inclusive classrooms. *Teaching Exceptional Children*, 28(3), 14–19.

Sternberg, R. J. (2007). Cultural dimensions of giftedness and talent. *Roeper Review*, 29, 160–165.

Tharp, R. G. (1989). Psychocultural variables and constraints: Effects on teaching and learning in school. *American Psychologist*, 44(2), 349–359.

Tharp, R. G., & Gallimore, R. (1988). *Rousing minds to life: Teaching, learning, and schooling in social context.* New York: Cambridge University Press.

Tomlinson, C. A. (Ed.). (2004). *Differentiation for gifted and talented students.* Thousand Oaks, CA: Corwin Press and the National Association for Gifted children.

Tomlinson, C. A., Brighton, C., Hertberg, H., Callahan, C. M., Moon, T. R., Brimijoin, K., Conover, L. A., & Reynolds, T. (2003). Differentiating instruction in response to student readiness, interest, and learning profile in academically diverse classrooms: A review of literature. *Journal for the Education of the Gifted*, 27, 119–45.

Tomlinson, C. A., Callahan, C. M., & Lelli, K. M. (1997). Challenging expectations: Case studies of high-potential, culturally diverse young children. *Gifted Child Quarterly*, 41, 5–17.

Tomlinson, C. A., & Eidson, C. C. (2003). *Differentiation in practice: A resource guide for differentiating curriculum.* Alexandria, VA: Association for Supervision and Curriculum Development.

Turnbull, A., Turnbull, R., & Wehmeyer, M.L. (2007). *Exceptional lives: Special education in today's schools* (5th ed.). Upper Saddle River, NJ: Merrill/Prentice Hall.

U.S. Department of Education, Office of Special Education and Rehabilitative Services, Office of Special Education Programs. (2005). *26th Annual (2004) Report to Congress on the implementation of the Individuals with Disabilities Education Act, vol. 1*, Washington, DC: U.S. Government Printing Office.

van Garderen, D., & Whittaker, C. (2006). Planning differentiated, multicultural instruction for secondary inclusive classroom. *Teaching Exceptional Children*, 38(3), 12–21.

Van Tassel-Baska, J. (2004). *The acceleration of gifted students' programs and curricula.* Waco, TX: Fastback series. Prufrock Press.

Wang, M. C., & Reynolds, M. C. (1997). *Progressive inclusion: Meeting new challenges in special education.* Philadelphia: Mid-Atlantic Lab for Student Success (ERIC Document Reproduction No. ED420134).

Yell, M., & Drasgow, E. (1999). A legal analysis of inclusion. *Preventing School Failure*, 43(3), 118.

Zentall, S. S., Moon, S. M. Hall, A. M., & Grskovic, J. A. (2001). Learning and motivational characteristics of boys with AD/HD and/or giftedness. *Exceptional Children*, 67, 400–519.

Zigmond, N. (2003). Where should students with disabilities receive special education services? Is one place better than another?, *Journal of Special Education*, 37, 193–199.

10

Gender

Terry Murray and Lorraine S. Taylor

Issues in Gender

Since the publication of the first edition of our text, there has been increasing attention to the plight of boys in our society and our schools. Thus, we have chosen to broaden this chapter to include important issues in the lives and schooling of boys. We begin with background information on girls and boys, followed by the cases of Cassie and Justin.

Seminal research by Brown and Gilligan (1992), Rogers (1991), Jordan (1997), Miller and Stiver (1997), Sadker and Sadker (1994), and others has expanded our understanding of girls' lives, their identity development, and factors affecting their school performance. This research has also provided a framework and tools for exploring the development and lives of boys in school.

In light of this awareness, much progress has occurred for girls as result of important research findings and new laws such as Title IX. Girls have "caught up," while boys have fallen behind. Gaps between the achievement of boys and girls in math, for example, have narrowed or closed (Lee, Grigg, & Dion, 2007). However, there is yet work to be done, particularly in areas such as the interaction of race and biased perceptions of girls' ability as in Cassie's case at the end of the chapter.

Nevertheless, researchers who have previously devoted their efforts to improving schooling and life choices for girls are now engaged in seeking answers to important issues in the educational and emotional development of boys. In fact, over the past decade, boys' lives, their school performance, and their role in school violence have been a predominant focus in research on gender and schooling.

Females and Mathematics

For more than four decades, researchers have been asking students to "Draw a scientist." In the 1950s high school students uniformly saw a scientist as a middle-aged or older man wearing glasses and a white coat and working alone in a lab.

Most recent trials with the Draw a Scientist Test (DAST) reveal little changes in the perception of the gender of a scientist. A study of undergraduates who were administered the DAST resulted in approximately 82 percent of both males and females drawing a male scientist (Thomas, Henley, & Snell, 2006). Some have argued that the directions are problematic. Maoldomhnaigh and Mholain (1990) changed the DAST instructions to "*Draw* a man or woman *scientist*" when testing between the ages of 11 and 16. Although boys in this sample almost exclusively drew males, 49 percent of the girls drew a female.

Interestingly, in a study conducted by Quita (2003), a diverse group of primarily preservice teachers who were enrolled in an elementary science course completed the DAST. The candidates were quite diverse including 70 percent Asian Americans, 20 percent Latinos, and 5 percent African Americans. Nineteen percent of the males and 35 percent of females drew female scientists. Rather than drawing the stereotypic White, male scientist, these teachers in training tended to depict ethnically diverse adults or children who were doing everyday "experiments" like cooking or gardening. Clearly, teachers who are involved in coursework that allow them to participate in science develop positive attitudes about their ability to be scientists and to implement successful science programs.

Other researchers have commented that if students today were asked to draw a mathematician, the chances are that they would also draw a man. In the words of Muller (1998), "The study of mathematics in the United States is stereotypically regarded as the domain of boys and a field in which girls have difficulty" (p. 336). Deborah Haimo (1997) supports Muller's position in the following comment: "Up until the past two or so decades, whereas males who indicated an interest and proficiency in mathematics were taken seriously and encouraged to continue in the field, women with like bent were not considered creditable and were largely ignored. . . . Indeed, the image of a mathematician prevalent throughout the world has been that of man" (p. 7).

It is reasonable to propose that images of the scientist and mathematicians as men that are held by so many students will not change until female mathematicians are widely recognized and respected as serious scholars. However, intervention programs have been designed to increase female participation in mathematics/science/technology careers. In fact, The Association for Women in Mathematics (AWM) was launched only in 1971. From the beginning they have worked to increase the participation and improve the position of women in mathematics (Blum, 1997). Blum (1997) has pointed out that while very few mathematicians in the 1970s were concerned with programs to increase the number of women in mathematics, a variety of intervention programs have now been established, especially at colleges and universities across the country, to increase the participation of women. The shift in focus in some programs from entry level students who might not have thought of going into mathematics to programs for students who have already shown talent in undergraduate mathematics has resulted in serious debate (Blum, 1997). While some mathematicians believe that programs should continue to focus on increasing the number of women in the field, others argue that the focus must shift to students who need encouragement and nurturing to continue at the graduate level.

Nevertheless, gender differences persist in the participation in mathematics, although differences in achievement are rapidly disappearing. For example, in higher education faculties, fewer females than males serve as faculty members in mathematics and science departments (Becker, 2003; Johnston, 2005; Spelke, 2005). Similarly, on the mathematics section of the SAT (SAT-M) in 2004, boys' scores averaged 537 compared with 501 for girls (Johnston, 2005). A difference has also been found among undergraduate majors in physics (Xie & Schuman 2003, cited in Spelke, 2005).

Johnston (2005) has pointed out that marital patterns have been suggested as a possible explanation for the paucity of females in higher education mathematics and science faculties. She stated that "43 percent of married female physicists are married to other physicists, while only 6 percent of male physicists have physicists as spouses" (p. 3). In families where there are two professionals, it is difficult for both to take advantage of their opportunities (Johnston, 2005). Women represent less than 15 percent of the employed scientists and engineers in computer science, mathematics, agricultural science, environmental science, chemistry, geology, physics and astronomy, economics, and engineering (National Science Foundation, 1996, cited in Becker, 2003).

Interestingly, Kleinfeld (1999) presents a somewhat different point of view based upon the notion of male and female "areas of strength." She notes that in high school science and mathematics, females simply do not do as well as males, although they are catching up. On the other hand, males do not do as well in literature or languages, which are female areas of strength (Kleinfeld, 1999). Yet recent research refutes these claims (Johnston, 2005; Spelke, 2005). However, Kleinfeld is most concerned about refuting much of the recent research on girls, especially the American Association of University Women Report, "How Schools Shortchange Girls," which created such a stir when it was published in 1992 because the schools' treatment of girls had not been previously publicized in that manner. With emphasis on the fact that the gender gap in mathematics is closing, Kleinfeld does note that, in her view, the main group of students that schools are truly failing are African American males—not females.

Nevertheless, among the possible influential variables considered by Leder (1990) at the beginning of the 1990s were school variables, teachers, peers, and learner characteristics. In fact, studies published during the 1980s and early 1990s focused on affective variables (Boswell, 1985; Clarkson & Leder, 1984; Fennema & Leder, 1990; Fennema & Sherman, 1977, 1978; Gittelson, Petersen, & Tobin-Richards, 1982) and peer influence (Leder, 1990), while later studies have focused on claims that innate gender differences in math exist.

Although almost twenty years have passed since the publication of Leder's work, the variables she identified continue to be investigated. Studies published during the intervening years have examined factors such as socialization practices (Clewell et al., 1992; Sadker & Sadker, 1994); teacher attitudes, beliefs, and behaviors (Evans, 1996; Grossman & Grossman, 1994; Singh, 1998; Tauber, 1998); peer influence (Ogbu, 1995); students' attitude toward mathematics (Ma, 1999); and parental involvement (Ma, 1999).

Socialization Practices

The family as a gendered institution that socializes its young to embrace gender roles is one of the factors identified earlier by researchers to explain the idea of male and female areas of study, careers, and professions (Clewell et al., 1992; Sadker and Sadker, 1994). Sadker and Sadker (1994) have pointed out that "even the most well-meaning adults can inadvertently let sexist expectations slip into their own behavior" (p. 251). As noted earlier, some studies have shown that boys and girls are given different toys: boys' rooms are filled with sports equipment, toy vehicles, and building kits, while girls have lots of dolls and kitchen utensils as their playthings (Sadker and Sadker, 1994). Thus, sex-typed play is encouraged, and girls are encouraged in nurturing and interpersonal skills while boys are developing spatial skills, among others (Sadker and Sadker, 1994). These early experiences may then contribute to female versus male areas of study and careers. One can see these gender-based expectations in the toy displays and commercials during the holidays.

Teacher Attitudes, Beliefs, and Behaviors

In the view of other social scientists, the gendered images may be due to the differential treatment by teachers who respond differently to boys and girls during mathematics instruction in the classroom (Tauber, 1998) or to teachers who believe that differences in gender are rooted in purely biological factors and that they should prepare girls to fulfill different roles (Singh, 1998). Increasing quantities of research literature suggest that gender issues underlie many classroom activities (Singh, 1998). For example, teachers' beliefs about the dominance or subordination of particular genders may determine whose ideas are heard or ignored in student discussions (Evans, 1996).

Teachers differ in their views of how they should address gender in the classroom (Singh, 1998). The different views are reflected in the work of Grossman and Grossman (1994), who have outlined four positions about the roles that educators think that teachers should play:

1. Since there are underlying biological differences between the sexes, teachers should prepare the genders to fulfill different roles.
2. Students should be prepared for gender-neutral or androgynous roles.
3. Teachers should help students to decide for themselves whether they want to conform to a particular gender role, since gender role socialization is mainly a function of the home.
4. Since some teachers may be uncomfortable dealing with gender issues, educators should decide if they want to prepare students for different gender roles or not.

The first position is often criticized because it limits individual freedom to make choices, while those who promote the second position believe that educators and schools should help to make the society less sexist (Singh, 1998). Among educators who believe that teachers should deal with gender issues, the question of gender equity or equality arises (Singh, 1996). Gender equality proponents believe that all students should receive the same opportunities to access resources and opportunities for learning, while equity proponents strive for having the same outcomes for all students. This means that students considered at-risk or less advantaged would receive unequal support to assure the same levels at the end of the class or course (Streitmatter, 1994).

On the National Assessment of Educational Progress, all 4th and 8th grade students showed improvement on the math assessment since the initial assessment in 1990

(Lee, Grigg, & Dion, 2007). While Blacks and Hispanics have made significant gains in math achievement since 1990, there is still an achievement gap between the performance of White students and Black and Hispanic students. Therefore, the question of equity or excellence may confront many teachers in diverse school populations or schools where these students are disproportionately represented. In view of the small numbers of African American and Hispanic persons represented in those careers that require advanced mathematics, the question is critical.

Teachers' expectations for gender differences can also interact with racial and ethnic differences, thus creating a self-fulfilling prophecy (Tauber, 1998). When teachers encounter African American female students in a mathematics class, expectations for achievement and gender role may interact and influence the teachers' behavior in the classroom. Research reveals that teachers form expectations of and assign labels to students based on such characteristics as body build, gender, race, ethnicity, given name and/or surname, attractiveness, dialect, and socioeconomic level (Good, 1987). Furthermore, studies show that teacher expectations can predict changes in student achievement and behavior beyond the effects of prior achievement and motivation (Jussim & Eccles, 1992). Thus, teachers who hold low expectations for African American students and also believe in specific gender roles may refuse to take an African American female's interest and proficiency in mathematics seriously, thus discouraging students through negative attitudes and behaviors. Peer influence and students' attitudes toward math will be discussed later.

Affective Variables

In the view of Fennema and Leder (1990), affective variables within the learner also influence participation and performance in mathematics. For example, in older studies, males in grades 6 through 12 consistently showed greater confidence than females in their ability to learn mathematics (Fennema & Sherman, 1977, 1978). Studies on the "fear of success" suggested that the lower performance of females in mathematics was due more to the internalization of and conforming to the expectations of others than to ability in and of itself (Boswell, 1985; Clarkson & Leder, 1984; Leder, 1982).

With respect to attributions of success and failure in earlier studies, females tend to attribute success to effort, while males tend to attribute it to ability. On the other hand, males tend to attribute failure to effort, while females attribute it to ability (Gittelson et al., 1982; Leder, 1984). In the words of Sadker & Sadker (1994),

> When children internalize success and externalize failure (the male approach), they are able to tackle new and challenging tasks with a mastery orientation, one that perseveres in the face of difficulty and leads to future achievement. Children who attribute success to effort and failure to lack of ability (the female approach) exhibit learned helplessness. When confronted with difficult academic material, they do not persist. (p. 97)

Furthermore, affective variables in the learner can also influence the course-taking patterns of females. Girls at the high school level are particularly concerned with being popular, and being bright is thought of as in conflict with being popular (Sadker & Sadker, 1994). Girls may even fake mediocrity in an effort to camouflage their abilities (Sadker & Sadker, 1994). The cost can be considerable, as noted more recently by Hofstetter (personal communication, 2000): "The aversion of many females to mathematics limits their career choices and results in limited understanding of and skills in a basic component of daily functioning."

Closely related to the student's attitude toward mathematics and mathematics self-concept is the pattern for dropping out of mathematics. A recent investigation of individual variables most strongly related to individuals dropping out of mathematics in grades 8 to 12 showed that, after taking account of SES, prior achievement, and prior attitude, females were 1.08 times as likely as males to participate in grades 8 to 11; however, in transitioning from grade 11 to 12, females were only 0.74 times as likely as males to participate, resulting in a considerable gender gap (Ma, 1999). When girls were asked why they dropped out of engineering in college, they gave three responses in order of ranking: (1) lost interest in an engineering major and switched, (2) curriculum overload, and (3) poor teaching (Johnston, 2005). That author also found that the effect of prior achievement in mathematics was much stronger than SES, particularly in the earlier high school grades. Later, it was the student's attitude toward mathematics that appeared to be most important. According to Ma, the significantly less positive attitude of females in grade 11 explained the gender difference in participation in grade 12.

Parental Involvement

In a study more specifically related to the gender achievement gap in mathematics, Muller (1998) used a database that included the base year for eighth-grade students and follow-up in grades 10 and 12. The results showed that girls talked more with their parents about school than boys, more frequently with their mothers than fathers. However, boys talked more with their fathers about their high school program than the girls did. Muller also found that parents restricted girls' out-of-school activities more than boys'; and parents intervened in their sons' lives more than their daughters', because boys enjoyed more freedom to get into difficulties. Interestingly, boys' test scores were higher in each grade in which the exam was administered, but girls' grades were higher, which raises questions about how teachers grade the male versus female student. The girls had higher educational expectations than the boys; however, the boys were more likely to report being in all kinds of mathematics sequences, including advanced mathematics, algebra, remedial mathematics, and higher level course work in grade 10 (Muller, 1998). The boys also had higher mathematics self-concepts that were closely associated with test scores. Muller's interpretation of the results included the facts that (1) parental involvement may mask some of the gender differences in grade 8 students' performance; (2) parental involvement was associated with test performance both positively and negatively; (3) talking with parents about school was positively associated with performance; (4) higher test scores were associated with parents' restriction of eighth grade students' activities; and (5) the strongest positive predictor of grade 10 mathematics scores was parental restriction of activities. Thus, while the higher scores of students in grade 8 were associated with talking with parents about school activities, in grade 10 it was restriction of activities with friends and of weekday television watching (Muller, 1998).

Minority Females and Mathematics

Clewell and colleagues (1992) have investigated barriers to minority as well as to female students' participation and performance in mathematics, science, and engineering. They identified important factors such as (1) negative attitudes and perceptions, (2) poor academic performance or achievement, (3) insufficient course and extracurricular preparation, and (4) limited knowledge of mathematics and science careers. It is important to note, however, that Clewell et al. did not consider poor teaching and other factors outside the students' control. Although the work of Clewell et al. did not directly focus on African American females, it did include minority students of both genders and is relevant to the issues of African American females in mathematics. A review of the barriers identified by Clewell et al. can be useful in our understanding of the issues.

Negative Attitudes and Perceptions

Research suggests that the positive attitudes of females and minorities toward mathematics and science begin to decline as they reach the level of junior high school (Ma, 1999). The change in attitudes has been attributed to a poor math self-concept, a negative perception of the usefulness of mathematics and science in real life, the stereotyping of mathematics and science as White male activities, and the influence of parents, teachers, and peers in discouraging participation (Oakes, 1990). Females may also respond to society's message that mathematics and science are unfeminine activities, thereby creating a conflict between their interest in the subjects and the desire to be popular (Bossert, 1981).

The stereotyping of mathematics and science as White male activities is related to Ogbu's (1995) work on cultural diversity and learning. Ogbu makes the important point that "the meaning and value students associate with school learning and achievement play a very significant role in determining their efforts toward learning and performance" (p. 584). Based on his theory that minorities may be subdivided into autonomous, voluntary, and involuntary minorities, he proceeds to explain the development of secondary cultural characteristics in opposition to the dominant group in control. Thus, involuntary (or castelike) minorities, those brought here against their will through the phenomenon that Ogbu labels "cultural inversion," regard certain forms of behavior, events, symbols, and meanings as inappropriate for them because these are characteristics of White Americans. In his words, "among involuntary minorities, school learning tends to be equated with the learning of the culture and language of White Americans, that is, learning of the cultural and language frames of reference of their 'enemy' or oppressors' " (p. 587). Most importantly, Ogbu points out that "unlike voluntary minorities, involuntary minorities do not seem to be able or willing to separate attitudes and behaviors that result in academic success from those that may result in linear acculturation or replacement of their cultural identity with White American cultural identity" (p. 588). It is important to point out that this is an abbreviated discussion of Ogbu's position, and it is essential to read a more extensive discussion of his work as cited in the references. Nevertheless, the implications are that some minority students may reject learning mathematics due to the attitude that it is a white activity.

Ogbu's discussion of variability in minority school performance (1996) also underscores his point that some minorities are successful in school "even though they face barriers in culture, language, and post school opportunities" (p. 88). Based on his comparative studies as an anthropologist, he notes that

> By comparing different minorities, it appears that the primary problem in the academic performance of minority children does not lie in the mere fact that children possess a different language, dialect, or communication style; it is not that they possess a different cognitive style or a different style of interaction; it is not even that the children face barriers in future adult opportunity structure. . . . The main factor differentiating the more successful from the less successful minorities appears to be the nature of the history, subordination, and exploitation of the minorities and the nature of the minorities own instrumental and expressive responses to their treatment, which enter into the process of their schooling. School performance is not due only to what is done to or for minorities; it is also due to the fact that the nature of the minorities' interpretations and responses makes them more or less accomplices to their own school success or failure. (p. 88)

Poor Academic Performance

Clewell, et al. (1992) attribute the underachievement of minority students to the negative attitudes described earlier; however, other factors may also explain the poor progress. For example, the instructional approaches and materials used may not be appropriate for the learning styles of many females and minority students, and poor schools and poorly trained teachers may also contribute to underachievement. In fact, the majority of mathematics teachers have not majored in mathematics in college. These important factors were discussed in Chapter 2 in the discussion of poverty schools and inequality in teachers.

Insufficient Course and Extracurricular Preparation

If students do not enter high school taking courses such as Algebra I or Geometry, they have little chance of taking advanced courses such as Calculus or Trigonometry. As noted by Clewell et al. differential patterns of course taking have been related to gender and ethnic differences in mathematics and science achievement. A review of the research literature has revealed that course-taking in high school mathematics can differ according to ethnicity (Davenport, Davison, Huang, Ding, Kirn, & Kwak, 1998). Traditionally, these groups (except Asian Americans) have enrolled in fewer optional or advanced courses than White male students. More recent research is revealing that the gender gap in advanced mathematics course-taking has closed, with females just as likely to take advanced courses as males (Freeman, 2004). However, the interaction of race and gender yields a more complicated picture. Riegle-Crumb (2006) analyzed the Adolescent Health and Academic Achievement data which reported on the content of high school transcripts to determine gender and racial patterns for taking math courses. African American and Latino students of both genders generally start high school in lower math courses compared to White peers despite the fact that diverse students are taking "harder courses" than in previous years. Black and Latino females who start high school with Algebra I progress to higher levels. Unfortunately, males from these groups who start high school with Algebra I often do not progress and fall short on the course-taking threshold needed for college.

The lack of availability of advanced courses in mathematics and science at the high school level for many minority students must be considered. In schools such as the one attended by Cassie in the case study to follow, few advanced placement courses are available.

Limited Knowledge of Mathematics and Science Professions

Minority students and their families may have insufficient knowledge of mathematics and related professions when making career choices. Career counseling is especially valuable for female minority students who may not be exposed to role models in careers involving mathematics and related fields. However, counselors will need an awareness of their own bias. Stereotypes and myths may result in low expectations and inappropriate advising as in Cassie's case. In addition, the use of inappropriate assessment instruments for diverse students can also lead to erroneous advice and guidance (Kerka, 1998).

In some cases, underfunded schools may be unable to provide adequate career counseling (Kozol, 1991). For example, one counselor in Cassie's high school described his situation in this way: "I have an overwhelming caseload of 300 students. How can I possibly help every one of these kids? I would love to do home visits, but when do I have time to?" (Ramirez, personal communication, 2001). Parents and families who lack information on careers in science and mathematics or who wish their daughters to enter more service-oriented, female careers might also influence the choice.

Peer Influence

Peers also provide influence and may become another important variable in the performance of females in mathematics. In the words of Leder (1990), "It [peer influence] acts as an important reference for childhood and adolescent socialization and further perpetuates sex-role differentiation through gender-typed leisure activities, friendship patterns, subject preference, and career intentions" (p. 17). As noted earlier, peer pressure from those who view mathematics as a "White" activity can also result in negative attitudes toward mathematics (Ogbu, 1993, 1995). However, successful programs around the country are increasing the numbers of minorities in math and science (see Table 10.1). At each transition in the educational pipeline, minority students may drop out of mathematics without intervention. Programs like those designed by Robert Moses (the Algebra Project) and Uri Treisman can increase the numbers of minority mathematicians and scientists.

African American Females and Mathematics

Research on African American females in mathematics is extremely scarce. Furthermore, the published studies that do involve African American females in particular are only indirectly related to our interests. A brief review of current research includes studies that are concerned with various aspects of adult education, teaching, and career and vocational preparation. Adenika-Morrow (1996) points out that where race and gender come together in the area of mathematics and science, African American girls have been more excluded than any other group. She underscores that statement as she notes that "Studies of women generally overlook women of color, and studies of students of color de-emphasize gender differences" (p. 80). This situation may also explain, at least in part, the scarcity of research specifically focused on African American females in mathematics.

Interestingly, Adenika-Morrow (1996) identifies two reasons for the situation: (1) African American women's lack of tools to negotiate the racism and sexism that damage the belief that they can succeed, and (2) the African American community's world view that "stresses the pragmatism of obtaining immediate employment. African American girls must go to work early and be practical in a career selection" (p. 80).

TABLE 10.1   *Common Themes in Successful Programs for Increasing Minorities in Mathematics*

1. Mathematics is related to students' daily lives, especially in early grades.
2. Cooperative learning is emphasized.
3. Intervention begins early.
4. The image of mathematics as a subject for "nerds" must be changed to "mathematics is for everyone."
5. Students learn about mathematicians who are from minority groups.
6. Teachers concentrate on successful learning of less material, rather than more content with less success.
7. Concrete examples are used to introduce abstract concepts.
8. Teachers are comfortable with mathematics.
9. Summer programs are used to help students to bridge the move between junior and senior high school.
10. At the college level, students are encouraged to study together in small groups.

Source: Selvin. (1992).

The author provides descriptions of two schools that target African American high school girls. One school offers a program that places the girls with science, mathematics, and engineering students at colleges and universities in Southern California. The girls also took science and mathematics courses that prepared them for college work. To elicit parents' support and understanding, students and parents completed a science project together. According to Adenika-Morrow (1996), the program helped the girls to realize that, with commitment and persistence, they could have careers in the sciences.

In another program, African American girls were extensively exposed to African American role models. Parent participation, guest speakers, and mentors were also included. Both programs involved high expectations and positive support from parents, teachers, counselors, principals, and peers, which gave the participants a solid foundation for the pursuit of a career in the sciences.

With respect to problems faced by those who do choose a career in mathematics as teachers, Brown, Cervero, and Johnson-Bailey (2000) conducted interviews of seven African American teachers of mathematics to investigate how their position in society affected their experience of teaching mathematics to adults in postsecondary institutions. Their findings also included reports of secondary school experiences by the women. Sadly, the women had all experienced marginality, isolation, discouragement, and devaluation as students in their mathematics classes. They reported feeling dumb and like an outsider. However, most of their observations related to experiences as undergraduate students, and it was difficult to separate the high school and college level experiences. Later, in teaching adults at the community college level, the women's *positionality*, a term used to denote status in the society, raised issues of credibility due to their race and gender and directly affected their classroom interactions and teaching strategies and philosophy. For example, because the women had experienced marginality in the society, they were especially sensitive to students who might feel this way. One of the interviewees stated that, since White males usually did most of the talking and questioning in the mathematics classroom, she called on females more often than males.

The authors concluded that these teachers had to draw on their own resources to develop teaching practices since they were influenced by their experiences of race and gender. They did not use universal teaching practices. Since the race and gender of the teachers influenced the students' perceptions of the teachers' credibility, it was necessary to find approaches to deal with these challenges. The findings agree with the view that teaching is not a neutral activity. It is permeated with values about individuality, knowledge, and society that reflect larger issues. In the words of Brown et al. (2000), "There are no universal teachers but there are teachers whose experiences are affected by their race and gender" (p. 286).

In summary, African American females who have interest and proficiency in mathematics will need teachers who have the knowledge, skills, and attitudes required to not only teach them effectively, but also to encourage, support, and expose them to career opportunities in mathematics or related fields in science and technology. African American female students are likely to face barriers such as peer pressure, family influence, limited availability of role models and mentors, and various affective factors. The availability of special intervention programs, advanced placement courses, and appropriate guidance and counseling can be most valuable for all talented females who deserve every chance to realize their potential. In view of the disproportionately small number of African American and other females with recognition in mathematics, we cannot afford to do otherwise.

The Foundations of Boys' Work

To understand current theories of boys' development, or boys' work, we must first consider research on gender over the past three decades. During this period, a growing number of researchers focused on gender and explored issues of identity, equity, violence, the interaction of gender, race and class, classroom life, and school achievement. This research has helped us understand the ways that the social construction of gender affects student learning and achievement (Biklen, 1995; Gilligan, 1993; Midgley, Feldlaufer, & Eccles, 1989; Sadker & Sadker, 1994; Thorne, 1993).

Much of the initial research on gender issues focused on girls' development. In considering what has been learned by researchers about girls and schooling, Reichert and Kuriloff (2004) commented:

> With regards to girls, we have learned to recognize the effects of our assumptions and biased preconceptions in science and math classrooms, in athletics, and in social interaction. Greater awareness has meant greater control over the expectations and images we offer girls in our schools, and ultimately, greatly enhances experiences for them. Though not nearly complete, the "revolution" in girls' education over the past several decades represents a huge advancement in children's rights and social ethics. (p. 2)

We now have an expanded awareness of the social, cultural, political, and economic disadvantages that girls and women have historically encountered, and an informed understanding of the impact of these inequities on their educational experiences. This research and the subsequent interventions it fostered provide an important foundation for exploring boys' development.

Over the past decade, boys' lives, their school performance, and their roles in school violence have been a predominant focus in research on gender and schooling. Weaver-Hightower (2003) has termed this focus a "boy turn." In commenting on this intense focus on boys' development in a social context, the researcher observed:

> . . . the boy turn in research has had some positive impact on our understanding of gender and education. Such work has provided a necessary complement to research on girls, increasing our recognition that gender inequity is not a deficiency in girls, but rather is caused by problematic masculinities and femininities. The boy turn, however, still has many contributions to make, including sometimes identifying problems that might place boys at a disadvantage—not overall, but in particular ways. (p. 490)

Educational and Social Indicators
of Boys' Problems

While the sources of boys' problems and how to address them are presently the subject of major public and academic debate, a sobering range of school and social indicators support the reality of these problems as they exist for boys and for those who care about and teach them. Sadker (2002) drew on national research done in 2002 by the National Center for Educational Statistics in highlighting school indicators of boy's problems:

- Male students perform significantly below female students, particularly in reading and writing.
- Males are more likely to be grade repeaters.
- Males have higher school dropout rates (13 to 10 percent).
- Males are the minority (44 percent) of students enrolled in undergraduate and graduate institutions and lag behind females in degree attainment at the associates (39 percent), bachelors (44 percent), and graduate (44 percent) levels.
- Male students are disciplined more harshly, more publicly, and more frequently than females when they violate the same rules.
- Parents of male students are contacted more frequently about their child's behavior or schoolwork than parents of female students (12 percent).
- Males constitute 71 percent of school suspensions.
- Males account for two-thirds of all students served in special education.

In focusing his research on youth violence, Garbarino (1999) explored the risk factors faced by boys in our culture that foster violent behaviors. These risks, Garbarino observed, can be found "in alienation from positive role models, in spiritual emptiness that spawns despair, in adolescent melodrama, in humiliation and shame, in the violent fantasy that seduces many of the emotionally vulnerable, and in the gun culture that arms our society's troubled boys" (p. 28).

As he explored youth violence, Garbarino (1999) also identified some social indicators that quantify violence in boys' lives. These include:

- Juvenile arrests for possession of weapons, aggravated assault, robbery, and murder rose more than 50 percent from 1987 to 1996.
- While the overall youth homicide rate dropped in 1997, the rate among small town and rural youth increased by 38 percent.
- In 1997, 28 percent of adolescent boys reported carrying a gun, knife, or club.
- In 1997, 20 percent of high-school-aged boys were in physical fights on school property.
- Child abuse and neglect rose from 14 percent per 100,000 in 1986 to 23 percent per 100,000 in 1993.
- Children who are abused are more than seven times more likely to develop problems with aggression.

Although Garabino (1999) discusses the impact of exposure to media violence through television, the Internet, movies, and video games in his writing, extensive research has clearly established the significant impact of this sustained exposure to media on children's attitudes and behaviors. Comprehensive research on youth violence by the U.S. Surgeon General (2001) and Anderson, Berkowitz, Donnerstein, Huesman, Johnson, Linz, Malamuth, and Wartella (2003) established a clear connection between violence in media and aggressive and violent behavior in youth. In describing this correlation, Anderson et al. explained that "well-supported theory delineates why and when exposure to media violence increases aggression and violence (in young viewers). Media violence produces short-term increases by priming existing aggressive scripts and cognitions, increasing physiological arousal, and triggering an automatic tendency to imitate observed behaviors. Media violence also produces long-term effects via several types of learning processes leading to the acquisition of aggressive scripts, interpretational schemas, and aggression-supporting behaviors." . . . (p. 81).

In addition to documenting and analyzing the effect of exposure to media violence, these reports also identified the inordinate amount of time that children and youth spend consuming media violence.

In the context of this discussion of boys' development and the research-documented impact of media violence on children, a range of studies have also documented many boys' fascination and deep engagement with media that contain elements of violence, fantasy, and action. Kendrick and McKay (2002), Anderson (2003), Williams (2004), Fletcher (2006), and Newkirk (2006) all describe their work with boys, their awareness of boys' "fascination with the spectacular and the grotesque" (Anderson, 2003, p. 223), and these boys' sustained engagement with video games and violent cartoons and movies.

A Critical and Relational Approach to Boys' Work

Although there is still much to learn about boys, their development, and their school performance, and conflicting perspectives on these issues still need to be resolved, it is apparent that much of what we do know is cause for great concern and for careful attention and thoughtful, theoretically grounded responses. The work of critical educational theorists, including Connell (1996), Gilbert and Gilbert (1998), Ferguson (2001), Martino and Pallotta-Chiarolli (2003), and relational psychologists and researchers including Brown and Gilligan (1992), Jordan (1997), Way (1997), Chu (2000), and Raider-Roth (2005) provide a humanistically, critically, and multiculturally grounded approach to boys' work. Key tenets of this integrated approach are:

- Although research has established that boys' and girls' brains are wired differently (King & Gurian, 2006), biology is not the sole determinant of boys' behavior and achievement in schools (Connell, 1996).
- How boys develop their social identity and the roles that schools play as sites of socialization in this process are critical dimensions to be identified and analyzed in understanding the social context of boys' lives. We need to identify and help

eliminate the restrictive social codes (Pollack, 2001), or "hegemonic masculinities" (Connell, 1996) that guide boys' socialization and limit their full development and achievement.

- To understand boys and their school performance, it is critical to understand teachers' relationships with boys and how these relationships shape teachers' practices and boys' learning and achievement. Research on teachers' relationships with male students suggests that as they work with boys, teachers are challenged to confront two tensions:

  - Their capacity to see boys as individuals and multifaceted learners, to be able to "locate, appreciate, and preserve boys' individuality while at the same time confronting the pressures that teachers face to act as forces of enculturation— to make them 'good boys'" (Raider-Roth, Albert, Bircam-Barkey, Gidseg, & Murray, 2008, p. 6).

  - Their ability to become aware of their own identity, particularly the way that gender shapes their own teaching identity, while at the same time "identifying the meaning that boyhood holds for their male students" (Raider-Roth et al., 2007, p. 6). Boys' development needs to be contextualized to include a consideration of the experiences of boys from diverse ethnic, racial, and socioeconomic backgrounds. It needs to consider "the ways in which the cultural identities and social contexts shape and are shaped by boys themselves" (Way & Chu, 2004), p. 2).

- Pitting boys against girls is a zero-sum game in which boys and girls lose. Concern for girls' development does not mean that we neglect boys. Rather than blame female teachers, curricula, and pedagogy, we need to focus on social messages about masculinity and on issues of poverty, racism, and classism (Brown, Chesney-Lind, & Stein, 2006).

Boys and Literacy

In addressing issues of boys and literacy, we must identify and understand the tensions and conflicting needs that exist in this educational terrain. As noted earlier in this section, as a group, boys experience difficulty with reading and writing in school, and this difficulty increases as they move from elementary to middle and high school. By the end of high school, there is a significant gender gap between male and female achievement in reading and writing. According to the National Center for Educational Statistics (2002), boys significantly outnumber girls in corrective and remedial reading programs, and this difficulty with writing tasks plays a major role in significantly higher high school dropout rates for males, particularly Black males.

Research by Newkirk (2006) illustrates a range of strategies that boys use in response to these reading difficulties. These self-protective strategies include avoidance and resistance, which are used to conceal their difficulty with literacy. Anderson (2003) documented how boys resist not only the processes of reading and writing, but also the types of literature that are most frequently are used in school. This researcher noted that boys and girls tend to be drawn to different types of literature. While girls favor stories that focus on relationships and nuance, boys tend to be drawn to themes of conflict, action, fantasy, and humor.

Although boys tend to be drawn to what they know, what they enjoy, and what experience through their often intense out-of-school interactions with their peers and with media, their life in school is restricted by codes intended to socialize boys away from science fiction, action, and violence, and toward character development in their reading and writing (Williams, 2004). Newkirk (2002) suggests that this is an approach to literacy education that focuses on "high culture" and is often considered "not only an intellectually superior form of literacy, but also a morally superior one" (p. 511). Newkirk further describes these implicit codes and explicit policies as part of a school's societal mission. In addition to their academic tasks, teachers are expected to "socialize boys away from violence, unruly behavior, and popular culture that celebrates such activities. . . ." (p. 512).

This social context that frames teaching and learning in the classroom creates significant dilemmas for teachers, particularly in a post-Columbine era when many schools have instituted blanket nonviolence policies for student writing. Teachers charged with helping students learn to read and write know that they need to motivate these students and to assist them in identifying and drawing on their "passions, interests, aspirations, and experiences" (Brozzo, 2006, p. 71). What happens for teachers and for boys when the students are not allowed to focus on themes of action and fantasy?

Accounts by Kendrick and McKay (2002), Anderson (2003), Williams (2004), Fletcher (2006), and Newkirk (2006) document the tensions, frustrations, doubts, and concerns that teachers often feel when restricted from using what Dyson (1993, as cited in Newkirk, 2006) describes as "a 'permeable curriculum' that embraces the 'unofficial worlds' of children—their hip-hop music, jump rope rhythms, television movies, professional sports, and other forms of popular and peer culture" (p. 64). Thinking and writing around these popular culture topics can provide a healthy means for students to personally explore their thoughts and feelings. "If students are experiencing violent thoughts and intentions, their writing might be a red flag to adults so that they can get much needed help" (Anderson, 2003, p. 228). Instead of fostering a classroom environment that students experience as a "construction zone," many teachers, in their work with boys, experience this environment as a "constriction zone." (Kendrick & MacKay, 2002). The work of Raider-Roth and colleagues (2007) documents these tensions as they describe teachers attempting to understand and interact with boys as unique individuals *and* as socialized children.

Finally, research has also begun to document the impact of restrictive school codes and policies on boys, their identity development, and their achievement. Kendrick and McKay (2002) document forms of resistance, as illustrated in children's drawings, in response to teacher restrictions around violent drawing and writing. In describing one student, Dustin, and his drawing of a dead, bleeding deer that he and his father had hunted and killed, they note: "[This drawing] appears to represent a small act of rebellion against [Dustin's] perception of his teacher's policy on violence" (p. 51). Citing Newkirk (2000), these researchers further note that this form of resistance may be especially appealing to boys who see "good students" as unmasculine and weak. These responses by male students, then, tend to draw them away from school behaviors and language practices that they perceive as threatening to their broader identities as boys, peers, and sons. These responses also tend to perpetuate a downward spiral of boys distancing themselves not only from literacy, but from school in general.

The Case of Cassie Brown

As she left the office of her mathematics teacher, Mr. Tempe, tears ran down Cassie's cheeks. In fact, she began to cry before Mr. Tempe had finished his advice to her. She had gone to him the second time for help with a difficult calculus problem, using logarithmic functions: $1.7(2.1)^{3x} = 2(4.5)^x$ after working on it for days.

Mr. Tempe reminded her, "Cassie, you told me earlier that you wanted to major in mathematics in college." Cassie turned to face him and he continued. "Are you really sure that you want to continue to study mathematics?" he queried. "There are not many minorities in this field and you are also female and African American. Are you sure that you don't want to reconsider your goal?"

Cassie responded firmly, "No, I'm going to study mathematics," and quietly left his office. Although she was shocked by his words and had wanted to say so, as a very shy person who had been reared to respect all adults, especially teachers, she simply took his advice as an honest opinion of her ability to succeed. Mathematics had been Cassie's favorite subject since she was in middle school.

Yet it was true that despite her usual persistence, which almost always paid off, she simply could not solve the problem and had become very frustrated. As she rode the bus home from school, she began to talk to herself silently, wondering what she should do now. She loved mathematics and computers more than anything and always thought of mathematics as her strongest subject. She did not want to give up. However, she just could not get it, even after Mr. Tempe explained the process twice.

As the older bus bumped along, she cried quietly as she thought, "Here I am in October of my senior year in high school, a student who has an average of 85, a member of the National Honor Society, and with 1300 on my SATs. I've received good grades in all my mathematics classes until now in precalculus, and Mr. Tempe is suggesting that I give up."

When she arrived home, Cassie was comforted by her parents, who encouraged her to stick to her plan to become a mathematics teacher. After all, they knew that Cassie had always loved school and wanted to be a teacher. Now, inspired mainly by her mathematics teachers in the middle school, she had chosen to study it after high school. Furthermore, since neither parent had been blessed with opportunities to go to college, they wanted all their children to accomplish that goal. But, perhaps she could not pass the class with Mr. Tempe!

After deciding that she must find someone to give her advice, Cassie chose to share her problem with the new minister of their church after the Sunday service. The family attended church together every Sunday without fail. Perhaps he could help her decide what to do. Although the new minister, Mr. Horton, had just arrived last week,

Cassie was accustomed to going to the former minister with her problems. She hoped that Mr. Horton would understand.

As she shook hands with the minister on Sunday, she smiled and said, "Remember, Mr. Horton, I met you last week with my parents. They were telling you about our family. Well, I'm feeling very upset about something that happened at school last week and I would appreciate your advice." After hearing a bit of Cassie's story, the minister encouraged her to arrange a meeting with the counselor at school and to ask if he could also attend the meeting.

On the following Wednesday morning, Mr. Horton drove to the high school counselor's office. As he drove through the fringes of the city, there were some attractive, middle-class homes and townhouse developments, which bordered on communities of surrounding suburbs. However, the closer he got to the center of the city, the more the buildings deteriorated. The main street of the inner city could be imagined as a "war zone" where, Mr. Horton had heard, drugs were bought and sold, homeless people regularly pushed their belongings in shopping carts, most businesses were boarded up, and young men who appeared to be without jobs hung out on corners. The high school was located on a street of small, neatly maintained older homes, which was not too far from the decaying, inner core of the city.

When he arrived at Jefferson High School, Miss Jensen introduced herself to Mr. Horton and greeted Cassie warmly. She then said to Mr. Horton, "I need about 15 minutes to handle a special problem. While you are waiting, would you like to read today's newspaper? There's an article about our district." Mr. Horton responded, "Yes, of course, thank you."

As Mr. Horton read, he discovered that the Jefferson School District in this community faced all the problems associated with urban schools, but on a smaller scale. Although the percentages for the city's population are 52.8 White, 35.7 Black, 0.4 American Indian, 1.6 Asian, 10.6 Hispanic, and 5.3 other, the public school population is predominately Black. According to the most recent demographics, the percentages for the students are approximately 64 Black, 6 Hispanic, 29 White, and 1 other. Seventy-five percent of the students in the district are eligible for free lunch and 2.0 percent of the students are English language learners. The most recent high school dropout rate is an encouraging 4.4 percent; however, the suspension rate is 17.2 percent. Although the total spending per student for 1999 was $11,542, all the school buildings are very old, overcrowded, and in need of repairs. No computers are available for students at any level. The administration does plan to present a bond proposal soon to fund a new elementary school.

The data for mathematics and science achievement from a recent "report card" published by the state's education department were included in the newspaper article. On the grade 4 math assessment the percentage of students at all district elementary schools who performed on grade level ranged from 1.35 in one elementary school to 21.3 at the top school. On the fourth-grade science assessment, the percent passing ranged from the lowest score of 42.86 to 71.56 in the highest school.

In the grade 8 mathematics assessment, 15.19 percent of the students at the middle school met the standards. Twenty-nine percent of the students at the high school passed the state biology exam, the lowest in the county, and 35 percent of the students passed the physics exam, again the lowest score in the county. Sixty-four percent of the students at the high school passed the chemistry exam and 40 percent passed the exam for Math I and 50 percent for Math III.

As Mr. Horton looked up from the paper, Miss Jensen came out of her office. "Thank you so much for your patience," she smiled to both Mr. Horton and Cassie. Miss Jensen invited them into her office and, as soon as they were seated, told Mr. Horton that Cassie was one of the best students at Jefferson High School, one who never had problems.

Miss Jensen turned to Mr. Horton. "How well do you know Cassie?"

When Mr. Horton replied, "Not very well," Miss Jensen proceeded to share the following information with him.

"I am so proud of Cassie. I encouraged her to participate in a special program, the Science and Technology Entry Program, which is provided by a cluster of state colleges in the Northeast. These programs have been very successful in recruiting, retaining, and encouraging minority and low-income students to pursue careers in mathematics, science, and technology" (Box 10.1).

Miss Jensen then turned to Cassie. "I was surprised when you came to ask for an appointment, Cassie, since I know that your program is set for your senior year and your decisions about college have been made. Please tell us about the problem."

BOX 10.1 • *The Science and Technology Entry Program*

The Science and Technology Entry Program (STEP) is in its thirteenth year. It is funded by the State Education Department and has as its mission the enhancement of the mathematics, science, and technology skills of diverse and low-income students. Ultimately, the goal is to encourage the participating students to continue their education after high school in the fields of mathematics, science, and technology.

Participants must belong to a minority ethnic group or meet low-income requirements to apply. Students must also be enrolled in a grade-level course in mathematics at their school, have an interest in technology (computers), science, or mathematics, and have the approval of a parent or guardian. STEP students receive instruction over a period of six Saturdays during the academic year.

Program components include large-group speaker presentations, a Saturday Academy comprising enrichment modules in science and math content, motivation, college preparation, acade-

mic tutoring and counseling, field trips, internship opportunities, and student monitoring and evaluation. It is expected that the program will foster student matriculation in college with a designated major leading toward a scientific, health, or health-related profession.

The accomplishments of the program to date have been due, in part, to altered instructional strategies as teachers have become more "hands-on," interdisciplinary, and inquiry based. They have also adopted or developed new curricular materials that are more engaging and transparently related to real-world issues and concerns. Secondary and postsecondary educators who deliver instruction, academic enrichment, and tutoring to the STEP students have critically examined their own biases, assumptions, and expectations of minority and low-income students as they witness such students excelling in programs that demand and expect excellence of them and provide them with the support that they need.

Cassie began: "Up until last week, I was totally convinced I wanted to be a math major in college. Then Mr. Tempe questioned my abilities and now I'm beginning to doubt everything I've believed about my abilities until now.

"If you remember, I was born in Jamaica, where I attended school until seven years ago. I began school there in kindergarten and continued through sixth grade. I came here in the middle of seventh grade. Teachers in Jamaica were very strict, yet motivating and encouraging. Punishment worked very well! The teachers there were very good, and I'm sure that if I had remained there I could have learned just as well. After all, when I came here I was immediately placed in eighth-grade mathematics! However, I would have had a real problem when it was time for high school in Jamaica, because you must pay for both tuition and books. In fact, kindergarten also requires tuition, but grades one through six are free.

"When my family moved here, I entered the Jefferson Middle School in seventh grade. I was immediately moved up to eighth-grade mathematics, and I continue to love mathematics. My grades have been good in all my mathematics classes, even though our high school teachers in mathematics have been very traditional; there is no such thing as 'hands-on.' Even so, my middle school mathematics teachers and several here at the high school have really inspired me to continue to study it and think about a career in mathematics. Although Mr. Tempe seems to doubt my ability now, I was in the top track in middle school and also now in high school."

Miss Jensen turned to Mr. Horton. "Mr. Horton, the tracking system separates students into those pursuing a regular or honors diploma."

Cassie continued, "I would like to have taken advanced placement courses, but we have very little advanced placement or AP courses available. Apparently, not many other girls want AP math classes. I have only one friend who has continued mathematics with me in twelfth grade. Although the numbers of males and females in my mathematics classes were almost even before grade 11, at that point we began to have more boys in class. Now, in my twelfth-grade mathematics class in precalculus, only five in fifteen students are females.

"I believed that my persistence, open-mindedness, and willingness to help others had paid off in my progress in mathematics. That is, until I reached Mr. Tempe's class. There have been times when I have persisted in solving a difficult problem for several days until I found the answer or solution! Open-mindedness has helped me to accept a different method in problem solving from a teacher after I have already learned another approach. When the teacher says, 'You learned an incorrect way to solve that kind of problem,' I am able to say, 'O.K.'"

"I know you're a very responsive student and a well-rounded student," Miss Jensen interjected. "Cassie, tell Mr. Horton about some of your extracurricular activities."

Cassie responded, "My main extracurricular activity in high school is the National Honor Society and, as a member, I sometimes do volunteer tutoring. Outside school, my social activities are connected with church. Sometimes, I have invited friends to church, but I usually see them only at school. I never did hang out, so peer pressure hasn't been a problem for me. In fact, my parents always taught us with the question, 'If you see someone jump off a bridge, would you jump?'"

"And what about the STEP program?" Miss Jensen asked.

"I enjoyed the program. For me, the most valuable thing that the program offered was the guest speakers. Although I liked the program, my personal opinion is that such a program is not the most critical factor in increasing diverse students' interest in mathematics. I think more encouragement from teachers, college recruitment beginning in high school (because that's when students drop out), more hands-on learning in mathematics, and parent involvement could make a difference. My parents did not spend a lot of time at the school, but they were very interested at home and we always had to finish homework before we could watch television."

Mr. Horton commented, "It seems that church has had a strong influence on you, Cassie. Are there other things that have helped you to succeed in school?"

"Yes," Cassie smiled, "Although teachers may not think of persistence when they think of the characteristics of successful students in mathematics, I believe that it is a very important trait. However, I can think of other characteristics, too. I would add, also, some type of religious involvement. As my grandfather says, 'What's wrong with all these children now is that they need Jesus.'

"Church has been a major focus in my family and we have had to go every Sunday. There are also social activities at church in which we participate. For example, we have had an award ceremony at church at which all children who passed or have good report cards or have graduated are recognized with an award. Sometimes, even during regular church service, our old minister would mention someone's grades or even someone's difficulties in school with which they need help.

"My parents have continued to encourage and support all three of us. My sister is now in college, and my brother, who is the youngest, is beginning high school. My brother says that he hates mathematics, so he calls on me for help with his homework. My sister is majoring in business. So, it looks like I'm the only one who has planned to major in mathematics.

"That is, until Mr. Tempe spoke to me on Friday. I went to him for help with several examples of a problem I just couldn't do. After he tried to explain what I was doing wrong, which I still don't understand, he discouraged me from continuing to study mathematics. He said that there are not many minorities in the field of mathematics and besides, I am also female and African American. Then, he asked me if I wanted to reconsider my plans for the future. He even pointed out that to become a mathematics teacher I'll need to take many more difficult courses. He obviously doesn't think that I have the ability.

"After I cried all weekend, my parents encouraged me to stick to my goals for the future. But, what do I do about this class? This teacher?"

Mr. Horton replied, "You have a difficult situation to deal with and I understand why you are so upset."

Miss Jensen interjected, "I wonder if he was simply trying to be helpful if he saw that you were upset. Of course, I'm not sure. We need to meet with him."

Cassie replied solemnly, "I don't see how a meeting will help me with the grade in his class and the decision I must make, although an apology would be considerate. Mr. Tempe may hold a stereotyped view of African Americans and their mathematical abilities."

Mr. Horton then interjected, "We should arrange a meeting with him and hear his point of view."

Miss Jensen agreed to arrange the meeting within the following week so that Cassie could resolve the issue before she lost too much time for planning. Mr. Horton thanked the counselor again for her interest and assistance.

Cassie left the meeting still saddened by the situation at this point in her high school experience and wondered how they could get Mr. Tempe to understand that he was wrong and should apologize.

Discussion Questions

1. What are the facts in Cassie's case?
2. What is Mr. Tempe's perception of Cassie as a student?
3. How does Mr. Tempe's perspective on Casssie's future differ from Cassie's perspective at this time?
4. What is Mr. Tempe's responsibility as Cassie's teacher in view of her difficulty with the math problem?
5. In deciding on an action plan, what are several major goals to help Cassie at this point? Can the goals be prioritized?
6. How would you describe Mr. Tempe's response to Cassie's difficulty? His comment?
7. What does research offer as a guide to understanding the issues in this case?

The Case of Justin Healy

"Fenrack, the giant mechanical spider attacked Axonn. His mouth was open and his sharp teeth showed. Axonn jumped out of the way at the last minute, but he dropped his magic ax! Axonn was doomed! But Brutaka came to the rescue. He bravely ran up and grabbed the magic ax. He tossed it to Axonn, who swung the weapon with all his strength. The ax hit Fenrack on the neck, and instead of blood, a giant ball of fire shot out of the wound. Fenrack was dead!"

Twelve-year-old Justin Healy wrote this passage. It was part of one of the countless stories he had written about his all-time favorites—*The Bionicle Heroes*. These fierce mechanical warriors had captured his attention over the last few months, and he and his friends played the *Bionicle Heroes* video games almost every afternoon after school. Although Justin rarely reads at home, he loves the challenge and excitement of video games like *Bionicle Heroes*, *Wartech*, and *Spiderman*. When he and his friends aren't playing video games indoors or war games on the playground, he checks out the cartoons on TV. Fantasy, action, and violence are at the center of Justin's world.

Justin is a fifth grader at Pine Hills Elementary School in the suburban community of Stafford Plains. A quiet, compassionate boy, Justin is generally compliant in school and has no history of behavior problems. He gets along well with his classmates and is part of a tight friendship group of boys in the class. On the playground and after school, Justin, Mark, Adan, Joey, and Amrit are inseparable.

His fifth-grade teacher, Mrs. Harwayne, is aware that Justin's life outside of school is dominated by his interest in video games and cartoons, many of which are violent in nature. Justin spends two or more hours each day after school watching TV or playing video games with his friends. As a result, though Justin consistently does his math, social studies, and science homework, he frequently comes to school without his writing assignments.

Although Justin is a bright student, he is a resistant writer. Mrs. Harwayne is consistently challenged to get Justin to write, and when he does, the topic of his writing always steers toward themes of action, fantasy, and violence. When she tries to guide him away from these topics, as the school district insists, he resists and loses interest in the assignment. As an experienced fifth-grade teacher, Mrs. Harwayne recognizes that Justin has already developed strategies to avoid writing. He will frequently complain about the topic, exclaiming "This is boring. Why do I have to write about this?" or delay the process by taking an inordinate amount of time to sharpen his pencil or arrange his desk.

As the school year has progressed, Mrs. Harwayne has become increasingly concerned with Justin's lack of interest in writing. She is keenly aware that his literacy skills are not developing and that he is falling behind academically. As she seeks to motivate and engage Justin in writing tasks, she continues to walk a fine line as a teacher. Given her principal's and district's expectations that she improve the test scores of all of her students and that she steer the boys in her class away from topics of fantasy and violence and toward more "noble" and school-sanctioned ones, she feels obligated to restrict and focus Justin. On the other hand, Mrs. Harwayne asks herself, "What happens when I don't allow boys to write about what they are interested in, that are part of their everyday life? Am I turning Justin off? How can I support his academic growth and still comply with school policies and practices?"

An event in far away Red Lake, Minnesota, in March of Justin's fifth-grade school year complicates this teaching–learning dilemma even further. On March 21, 2005, Jeffrey Weise, a student at Red Lake High School, killed seven people, including five students, a teacher, and a security guard. Weise also wounded seven other people in this school massacre. When police cornered Weise inside the school, he shot and killed himself. Police and family members were never able to discover Weise's motivation for the shootings and suicide.

News of this tragedy, one of the deadliest school shootings in U.S. history, quickly circulated on TV, the Internet, and in newspapers nationwide. There was no indication that Justin Healy had heard about, much less been affected by, this tragedy until Justin submitted a writing assignment as part of a classroom writing workshop two days later. When Mrs. Harwayne read Justin's paper, she was shocked and deeply concerned. Rather than write another variation on *The Bionicle Hero* adventures, Justin had written a story about a boy who takes a pistol borrowed from his father's collection to school and subsequently shoots and kills several classmates and his teacher. In the graphic detail that Mrs. Harwayne had become accustomed to from Justin's previous stories, this 12-year-old boy describes these shootings and his subsequent capture by state troopers.

Mrs. Harwayne's initial reaction is to take Justin aside and talk to him privately about his story, his motivation for writing it, and her intent. But, given the nature of this student's writing, his dramatic change in writing topic to a real-life event, and the district's zero tolerance policy that strictly prohibits "frightening and intimidating acts," she realizes that she is obligated to report this incident to her principal, Mr. Sanchez.

The remainder of this case study describes the events that subsequently unfold in response to Justin's story from the perspectives of Principal Paul Sanchez, Superintendent of the Stafford Plain School District; Dr. Kathryn Short; and Justin's father, Quentin Healy.

Paul Sanchez

When Jayne Harwayne came to his office and shared Justin's story with him, Principal Paul Sanchez's stomach knotted. "Oh, no . . . here we go," he thought to himself. Before he even talked with Jane about Justin and the context for this writing, he knew that he had to report this incident to Dr. Short, the Stafford Plains Superintendent of Schools. Given the Student Conduct/Zero Tolerance Policy that the Stafford Plains School District had adopted in 1993 and subsequently revised and expanded over the next nine years, this was surely an example of a "frightening or intimidating act." According to the District's Student Code of Conduct, violation of this or any one of the other thirty rules in the code could result in the suspension, expulsion, or emergency removal of the student.

Paul Sanchez had been the Principal of Pine Hills Elementary School for three years. Prior to moving into school administration, Paul had worked as a sixth-grade teacher in the Stafford Plains school district for ten years. He knew Jane Harwayne to be a committed, effective teacher who rarely referred students to him for disciplinary reasons. Although Paul could picture Justin in his mind, he did not know much about him other than the fact that he had not previously had any behavioral problems that had brought him to Paul's office.

Although Paul firmly believed that all schools need good discipline and student behavior in order to create a safe learning climate and for students to flourish, he favored a focus on preventive measures in managing student behavior more than lockstep disciplinary measures. He also knew from experience that it was critical to provide follow-up support after an incident of student misbehavior. From Paul's perspective, the District's policies did not address either of these dimensions sufficiently.

Jayne Harwayne described Justin and the context of Justin's violent story. She characterized Justin as a 12-year-old boy who was fascinated with action, fantasy, and violence in his imaginary world, like many of her male students, but now was clearly frightened and confused by the real-life violence in a public school that had forced itself into his world. She believed that he was not a threat to the school or the community. As he listened to this concerned teacher, Paul tended to agree with her assessment, but did not voice his opinion. He knew that, as principal, he had an assigned role to play in the disciplinary process that was about to unfold.

Paul explained to Jayne that given the District's Student Code of Contact/Zero Tolerance Policy, he was obligated to report this incident to the Superintendent. Justin could be suspended or expelled from school. Paul further explained that Justin's parents would be notified by phone and in writing of their son's violation of the District's Code of Conduct/Zero Tolerance Policy.

When an obviously frustrated Jayne Harwayne had left his office, Paul reflected on his own frustrations around the District's disciplinary policies. Once again, the rigidity of the District's disciplinary policies seemed to undermine the tone that he was trying to set in the school and limit his role and his professional discretion as a principal. Zero Tolerance policies in response to student behaviors were an understandable but misdirected reaction to school violence.

Dr. Kathryn Short

In the days following the student violence at Red Lake High School, District Superintendent Kathryn Short had spent a good deal of her time talking with Stafford Plains Board of Education members, concerned parents, and the president of the Stafford Plains Teachers Association. They all wanted to be assured that the District had plans and policies in place that would protect the community's children from this type of senseless violence. She was exhausted and on edge, but working hard at appearing calm and in control.

Paul Sanchez' call could not have come at a worst time. Given the current climate of fear and concern, she knew that she had to handle this incident firmly, to follow the District's Student Code of Conduct/Zero Tolerance Policy to the letter. Dr. Short requested that Paul contact Justin's parents to come to school and pick him up. Until this matter was resolved, she was suspending Justin from school. Once he had successfully contacted Justin's parents and the student had been taken home, Paul was to come to the District Offices immediately and bring Justin's writing with him.

After hanging up, Kathryn Short pulled her copy of the Student Code of Conduct/Zero Tolerance Policy out of her desk. She wanted to review the policies and established procedures before she drafted the required letter to Justin's parents. She shuffled through the document and found rule seventeen, which clearly applied here:

> Frightening or Intimidating Acts—A student shall not knowingly or with reckless disregard engage in any act or conduct that causes another person to reasonably believe that such student will cause physical harm to the person or the property of such a person.

From what Principal Sanchez had described, Justin's writing was surely frightening and intimidating. After reading the story herself and meeting with Paul, Justin, and Justin's parents, she would have to decide what to recommend to the Board of Education. Kathryn had the authority to suspend, expel, or remove this student from the District.

Kathryn Short did not relish this aspect of her role as Superintendent of Schools but recognized how critical it was for the public to feel that their children are safe from harm as well as achieving at their highest ability. While not perfect, she supported the District's Zero Tolerance Policy as a no-nonsense approach to school discipline. The goal of zero tolerance is to send a message to potential troublemakers that a comprehensive range of specific behaviors will not be tolerated.

Quentin Healy

When Quentin Healy received Principal Sanchez's phone call at work, he was dumb-founded. "Frigthening, intimidating writing? My son a threat? Concerns about possible violent behavior? Expulsion from school a possibility? You've got to be kidding! My son would never hurt anyone! This is ridiculous!"

After calling his wife, Ada, who was working a 12-hour shift as a nurse at the local hospital, he headed to Pine Hills Elementary School to pick up Justin. As he drove, his mind reeled. "Sure Justin is fascinated with action and violence. Aren't all boys his age? My god, at his age I was enthralled by Star Wars and guns. I loved to play war, but like all boys I grew out of the guns-and-war stage." Recalling his conversation with Principal Sanchez, Quentin couldn't believe that they were reacting to Justin's story so rashly. "Sure I agree that a school needs strict policies for misbehaving kids, but those are policies for troubled kids and that's not our Justin!"

Quentin and Ada Healy had conscientiously monitored Justin's TV viewing and the videos he watched as a kid. But he always loved action, superheroes, and guns. Although they monitored for these things, action-oriented and violent images seemed to be everywhere outside their home—in the stores, on food packaging, on t-shirts—everywhere. As he grew, Justin was a good kid. He was kind to his younger sister, got along with his friends, didn't get into fights . . . nothing.

"Okay," Quentin admitted to himself, "Maybe he spends to much time now watching TV and playing video games with his friends. But he seems to get his schoolwork done. Except for his reading grades, he seems to be doing just fine in school."

As Quentin Healy's emotions settled a bit, another aspect of this situation caught his attention. Why had his son written a story about a boy killing his classmates and teacher? This was so atypical of Justin. Quentin frequently listened to and read some of Justin's *Bionicle Heroes* stories. They were amusing and mildly entertaining, but never seemed a cause for alarm. "Why the shift?" Quentin wondered "Why did he suddenly write a story about a real, violent event?"

As Quentin thought back to the news announcements earlier in the week about the student killer in Red Lake, Minnesota, he recognized that he had been deeply troubled, but realized that he hadn't paid attention to Justin's reaction to this news. His son had been in the living room when the shooting were first reported, but hadn't said anything and didn't seem to react. "Perhaps," Quentin thought, "I was hoping that he wasn't paying attention, that the reality that this frightening wave of kids killing kids and adults in schools was continuing."

As Quentin approached Pine Hills Elementary School, he knew that he and Ada had the right to state their case at a hearing, and to appeal the Superintendent's decision, and they would do just that. Their son was not a menace or a threat, not a time bomb waiting to go off! Quentin Healy knew that he would stand up for his son and fight this asinine policy.

Discussion Questions
1. What are the facts in Justin's case?
2. What assumptions are being made by the teacher, the principal, the superintendent, and Justin's father?

3. What are the key issues that need to be addressed in discussing this case? Which of these issues is most important for you and why?

4. What internal tensions are being experienced by each of the adults in this situation?

5. Justin's voice is not heard in this story. How do you imagine that Justin would describe this experience as it is unfolding?

6. Given the information provided, what do you think will be the outcome of the superintendent's hearing? How do you feel about this outcome?

7. What outcome would best suit Justin's needs?

8. What does the research offer as a guide to understanding the issues in this case?

References

Adenika-Morrow, T. J. (1996). Lifeline to science careers for African American females. *Educational Leadership, 53*(8), 80–83.

Anderson, C., Berkowitz, L., Donnerstein, E., Huesmann, L.R., Johnson, J., Linz, D., Malamuth, N., & Wartella, E. (2003). The influence of media violence on youth. *Psychological Science in the Public Interest, 4(3)*, 81–110.

Anderson, M. (2003). Reading violence in boys' writing. *Language Arts, 80(3)*, 223–231.

Becker, J. (2003). Gender and mathematics: An issue for the twenty-first century. *Teaching Children Mathematics, 9*, 470–473.

Biklen, S.K. (1995). *School work: Gender and the cultural construction of teaching.* New York: Teachers College Press

Blum, L. (1997). Women in mathematics: Scaling the heights and beyond. In D. Nolan (Ed), *Women in mathematics: Scaling the heights* (pp. 2–6). Washington, DC: Mathematical Association of America.

Bossert, S. T. (1981). Understanding sex differences in children's classroom experiences. *Elementary School Journal, 81*, 254–266.

Boswell, S. L. (1985). The influence of sex-role stereotyping on women's attitudes and achievement in mathematics. In S. F. Chipman, R. L. Brush, & D. M. Wilson (Eds.), *Women and mathematics: Balancing the equation* (pp. 175–198). Hillsdale, NJ: Erlbaum.

Brown, A., Cervero, R., & Johnson-Bailey, J. (2000). Making the invisible visible: Race, gender, and teaching in adult education. *Educational Quarterly, 50*(4), 273–288.

Brown, L., & Gilligan, C. (1992). *Meeting at the crossroads: Women's psychology and girls' development.* Cambridge, MA: Harvard University Press.

Brown, L., Chesney-Lind, M., & Stein, N. (2006, June 7). What about the boys? *Education Week*, 40.

Brozzo, W. (2006, September). Bridges to literacy for boys. *Educational Leadership*, 71–74.

Chu, J. (2000). *Learning what boys know: An observational and interview study with six four-year-old boys.* Cambridge, MA: Harvard Graduate School of Education, unpublished dissertation.

Clarkson, P., & Leder, G. C. (1984). Causal attributions for success and failure in mathematics: A cross-cultural perspective. *Educational Studies in Mathematics, 15*, 413–422.

Clewell, B., Anderson, B., & Thorpe, M. (1992). *Breaking the barriers: Helping female and minority students succeed in mathematics and science.* San Francisco: Jossey-Bass.

Connell, R.W. (1996). Teaching the boys: New research on masculinity, and gender strategies for schools. *Teachers College Record, 98*(2), 206–235.

Davenport, E., Davison, M., Kuang, H., Ding, S, Kim, S., & Kwak, N. (1998). High school mathematics course-taking by gender and ethnicity. *American Educational Research Journal, 35*(3), 497–514.

Evans, K. (1996). Creating spaces for equity? The role of positioning in peer led literature discussions. *Language Arts, 73*(3), 194–202.

Fennema, E., & Leder, G. (1990). *Mathematics and gender.* New York: Teachers College, Columbia University.

Fennema, E., & Sherman, J. A. (1977). Sex-related differences in mathematics achievement, spatial visualization and affective factors. *American Educational Research Journal 14*, 51–71.

Fennema, E., & Sherman, J. A. (1978). Sex-related differences in mathematics achievement, spatial visualization and related factors: A further study.

Journal for Research in Mathematics Education 9, 189–203.

Ferguson, A. (2001). *Bad boys*. Ann Arbor: University of Michigan Press.

Fletcher, R. (2006). *Boy writers: Reclaiming their voices*. Portland, ME: Stenhouse Publishers.

Freeman, C. (2004). *Trends in gender equity for girls and women: 2004* (NCES 2005-016). U. S. Department of Education, National Center for Education Statistics. Washington, DC: Government Printing Office.

Garbarino, J. (1999). *Lost boys: Why our sons turn violent and how we can save them*. New York: The Free Press.

Gilbert, R., & Gilbert, P. (1998). *Masculinity goes to school*. London: Routledge.

Gilligan, C. (1993). *In a different voice: Psychological theory and women's development*. Cambridge, MA: Harvard University Press.

Gittelson, I. B., Petersen, A. C., & Tobin-Richards, M. H. (1982). Adolescents' expectancies of success, self-evaluations, and attributions about performance on spatial and verbal tasks. *Sex Roles, 8*, 411–420.

Good, T. L. (1987). Two decades of research on teacher expectations: Findings and future directions. *Journal of Teacher Education, 38*(4), 32–47.

Grossman, H. & Grossman, S. H. (1994). *Gender issues in education*. Boston: Allyn and Bacon.

Haimo, D. (1997). Excellence in mathematics. In D. Nolan (Ed.), *Women in mathematics: Scaling the heights* (pp. 7–12). Washington, DC: Mathematical Association of America.

Johnston, T. (2005). No evidence of innate gender differences in math and science. Stanford Report, Institute for Research on Women and Gender, Stanford University. Retrieved August, 2007 from: http://news-service.stanford.edu/news/2005/february9/math-020905

Jordan, J. (1997). A relational perspective for understanding women's development. In J. Jordan (Ed.), *Women's growth in diversity*. New York: Guilford.

Jussim, L., & Eccles, J. (1992). Teacher expectations: II. Construction and reflection of student achievement. *Journal of Personality and Social Psychology 63*(3) 947–961.

Kendrick, M., & McKay, R. (2002). Uncovering literacy narratives through children's drawings. *Canadian Journal of Education, 27*(1); 45–60.

Kerka, S. (1998). Career development and gender, race and class. (ERIC Digest No. 199 ERIC Document Reproduction No. ED421641).

King, K., & Gurian, M. (2006, September). Teaching to the minds of boys. *Educational Leadership*, 56–60.

Kleinfeld, J. (1999). Student performance: Males versus females. *Public Interest, 134*, 3–20.

Kozol, J. (1991). *Savage inequalities*. New York: Crown.

Leder, G. (1982). Mathematics achievement and fear of success. *Journal for Research in Mathematics Education, 13*, 124–135.

Leder, G. (1984). Sex differences in attributions of success and failure. *Psychological Reports, 54*, 57–58.

Leder, G. (1990). Gender differences in mathematics: An overview. In E. Fennema & G. Leder (Eds.), *Mathematics and gender* (pp. 10–26). New York: Teachers College Press.

Lee, J., Grigg, W., & Dion, G. (2007). *The nation's report card: Mathematics 2007*. (NCES 2007-494). National Center for Education Statistics, Institute of Education Sciences, U.S. Department of Education, Washington, DC.

Ma, X. (1999). Dropping out of advanced mathematics: The effects of parental involvement. *Teachers College Record, 101*(1), 60–81.

Maoldomhnaigh, M. O., & Mhaolain, V. N. (1990). The perceived expectation of the administrator as a factor affecting the sex of scientists drawn by early adolescent girls. *Research in Science & Technological Education, 8*(1), 69–74.

Martino, W., & Pallotta-Chiarolli, M. (2003). *So what's a boy?* Buckingham, UK: Open University Press.

Midgley, C., Feldlaufer, H., & Eccles, J.S. (1989). Student/teacher relations and attitudes before and after the transition to junior high school. *Child Development, 60*, 981–992.

Miller, J., & Stiver, I. (1997). *The healing connection: How women form relationships in therapy and life*. Boston: Beacon Press.

Muller, C. (1998). Gender differences in parental involvement and adolescents' mathematics achievement. *Sociology of Education, 71*, 336–356.

National Center for Education Statistics. (2000). *Trends in educational equity for girls and women*. Washington, D.C.: U.S. Department of Education.

National Center for Educational Statistics. (2002). *The nation's report card: Writing*. Washington DC: Author.

Newkirk, T. (2000). Misreading masculinity: Speculations about the great gender gap. *Language Arts, 77*, 294–300.

Newkirk, T. (2002). *Misreading masculinity: Boys, literacy, and popular culture*. Portmouth, MA: Heinemann.

Newkirk, T. (2006, September). Media and literacy. *Educational Leadership*, 62–66.

Oakes, J. (1990). *Multiplying inequalities: The effects of race, social class, and tracking on opportunities to learn mathematics and science.* Washington, DC: National Science Foundation.

Ogbu, J. (1993). Differences in cultural frame of reference. *International Journal of Behavioral Development 6*(3), 483–506.

Ogbu, J. (1995). Understanding cultural diversity and learning. In J. A. Banks & C. A. McGee Banks (Eds.), *Handbook of research on multicultural education* (pp. 582–596). New York: Macmillan.

Ogbu, J. (1996). Variability in minority school performance: A problem in search of an explanation. In E. Jacob & C. Jordan (Eds.), *Minority education: Anthropological perspectives* (pp. 83–111). Norwood, NJ: Ablex.

Pollack, W. (2001). *Real boys' voices.* New York: Henry Holt and Company.

Quita, I. (2003). What is a scientist? Perspectives of teachers of color. *Multicultural Education*, 11(1), 24–31.

Raider-Roth, M. (2005) *Trusting what you know: The high stakes of classroom relationships.* San Francisco: Jossey-Bass.

Raider-Roth, M., Albert, M., Bircam-Barkey, I., Gidseg, E., & Murray, T. (2008). Teaching boys: A relational puzzle. *Teachers College Record, 110*(2), 443–481.

Reichert, M., & Kuriloff, P. (2004). Boys' selves: Identity and anxiety in the looking glass of school life. *Teachers College Record, 106*(3), 547–576.

Riegle-Crumb, C. (2006). The path through math: Courses sequences and academic performance at the intersection of face-ethnicity and gender. *American Journal of Education, 113*, 101–122.

Rogers, A. (1991). Voice, play, and practice of courage in ordinary girls' and women's lives. In C. Gilligan, A. Rogers, & D. Tolman (Eds.), *Women, girls, and psychotherapy: Reframing resistance* (pp. 265–294). New York: Harrington Park Press.

Sadker, D. (2002, November). An educator's primer on the gender war. *Phi Delta Kappan*, 235–245.

Sadker, M., & Sadker, D. (1994). *Failing at fairness: How America's schools cheat girls.* New York: Charles Scribner's Sons.

Selvin, P. (1992) Math education: Multiplying the meager numbers. *Science, 258*. (5085), 1200–1202.

Sharp, R. M., Sharp, V. F., & Metzner, S. (1995). *Scribble scrabble: Ready in a minute math game.* Blue Ridge Summit, PA: TAB Books.

Singh, M. (1998). Gender issues in the language arts classroom. (ERIC Digest. ERIC Document Reproduction number ED 426409).

Spelke, E. (2005). Sex differences in intrinsic aptitude for mathematics and science? A critical review. *American Psychologist*, 60(9) 950–958.

Streitmatter, J. (1994). *Toward gender equity in the classroom: Everyday teachers' beliefs and practices.* Albany: State University of New York.

Tauber, R. (1998). Good or bad: What teachers expect from students they generally get. (ERIC Digest. ERIC Document Reproduction number ED426985).

Thomas, M., Henley, T. & Snell, C. (2006). The draw a scientist test: A different population and a somewhat different story. *College student journal*, 40(1), 140–148.

Thorne, B. (1993). *Gender play: Girls and boys in school.* Brunswick, NJ: Rutgers University Press.

U.S. Surgeon General. (2001). *Youth violence: A report of the Surgeon General.* Retrieved on 6/21/07 from http//mentalhealth.samhasa.org.gov/youthviolence/surgeongeneral/SG_Site

Way, N. (1997). Using feminist methods to understand the friendships of adolescent boys. *Journal of Social Issues, 53*(4), 703–723

Way, N., & Chu, J. (2004). *Adolescent boys: Exploring diverse cultures of boyhood.* New York: New York University Press.

Weaver-Hightower, M. (2003). The "boy turn" in research on gender and education. *Review of Educational Research, 73*(4), 471–498.

Williams, B. (2004). Boys may be boys, but do they have to read and write that way? *Journal of Adolescent & Adult Literacy, 47*(6), 510–515.

11

Sexual Orientation

Jane M. Sileo and Catharine R. Whittaker

The issue of sexual orientation is undoubtedly one of the most controversial topics in U.S. society today. The horrendous killing of Matthew Shepard, a gay college student, in 1998 brought to national attention the glaring fact that the number of hate crimes committed against gay men and lesbians is increasing in the United States (Human Rights Campaign, 2001). In 2006 the U.S. government reported that about 14 percent of the hate crimes committed in the past year were motivated by sexual orientation bias (Federal Bureau of Investigation, 2006). While virtually all Americans stand in opposition to such unconscionable acts, the degree to which they are willing to allow homosexuals the same rights and privileges granted to heterosexuals varies according to the issue. Nine out of ten Americans believe that homosexuals should have equal rights in terms of job opportunities; less than 60 percent believe that homosexual relations between consenting homosexuals should be legal (Gallup Poll, 2007).

The public schools represent a microcosm of this debate. In fact, an argument can be made that the discrimination faced by teens who are not heterosexual is more intense than that faced by gay adults. More than three-quarters of students in middle schools report that students in their schools have a negative attitude toward students who are thought to be gay, lesbian, or bisexual (Markow, Liebman, & Dunbar, 2007). Middle school might be the worst school setting for harassment. An earlier survey found that 47 percent of middle school students consider bullying and harassment a somewhat or very serious problem at school, compared to only 35 percent of high school students (Harris Interactive and GLSEN, 2005).

To understand these results and discuss the issues relating to sexual orientation in the public schools, it is useful to understand the terminology used in the discourse. *Sexual orientation* is a term used to describe the attraction one feels toward either or both sexes, since individuals may be homosexual, heterosexual, or bisexual (GLSEN, 1999; Lugg, 2003). Just as is the case with heterosexuals, adults who are nonheterosexual report that they have little control over their sexual orientation (Pharr, 1988). *Sexual behavior* involves the sexual activities in which individuals engage. While the median age for recognizing one's sexual orientation is 13, sexual behavior may or may not accompany this awareness. *Sexual identity* is a broader concept than sexual orientation, involving a multitude of issues related to gender. Unlike most individuals struggling with their racial identity, youth forming their sexual identity can be recognized by others as having a different sexual identity than the one that the individual eventually determines. Others generally assume heterosexuality until a person "comes out" as gay or bisexual. *Homophobia* has been defined as "prejudice, discrimination, harassment, or acts of violence against sexual minorities, including lesbians, gay men, bisexual, and transgendered persons, evidenced in a deep-seated fear or hatred of those who love and sexually desire those of the same sex" (Sears, 1997, p. 16). The fears, misunderstandings, and discriminatory behavior of heterosexuals directed toward gay, lesbian, bisexual, and transgendered (GLBT) individuals are well documented (GLSEN, 1999; Harris Interactive and GLSEN, 2005). The intensity of these negative feelings and behaviors is correlated with a variety of personal, geographic, religious, and educational factors (Sears, 1997). *Heterosexism* is "a belief in the superiority of heterosexuals or heterosexuality evidenced in the exclusion, by omission or design, of nonheterosexual persons in policies, procedures, events, or activities" (Sears, 1997, p. 16). This is the pervading view in school and society and, despite an increased awareness of the injustice of such a view, the majority of school personnel are often inactive in changing behaviors that place GLBT students at risk daily.

Risk Factors for GLBT Students

The overriding risk factor for all teens is the lack of communication or support from one or more of their multiple worlds: family, school, religious institution, community, and peers. Many GLBT students experience significant stress knowing that there is little if any support in any of these circles for a nonheterosexual orientation.

The consequences for coming out can be severe, ranging from verbal harassment and social ostracism to physical abuse (Remafedi, 1994). Being the recipient of verbal abuse is almost guaranteed, with 52 percent of youth reporting that they hear homophobic epithets in school (Harris Interactive and GLSEN, 2005). "That's so gay" has become a commonly used phrase in which "gay" means something bad or devalued. The low self-esteem and feelings of isolation and depression that GLBT youth experience are tied to any number of risky behaviors, including school absenteeism, dropping out, homelessness, substance abuse, risky sexual behavior that can lead to HIV infection, and suicide (GLSEN, 1999; Harbeck, 1997; Hunter, 1996; Remafedi, 1994).

The statistics for 2004 indicate that 7.8 percent of adolescent deaths were due to suicide (Hamilton, Minino, Martin, Kochanek, Strobino, & Guyer, 2007). There is a significantly higher rate of suicide ideation and attempts among GLBT adolescents and young adults (ages 15 to 24) compared to heterosexual individuals (NEA, 2006; O'Conor, 1995; Remafedi, 1994). While there is some controversy regarding the extent of this problem due to sampling issues (Unks, 1995), perhaps the most important message is that higher rates of attempted suicide and actual suicide among homosexual teens are not due to an inherent mental instability, but to a predictable reaction to a hostile environment.

Characteristics of GLBT Youth

Estimates of the number of GLBT adolescents in the United States varies from 1 to 30 percent, although a range of 5 to 10 percent is most commonly reported (Ginsberg, 1999; Harbeck, 1997). As mentioned previously, gay teens usually report being aware of being more attracted to persons of their own sex between ages 12 and 14, although individual reports vary widely (Anderson 1995; Ginsberg 1999; Sears, 1991). Most homosexuals recall a period of intense anxiety when they realize that they belong to a stigmatized group and often go through a period of trying to change their orientation. They may begin or continue heterosexual activity despite an awareness of their orientation. Again, it is important to point out that sexual orientation is distinct from sexual behavior and that, despite the presumption of promiscuity that colors much of the public debate about homosexuality, studies have shown that GLBT students' sexual experiences are similar to those of their heterosexual peers (Ginsberg, 1999).

For many GLBT teens, coming out is an all-consuming issue that is rooted in a strong need for emotional support and often takes precedence over the many curricular and extracurricular activities that are associated with success in high school (Ginsberg, 1999). Students most frequently come out to trusted GLBT peers first, then close heterosexual peers or family members, although some may rely on a teacher, counselor, or coach (GLSEN, 1999; Kosciw & Diaz, 2006). Coming out to a sibling or parent can be very threatening, depending on the family members' beliefs and expectations. Parental responses can range from confusion or denial to threats of disowning the child or physical violence if the child does not "change" (Ginsberg, 1999).

Some of the negative responses that parents display are rooted in the belief that a child can change his or her sexual orientation. To some extent, this belief is tied to the controversy over the factors that determine sexual orientation. There continues to be debate over the biological basis for sexual orientation (Jones, 1999; Lipkin, 1996). Some studies suggest that when one identical twin is gay there is a higher likelihood that the other twin is gay than with fraternal twins, suggesting a biological link. Furthermore, the sexual orientation of adopted children is unrelated to the orientation of the parents, suggesting that the trait is not socially rooted. Nevertheless, there is no foolproof way to identify sexual orientation, despite an array of theories based on genetic makeup, hormonal levels, socialization, and environment (Pharr, 1988). However, both heterosexual and homosexual adults report having little control over their sexual orientation.

One group that faces even greater risk is students who are both gay and people of color. They are more vulnerable to antigay harassment and face a more complex set of issues in coming out (Adams & Carson, 2006; Johnston, 1999; Sears, 1995, 1997). Although there are individual reports that the Black community is less accepting of homosexuality than the White community, there is little empirical support for this belief. Nevertheless, these youth often feel extreme isolation in trying to keep separate the three worlds in which they reside: the homosexual community, their racial community, and the society at large.

Gay Teachers

The gender of the teaching profession has an interesting development in the United States. Males dominated the field until the mid-nineteenth century, when a burgeoning public schools movement required many teachers and small salaries (Blount, 2000). Rather than continuing to hire men, school districts preferred hiring young, single women. When these women did not marry, or became "spinsters," they were suspected of lesbianism. By 1920 men occupied only 14 percent of the education workforce, including administration. Males who remained, particularly those working with young children, were often viewed as "sissies." Many considered effeminate men to be homosexuals who would be a bad influence on their students. In the 1950s and 1960s a campaign began to attract "masculine" males to the profession with a promise of a fast track to administrative positions. Simultaneously, in many places teachers who were suspected of being gay were charged with largely trumped-up charges and fired (Lugg, 2003; Marcus, 1992).

In the 1970s Anita Bryant started the "Save Our Children Movement" campaign largely in response to a newly passed Miami ordinance protecting gays from discrimination in housing and some employment (Harbeck, 1997). Bryant also supported a national law that would keep gays out of the teaching profession. The specter of gay teachers enabled her to mobilize conservative Christians and politicians to win a rescinding of the ordinance. This is but one example of numerous ballot initiatives and laws that have attempted to ban those suspected of being GLBT from working in public schools (Lugg, 2003).

School employment remains gender-polarized today. Women comprise about 75 percent of the teaching profession and most men teach in upper grades, coach, or hold administrative positions (Blount, 2000). Openly gay teachers can still be denied employment in many states. The Employment Non-Discrimination Act, prohibiting employment discrimination on the basis of sexual orientation, was introduced and strongly supported during the Clinton administration, but it has not been passed to date (NEA, 2006). Therefore, it is up to state law whether sexual orientation is a protected category, and only sixteen states have enacted such legislation. "In the vast majority of American states, queer educators can be fired for their status, and they have no legal recourse" (Lugg, 2003, p. 117). Federal district courts have ruled that it is unconstitutional for a school district to discriminate against a gay or lesbian teacher (NEA, 2006). Although case law has supported the rights of gay and lesbian teachers whose districts have attempted to terminate their employment on the basis of sexual orientation, questions remain regarding a possible line between public and private behavior (NEA, 2006; Zirkel, 1999). Many gay and lesbian teachers have come out and taken a strong stand for the rights of GLBT teachers, often at great personal and professional cost (Anderson, 1996; DeJean, 2004; Jennings, 1996; Prince, 1996; Toynton, 2006). However, it is unclear whether gay teachers can come out to their students safely. Often this depends upon the collective bargaining agreement in place and the actual "GLBT-related" speech used by the teacher.

Rationale for a School and Community Response

There are a variety of strong educational, psychological, legal, and ethical reasons for supporting students who are GLBT in the schools. Obviously, these are students who are at risk, and their existence is often denied by the school culture and curriculum (Kosciw & Diaz, 2006; Unks, 1995). The public school culture—the newspaper gossip columns, the school yearbook signings, class ring exchanges, Valentine's celebrations, the prom—is based on a heterosexist view. Furthermore, like other diverse groups, the lives, literature, art, and music of GLBT individuals is either absent from the pages of elementary and secondary texts or not identified as such.

Many national educational, medical, and mental health organizations have written policy statements supportive of the rights of GLBT students and educators. For example, the National Association of State Boards of Education, representing the fifty state boards of education, voted that "State boards should provide leadership in eliminating the stereotypes and discrimination on the basis of sex, age, disability, race, religion, sexual orientation, ethnic background or national origin in curriculum materials, counseling methods and other education processes" (Harbeck, 1997, p. 18). Similarly, since 1974 the National Education Association has issued strong statements opposing employment discrimination on the basis of sexual orientation. The position statement of the National Association of School Psychologists (1999) supports sexual minority youth in public and private schools by endorsing (1) education of students and staff, (2) direct counseling, (3) advocacy, (4) research, and (5) programs for HIV prevention directed toward GLBT youth.

Those who view homosexuality as abnormal or immoral can exacerbate the psychological stress that may accompany coming out. The psychological implications of reparative therapy present another issue that has caused professional organizations to respond. *Reparative therapy* refers to psychotherapy aimed at eliminating homosexual desires and the belief that homosexuality is a mental disorder (GLSEN, 2002). *Transformational ministry* is an approach used by some Christian groups to attempt to eliminate homosexual desires. The American Psychiatric Association declassified homosexuality as a mental disorder in 1973; all major health professional organizations have supported this. In addition, the Surgeon General's Report determined that homosexuality is not a reversible lifestyle choice (Satcher, 2001). Furthermore, ten national education, health, and counseling organizations have supported a statement in opposition to reparative therapy and transformational ministry, saying that its promotion is likely to exacerbate the risk of harassment, harm, and fear.

Although there is considerable case law regarding homosexual students and teachers, the Nabozny case stands out. In 1995 Jamie Nabozny, a gay former student, sued the Ashland School District in Wisconsin for not protecting him against harassment (Jones, 1999). Jamie was mock-raped in a classroom, urinated upon in a bathroom, and kicked so badly that he required surgery to stop the internal bleeding. In this landmark case, the Seventh U.S. Circuit Court of Appeals ruled that the district pay Jamie Nabozny $900,000 in damages for violation of the Fourteenth Amendment Equal Protection Clause.

While no federal law protects students simply on the basis of their sexual orientation, Title IX applies to cases of sexual discrimination in which sexual orientation issues may be present. The Office of Civil Rights has issued extensive guidance for school districts that outlines a school's responsibilities under Title IX, including grievance procedures and prevention (Office for Civil Rights, 2001). Massachusetts was the first state to ban discrimination on the basis of sexual orientation in public schools (Commonwealth of Massachusetts Governor's Commission on Gay and Lesbian Youth, 1993; Jennings, 1996).

The ethical dimensions of the homosexual controversy in U.S. society are extremely complex, especially given the plurality of religious beliefs. However, there are issues on which many faith organizations can agree, especially the right of individuals not be discriminated against on the basis of sexual orientation in areas such as safety and employment (Interfaith Alliance Foundation, n.d.). Furthermore, it is not true that all religious organizations are opposed to homosexual orientation and behavior. Some organizations have openly supported homosexuality as healthy and acceptable (PFLAG, n.d. a), whereas in other major denominations there are groups within the denomination that are openly accepting of gay and lesbian individuals regardless of official church doctrine (Crew, 1997; Nugent, 1997). Nevertheless, it is clear that many conservative Christian denominations view homosexuality as sinful. However, the debate over the biblical view of homosexuality is far from resolved in most major Protestant denominations (see Box 11.1).

A final rationale for addressing sexual difference in schools is that all students benefit from gaining factual information. Homophobia hinders all students by confining people in rigid gender roles and inhibiting close personal relationships with members of the same sex (Kosciw & Diaz, 2006). All students, whether gay or straight, are

BOX 11.1 • *Homosexuality and Christianity*

There is an ongoing dialogue among Christian theologians across the United States regarding many issues relating to the acceptance of gays in the church, the clergy, and the sacrament of marriage. Protestant denominations traditionally viewed as more liberal, such as the Episcopal Church, are allowing this dialogue to continue without resolution in sight. For example, in 2003, the Episcopal's House of Bishops consented to the election of the Rev. V. Gene Robinson, an openly gay minister, as the bishop of New Hampshire. However, many within the church still oppose his election. On the other hand, the Catholic church and many conservative Protestant denominations are firmly opposed to such changes, choosing to "love the sinner, but hate the sin" (Rosik, Griffith, & Cruz, 2007).

The issues surrounding gay individuals within the church carry with them far-reaching implications for church doctrine. By anyone's standard, the number of passages in the Old and New Testament that speak directly to the issue of homosexuality is a very small portion of the overall Bible (White, n.d.). However, these few passages, if read literally and without consideration for the cultural and historical setting, appear to condemn homosexuality. Christians who see the Bible as the infallible word of God have a strict interpretation of these passages and thus oppose the practice of homosexuality (Gagnon, 2002; Jones & Yarhouse, 2000). They view the attempt by theologians and church leaders to interpret them differently as a Pandora's Box that opens the door for doctrinal relativism on a host of issues. Those willing to welcome gays into the church respond that Jesus said nothing about homosexual behavior, and Biblical texts that appear to condemn it are not referring to homosexual behavior as we know it today (Countryman & Ritley, 2001; Helminiak, 2000; Rogers, 2006; Wink, 2002). They emphasize the overall Biblical message of love within a committed and trusting relationship.

vulnerable to homophobic slurs, regardless of their sexual orientation (Kosciw & Diaz, 2006; Sattel, Keyes, & Tupper, 1997). Although the issue is constantly appearing in the media in ways that may or may not be helpful or accurate, many community groups avoid the topic due to its controversial dimensions. Unless public schools respond to the void of information available, students will continue to rely on hearsay.

Staff Training and Resources

Although most teachers and support staff are aware that there are GLBT youth in their classrooms, they admit that they do not meet these students' needs due to their lack of professional training, their own homophobic feelings, or their fear that colleagues will think that they were gay or lesbian, thus potentially compromising their reputation or employment (Jennings, 2005; Sears, 1992). These responses indicate that, like their students, teachers and other school staff are in need of information about GLBT youth, as well as strategies for working with these students.

It is not reasonable to expect gay and lesbian teachers to become the standard bearers for change. It is important that all preservice and in-service teachers receive relevant information. In 1994 Massachusetts became the first state to establish an Advisory Commission on Gay and Lesbian Youth that must ensure that all teacher certification programs include information about serving GLBT youth (Harbeck, 1997). Workshops that address homophobia and address sensitivity training will certainly help many in-service educators to feel more comfortable about addressing these issues with students. In addition, many resources, such as speakers, brochures and books, policy statements, and videos, are available through organizations such as Parents, Families, and Friends of Lesbians and Gays (PFLAG, n.d. b) and Gay, Lesbian, and Straight Education Network (GLSEN, 2006; Jennings, 1996) (see Table 11.1). At minimum, staff must understand the federal and state laws that govern their behavior toward students and follow accompanying procedures established by the school district. Although guidance counselors, social workers, health teachers, and coaches may have a higher likelihood of coping with students who are victims of harassment, school staff can encounter antihomosexual epithets from students and peers and must deal with them appropriately.

School districts should adopt anti-harassment policies that specifically name sexual orientation as a protected group and outline grievance procedures and collective action (Harris Interactive and GLSEN, 2005; Mukilteo School District, n.d.).

Name calling, bullying, and sexual harassment are commonplace among teens in our society. GLBT teens report hearing "faggot, dyke, and that's so gay" at school (Harris Interactive and GLSEN, 2005). Teachers clearly need to immediately address bullying and harassment, and Box 11.2 provides some ideas for doing so.

Curriculum Issues

While school staff are generally aware of the need to enforce antidiscrimination policies in the public schools, the process of including information about homosexuality and the histories, literature, art, and music of GLBT individuals in the curriculum continues to

TABLE 11.1   *Organizations that Support Gay, Lesbian, Bisexual, and Transgendered Youth*

Gay, Lesbian, and Straight Education Network (GLSEN)
www.glsen.org email: glsen@glsen.org
212-727-0135

GLBT National Help Center
www.glnh.org email: info@GLBTNationalHelpCenter.org
1-888-843-4564

Hetrick Martin Institute
www.hmi.org email: info@hmi.org
212-674-2400

Human Rights Campaign
www.hrc.org email: hrc@hrc.org
1-800-777-4723

National Youth Advocacy Coalition
www.nyacyouth.org email: nyac@nyayouth.org
1-800-541-6922

Parents, Families, and Friends of Lesbians and Gays (PFLAG)
www.pflag.org email: info@pflag.org
202-467-8180

Project10
www.project10.org email: project10@hotmail.com
626-577-4553

The Family Pride Coalition
www.familypride.org email: info@familypride.org
202-331-5015

be a source of controversy across the country. However, individual teachers and school districts have implemented curriculum change in a number of ways. For example, the Minnesota State Board of Education requires every school to submit a plan for including multicultural, gender-fair, disability-sensitive material and resources throughout the curriculum. Some districts include sexual orientation as part of the gender fairness concept (Sattel et al., 1997). Districts include this content within courses or units on justice, equity, and prejudice reduction; health; and the history or psychology of sport. Sexual orientation can be appropriately discussed in a variety of content areas (Lipkin, 2000; Lugg, 2003; Roy, 1997). Students should learn in social studies courses that gays were targets during the Holocaust and the McCarthy era. In science classes the study of genetics provides a logical discussion of the range of XX and XY combinations (Lugg, 2003). When gay authors are discussed in English classes, gender orientation is relevant bio-

BOX 11.2 • *How Teachers Can Address Bullying and Harassment of GLBT Students*

1. Adopt ground rules for responsible classroom behavior.
2. Wear a supportive pin; hand a poster; put a "safe space" logo on your door
3. Watch for signs of bullying and harassment.
4. Invite students to talk with you.
5. Intervene when you witness something inappropriate.
6. Learn a short response such as:
   " '_____' is a word that insults gay and lesbian people. I want to remind you that there are or there may be gay and lesbian people at this school, and when you use words like that you make them feel unsafe and unwelcome. It is important to me that everyone at this school feel safe and welcome. I don't want you to use that word anymore."
7. Examine ways in which you may unconsciously pass messages about GLBT people.
8. Monitor your own language regarding GLBT individuals.

Sources: GLSEN, 2002; National Education Association (2006).

graphical information. Furthermore, there is a range of young adult literature available that either deals with the issues of coming out or simply includes gay characters without making gender orientation a source of conflict (Blackburn & Buckley, 2005; Daniel, 2007).

Sexuality education should be inclusive, accurate, and culturally sensitive. A strong curriculum should introduce content regarding sexual maturation for a range of identities, conception and contraception, maintaining sexual health, and how to prevent sexually transmitted diseases at developmentally appropriate levels (Lugg, 2003). Unfortunately, even including a statement that homosexuality is neither a disease nor a mental illness in the curriculum is a challenge in some districts (de Vise, 2007), while other districts require an abstinence-only education model.

Most recently, educators are exploring the need for addressing these issues on the elementary level (Boyd, 1999; Letts & Sears, 1999; Schall & Kauffmann, 2003). The video *It's Elementary: Talking about Gay Issues in School* is a powerful resource for students and teachers (Cohen & Chasnott, 1997). An increasing body of information is available for districts seeking to make their curriculum more inclusive and is available through many of the organizations mentioned above (Lipkin, 2000; Schniedewind & Davidson, 2006).

There are many ways in which individuals who are GLBT can be represented in the curriculum for the contributions they have made to society in particular content areas. Regardless of their content area or grade level, researchers (GLSEN, 2002; Sileo, 2004) suggest that educators (a) not assume heterosexuality, (b) guarantee equality by creating a safe environment, (c) provide support for students by being a role model, (d) be knowledgeable about GLBTQ issues, and (e) include Gay-Straight Alliances (GSA) as an extracurricular group.

School and Community Support Groups and Programs

Support groups for GLBT youth are known by a variety of names (e.g., Gay–Straight Alliance, BIGAYLA, Allies). Many of these groups have grown out of GLSEN because the organization emphasizes education, action, and the inclusion of people of all sexual orientations (GLSEN, 2006). Each group or chapter sets its policies and procedures; however, a universal policy is that youth are not required to declare their sexual orientation. GSAs are a place where students can meet and discuss GLBTQ issues (Kosciw & Diaz, 2006). Often groups meet on campus after school, but other groups are sponsored by a variety of service organizations and may meet in community buildings. The federal law known as the Equal Access Act requires school districts that recognize student clubs that are not related to the curriculum (e.g., a chess club) to also recognize GLBT-related groups (NEA, 2006).

Another organization that is helpful to youth and their families is PFLAG. Its mission is to support the needs of parents and friends of lesbians and gay men, to educate them and others, and to advocate equality for their gay and lesbian children (Durgin-Clinchard, 1997). In addition to sponsoring 500 affiliates, PFLAG provides newsletters, help lines, programs, brochures, and advocacy activities (PFLAG, n.d. b).

Two fairly comprehensive district programs that have been created to address the needs of GLBT teens are Project 10 at Fairfax High School in the Los Angeles Unified School District and the Hetrick-Martin Institute, home of the Harvey Milk School in New York City.

Project 10 began in 1984 to address the needs of GLBT youth by focusing on "education, reduction of verbal and physical abuse, suicide prevention, and dissemination of accurate AIDS information" (Uribe, 1995). The centerpiece of the model is a weekly support group averaging ten to twelve students for students who are suffering the effects of stigmatization and discrimination based on sexual orientation. The adult cofacilitators are trained through workshops and must be nonjudgmental with regard to sexual orientation. When appropriate, students are referred to community agencies for additional services. Project 10 also includes a district resource center, a paid coordinator, ongoing workshops for school staff, school support teams, lists of books for school librarians, enforcement of nondiscrimination policies, and advocacy for gay and lesbian student rights through the school system and community. This program has been successful partially due to its collaboration with social service agencies in Los Angeles that offer discussion groups, a youth hotline, emergency shelter for homeless gay youth, and group homes and foster placements for teens rejected by their families (Gover, 1996).

The Harvey Milk School, opened in 1985, grew out of the same concerns for gay and lesbian youth that spawned Project 10 (Gover, 1996; Hunter, 1996). It is a small alternative school in Manhattan that, in addition to a traditional curriculum, offers substantial social services, including a family counseling program. Serving students primarily between the ages of 12 and 21 and their families, Harvey Milk is a transitional school that encourages students to return to traditional schools when ready.

The debate over how our governmental, economic, religious, and educational institutions should respond to the issue of sexual orientation will undoubtedly continue over the next decade. All school personnel, regardless of the age level of the students they serve, will confront these difficult issues. The case of Renee Fischer involves resistance to the formation of a GSA on the high school level, whereas the case of Sam Meyers is about a new early childhood teacher who is gay. We believe that grappling with both of these cases will help you to consider many of the important concerns related to sexual orientation in public schools.

The Case of Renee Fischer

As a social worker, I've always been concerned about the need to support students who are struggling with sexual identity, especially those who think that they may be gay, lesbian, bisexual, or transgendered. However, it wasn't until last spring that a real opportunity to reach some of these kids presented itself.

I got an announcement of a conference to be held at Abington University for high school students in a four-county area encompassing about twenty schools. It was sponsored by a state-funded agency for safe schools and Kevin Jennings, the director of the Gay, Lesbian, and Straight Education Network (GLSEN) was the keynote speaker. To be honest, I didn't know much more about the conference than that, but I saw it as a way to get kids to identify themselves as interested in these issues. I wasn't asking them to declare their sexual orientation; that was up to them. I was just providing them with an opportunity to gain information in a supportive atmosphere.

I talked to George Foster, our principal, about advertising the conference, and he didn't hesitate at all. He didn't hold a faculty meeting to explain his rationale or consult with the superintendent. George lives by the motto, "It's easier to ask for forgiveness than permission."

He simply said, "This looks like a way to identify those students who we know are out there, Renee. Since it's off campus, they may feel safe enough to come to you and find out the details. Get some fliers up right away, and we'll see what happens."

I had enough neon pink fliers printed to cover every bulletin board in every hall in the high school. There was no way that anyone—students, teachers, administrators, or staff—could say that they hadn't heard. I was somewhat apprehensive, but excited. I guess that's why I'm still a school social worker, despite the stress of the job; I believe that it's possible to make an impact on the lives of adolescents that can have long-term positive outcomes. O.K., I admit it. Challenges like these take me back to my 1960s activist days when marchers sang "We shall overcome" and believed it. But this decision wasn't about me—it was about supporting kids who deserved a place where they could talk freely and be taken seriously without threat of harassment.

I came in at 7:00 that morning before any students and most faculty and staff were in the building. Even if you were still asleep, these fliers would wake you up:

CONFERENCE ON
MAKING SCHOOLS SAFE FOR GAY, LESBIAN,
BISEXUAL, AND TRANSGENDERED KIDS

MAY 5
ABINGTON STATE UNIVERSITY

SEE MS. FISCHER FOR MORE INFORMATION

That's all the fliers said, but it was enough to get the basic information across and let students who were interested contact me without having to take a major risk. Sure, they'd have to let me know they wanted to go, but I would keep it confidential.

George and I had been talking about the need to support GLBT students for five years—as long as we've worked together. Our major goal has always been to provide a safe educational environment for students. We were concerned about safety and violence prevention long before people were talking about it on the state and national level. Our high school is an urban school and the student population is diverse: 80 percent African American or Caribbean American, 7 percent Mexican American, 10 percent European American, and 3 percent "United Nations." When racial violence threatens to erupt due to local or national issues, we address it immediately through forums, class discussion, and counseling.

I've heard George state his philosophy to teachers and community groups so many times now I can give it myself.

> In order to provide a safe environment in this high school, we have to open up as many communication channels as we possibly can. The students who have difficulties here are students that don't have a place where they feel they belong. They are alienated from peers, counselors, teachers, administrators, and parents. They feel alone and misunderstood. It's our job to identify the risk factors that break down communication and create new ways for students to let us know that they need support. We can't ignore the facts; our job is to keep kids in school and learning.

That's not to say it's been easy for George to back an initiative to support GLBT students. He's honest with me about having to deal with his own homophobia, although this is something he doesn't discuss publicly. There's plenty of pressure for a high school principal in an urban school to present a tough persona, and George is aware of that. But George is tough in the right way. He's assertive and willing to make hard decisions that he believes are right and then take the flack that inevitably follows.

So plastering the halls with these neon fliers was the culmination of a lot of events in this building that most students and teachers hadn't really had on their radar screens. I suppose it became more apparent to us that we had an issue in the school after we initiated the pizza lunches for students. The purpose of these lunches was to keep communication lines open. Every Wednesday we would have a free pizza lunch for a different homeroom group. During lunch we would open the discussion up to the students, and they could talk about whatever concerns they had. All students were given the chance to come over the course of the school year. The discussion would range from no soap in the bathrooms to climate in the building, sexual harassment, bullying, cafeteria food, pass time between classes, and locker room stink. The topic of GLBT kids came up once in awhile. I remember one lunch at which kids were making comments like, "Can you imagine two girls doing it? How disgusting!"

Later, George had the idea that we should start an Adopt-a-Clergy Program. It was part of his goal to increase communication with the community and provide students with another means of support. The purpose was to introduce priests, pastors, rabbis, and ministers to students so that they could get to know each other. The clergy would come to the pizza lunches and help to facilitate the discussions. Then, if the students wanted to talk to the clergy further on any issues, they could call their "clergy of choice" on their own. Phone numbers were available, but it was up to the kids. It became a type of mentoring program.

People were a little suspicious of having clergy talking with students at first. They wanted to know about the First Amendment and the separation of church and state. But George got the clergy to sign a memorandum of agreement pledging to participate in the program without proselytizing. There were ground rules that they had to adhere to. The clergy involved were part of the Interfaith Clergy Council, so we had all faiths involved.

The Adopt-a-Clergy Program was another step toward assisting students with a broad range of needs, but we still didn't have any way to give students the opportunity to discuss issues around sexual orientation. As far as we knew, the only one on the faculty who was talking about homosexuality in the classroom was the health teacher. In fact, it seemed to be a topic that everyone else avoided. We knew from the educational literature that as many as 10 percent of our students could be dealing with questions about being gay, lesbian, bisexual, or transgendered. However, we didn't know who these students were and, if the discussion was taking place, we hadn't heard about it. These students were invisible to us and the rest of the school.

That's why the conference seemed like a logical next step. After putting up the fliers, I headed to my office in the guidance department. I had a busy day. There were about six students to see and a mile-long list of phone calls to return. Somewhere around 11:00 while classes were in session, I finally emerged from my office to take a break and headed down the hall toward the main office. In every direction I saw neon fliers that had been ripped up, stepped on, and mutilated all over the floor. I turned the corner toward the cafeteria and the scene was identical. On every floor and hallway I checked neon confetti littered the hallway.

I hurried back to George's office and, as usual, there was a line waiting to see him. I asked Mona, his secretary, if there was a chance I could get in to see him.

"I don't know. I'll ask him as soon as he's done with Mr. Ritter. He's had a lot of unscheduled meetings this morning."

As I turned to go back to my office, George opened the door and Harold Ritter, one of the senior history faculty, was emerging. Neither one of them looked happy.

Before Mona could get a word in, George said, "Ms. Fischer, do you have a minute?"

I entered the office and sat down at the long conference table that extended down from George's desk. As always it was piled with stacks of proposals, state laws and regulations, and reports. His phone was ringing and several lines were blinking. Today the room felt like more of a war room than a principal's office.

"Have you seen the hallways?" he asked.

"That's why I'm here."

"I've had a few visitors. Harold Ritter wanted to know why we wanted kids to go to a conference on homosexuality. He wanted to know what our goals were. When I said we wanted to set up a support system for students who were gay, lesbian, and bisexual, he said he didn't have any of those kids in his classes. He wants to know if this is something particular kids have been asking for or just our attempt to be politically correct. Harold says we don't have any problems with gays and lesbians in the school now and this could easily incite something. 'Those fliers on the floor are just the beginning of your problems, George,' he says to me. 'The students are trying to tell you something and you better listen to them. We've got enough fire kegs in this building ready to explode over racial issues. We don't need to start our own fire.'"

"Did you tell him that there ARE gay kids in this school? There are gay kids in every school in the United States!"

"Sure, I did. But I can't honestly say that they've come to us and asked for this, can I? I told him it was just like trying to reduce heart disease. We know what you do to reduce the risk of a heart attack: stop smoking, get exercise, and watch your diet. We also know that kids who are struggling with their sexual orientation are at risk for dropping out of school, drug abuse, suicide, and a lot of other things. So we have to figure out what we can do to reduce the risk that they'll choose those options. We need to help them get answers to their questions in a safe environment where peers and staff won't harass them."

"Harold doesn't like conflict. He doesn't understand the issues and thinks they'll go away if we ignore them."

"Harold was mild compared to our arch conservative John Askew. John asked me how I could possibly endorse the idea of the high school supporting attendance at a conference on sexual immorality. He says, 'You might not think so, George, but there are still a lot of people in this community, including me, that believe that homosexuality is an abomination. You're going to raise a lot of hackles if you try to promote a lifestyle that many people in this community view as immoral. You can put your foot down and squash this right now.' I realized he was here to deliver his opinion and wasn't about to listen. I tried to talk with him but his is the last mind I'm going to change."

"Have you had any students down here complaining?" I asked.

"Not yet. Have you heard from any students who want to go?"

"No, but I'm not surprised. Given the condition of those fliers, I'm sure any kids who thought about wanting to go are having second thoughts."

"Seems like we have to just wait it out. I've only heard from a few teachers. I'm expecting phone calls from parents once the kids go home. Just let me know if you hear kids talking. And let me know right away if anyone wants to go."

"George, I have an idea. Tomorrow is the pizza lunch and three clergy members are planning on attending. Why don't I ask the students what they think about starting an Allies group to discuss GLBT issues?"

"I'm sure the topic will come up whether you initiate it or not, so you might as well structure it to see what the students are thinking. It might be a chance to educate a few kids about the needs."

"Makes sense. I'll prepare some questions that allow them to talk but also help them to consider the value of such a group. I'll also call the clergy so they know what the topic will be and have a chance to think about it ahead of time."

I thought I had better see if George and I were on the same page for the long run.

"Of course, if there are kids that want to go to this conference, they are going to hear about other schools that have started Gay–Straight Alliances. Other schools have been able to enlist faculty or staff who will act as sponsors for the group. At minimum, they have to be willing to provide a safe room for the kids to meet after school. An advisor should help moderate the discussions and assist with activities the kids may want to be involved in," I reminded him.

"Well, I don't have an answer to that. Can you do it, Renee?"

"George, I'm already running four support groups in this school. I can't be seen as the only person who deals with identity issues."

"O.K. Who would be an advisor?"

"Right now we don't have any teachers in this school who have identified themselves publicly as gay or lesbian. I know they exist, but it could be too threatening for them to be seen as promoting a particular orientation. Besides, it's not necessarily good to expect gay or lesbian teachers to be the standard bearers for these things. But I don't know of any straight teachers who are willing or able to stick their necks out. The teachers who might support this idea are already involved in one or more extracurricular activities and they're feeling overwhelmed. The rest are afraid that they'll be suspected of being gay themselves. We may need to use community resources."

"As far as I'm concerned, the more we work with community agencies, the better. But I have to know that students want this first."

At the pizza luncheon the next day, clergy from Jewish, Lutheran, and Unitarian traditions attended. I prepared a series of questions that I thought would ground the discussion. The clergy and I primarily facilitated the meeting and listened to student response, although we all asked thought-provoking questions when it seemed appropriate. First, I explained that some high schools across the country had established Allies groups for students who were interested in discussing GLBT issues and asked if they thought we should start such a group. The students didn't need much prompting; their responses followed each other in rapid fire.

"I think we should have a group like this. Everybody should be open in our school."

"What? You are looking to start trouble. What if students are against this group?"

"Yeah, the administration won't let us have a KKK group, so why have a homosexuality group?"

"We can't have a hate group on campus, so why is it O.K. to have an Allies group? What if someone wanted to start an Anti-Allies group?"

Then I asked what the reasons might be for having such a group.

"For one thing, high school prepares you for college where you are exposed to all kinds of people."

"True, and what about right now? Where else do kids who want to know about homosexuality have to gather and meet?"

"I think it would be more negative than positive. There are some things I don't need to know. What about being in the locker room changing? I'd be very uncomfortable knowing someone was gay."

I asked them what they were fearful of.

"I think we shouldn't be afraid. It's worse to be ignorant regarding sexual matters."

"But if we're not comfortable, why *force* us to accept it?"

"No one was comfortable when women and Blacks started fighting for their rights!"

"Those are two different things."

"Are they? What about the fact that the largest number of adolescent suicides is among young people with gender diversity?"

I asked them if it would be worthwhile to have an Allies club in school if it saved a life.

"Of course!"

"That's what they have psychiatrists for. School is calm now. It will start problems if 'they' are here."

" 'They' are the same people you know now."

"No one is trying to push homosexuality on anyone else. It's about keeping people from being alone and isolated."

Finally, I asked them what the goals of such a group should be if we were to establish it.

"Well, first, it shouldn't be an administrative decision. It should be up to a student vote."

"The goal is to provide a safe environment for everyone."

"Yeah, it's about getting educated so we won't be uncomfortable."

"Besides, if any group disrupts the education process, they will be asked to leave."

"This is the same discussion they had when they desegregated schools in Kansas and when we talk about gays in the military."

"I used to be uncomfortable around gays. I had strong negative feelings about seeing guys holding hands and kissing. *I* had to learn, too."

Although the clergy didn't have much of a chance to speak, they did occasionally share their experiences. It was clear that at least two of the clergy had dealt with the issue within their respective congregations. They talked about family members who weren't straight or mentioned that they were Parents, Families, and Friends of Lesbian's and Gays (PFLAG) members. It would have been a lot harder being the only adult in the discussion. There was no doubt that student opinions were all over the map. While some may have thought twice about their beliefs, it was obvious that many held the same position coming out of the session as they did coming in.

After that discussion, a few of the students had regular contact with the clergy who were sensitive to GLBT issues. The clergy were open to these discussions and, although we didn't know who the kids were or what their interests or concerns were, we knew that they were contacting the clergy about gender diversity.

On Thursday I typed up my notes from the meeting and shared them with George. I was surprised to hear that he hadn't gotten any complaints from parents. Maybe kids weren't about to talk about this with their parents. However, I still hadn't heard from any students who wanted to go to the conference.

During last period our secretary, Helen, buzzed me and said that Stacey Whitman wanted to talk with me but wouldn't say what she wanted. I thought she might have heard that she was admitted to one of the highly selective colleges she had applied to.

Stacey stopped by after school. She came into the office and simply said, "Ms. Fischer, I want to go to the conference and so does Alisha Hammond."

By the next day there were two other female students who wanted to go. I gave them each information about the conference that was to be held the following Friday at Abington State University, and they were excused from classes for the day.

The Monday morning after the conference the four girls were in my office.

"Ms. Fischer, that conference was fantastic!" they chimed.

"Yeah, there were kids from high schools and colleges all over this area. Did you know they already have an Allies group at Plainsville High School?"

"It was so exciting to hear Kevin Jennings talk about his experience as a high school teacher and then what's happening all over the United States!"

"Ms. Fischer, we want to start an Allies group here. We're not the only ones who think this is important."

Later that morning I got in to see Mr. Foster.

"George, there are four students who want to start an Allies group. I have so many concerns regarding safety, policies, procedures, and staffing. And I just can't take on one more advising responsibility now. What should we do?"

Discussion Questions

1. What is the impetus for starting a group for students who want to discuss issues around gender diversity?
2. What are the attitudes of teachers, students, and administration toward the establishment of a support group for students who are GLBT?
3. What do we know from research about adolescents and sexual identity that would support or dispute the establishment of a support group for students who are GLBT?
4. What responsibilities do teachers (both gay and straight) have with regard to students who have questions about sexual orientation?
5. What can be done in schools and in the community to promote a greater understanding of the issues related to gender diversity and the implications for our society?
6. How can the public schools work in a constructive manner with parents, community groups, and religious organizations that disagree with a homosexual lifestyle on a moral basis?

The Case of Sam Meyers

He was so excited. He had finally made it—his first teaching position. Wow! His partner Jesse had been encouraging him to become a teacher for a long time now, so they went out to celebrate once Sam received his teaching contract in the mail.

Sam did not fit the typical early childhood special educator stereotype. For one thing, Sam decided to become a teacher late in his career. Prior to teaching, he worked at a hospital in the clerical field. For another, he was male and older. Born with a degenerative eye disease, Sam also had a visual disability. As a result, he was considered legally blind. He had had eye surgery, which helped with his vision; however, he still wore coke bottle glasses.

The interview process was difficult for Sam. His first interview was with a panel that included district office personnel, principals, and teachers. One of the principals on the panel, Cameron, was in his second year. He is a commanding principal who has high expectations. When members of the community are asked about him, they often reply, "He's tough." Prior to becoming a principal he taught for twenty years.

Sam was nervous during his panel interview. He stumbled with his answers and he didn't fit the typical teacher stereotype. Cameron didn't want to hire him. He didn't think that Sam would be a good teacher. As a result, he almost didn't get the job. However, despite Cameron's objection, the panel decided to take a chance on Sam. They could see his potential and approved him for the next round of interviews. Sam now had several interviews at school sites with various principals in the district.

During this time, Sam interviewed at Howe Elementary with Mrs. Morehead, who was finishing her first year as principal. She had been hired the previous January when the prior principal moved on to open a new elementary school. Mrs. Morehead was very different from the prior principal, and as a result the parents were skeptical. She was still learning the ropes. Mrs. Morehead had heard good things about Sam from the first-grade teacher where he had done his student teaching.

"He's a great teacher," the cooperating teacher said. "He really knows his stuff. He got along great with the kids and their parents."

Mrs. Morehead was thrilled. "That's wonderful! Thanks." She had found a teacher. Finally, Sam was offered a job as an early childhood special educator working with young children with autism.

The families of the children who attended Howe Elementary School were primarily from the lower socioeconomic level. It was located in a suburban area of a popular vacation destination. In the past, the school had been considered an award-winning school; however, over time, the achievement scores at the school declined. Most of the families in the neighborhood were conservative Christian, as were many of the families throughout the county. The majority of the parents worked in the tourism industry and often worked second or third shift. Many of the parents did not have any formal education past twelfth grade, as the local industry made it easy for them to get jobs without a postsecondary education.

As a result of the arduous interview process, Sam was even more eager to start his new career. New teachers to the district report fifteen days prior to the first day of school. This time is spent attending new teacher meetings, getting the lay of the land, and setting up their classrooms. Sam also spent time with the other new teachers, sharing his enthusiasm for starting a new career. About ten days in, the returning teachers came back to school. That first day as everyone was being introduced, Sam was introduced to Hannah. "Hi. It's nice to meet you," she said.

"It's nice to meet you too," replied Sam. "I'm really excited to be here."

"I guess I'm going to be your mentor," she said. This additional assignment had caught her by surprise. Along with teaching full-time, Hannah was also enrolled in a doctoral program in special education at the local university. Hannah was in her ninth year of teaching, her first in an early childhood special education program. Sam was to be her first mentee.

"We're going to have a blast this year," she said. "My classroom is right next to yours. I'd be happy to share anything I have."

Paraprofessionals report two days before school starts. Therefore, when it was finally time to meet his new assistants, he was ready. Julia arrived first. Most of the staff considered Julia to be a straight arrow. She was a conservative Christian. Most of her conversation with the staff revolved around her church activities and her Christian faith. She was the mother of three and devoted to her family.

Miley entered next. She was married and the mother of two small children. Although Miley was also a member of a conservative Christian church, her lifestyle was more liberal than Julia's. She drank, used profanity, and had tattoos. Even though Miley identified herself as a Christian, she didn't fit the same profile that Julia did.

Sam said hello and welcomed them to the new year.

"Good morning, I'm so glad you're here. I'm really looking forward to teaching with you this year. My name is Sam and this is my first year. I've spent the past fifteen years working in a hospital as a clerk."

Julia was the first to introduce herself.

"I'm Julia." she said. "I'm married and have four children. I've been working in this classroom for two years," Julia told Sam.

"And I'm Miley. I'm married and have two young girls. I've been working in this classroom for the past year."

Throughout the day, they each shared a bit more about themselves. At lunch Julia talked about her church.

"We're going to have such a busy weekend at church. The younger children are putting on a play for the older ones before they go off on their mission trip to the inner city. We're also having a barbeque at the church. The kids leave next week."

"Wow!" Sam replied. "You sound busy. My weekend will be filled with taking the dogs to the dog park and having a pool party on Sunday afternoon. Jesse and I have been together for almost twenty years and thought we should celebrate with a party for all of our friends. We're going to Disneyworld for our anniversary in December, but decided we'd have a party now, since most of our friends are off for the summer."

Well, Julia gasped! She had never worked with a gay man before. She was unsure of how Sam would do teaching young children with disabilities. He was so different from the teacher she had worked with last year. The previous teacher had shared the same religious beliefs.

Julia thought to herself, "I'm not sure I can do this. I'm not supposed to work with gay men. Can I even be in the room alone with him?"

Her belief system condemned homosexuality. Other than that it was wrong in the eyes of God, she knew little about homosexuality and questioned whether he would molest the children or whether they could "catch" homosexuality from him. Julia did not deal well with change and the prospect of working with Sam made her very nervous.

Julia made it through the day, but couldn't wait to go home and tell everyone about the gay teacher she was working with. Julia shared her day with her husband and family.

"Oh my goodness, the man I'm working with is a homosexual!" she exclaimed. "What am I supposed to do now? Does our faith allow me to be in a room alone with him?" she asked her husband.

"Yes," he replied. Julia's husband knew of other women at their church that worked with gay men. He also knew that they couldn't afford for Julia to quit her job. This response did not settle Julia's nerves. She was still very nervous about working with Sam.

Julia not only talked to her family about Sam, but also gossiped about Sam to other members of the community. In fact, the next day Julia was picking her daughter up who was babysitting for Joey, one of the students who would be in Sam's class.

As she came in the door, she immediately told Joey's mom, "The new teacher is gay. He just came out and told me. I couldn't believe it. This is not a good way to start off the year. I mean really, homosexuality is wrong! Doesn't he believe in God? I'm not sure how this year is going to go."

Well, what a chain of events this set off!

The parent was shocked. What did this mean? Could a gay man teach? How was this going to affect her son? The mom talked it over with her husband. She told him what Julia had told her, and they decided to call the school. She called Mrs. Morehead and was assured that Sam was a good teacher and that everything would be fine.

Unfortunately, she wasn't satisfied with the answer, and before the first day of school had even arrived, the mom called Sam. She told him that under no circumstances was he allowed in the bathroom alone with her son.

Sam was so stunned he could hardly respond. All he could say was, "I'll have to talk with the principal about this."

He ended the conversation as quickly as possible. Suddenly all the excitement of a new job popped like a giant balloon. He felt deflated, stigmatized, and confused. While he was not naïve about the possible objections there might be in this conservative town regarding his sexual orientation, he hadn't expected it to become an issue before school even started. He wondered how that parent had even heard that he was homosexual. Was it Julia or Miley who had contacted this family?

That night, as soon as Jesse got home, he talked to him about it.

"What should I do? I knew there was a possibility of being discriminated against because I was gay, but I didn't think it would happen. It's the Twenty-first Century! It's like when I was a kid and being discriminated against because of my vision all over again, except this time, the stakes are higher! What should I do?"

Jesse thought for a while and replied, "I'm not sure. Is there someone you could talk to at school? Perhaps you should talk to your principal about this."

"I told you about Hannah yesterday. Maybe I could talk to her. She might know what to do or be able to steer me in the right direction."

"O.K," Jesse replied. "I can't believe this has happened to you. I'm really sorry. I know how much you've wanted to become a teacher."

The next morning, after dropping his stuff in his room he headed right for Hannah.

"Joey's mom called yesterday. She told me, 'Under no circumstances are you allowed in the bathroom with my son.' What should I do? I can't believe it. I was so excited about my new job and now this."

Hannah couldn't believe it either! She reassured Sam that everything would be O.K. "You should go talk to Mrs. Morehead and tell her about the conversation. Maybe she can help."

"Thanks," Sam replied. "I'll think about it." Sam realized he probably needed to talk with the principal, but he didn't want to. After all, this was his first teaching job and he didn't want to mess it up.

Discussion Questions

1. What are the issues regarding sexual orientation that Sam, the other teachers, the families, and school must address?
2. What are the beliefs about sexual orientation held by the major stakeholders in the case?
3. What legal precedents and established standards of practice can be used as guidelines for those involved?
4. What resources and supports are available for Sam, the family involved, and the school district?
5. What short- and long-term goals can be set that will assist all parties to deal with similar situations in the future?

References

Adams, D. C., & Carson, E. S. (2006). Gay-straight alliances: One teacher's experience. *Journal of Poverty, 10*(2), 103–111.

Anderson, D. A. (1995). Lesbian and gay adolescents: Social and developmental considerations. In G. Unks (Ed.), *The gay teenager* (pp. 17–28). New York: Routledge.

Anderson, J. D. (1996). Out as a professional educator. In D. R. Walling (Ed.), *Open lives, safe schools* (pp. 17–28). Bloomington, IN: Phi Delta Kappa.

Blackburn, M. V., & Buckley, J. F. (2005). Teaching queer-inclusive English language arts. *Journal of Adolescent & Adult Literacy, 49*(3), 202–212.

Blount, J. M. (2000). Spinsters, bachelors, and other gender transgressors in school employment, 1850–1990. *Review of Educational Research, 70*(1), 83–99.

Boyd, B. F. (1999). Should gay and lesbian issues be discussed in elementary school? *Childhood Education, 76*(1), 40.

Cohen, H. S. (Producer) & Chasnott, D. (Producer & Director). (1997). *It's elementary: Talking about gay issues in school* [Motion picture]. (Available from Women's Educational Media, San Francisco)

Commonwealth of Massachusetts Governor's Commission on Gay and Lesbian Youth. (1993). Making schools safe for gay and lesbian youth: Breaking the silence in schools and in families. Boston: Author. In G. Remafedi (Ed.), *Death by denial: Studies of suicide in gay and lesbian teenagers.* Boston: Alyson Publications.

Countryman, L. W., & Ritley, M. R. (2001). *Gifted by otherness: Gay and lesbian Christians in the church.* Harrisburg, PA: Morehouse Pub.

Crew, L. (1997). Changing the church: Lessons learned in the struggle to reduce institutional heterosexism in the Episcopal Church. In J. T. Sears & W. L. Williams, (Eds.), *Overcoming heterosexism and homophobia: Strategies that work* (pp. 341–353). New York: Columbia University Press.

Daniel, P. L. (2007). Invitation to all: Welcoming gays and lesbians into my classroom and curriculum. *English Journal, 96*(5), 75–80.

DeJean, W. (2004). Gay male high school teachers. *Encounter, 17*(3), 19–23.

deVise, D. (2007, June 8). New sex-ed curriculum is urged for all schools. *The Washington Post*, p. B02.

Durgin-Clinchard, E. (1997). A three-legged stool: PFLAGs support, education and advocacy. In J. T. Sears & W. L. Williams (Eds.). *Overcoming heterosexism and homophobia: Strategies that work* (pp. 141–147). New York: Columbia University Press.

Federal Bureau of Investigation. (2006). *Uniform crime report: Hate crime statistics.* Washington, DC: U.S. Department of Justice, Federal Bureau of Investigation.

Gagnon, R. A. J. (2002). Gays and the Bible: A response to Walter Wink. *The Christian Century, 119*(17), 40–43.

Gallup Poll. (2007). *Homosexual relations.* Retrieved July 29, 2007, from http://www.galluppoll.com

Gay, Lesbian, and Straight Education Network. (GLSEN) (2002). *Ten things educators can do . . . Ten action points to ensure respect for all is taught in your school.* Retrieved July 25, 2007, from http://www.glsen.org

Gay, Lesbian, and Straight Education Network. (GLSEN) (1999). *Homophobia 101: Teaching respect for all.* Retrieved July 29, 2007, from http://www.glsen.org

Gay, Lesbian, and Straight Education Network. (GLSEN) (2006, March 14). *How to start a GLSEN chapter.* Retrieved July 29, 2007, from http://www.glsen.org/

Ginsberg, R. W. (1999, Fall). In the triangle/out of the circle: Gay and lesbian students facing the heterosexual paradigm. *Educational Forum, 64,* 46–56.

Gover, J. (1996). Gay youth in the family. In D. R. Walling (Ed.), *Open lives, safe schools* (pp. 173–182). Bloomington, IN: Phi Delta Kappa.

Hamilton, B. E., Minino, A. M., Martin, J. A., Kochanek, K. D., Strobino, D. M., & Guyer, B. (2007). Annual summary of vital statistics: 2005. *Pediatrics, 119,* 345–360.

Harbeck, K. M. (1997). *Gay and lesbian educators: Personal freedoms, public constraints.* Malden, MA: Amethyst Press.

Harris Interactive and GLSEN. (2005). *From teasing to torment: School climate in America, a survey of students and teachers.* New York: GLSEN.

Helminiak, D. (2000). *What the Bible really says about homosexuality.* Tajique, NM: Alamo Square Press.

Human Rights Campaign. (2001, February 13). *HRC calls on Congress to pass comprehensive hate crimes legislation as FBI releases final report detailing problem.* Retrieved March 18, 2001, from http://hrc.org/hrc/hrcnews/2001/010213FBIreport.asp

Hunter, J. (1996). New directions for lesbian, gay, and bisexual youth: Reflections on the Harvey Milk School. In L. M. Bullock, R. A. Gable, & Ridky, J. R. (Eds.), *Understanding individual differences: Highlights from the National Symposium on What Educators Should Know about Adolescents Who Are Gay, Lesbian, or Bisexual* (pp. 24–27). New York: Council for Exceptional Children.

Interfaith Alliance Foundation. (n.d.). *Discrimination against gays and lesbians in housing, employment, and education.* Retrieved July 11, 2002, from http://www.interfaithalliance.org

Jennings, K. (Ed.). (2005). *One teacher in 10* (2nd ed.). Los Angeles, CA: Alyson Books.

Jennings, K. (1996). "Together for a change": Lessons from organizing the Gay, Lesbian, and Straight Teachers Network. In D. R. Walling (Ed.), *Open lives, safe schools* (pp. 251–260). Bloomington, IN: Phi Delta Kappa.

Johnston, A. (1999). Out front. *Rethinking Schools, 13*(2), 1–7. Retrieved July 18, 2007 from http://www.rethinkingschools.org/archive/13_02/gay.shtml

Jones, R. (1999). "I don't feel safe here anymore." *American School Board Journal, 186,* 26–31.

Jones, S. L., & Yarhouse, M. A. (2000). *Homosexuality: The use of scientific research in the church's moral debate.* Downers Grove, IL: InterVarsity Press.

Kosciw, J. G., & Diaz, E. M. (2006). *The 2005 national school climate survey: The experiences of lesbian, gay, bisexual and transgender youth in our nation's schools.* New York: GLSEN.

Letts, W. J., & Sears, J. T. (1999). *Queering elementary education: Advancing the dialogue about sexualities and school.* Lanham, MD: Rowan and Littlefield.

Lipkin, A. (1996). The case for a gay and lesbian curriculum. In D. R. Walling (Ed.), *Open lives, safe schools* (pp. 47–69). Bloomington, IN: Phi Delta Kappa.

Lipkin, A. (2000). *Understanding homosexuality, changing schools.* Boulder, CO: Westview Press.

Lugg, C. A. (2003). Sissies, faggots, lezzies, and dykes: Gender, sexual orientation, and a new politics of Education? *Educational Administration Quarterly, 39*(1), 95–134.

Marcus, E. (1992). *The struggle for gay and lesbian equal rights, 1945–1990, an oral history.* NY: Harper Collins.

Markow, D., Liebman, M., & Dunbar, J. (2007, May 14). *Middle school poll.* National Association of Secondary School Principals and Phi Delta Kappa. Retrieved July 29, 2007 from http://www.pdkintl.org

Mukilteo School District. (n.d.) *Respect policy.* Retrieved July 29, 2007, from http://www.tolerance.org/rthas/section4_2_1.jsp

National Association of School Psychologists. (1999). *Position statement: Gay, lesbian, and bisexual youth.* Bethesda, MD: Author. (ERIC Document Reproduction Service No. ED 431 983)

National Education Association. (2006). *Strengthening the learning environment: A school employee's guide to gay, lesbian, bisexual, and transgender issues* (2nd ed.). Washington, DC: Author.

Nugent, R. (1997). Homophobia and the U.S. Roman Catholic clergy. In J. T. Sears & W. L. Williams (Eds.), *Overcoming heterosexism and homophobia: Strategies that work* (pp. 354–370). New York: Columbia University Press.

O'Conor, A. (1995). Breaking the silence: Writing about gay, lesbian, and bisexual teenagers. In G. Unks (Ed.), *The gay teenager* (pp. 13–17). New York: Routledge.

Office for Civil Rights. (2001, January). *Revised sexual harassment guidance: Harassment of students by school employees, other students, or third parties.* Washington, DC: Department of Education. Retrieved March 18, 2001, from http://www.ed.gov/offices/OCR

Parents, Families, and Friends of Lesbians and Gays. (PFLAG) (n.d. a). *Is homosexuality a sin?* Retrieved March 10, 2002, from http://www.pflag.org/store/resources/isitasin.html.

Parents, Families, and Friends of Lesbians and Gays. (PFLAG) (n.d. b). *About PFLAG.* Retrieved July 29, 2007, from www.pflag.org

Pharr, S. (1988). *Homophobia: A weapon of sexism.* Little Rock, AR: Women's Project, Chardon Press.

Prince, T. (1996). The power of openness and inclusion in countering homophobia in schools. In D. R. Walling (Ed.), *Open lives, safe schools* (pp. 29–34). Bloomington, IN: Phi Delta Kappa.

Remafedi, G. (Ed.). (1994). *Death by denial: Studies of suicide in gay and lesbian teenagers.* Boston: Alyson Publications.

Rogers, J. B. (2006). *Jesus, the Bible, and homosexuality: Explode the myths, heal the church.* Louisville, KY: Westminster John Knox Press.

Rosik, C. H., Griffith, L. K., & Cruz, A. (2007). Homophobia and conservative religion: Toward a more nuanced understanding. *American Journal of Orthopsychiatry, 77*(1), 10–19.

Roy, A. (1997). Language in the classroom: Opening conversations about lesbian and gay issues in senior high English. In J. T. Sears & W. L. Williams (Eds.), *Overcoming heterosexism and homophobia: Strategies that work* (pp. 209–217). New York: Columbia University Press.

Satcher, D. (2001). *The Surgeon General's call to action to promote sexual health and responsible sexual behavior.* Retrieved July 29, 2007 from http://www.surgeongeneral.gov/library/sexualhealth/call.htm

Sattel, S., Keyes, M., & Tupper, P. (1997). Sexual harassment and sexual orientation: The coaches' corner. In J. T. Sears & W. L. Williams (Eds.), *Overcoming heterosexism and homophobia: Strategies that work* (pp. 233–246). New York: Columbia University Press.

Schall, J., & Kauffmann, G. (2003). Exploring literature with gay and lesbian characters in the elementary school. *Journal of Children's Literature, 29*(1), 36–45.

Schniedewind, N., & Davidson, E. (2006). *Open minds to equality: A sourcebook of learning activities to affirm diversity and promote equity* (3rd ed.). Milwaukee, WI: Rethinking Schools.

Sears, J. T. (1991). *Growing up gay in the South.* New York: Haworth.

Sears J. T. (1992). Educators, homosexuality, and homosexual students: Are personal feelings related to professional beliefs? In K. M. Harbeck (Ed.), *Coming out of the closet: Gay and lesbian students, teachers, and curricula* (pp. 29–79). New York: Haworth.

Sears, J. T. (1995). Black–gay or gay–black? Choosing identities or identifying choices. In G. Unks (Ed.), *The gay teenager* (pp. 135–158). New York: Routledge.

Sears, J. T. (1997). Thinking critically/intervening effectively about homophobia and heterosexism. In J. T. Sears, & W. L. Williams, (Eds.), *Overcoming heterosexism and homophobia: Strategies that work* (pp. 13–48). New York: Columbia University Press.

Sileo, T. W. (2004). *Educational equity and social justice for all students.* Paper presented at the 2004 Council for Exceptional Children Annual Convention and Expo, New Orleans, LA.

Toynton, R. (2006). "Invisible other": Understanding safe spaces for queer learners and teachers in adult education. *Studies in the Education of Adults, 38*(2),178–194.

Unks, G. (1995). Thinking about the gay teen. In G. Unks (Ed.), *The gay teenager* (pp. 3–12). New York: Routledge.

Uribe, V. (1995). Project 10: A school-based outreach to gay and lesbian youth. In G. Unks (Ed.), *The gay teenager* (pp. 203–210). New York: Routledge.

White, M. (n.d.) *What the Bible says—and doesn't say—about homosexuality.* Retrieved August 21, 2007, from www.soulforce.org

Wink, W. (2002). To hell with gays? *Christian Century, 119*(12), 32–34.

Zirkel, P. A. (1999). Are you gay? *Phi Delta Kappan, 81*(4), 332–333.

12

Religion

Just as ethnic, linguistic, and cultural diversity in the United States is expanding, so is the U.S. religious landscape. Some would argue that no other nation on Earth has experienced such wholesale changes in its religious composition as has the United States (Eck, 2001). This assertion is based primarily on the numbers of individuals reporting allegiance to various religious groups since colonial times (Ostling, 1999). Others suggest that diversity of religious affiliation has always been a hallmark of the United States, especially in the last century, but the shifting content of beliefs within and between the various denominations and religions constitutes the most significant changes on the religious landscape (Williams, 2000). Whether change is viewed in terms of numbers or content of belief, we agree with Sewall (1999) that religion is not simply a cultural artifact. It is a separate entity in the kaleidoscope of diversity that warrants considerable attention from educators. In using the term religion we do not reject the idea of spirituality, which is increasingly under discussion as an important component of the education process. Rather, we recognize that religious affiliation with a particular group, no matter how tenuous, is an important marker that distinguishes individuals from those who report having no religion. However, spirituality may be present or absent, regardless of religious affiliation.

A person's religious and spiritual convictions often shape his or her belief system or world view. As we have stressed in the "reframe the problem" step of the Decision-Making Scaffold, people are most likely to work toward accomplishing educational goals that are aligned with their belief system. Conversely, they can be expected to oppose school-based decisions or programs that they perceive as antithetical to their beliefs. The public schools must establish and maintain a broad range of policies that are not value neutral. These include statements regarding curriculum content, discipline, attendance, extracurricular clubs, holiday celebration, school-sponsored events, dress codes, and nutrition. As we will discuss, there is considerable agreement by religious and educational leaders about many of these issues. Nevertheless, the diversity of religious and spiritual beliefs within the community can be one predictor of the types of disagreements that may emerge. Therefore, it is helpful to understand the changing religious landscape in the United States to better address the concerns of families that the public schools serve.

Religious Diversity in the United States

One primary reason that Europeans came to the United States was to escape religious persecution. A 1776 survey of American religious congregations found British groups dominant. Congregationalists, Presbyterians, Baptists, Episcopalians, and Quakers constituted almost 80 percent of America's congregations (Ostling, 1999). Catholics had 65 congregations and Jews had 5 synagogues. By 1890, Catholics claimed first place with 7.3 million, a place that they have kept ever since due to the diversity of Protestant denominations. When asked, "What is your religion, if any?" individuals responded as displayed in Table 12.1. Americans today report a high degree of religiosity, with anywhere between 60 and 90 percent of individuals reporting affiliation with some religion, depending on how the question is posed (Kosmin, Mayer, & Keysar; 2001; Ostling, 1999; Pew Forum, 2002). However, only about half of the population attend church weekly (Gollnick & Chinn, 2006).

TABLE 12.1   *Self Described Religion Identification of U. S. Adult Population in 2001[*] (Weighted Estimate of Top Twenty Responses)*

Religious Group	Number	Percentage
Catholic	50,873,000	24.5
Baptist	33,830,000	16.3
Christian—no denomination supplied	14,190,000	6.8
Methodist/Wesleyan	14,150,000	6.8
Lutheran	9,580,000	4.6
Presbyterian	5,596,000	2.7
Protestant—no denomination supplied	4,647,000	2.2
Pentecostal/Charismatic	4,407,000	2.1
Episcopalian/Anglican	3,451,000	1.7
Jewish	2,831,000	1.3
Mormon/Latter-Day Saints	2,787,000	1.3
Churches of Christ	2,503,000	1.2
Nondenominational	2,489,000	1.2
Congregational/United Church of Christ	1,378,000	0.7
Jehovah's Witness	1,331,000	0.6
Assemblies of God	1,106,000	0.5
Muslim/Islamic	1,104,000	0.5
Buddhist	1,082,000	0.5
Evangelical	1,032,000	0.5
Church of God	944,000	0.5

[*]Total US Adult Population 18+ was 207,980,000
Source: Kosmin, Mayer, & Keysar (2001).

Non-Christian religions also are part of our diversity. The Jewish community constitutes about 3 percent of the population, although only about half identify with Judaism as a religion (Kosmin et al., 2001). Younger American Jews marrying Gentiles are now a majority for the first time in history (Ostling, 1999; Williams, 2000). Estimates indicate that currently there are between 6 and 8 million Muslims, between 1 and 4 million Buddhists, and about a million Hindus in the United States (Moore, 2005; The Pluralism Project, n.d) although publicists for these groups give much greater estimates. This is often because these groups have comparatively little organizational infrastructure.

There is relatively little reliable survey data on the views of U.S. youth toward religion. While an increasing number of adults identify themselves as not having a religion or consider themselves atheist, agnostic, humanist, or secular (Kosmin et al., 2001), this trend is not clearly observed in the best data available on the religious beliefs of U.S. teenagers (Smith, Denton, Faris, & Regnerus, 2002). Interestingly, while measures of religious affiliation have declined somewhat from 1976 to 1996, measures of subjective religiosity are relatively stable. For example, during those years a majority of U.S. adolescents consistently reported that religious faith is important to them, and nearly two-thirds said they prayed daily or weekly. Furthermore, females exhibited more subjective religiosity than males, and Blacks said religion was important more than Whites, Hispanics, or Asians. Two-thirds closely agreed with the religious ideas of their parents. As more reliable research is conducted, it will be interesting to see if the trend toward "spirituality" rather than "religion" among adults (Ostling, 1999) is also true of youth. Regardless of how Americans define their beliefs, there is a growing consensus that these beliefs cannot be left at the schoolhouse door.

Why Religion Is an Issue in Public Schools

Many scholars interested in public education and the law are convinced that new models for understanding the relationship of religion and education, or church and state, must be developed. Charles Haynes, a senior scholar with the Freedom Forum First Amendment Center, has emphasized this concern by stating, "If we are going to sustain the American experiment—E Pluribus Unum—then we can't afford culture wars in our schools that rend apart the fabric of our communities and undermine the education of our children. We need a fresh, bold approach to the conflicts—an approach that enables us to live with even our deepest differences" (Haynes, 1999, p. 7).

This need for a new approach is apparent in many arenas. This is especially apparent when considering the acrimony that has grown up between public educators and the Religious Right (Brown, 2002; Herrington, 2000; Sewall, 1999). Conservative Christian groups have been viewed by many educators as irrelevant and by others as sinister. Nevertheless, there has been a resurgence of conservative religion in the United States. Conservative churches such as Southern Baptists, Assemblies of God, Seventh-Day Adventists, and Church of the Nazarene have experienced significant increases in membership while more mainline churches have lost members steadily (Nord, 1995). In fact, two-thirds of Americans are reported to believe that, "Liberals have gone too far in trying to keep religion out of the schools and government" (Lupu, Elwood, Davis, Masci, Tuttle, & Bert, 2007). There is little doubt that a conservative Christian agenda continues to have broad-based support in the United States. In addition, public school personnel sometimes view the beliefs and customs of adherents to Islam as conservative and intrusive.

The fear and prejudice resulting from terrorist attacks by Muslim extremists around the world and in the United States on September 11, 2001 have cast a spotlight on the growing Muslim population in the United States. While unsettling incidents of anti-Muslim or anti-Arab hate crimes have been reported (Lynch, 2007), many political and religious leaders and communities have rallied to support their Muslim, Middle Eastern, and Arab neighbors (and Muslims have reciprocated in the dialogue (Nahi-Tobias & Garfield, 2003; Southern Poverty Law Center, 2001). Many Americans are motivated like never before to gain a better understanding of the tenents of Islam. Nevertheless, many Muslims feel that some Americans act in prejudicial ways toward them simply due to their religious affiliation, country of origin, or physical appearance (see Box 12.1).

Failed Models of Religion in the Public School

To evaluate models that describe the relationship of religion to public education, one must have knowledge of constitutional law. The Constitution does not speak about religion, apart from a statement that no religious test be required for public office, because the framers believed that the federal government had no power to infringe on religious liberty (Nord, 1995). However, the states did not agree that religious liberty was assured by the Constitution, and therefore the First Congress added the Bill of Rights, including the First Amendment, which states that: "Congress shall make no laws respecting an establishment

BOX 12.1 • *Iraqi American Teenager Faces Discrimination*

On the final day of school at Mesquite Junior High School in Phoenix, Arizona, 13-year-old Mustafa Abdul Razzaq decided to stay home because it was a halfday. His mother got a phone call from the police investigating a school bomb threat that he allegedly instigated. A parent had found the threat written in her son's yearbook, although it was later determined that another student signed Mustafa's name. While the police viewed it as a prank, the family believes it is a religious bias incident that was one of many over the years that have targeted the boy because he is a Muslim.

The young Iraqi American told the police through tears that another boy had written the yearbook comment, and he had confronted the boy when he heard about it. The boy only laughed and walked away.

This is just one of many times Mustafa's been humiliated or labeled a terrorist since September 11, 2001. He says kids have told him to "go hijack a plane and run into a building" verbally and on notes left on his desk.

Last year Mustafa was made fun of when he came to school dressed in traditional Saudi Arabian garb for a class assignment. They called him Osama bin Laden and said his parents were terrorists.

"Some of the teachers in the junior high don't care," Mustafa says of the discriminatory teasing he's endured. "They don't want to get into this kind of stuff."

Source: Lynch (2007).

of religion, or prohibiting the free exercise thereof." The first part of the amendment has come to be called the establishment clause and the second part the free exercise clause.

Given these legal principles, it becomes easier to understand why two models of schooling have failed (Haynes, 1999; Haynes & Thomas, 2001). The *sacred public school* was one in which one religion, that of the dominant culture, dictated school policy. While this model was prevalent in the early history of the United States, many problems were encountered. For example, Catholics and Protestants argued over which versions of the Bible and which prayers should be used in public schools in the 1840s (Lupu et al., 2007). The sacred public school has been determined unconstitutional and decried as unjust today. More recently, the *naked public school* model has been espoused. This model promotes a strict interpretation of the idea of separation of church and state and, therefore, declares schools to be religion-free zones. While the intention of this model was to eliminate conflict based on a determination that the state must be neutral on issues of religion, some have charged that this approach is equally as unjust as the sacred school and possibly unconstitutional. Critics of the naked public school model point out that eliminating religion from the curriculum is, in fact, a violation of neutrality in that secularism becomes the de facto curriculum (Nord, 1995). Few educators would deny that concepts of history such as nationalism, imperialism, slavery, and capitalism have important religious aspects (Douglass, 2002; Sewall, 1999). Furthermore, difficult issues such as anti-Semitism or evolution must be discussed rather than avoided in the context of their religious dimensions. In fact, critics of the naked school argue that schools have a responsibility to teach values and the religions that have established the moral foundations of our civilization. Because they do not, silence on issues of religion is equally as discriminatory as silence on issues of gender, race, and culture.

The Civil Public School

The *civil public school* is a model that holds promise for fair application of First Amendment principles in public education. This model avoids inculcation of religious views while promoting respect for religious belief or unbelief. Furthermore, the civil public school recognizes the importance of study about religion as part of a good education. Remarkably, twenty-four religious and educational groups have issued a joint statement entitled "Religious Liberty, Public Education and the Future of American Democracy: A Statement of Principles" (Haynes & Thomas, 2001) that outlines the commitments of the civil public school. Organizations as disparate as People for the American Way, the National Association of Evangelicals, the Anti-Defamation League, and the Council on Islamic Education have endorsed this statement.

Current Religious Issues in the Public Schools

Many issues related to religion have caused tremendous controversy in public schools. Some of these issues, such as student religious discussion, religious activity in schools, religion in the curriculum, religious holidays, released time for religious observance and instruction, and student dress, have been either challenged in the courts or addressed by presidential directives and appear to have resolution. Of course, challenges to these resolutions continue, but adequate consensus from legal and educational sources exists to guide the development and implementation of good policy on these issues. Other thorny issues such as the teaching of evolution or sex education continue to reappear in the national news and on school board agendas. While guidance regarding these issues may be available, the results have not been adequate to satisfy many parents, teachers, students, and religious leaders. Furthermore, issues are emerging that relate to minority religions in the United States, such as Islam, that have only begun to surface nationally.

Legal guidance on any number of issues regarding religion and the schools is available from a variety of sources (Haynes & Thomas, 2001). In addition to the "Statement of Principles" just mentioned, another document entitled "Religion in the Public Schools: A Joint Statement of Current Law" (Religion in the Public Schools, 1995) was endorsed by 35 religious organizations (see Box 12.2). This statement addresses what is and is not permissible under the First Amendment. In a 1995 speech on religious liberty, President William Clinton stated that "The First Amendment does not . . . convert our schools into religion-free zones. . . . There are those who do believe our schools should be value neutral and that religion has no place inside the schools. But I think that wrongly interprets the idea of the wall between church and state. They are not the walls of the school" (Jurinski, 1998, p. 97). Clinton directed the U.S. secretary of education, Richard Riley, to issue guidelines regarding religious expression in public schools that reflected the Joint Statement (Riley, 1998). The purpose of these guidelines is to encourage the development of school district policy regarding religious expression and to inform teachers, students, and parents of their responsibilities. Many school districts have undertaken such policy development, and their efforts are instructive (Haynes & Thomas, 2001).

Consensus Issues

While nothing can preclude further challenges to any issues regarding the place of religion in schools, school districts that establish reasonable policies that involve all stakeholders are less likely to face ongoing disputes. For example, there are definite parameters under which student prayer and religious discussion can occur in public schools (Haynes & Thomas, 2001). Two Supreme Court cases deal directly with these issues (Lupu et al., 2007). In *Engel v. Vitale* (1962), the Supreme Court ruled that schools could not require students to say nonsectarian prayers in school since it violates the Establishment clause. The following year in *Abington School Board v. Schempp* (1963), the high court extended this ruling, deciding that a school-sponsored program of Bible reading was unconstitutional. Students may pray in a nondisruptive manner individually or in a group when not engaged in school activities or instruction. In fact, although the Supreme Court ruled in *Wallace v. Jaffree* (1985) that the state of Alabama could not require schools to set aside a moment of silence for prayer each day, schools may give students a moment of silence if the purpose is secular and does not emphasize prayer over other types of meditation. Furthermore, school officials may not mandate or organize prayer at graduation nor organize religious baccalaureate ceremonies. They must remain neutral regarding all religious activity. However, there are still issues of

BOX 12.2 • *Excerpt From "Religion in the Public Schools: A Joint Statement of Current Law"*

The Constitution permits much private religious activity in and about the public schools. Unfortunately, this aspect of constitutional law is not as well known as it should be. Some say that the Supreme Court has declared the public schools "religion-free zones" or that the law is so murky that school officials cannot know what is legally permissible. The former claim is simply wrong. And as to the latter, while there are some difficult issues, much has been settled. It is also unfortunately true that public school officials, due to their busy schedules, may not be as fully aware of this body of law as they could be. As a result, in some school districts some of these rights are not being observed.

We offer this statement of consensus on current law as an aid to parents, educators and students. . . .

Student Prayers

Students have the right to pray individually or in groups or to discuss their religious views with their peers so long as they are not disruptive. Because the Establishment Clause does not apply to purely private speech, students enjoy the right to read their Bibles or other scriptures, say grace before meals, pray before tests, and discuss religion with other willing student listeners. In the classroom students have the right to pray quietly except when required to be actively engaged in school activities (e.g., students may not decide to pray just as a teacher calls on them). In informal settings, such as the cafeteria or in the halls, students may pray either audibly or silently, subject to the same rules of order as apply to other speech in these locations. However, the right to engage in voluntary prayer does not include, for

example, the right to have a captive audience listen or to compel other students to participate.

Teaching About Religion

Students may be taught about religion, but public schools may not teach religion. As the U.S. Supreme Court has repeatedly said, "[i]t might well be said that one's education is not complete without a study of comparative religion, or the history of religion, and its relationship to the advancement of civilization." It would be difficult to teach art, music, literature and most social studies without considering religious influences. The history of religion, comparative religion, the Bible (or other scripture) as literature (either as a separate course or within some other existing course), are all permissible public school subjects. . . .

These same rules apply to the recurring controversy surrounding theories of evolution. Schools may teach about explanations of life on Earth, including religious ones (such as "creationism"), in comparative religion or social studies classes. In science class, however, they may present only genuinely scientific critiques of, or evidence for, any explanation of life on Earth, but not religious critiques (beliefs unverifiable by scientific methodology). Schools may not refuse to teach evolutionary theory in order to avoid giving offense to religion nor may they circumvent these rules by labeling as science an article of religious faith. Public schools must not teach as scientific fact or theory any religious doctrine, including "creationism," although any genuinely scientific evidence for or against any explanation of life may be taught. Just as they may neither advance nor inhibit any religious doctrine, teachers should not ridicule, for example, a student's religious explanation for life on Earth.

Source: Religion in the Public Schools (1995)

student religious expression where the U.S. courts appear to send conflicting messages (see Box 12.3) (Lynch, 2007).

Students may speak to their peers about religious topics as long as this speech does not constitute harassment of others. Students may participate in before- or after-school events with religious content, but school officials may neither discourage nor

BOX 12.3 • *Graduation Speech Dilemma*

Situation

One of your students is giving this year's valedictorian's address. She has finished writing the speech and has asked you, her favorite teacher, to read it over and give her your opinion. The speech includes the following statement in the final paragraph, "We all should be grateful to those who have helped us get to this important point in our education. It is because of the love of my family and my savior Jesus Christ that I stand before you today. I would encourage you to consider who you need to thank and not miss the opportunity to do so today."

Case Law

Supreme Court   *Lee v. Weisman* (1992): The practice by a school in Providence, Rhode Island, of allowing principals to ask members of the clergy to give commencement invocations and benedictions was prohibited.

   Santa Fe Independent School District v. Doe (2000): The Texas School District's policy permitting a student-elected chaplain to offer a nonsectarian, nonproselytizing prayer over the loud speaker at football games violates the Establishment Clause.

Lower Courts   In *Adler v. Duval County School Board* (2001): In Duval County, Florida, school officials adopted a policy letting high school seniors decide whether to choose a fellow student to give a brief opening and/or closing uncensored message at graduation. The Eleventh U.S. Circuit Court of Appeals ruled that the system for choosing the

student was permissible and, therefore, the school was not responsible for the religious content since they neither were responsible for the choice of the student nor screened the speech.

   ACLU v. Black Horse Pike Regional School District (1996): A similar procedure for choosing a commencement speaker in a New Jersey high school was invalidated by the Third U.S. Circuit Court of Appeals. As in the Florida school, the students chose the commencement speaker in advance of knowing the content of the speech. The student lead the attendees in prayer. The court ruled that the high school could not allow religious speech in the address. Citing *Lee V. Weisman* (1992), they argued that having a student lead in prayer was just as coercive as having a clergy person do so.

   Now Supreme Court Judge Aileto was on the Third U.S. Circuit Court at the time of the decision. He wrote the dissenting opinion, which held that the individual rights of the student to free expression should prevail over concerns about the establishment of religion.

Questions

1. What do recent court decisions regarding religious expression by students in school-sponsored events appear to agree and disagree upon?
2. What do you believe about a student's right to religious expression in public schools?
3. What would you do in the situation described above?

Sources: Dowling-Sendor (2001), Lupu et al. (2007), Mauro (2001).

---

encourage participation in such an event. The Equal Access Act gives student religious activities, including prayer and worship, the same access to public school facilities as are given to student secular activities.

   Legal decisions and state and professional standards encourage teachers to include religion in the school curriculum (Douglass, 2002; Elhoweris, Salend, & Whittaker, in press; Nord & Haynes, 1998). While public schools may not provide religious instruction, they may dismiss students to off-premises religious instruction. Teachers may teach *about* religion, including the Bible and other scripture. Therefore, both elementary and secondary teachers may teach the history of religion or the role of religion in history (Ayers & Reid, 2005; Moore, 2006). Similarly, they may discuss the influence of religion on art, music, and literature. Certainly this requires teachers to carefully research their content or provide guest speakers who are better acquainted with the topic. It is permissible to invite religious leaders to speak in public schools when their expertise is relevant to the curriculum, as long as they do not proselytize (Elhoweris et al., in press). It is the responsibility of educators to provide guest speakers with background on the students' developmental level and how the content of the presentation relates to the curriculum.

Consensus statements are also available regarding teaching civic values, student assignments, and clothing. Although schools must be neutral with respect to religion, they may teach civic values and virtue and the moral code that holds a community together. Furthermore, students may express their beliefs about religion in their assignments, and these products must be judged by ordinary academic standards. In regard to clothing, schools can adopt policies relating to student dress, but cannot prohibit religious attire. In addition, students may display religious messages on items of clothing to the same extent that they are permitted to display comparable secular messages. The First Amendment Center and the Freedom Forum are both rich resources for current updates on these topics.

One attribute of a civil public school is that students learn to discuss their fears of or prejudice against those they perceive as "other." Sometimes students will, intentionally or unintentionally, show disrespect toward another student's religious beliefs or practices (Elhoweris et al., in press). Responses to such acts of insensitivity and intolerance will vary depending upon the school's policies; the nature and setting of the act; and the history, age, and intent of the individuals involved. If the intent of the act was not to hurt others, teachers might want to deal with students privately or present the situation confidentially at a class meeting to discuss ways to avoid similar insensitive acts and to respond in a just and caring manner.

Unfortunately, educators also are likely to encounter students being intentionally intolerant of others, such as making disparaging remarks about sacred symbols, clothing, and jewelry. When this occurs, educators can act promptly and decisively to help their students learn that discriminatory and hurtful behaviors are unacceptable. Prompt, consistent, and firm responses to all acts of intolerance, harassment, and exclusion can minimize their negative effects and serve as a model for how students can react to them.

Controversial and Emerging Religious Issues in the Public Schools

Clearly, there has been tremendous progress in our understanding of the delicate relationship of religion and public education. While some would argue that the wall of separation is too high and others too low, the courts have produced enough case law on some issues to assist us in at least knowing where the wall stands. However, contentious issues remain. Often this is because the issues involved get to the core of religious belief for some, and they are unwilling to let the state make statements that they view as either immoral or false.

The teaching of evolution is one such issue that reappears over and over again, despite legal battles. Americans are divided on this issue. In a recent survey of religious belief in the United States, 51 percent agreed with the statement "Humans and other living things have evolved over time," whereas 42 percent believed they have existed in their present form only (Pew Research Center, 2006). Individuals who consider themselves religiously liberal are more likely to agree with the former statement than those who consider themselves to be religiously conservative. Consequently, it is important for teachers to understand the legal, educational, and philosophical factors affecting this debate.

The Teaching of Evolution.   In 1925 the famous "monkey law" trial took place in which John Scopes was convicted and fined for teaching evolution when Tennessee law made it a crime to teach anything but the biblical version of creation (Larson, 2006). Since then two Supreme Court and lower court decisions have involved the teaching of "creation science" alongside evolution theory (Nord, 1995)(see Box 12.4). Creation science teaches that Earth and most life forms came into existence suddenly about 6,000 years ago based upon a literal reading of the Biblical account. More recently, the Tagipahoa Parish Board of Education in Louisiana decided on a close vote to reject a proposal to teach creation science in its school. Subsequently, they crafted a disclaimer to be read by teachers in the district to students about to study the theory of evolution. In 1999 the Fifth Circuit Court of Appeals ruled that this disclaimer must be struck down because it had the effect of promoting religion. The Supreme Court refused to hear the case, although Justice Scalia, writing for the three dissenting judges, criticized the court for not allowing a school district to even suggest to students that other theories besides evolution are worthy of consideration.

Another battleground was established when the ten-member Kansas Board of Education voted to adopt new science standards that de-emphasize evolution in science classes and permit school boards to allow the teaching of theories of intelligent design (Haynes, 1999). Intelligent design posits that biological life is so complex that it must have been designed by an intelligent source, but does not explicitly identify the source as God. The American Civil Liberties Union responded by warning that they would take legal action if teaching this theory was permitted. Subsequently, Kansas voters removed conservative members of the State Board of Education, which has since repealed science guidelines questioning evolution, putting into effect new ones that reflect mainstream scientific views (Associated Press, 2007a). Their decision was undoubtedly influenced by the federal court ruling striking down a policy adopted by the Board of Education in Dover, Pennsylvania (Goodstein, 2005). Allies such as the National Council of Science, the National Association of Biology Teachers, and the American Civil Liberties Union oppose the Creation Science Association, which holds that there is a vast amount of scientific evidence that supports the biblical creation account (Matsumura, 1999). The Public Broadcasting System has produced an excellent series on evolution that discusses many of these issues in the schools and provides teachers and students with additional thought-provoking material (Public Broadcasting System, 2007).

Although the principles set forth by case law assist teachers in making informed decisions regarding this issue, there will undoubtedly be legal challenges in the future. The Supreme Court has refused to review recent cases, but a change in the composition of the justices could easily open the door to reversals of lower-court rulings that now stand. Furthermore, the shifting of positions regarding the relationship of science and religion in the academy and the general public may further activate this national discussion. Therefore, it is important for teachers to be informed about the controversy and consider how they might respond to situations in the classroom (see Box 12.4)

BOX 12.4 • *Debate on Evolution*

Situation

You have given the students in your high school Social Studies class an assignment to participate in a debate on a controversial issue that has made national news in recent years. They are to work in teams of four to give an oral presentation to the class. They may choose their topic but must argue both sides of the issue. One group decides they want to debate the issue of teaching Intelligent Design in public schools. You know that two of the students in this group attend the same conservative Christian church and their parents have been actively petitioning the Board of Education to include Intelligent Design in the school biology curriculum.

Case Law

Supreme Court   *Epperson v. Arkansas* (1968): Arkansas could not eliminate from the high school biology curriculum "the theory that mankind descended from a lower order of animals." The court reasoned that by showing a preference for the Genesis account of creation, the state was not maintaining religious neutrality.

   Edwards v. *Aguillard* (1987) barred the Louisiana law requiring the teaching of "creation science" alongside evolution theory. The court said the purpose was to single out a particular religious belief and promote it as an alternative to accepted scientific theory.

Lower Courts   *Freiler v. Tangipahoa Parish Board of Education* (1999): The Fifth Circuit Court struck down a disclaimer that teachers must read at the start of a lesson on evolution that advises students that the lesson is "presented to inform [them] of

the scientific concept and not intended to influence or dissuade the Biblical version of Creation or any other concept." The court held the disclaimer unconstitutional for *not* being neutral.

   Selman v. Cobb County School District (2005): The federal district court ruled that district could not continue the school board policy that a sticker be placed in science textbooks that read, "This textbook contains material on evolution. Evolution is a theory, not a fact, regarding the origin of living things. This material should be approached with an open mind, studied carefully, and critically considered." The court stated that the sticker "has the effect of implicitly bolstering alternative religious theories of origin by suggesting that evolution is a problematic theory even in the field of science."

   Kitzmiller v. Dover Area School District (2005): The judge struck down a Pennsylvania school board policy of informing high school science students about intelligent design as an alternative to evolution. The federal district court concluded that the policy violates the Establishment Clause because intelligent design is a religious not a scientific theory.

Questions

1. What do recent court decisions regarding the teaching of creationism or intelligent design appear to agree and disagree upon?
2. What do you believe about a student's right to learn about and discuss intelligent design in public schools?
3. What would you do in the situation described above?

Sources: Hudson (2007), Larson (2006), Lupu et al. (2007).

Emerging Issues in the Public Schools.   There are many emerging issues regarding religion in the schools. One is that of character or values education (Sizer & Sizer, 1999). A primary educational concern of many U.S. families is school safety. One suggested remedy for the incivility displayed by some students is character education. However, there is an ongoing debate about the appropriateness and content of moral education in the public schools. It appears to be the case that schools may teach civic virtues (e.g., honesty, good citizenship, courage, respect for others, moral conviction, tolerance), but may not teach them as religious tenets. The fact that most religions also teach these values does not make it unlawful for schools to teach them (American Jewish Congress, n.d.). Values education is sometimes contrasted with some educators' discussions of the need for a consciousness of spirituality in the schools. While educators such as Palmer (1998–1999) and Scherer (1998–1999) reject the imposition of any religion in public education, they encourage the exploration of the spiritual dimensions of teaching and learning. Of course, a clear definition of what constitutes spiritual content and how it might overlap or conflict with values education is yet to be fully determined.

Another current issue is exactly how the Bible can be taught in schools. New textbooks on the Bible have recently been published. Some schools have offered courses in the Bible as literature as an elective in the high school curriculum, and families are suing. The state school board of Georgia approved curriculum in 2007 for teaching the Bible in high school, but only a handful of the state's 180 school districts have agreed to offer the elective classes to date (Associated Press, 2007b). State sponsorship of a Bible curriculum promises to ignite new litigation. The list of emerging issues could go on. As one example of emerging issues of religion in the schools, we have chosen to present a case about a The Higher Ground Academy, a school with a population of students who are predominantly immigrants from Somalia and practice Islam.

Muslims in the Schools.   Islam is one of the fastest growing religions in the world with over 1 billion adherents worldwide (Moore, 2005). In the United States, it is estimated that Muslims constitute 1.4 percent of the population, and they are concentrated in the states of California, New Jersey, New York, Ohio, Michigan, and Illinois (Curtiss, Alamoudi, Johnson, & Reda, 1999). Of the estimated 6 to 8 million Muslims in the United States, about 42 percent are African American, 25 percent are South Asian, and 12 percent are Arab. There have been Black Muslims in the United States for over 100 years, but the movements within that group have changed political and religious commitments over time (Gollnick & Chinn, 2006). South Asian Muslims come from countries such as Pakistan and India. Arab Americans represent twenty countries in the Middle East and Northern Africa and represent a variety of religions including Christianity, Islam, and Judaism (Al-Khatab, 1999). This diversity of national origins and religions in the United States presents many dilemmas to those trying to forge an identity. At the same time, it is noteworthy that the number of U.S.-born Muslims exceeds the number of immigrant origin (Nahi-Tobias & Garfield, 2003).

Muslim families are facing new challenges as they attempt to follow the tenets of their faith in a country that practices religious pluralism. While many Muslim youths in the United States are questioning the strict rules of the Qur'an (or Koran), they also are proud of their faith and the moral stance that it upholds. The place of women in Muslim society is certainly changing. Women who would have prayed at home rather than at the mosque in their country of origin now go to the mosque to pray. Teenagers question the rationale for arranged marriages. Although it is not yet clear how second- and third-generation Muslims will acculturate, it is certain that teachers and administrators will need to address the challenges that Muslim students bring to the public schools. While there are now over 200 Islamic schools in the United States (Moore, 2005), the majority of U.S. Muslims will attend public schools.

In many countries around the world, Muslims attend a *madrasa*, the Arabic word for a school devoted to Islamic instruction (Ayoub, 2007). These schools vary tremendously in organization and curriculum depending upon the country and population served. Thousands of other students attend Islamic weekend schools (Nahi-Tobias & Garfield, 2003). The goal of these schools is to preserve Muslim character and develop spirituality, ethical values, independence, and love of learning. Usually these schools teach Arabic so that children can learn to read the Qur'an themselves (Seymour-Jorn, 2004). Sometimes parents pay to send their children to Islamic institutions because the children have experienced religious discrimination like Mustafa. Increasingly, there are public schools across the United States whose students are primarily Muslim. Often this is because the district has decided to start a charter school that espouses values that are complimentary to those of Islam or because the school promotes Arab culture. For example, in the fall of 2007 New York City began a school dedicated to the study of Arabic language and culture (Marks, 2007). The announcement of the opening of the school caused mixed reactions, although the city already has sixty-five dual-language schools.

Muslims believe that there is one god, Allah, and that Islam was the faith of all God's prophets from Adam to the last prophet, Muhammad (Breuilly, O'Brien, & Palmer, 1997). Muhammed revealed God's final words to mankind in the Qur'an. The only authorized version of the Qur'an is in Arabic and translations are never used in worship. Learning to read and recite the Qur'an is an important part of a child's education. Because Muhammed is believed to have interpreted the word of God in his actions, the stories and sayings of Muhammed are collected in the Hadith, which is also a source of guidance.

The five pillars, or basic beliefs, of Islam must be practiced by all Muslims (Breuilly, O'Brien, & Palmer, 1997; Moore, 2006). The first is the *shahada* or affirmation that there is no god but Allah and Muhammad is his prophet. So, like Christianity and Judaism, Islam holds to monotheism. The second is *salah*, five daily prayers that each individual is obliged to offer unless ill or traveling. These prayers involve a variety of important rituals such as washing the body, or ablution. Prayers are said communally at the mosque each Friday afternoon. Fasting, or *sawm*, is performed during the ninth Muslim month known as Ramadan. During this month an adult Muslim refrains from eating, drinking, smoking, and conjugal relations from dawn to sunset. Children under the age of puberty are exempt, but may partake in a limited fast. The Eid ul-Fitr celebrates the end of this fast, and special prayers, foods, and festivals accompany this holiday. The fourth pillar is *zakat*, a welfare tax for the needy. It is believed that the Muslim community has the right to surplus wealth, which is calculated as a minimum of 2.5 percent of the annual family income. Finally, once in a lifetime a *Hajj* or pilgrimage to the holy city of Makkan (Mecca) is expected of all Muslims who are able to travel and can afford to go without risking the family's well-being.

While there are central tenets of Islamic faith, like all religions, Islam has competing schools of thought regarding theology, rituals, and practices (Moore, 2005). There are two major sects within Islam that have profound theological and political differences: Sunni Muslims constitute the largest group, whereas Shiite Muslims are smaller, but highly visible (Gollnick & Chinn, 1997). This is due, in part, to their belief that the state should adhere to Islamic law. It was a radical group of Shiite Muslims, followers of the Ayatollah Komeni, who overthrew the shah of Iran and later seized U.S. hostages. Subsequent terrorist attacks against Western countries have led to ongoing political mistrust. Unfortunately, this situation has led to negative reactions from some Americans against individuals with Arab backgrounds (Schwartz, 1999).

Certain rituals separate Muslims from non-Muslims (Moore, 2005; Weiss, 1995). Muslims do not eat pork or drink alcoholic beverages. They require that animals be slaughtered in a ritual manner. Another practice is that their sons should be circumcised. Traditionally, boys and girls are educated separately, so co-ed classrooms and physical education are viewed unfavorably by many Muslims. Girls are required to wear modest clothing, including a head covering (see Figure 12.1). However, cultural

FIGURE 12.1   Types of Muslim Head Coverings
Sources: http://news.bbc.co.uk/1/shared/spl/hi/pop_ups/05/europe_muslim_veils; http://www
.khrn.org/veil.htm; http://seattletimes.nwsource.com/news/nation-world/crisis/theregion/veils
.html; http://www.psames.uiuc.edu/outreach/Dress/Middle%20Eastern%20Dress%20
Vocabulary.pdf.

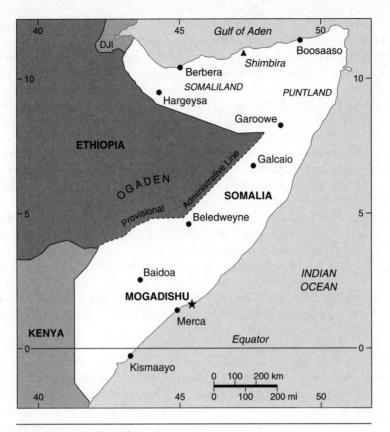

FIGURE 12.2   Somalia

and religious norms are not necessarily identical. While Islam does not require a woman or girl to cover her head, apart from during religious worship, some cultural groups do require it. Therefore, it is important to try to determine the cultural norms that particular families adhere to.

School leaders must be aware of the personal and religious rights of Islamic students. There is certainly a need to counteract possible harassment of Arab American students by including the contributions of Arab culture and Muslim religion fairly and accurately in the curriculum (Moore, 2006; Schwartz, 1999). Similarly, educators should accommodate Islamic practices such as fasting, prayer, and dress. Students should be allowed access to a room other than the cafeteria if they are fasting, and pork products in the cafeteria should be labeled. Just as student prayer is allowed for other religious groups, Muslims should be able to pray. Girls should not be harassed for wearing head coverings or traditional dress. In some places where there is a concentrated population of Muslims, schools offer separate physical education classes for girls. Some would argue that if such classes cannot be provided then Muslim children should not be required to participate in physical education, since taking group showers and wearing typical gym clothes may violate the Muslim tradition of modesty.

The religious beliefs of students have a significant effect on their behavior both in and out of school. It is critical that teachers understand and respect their students' beliefs and include information about religion in the curriculum when appropriate. Educators must be aware of the bias against Arabs that is portrayed in some textbooks and children's literature and some writers' tendency to conflate, essentialize, or normalize the culture (David & Ayouby, 2005). For example, making a distinction between the "Muslims" and the "Arabs" avoids conflation and helps students understand that all Arabs are not Muslims and vice versa. Essentializing involves referring to some cultural, social, religious, or other essence that supposedly describes all individuals in a group. To avoid essentializing, teachers should emphasize the intergroup differences amongst Muslims such as their country of origin or first language. Normalizing a culture or religion means trying to make it seem like the group is "just like everyone else." A lesson that encourages students to critically examine social pressures to follow current clothing trends juxtaposed against the freedom some Muslims experience by wearing a head covering avoids normalization.

Therefore, it is important to acquire accurate materials and discuss materials that may promote stereotypes. Resources are available through the American Forum for Global Education (Kelahan & Penn, 1996), the Arab World and Islamic Resources and School Services (Shabbas, 1998), the American-Arab Anti-Discrimination Committee, and the Islamic Service Foundation (Zehr, 2007).

Somalia.   Somalia is a predominantly Sunni Muslim country from which an increasing number of individuals have immigrated to the United States in recent years due to civil war. Few Americans know much about the physical location, political climate, or educational system of this country in East Africa (see Figure 12.2).

The recent history of Somalia has been one of upheaval, resulting in a weak educational system. Although both the British and Italians had claims on Somalia after World War II, the country finally gained full independence in 1960 as a Western-style parliamentary democracy (Somalia, 2007). While the country enjoyed a brief period in which there was hope for an equitable government, internal and external conflicts escalated during the next thirty years. According to a UN report, the beginning of the civil war in 1988 marked a time when Somalia came apart (Eversmann, 2000–01). In 1991 a de facto government declared the formation of an independent Republic of Somaliland in the northeast; similarly, in 1998 the autonomous region of Puntland was self-proclaimed in the northeast (Somalia, 2007). Both regions are not officially recognized. Between 1991 and 1998 sporadic fighting and wars among various groups and regions of the country resulted in hundreds of thousands of deaths and over a million people being displaced out of a total prewar population of about 6 million. The formal system of education was almost completely destroyed.

As late as 1972 during a period marked by educational innovation, the government introduced the first Somali alphabet based on the Latin script, and the Somali language was made the official language of the schools (Eversmann, 2000–01). In the mass literacy campaign that followed, the school enrollment rate never increased beyond 50 percent, but those gains were lost during the 1980s. However, the education system survived to a very limited extent, with the assistance of the international community. United Nations agencies have played an important role in its survival.

However, instability in the government due to assassinations and military coups, internal warfare between clans and warlords fighting for power, civil wars, natural disasters that limited the food supply, and general poverty have plagued the country for the past three decades and forced more than a million Somalis to seek refuge in the refugee camps of Kenya and Ethiopia. Hostile relations with Ethiopia lasted a decade following a war in 1977–78 over the Ogaden area of Ethiopia, where ethnic Somalis have lived (Arabic-German Consulting, 2007). Many Americans are familiar with Somalia because of the conflict that occurred in 1993 in Mogadishu, the capital of Somalia, where nineteen U.S. soldiers lost their lives. The book and subsequent movie— *Blackhawk Down*—retell this unfortunate incident in which as many as 1,500 Somalian militia and civilians also lost their lives.

Somalia's current government is best described as transitional. The country has an interim prime minister who recently nominated a new cabinet of thirty-one members (BBC News, 2007). Since the Prime Minister, Ali Mohamed Ghedi consulted with the President and the speaker of parliament, his nominations for the cabinet are likely to be accepted by parliament (BBC News, 2007). This is seen as a hopeful sign. Another positive development is that the Islamic Courts have helped to exclude the warlords, who used to control Mogadishu, from the government. In a country that has had continuous turmoil since it declared independence, a stable government is desperately needed. Mogadishu itself was divided among three warring groups in the late 1990s.

The disorder in the country is reflected in the education of Somali's children. Reports from the United Nations sum up the current status of Somalia's education system as one of the worst in the world (Eversmann, 2000-2001; UNICEF, n.d.). The Survey of Primary Schools in Somalia for 2003–2004 shows that fewer than 20 percent of children ages 6 to 17 were enrolled in formal schools. Some private schools have managed to function since the civil war, as have some schools in the Republic of Somaliland and Puntland (Somalia, 2007). The story of Fooishya, who attends a government-run school, describes the value of education for such children (see Box 12.5). However, many individual schools operate much on their own, without a national administrative infrastructure or national curriculum. Schools are using Arabic, pre-war Somali, Kenyan, and/or Western curricula. While children in Somalia often attend Islamic schools or *dugsis*, most students have never attended a formal, secular school where academic subjects are taught.

There are considerable disparities within Somalia regarding access to and quality of, primary education, due to socioeconomic, cultural, and political realities. For example, there are gender-related disparities resulting in a gender-gap in school enrollment. Only 35 percent of all students are girls, and fewer than 13 percent of teachers are female (Eversmann, 2000-2001; UNICEF, n.d.). Furthermore, nomadic children have been hard to reach. Nomadic people constitute about 6 percent of the population in Africa and are found in at least twenty countries (de Souza, 2007). Nomadic societies are marginalized and often unrepresented minorities (de Souza, 2007). Girls and nomadic children are the target of recent UNICEF educational programs due to the inequities that currently exist. The goal of UNICEF and UNESCO in Somalia is to adapt the new educational methods developed for primary education to access nomadic children and the unreached and hardest-to-reach Somali children in the 6 to 14 age group (UNICEF, 2005a).

BOX 12.5 • *Foosiya's Story*

Foosiya, age 12, lives in Hargeysa, the capital of the self-declared Republic of Somaliland. She lives in the center of the city with eight siblings. Her father, a former history teacher, runs a small garage while her mother looks after the children at home. Foosiya, who is in sixth grade, attends a government primary school where 22 of the 83 students in her class are girls. She pays a dollar each month in school fees. Her studies include Arabic, English, Islamic studies, math, Somali, science, and social studies.

She is a bright and outgoing girl doing well in her studies. Foosiya hopes to continue at a government secondary school and one day become a secretary. While her older siblings attend private schools, the family cannot afford the fees required for her and the younger siblings.

Foosiya's day starts at 6:00 AM when she gets up to pray with her mother and the other children. She then has breakfast and walks to her school. Classes begin at 7:30 AM and end at noon. In the afternoon she helps her mother with the younger children and household chores. Once a week she plays basketball at a sports center for girls, the first of its kind in Somaliland.

Source: UNICEF (2005a).

International organizations have been working in Somali to make improvements in the educational system. UNICEF introduced Education Kits into the country beginning in 1994, and UNESCO has provided teacher training. The UNICEF kits are packages of such basic educational materials as pens, pencils, and notebooks, designed as a preparedness strategy to support schooling for populations caught in complex emergencies (Eversmann, 2000-2001). Research on the use and effectiveness of the kits was conducted in Somalia and two other countries between 1994 and 1997, and the program has received mixed reviews (Eversmann, 2000-2001). While UNICEF views the kits as a "stop-gap" measure, UNESCO also has designed kits as a short-term basic literacy and numeracy education course.

As areas of the country become free of conflict, new schools are opening (Eversmann, 2000-2001). In 2002 a new lower primary school curriculum was developed and a curriculum for grades 5 to 8. During that year over 7,000 teachers received in-service training, and classroom practices and children's learning levels were improved by a pilot mentoring project (UNICEF, 2005b). However, there are still people living in refugee camps within Somali. As the story of Murayo illustrates, nongovernmental organizations are working to educate these children (see Box 12.6).

UNICEF does plan a broader focus that will target system-wide education reforms in Somalia. Plans include the development of a curriculum in the Somali language, textbooks, improving the standards of learning, and developing Education Management Information Systems (EMIS) that will provide more reliable educational data (UNICEF, n.d.). In order to reach nomadic children, the Kenyan government, in collaboration with OXFAM Great Britain and UNICEF, has been piloting a system of mobile schools modeled on the local system of *dugsi* schools whereby a Koranic teacher travels within each community and provides religious instruction at hours convenient

BOX 12.6 • *Murayo's Story*

It is December 2005 on a hot, dusky morning in the Askar Internally Displaced Persons Camp where Murayo has grown up. The camp has grown larger as Somali refugees have returned from Ethiopia and Kenya. Most dwellings in the camp are made of cartons and polyethylene on twig and branch frames. Occasionally a mattress is thrown on top, risking a fire. Fires are a constant threat, fanned by winds from the sea. A fire in 2005 injured two people and destroyed 70 homes.

This morning Murayo, 11 years old, is cooking *anjera*, a Somali delicacy, as her mother hangs out the laundry to dry. Reyo, Murayo's mother, has seven other children. Abdi, 2 years old, is trotting after his mother.

At 7:30 AM Murayo grabs her black bag, dons her blue hijab and enters the dusty compound where her classroom is located. There are four classrooms made of mud caked onto stave and twig frames with an orange tarpaulin as a roof. The school was founded only in 2004 by a nongovernmental organization that helps children in the camps. Training for teachers and supplies were provided by UNICEF. The school has 170 students and four teachers. Ninety-two of the students are girls. The school day ends at 10:30 A.M. to accommodate the families who need income and other help. Children work as shoe shiners and manual laborers.

Source: UNICEF (2005b).

---

for the children, in the context of their family labor responsibilities. This model may provide the answer to nomadic societies in Somalia.

Despite the efforts of many organizations, only a small minority of children in Somalia receive any type of education. An understanding of the enormous cultural, religious, and educational differences that face Somali refugees who come to the United States is critical to analyzing the case of The Higher Ground Academy.

The Case of The Higher Ground Academy

Two colleagues, Mr. Wilson and Mr. Jones, came together in 2000 to find a solution to the dismal achievement picture of many African American students in the public schools of St. Paul, Minnesota. The result of much brainstorming and long evenings together in discussions was a proposal to the state to establish a K-12 charter school, which they strongly believed could make a difference for at least some of the failing students. A charter school would allow them the freedom and flexibility to create their vision of an ideal educational environment, with appropriate curriculum and staff.

The site they chose for the school is located on the fringe of a neighborhood where a concentration of African Americans have always lived. They chose an older building in which the school would be housed. As Mr. Wilson and Mr. Jones surveyed the school, they planned for an appropriate number of classrooms and space for extracurricular activities that would provide the best possible educational program for their students.

Charter schools offer an unprecedented combination of freedom and accountability (U.S. Department of Education, 2004). The schools are underwritten with public funds but run independently. As a charter school, they could lengthen the school day, decide on an organizational structure including their governing board, decide what and how they would teach, decide where and how they would use their budget, and decide who they could hire and fire. They realized that in return, they would be held strictly accountable for their academic and financial performance, since no charter is permanent; it must be renewed at regular intervals (U.S. Department of Education, 2004). One of the most appealing aspects was the freedom to experiment by trying out innovations, as long as they remained true to the school's mission and their students met the state standards.

As of January 2004, there were 2,996 charter schools operating in the United States. Across forty states and the District of Columbia, about 750,000 students were participating in them under varying charter laws (U.S. Department of Education, 2004). The first charter school legislation was passed in Minnesota in 1991, and there are currently over 170 charter school locations in that state (Minnesota Department of Education, 2007). Parents choose to enroll their children in charter schools, and the number of children enrolled at any given time can be one measure of the school's success. In fact, continued funding is tied to student enrollment (U.S. Department of Education, 2004).

The two colleagues received approval from the Minnesota State Department of Education, and the city school district became the major sponsor of the school. Thus, The Higher Ground Academy opened in 1997, and 250 African American students entered the first year. As is true for other charter schools around the country, the state standards became goals of the Academy and objectives were designed to meet the state's goals and assure that the Academy's students would pass the state tests.

However, the school's mission also includes "dedication to the creation of a socially committed, morally responsible, and ethnically diverse learning environment where students are valued both individually and collectively." Its goal is to encourage students' intellectual and leadership development to meet the twenty-first-century standards of education. Preparation for the students to pursue postsecondary and postbaccalaureate studies is viewed as crucial and enables them to meet the school's requirement of admission to a postsecondary educational program in order to graduate. Thus, the curriculum is broader than "preparation for the state tests," and includes the traditional subjects of language arts, social studies, math, science, but also a requirement for service learning. Service learning, a popular initiative around the country at this time, is an integral part of Higher Ground's philosophy that "learning is in doing." Actually, one of the school's goals for 2006–2007 was to enroll 100 middle and high school students in a year-long credited service learning course that engages older students as tutors of younger students in math, language arts, and Arabic.

To the surprise of the staff and directors, Somali children and a smaller number of Oromo students began to seek admission to the school in 1999. As the number of Somali students increased, the population of African American students gradually decreased to 20. In the 2005–2006 school year, student demographics were the following:

Grade Level	Somalis	Americans	Oromos	Hmongs
K-3	141	16	24	0
4-6	45	19	12	0
7-12	127	33	21	2

The Oromos, whose language is Oromo, are an indigenous African ethnic group located in Ethiopia and to a lesser extent in Kenya and Somali. The Hmong students are immigrants from Laos who began coming to the United States in 1975 after the Vietnamese War.

It appeared that The Higher Ground Academy was moving toward a mostly homogeneous student population. The positive result was that students could help each other with language and other requirements. It also would be a school in which students were largely devoted to Islam and practiced the beliefs of that faith. However, the school's mission to "create an ethnically diverse learning environment" was in question. Nevertheless, at that point Mr. Wilson thought to himself, "Our greatest challenge will be in addressing the following two questions: How can we accommodate the culture and how can we be an open and welcoming receptacle for them?"

The language needs of the Somali and Oromo students would also be challenging. In the 2005–2006 school year, 164 or 37 percent were English Language Learners (ELL) (The Higher Ground Academy, 2005–2006). Of 313 Somali students, almost 32 percent were ELL as were 53 percent of the Oromo students. In fact, Mr. Wilson and Mr. Jones were faced with changing their vision to that of planning for students of a different and unfamiliar culture and religion. They needed, first, to recruit and hire staff who, if at all possible, could understand the Somali or Oromo language and were familiar with the culture. Fortunately, the sizable number of Somali immigrants in the city allowed them to hire teachers who shared many aspects of the Somali culture, language, diet, and Islam as a religion. The cafeteria, in fact, was staffed by East African people familiar with foods that were allowed by Islam, or *halal*, and those that were banned. The two directors, with the school psychologist, also developed necessary procedures for admission and establishing a student's level of English proficiency (see Box 12.7). Furthermore, they heard about lectures to be given in the community about Somalia and the Somali religion and culture, so they felt they had to attend.

After the lecture series on Somalia, the directors of Higher Ground Academy made the decision that the staff would learn about the Somali culture as they worked with and planned for the students and their families or guardians, and the directors also would continue to learn. They would not organize a formal staff development program. There also were courses available at the colleges and universities as well as ongoing lectures in the community.

The directors also recognized that having Somalian students who also were Muslim would mean making arrangements of space for their prayers, changing the diet at lunchtime to respect their food restrictions, and hiring an additional English as a Sec-

BOX 12.7 • *Higher Ground Admission Procedures*

When a student arrives at the Academy, he or she usually speaks little English. The student and family are introduced to the staff. The school psychologist informally assesses the student's level of English proficiency. The student is then placed in a multi-level group to learn English and monitored to determine when he or she is ready to be mainstreamed into classes in English. Support also is provided for the retention of the student's home language.

ond Language teacher. They modified the art curriculum and projects to eliminate drawing human figures since Muslims are prohibited from creating any type of image. This is due to the interpretation of various Muslim traditions and texts that hold that adherents are prohibited from representing the divine, including the human form (Grabar, 2003). They even reexamined the floor plan of the school to set aside one classroom as a place in which students could pray together at the same time of day.

During the first two to three weeks of the 2006 school year, the climate was positive and friendly among the students. The 350 students were evenly divided between girls and boys. Although some girls were Protestant or of unknown religion, 125 of the girls were of the Islamic faith. This meant that the directors had to provide a schedule and room that could accommodate 125 girls for prayer. They also had to assume that the girls would cooperate with each other in using the facilities available.

One morning as Mr. Jones approached his office, it appeared that a small group of girls in Western clothing waited at his door. Mr. Jones could not imagine what the problem might be, yet he knew that it was serious when so many of the usually quiet students seemed upset. As he opened the office door, the students rushed into the limited space and surrounded him. One girl, who often stopped by to tell Mr. Jones how pleased she was to be at the school, stepped forward as the spokesperson for the group. "Mr. Jones, she began, "we have a difficult situation here. Every day when we try to use the girls' bathrooms in the afternoon, we must pick up paper towels, try to dry wet, slippery floors, and clean up the liquid soap that spills from broken soap dispensers in the sinks and sometimes on the floor. Iris slipped and fell one day. Something will have to be done."

Mr. Jones summoned his friend and colleague, Mr. Wilson to discuss the bathroom problem with him. He also asked one of the teachers to ask her student, Yasmin, to stop at his office after classes. He hoped that Yasmin, a very pleasant and religious eleventh-grade student (Box 12.8), could help them to understand the bathroom issue.

Yasmin was glad for the opportunity to explain the needs of the students who were of the Islamic faith. "Before we pray each time, Mr. Jones, we must cleanse ourselves. It is necessary to wash all the parts of the body which are generally exposed to dirt or dust or smog, not just our hands. It is very hard to do that with just one bathroom with a few sinks and so many girls. I don't think anyone means to be messy, but we have so little time. We need to follow Islamic law if Allah is to hear our prayers."

Both men looked at each other with raised eyebrows.

"Thanks for your help, Yasmin," said Mr. Jones.

"We have a better understanding of the religious importance of cleansing after your explanation. Have a good evening," added Mr. Wilson.

Once Yasmin had left, the two men continued their conversation.

"Well, this is a new twist," said Mr. Jones. "Just how far do you think we need to go to accommodate the religious needs of our students? We are a public school."

Mr. Wilson responded, "We really need to think about this. Let's get together tomorrow and see what we come up with."

Mr. Jones agreed and then expressed an even more perplexing thought, "Do you think these kids would be better off in a regular public school where they would have more contact with mainstream Americans, African Americans, and children from other cultures that don't attend this school? Are we doing them a disservice by not exposing them to mainstream cultural, conversational, or social behaviors?

BOX 12.8 • *Yasmin's Story*

Yasmin, a tall, slim student at Higher Ground Academy, is in her third year at the school and in eleventh grade. Yasmin is from Somalia and, as a devout Muslim who practices the Islamic faith, she wears traditional clothing of Muslim women. She wears an Al-Amira over her head. In school, like many of the female students at Higher Ground, her face is uncovered and she also wears gloves. The Higher Ground Academy is the first formal, secular school that she has ever attended. She did attend a *dugsi* in Somalia.

She left Somalia in 1998 and traveled to Nairobi, Kenya, and then to the United States with her "adoptive" family in 2004. Yasmin left her biological family of four brothers and six sisters and her parents in Somalia. In St. Paul she lives with an uncle and his family.

Yasmin describes her initial impressions of the United States as "scary." In her words, "There were so many people, so strange, and I didn't know anyone." The smell of the foods made me sick, and I spent my first weeks at Higher Ground alone, in a room, without food, at lunchtime."

In contrast, her first impressions of the school were "very happy." She continued to smile as she commented that "there were lots of students like me; they all spoke my language and could translate for me, and the girls were all dressed like me. We help each other in whatever

way we can. I spoke both Somali and Oromo when I arrived; English was totally unfamiliar to me, and it sounded strange. I was placed in the ESL class at first. Now, I am making progress, and my eleventh grade program consists of math, chemistry, history, and English where I am reading George Orwell's *1984*, studying poetry, and keeping a journal. My program also includes service learning where I help first graders. I love this school and I am considering vocational education as a future career. I would like to be able to help young people in their choice of and preparation for a career."

Although she has been in this country three years, she has no American or African American friends. She does have several Somali girlfriends with whom she visits sometimes. Yasmin describes her neighbors as people who stay in their houses all the time, so she knows none of the people in her neighborhood.

"In Africa," Yasmin explained, "we all lived so close together that it was easy to know everyone. Now, my time after school is usually filled with chores and homework, and I read the Koran every day. I spend three hours on Saturday and three hours on Sunday at the *dugsi*. Only now, I teach younger children."

In Somalia, students attend the *dugsis* six or seven days each week. For many children it is the only source of education.

"Our mission statement includes our creation of an ethnically diverse environment, and we both believe that we should respect their culture and religion. We expect that they may eventually become bicultural. However, will they be able to do so without a more diverse educational experience? How do we respect their culture and religion while still providing them with the opportunity to experience diversity?"

Discussion Questions
1. How would you respond to the questions raised by Mr. Jones and Mr. Wilson?
2. What is your reaction to the discrepancy between the school's mission statement and the extent of diversity in the student population?
3. How do educators in public schools draw the line between accommodating and promoting any one religion?

4. Is it possible to learn about students' cultures as you work with them in the school setting? Are there advantages in learning this way or would you favor an in-service program that would provide information and understanding?
5. Would you choose to teach at this type of school? Why?
6. If you were the principal of The Higher Ground Academy, what long-term goals would you work to implement?

References

Abington School District v. Schempp, 374 U.S. 203 (1963).

ACLU v. Black Horse Pike Regional Board of Education, 84 F.3d 1471 (3d Cir. 1996).

Adler v. Duval County School Board, 250 F.3d 1330 (11th Cir. 2001).

Al-Khatab, A. (1999). In search of equity for Arab-American students in public schools of the United States. *Education, 120*(2), 254–266.

American Jewish Congress. (n.d.). *Religion in the public schools: A joint statement of current law.* Retrieved October 21, 2001, from http://ajcongress.org/clsa/clsarips.htm

Arabic-German Consulting. (1998–1999). *Somalia-History.* Retrieved September 13, 2007, from http://www.arab.de/arabinfo/somalihis.htm

Associated Press. (2007a, February 14). Kansas: Anti-evolution guidelines are repealed. *New York Times.* Retrieved July 11, 2007, from http://www.nytimes.com

Associated Press. (2007b, May 3). *Ga. schools cautious on state-funded Bible classes.* Retrieved July 13, 2007, from http://www.firstamendmentcenter.org/news.aspx?id=18510

Ayers, S. J., & Reid, S. (2005). Teaching about religion in elementary school: The experience of one Texas district. *The Social Studies, 96*(1), 14–17.

Ayoub, N. C. (2007, April 6). Schooling Islam: The culture and politics of modern Muslim education. *Chronicle of Higher Education, 53* (31)15–15.

BBC News. (2007). *Africa/Somalia prime minister names new government.* Retrieved August 21, 2007, from http://news.bbc.co.uk/2/hi/africa/5270236.stm

Breuilly, E., O'Brien, J., & Palmer, M. (1997). *Religions of the world: The illustrated guide to origins, beliefs, tradition, and festivals.* New York: Facts on File.

Brown, S. P. (2002). *Trumping religion: The new Christian right, the free speech clause, and the courts.* Tuscaloosa, AL: The University of Alabama Press.

Curtiss, R. H., Alamoudi, A., Johnson, J. W., & Reda, H. (1999). Symposium: American Muslims and U.S. foreign policy. *Middle East Policy, 7*(1), 1.

David, G. D., & Ayouby, K. K. (2005). Studying the exotic other in the classroom: The portrayal of Arab Americans in educational source materials. *Multicultural Perspectives, 7*(4), 13–20.

de Souza, A. (2007) *Forum on flexible education: Reaching nomadic populations in Africa: Summary report.* Vancouver, British Columbia: Commonwealth of Learning.

Douglass, S. L. (2002). Teaching about religion. *Educational Leadership, 60*(2), 32–37.

Dowling-Sendor, B. (2001). A prayer by any name. *American School Board Journal, 188* (11), 52–53.

Eck, D. L. (2001). *A new religious America: How a "Christian Country" has become the world's most religious diverse nation.* San Francisco, CA: Harper.

Edwards v. Aguillard, 482 U.S. 578 (1987).

Elhoweris, H., Salend, S. J., & Whittaker, C. R. (in press). Religious diversity in schools: Addressing the issues. *Intervention in School and Clinic.*

Engel v. Vitale, 370 U.S. 421 (1962).

Epperson v. Arkansas, 393 U.S. 97 (1968).

Eversmann, E. (2000–2001). *Education kits in Somalia.* Retrieved August 31, 2007, from http://web.mit.edu/cis/www/migration/pubs/mellon/3_somalia.html

Freiler v. Tangipahoa Parish Board of Education, 185 F.3d 337 (5th Cir. 1999).

Gollnick, D. M., & Chinn, P. C. (2006). *Multicultural education in a pluralistic society* (7th ed.). Englewood Cliffs, NJ: Pearson.

Goodstein, L. (2005, December 21). Judge rejects teaching intelligent design. *New York Times.* Retrieved July 11, 2007, from http://nytimes.com

Grabar, O. (2003). From the icon to aniconism: Islam and the image. *Museum International, 46*(8), 46–53.

Haynes, C. C. (1999). Religion in the public schools. *School Administrator, 56*(1), 6–10.

Haynes, C. C., & Thomas, O. (2001). *Finding common ground: A guide to religious liberty in public schools.* Arlington, VA: First Amendment Center.

Herrington, C. D. (2000). Religion, public schools and hyper-pluralism: Is there a new religious war? *Educational Policy, 14,* 548–563.

Hudson, D. (2007, January 24). *Evolution and creation.* Arlington, VA: The First Amendment Center. Retrieved July 13, 2007, from http://www.thefirstamendmentcenter.org

Jurinski, J. J. (1998). *Religion in the schools: A reference handbook.* Santa Barbara, CA: ABC-CLIO.

Kelahan, B., & Penn, M. (Eds.). (1996). *Spotlight on the Muslim Middle East—Crossroads. A student reader and teacher's guide.* New York: American Forum for Global Education (ERIC Document Reproduction Service No. ED 415 144).

Kitzmiller v. Dover Area School District, 400F. Supp. 2d 707 (M.D. Pa. 2005).

Kosmin, B. A., Mayer, E., & Keysar, A. (2001). *American religious identification survey.* New York: The Graduate Center of the City University of New York.

Larson, E. J. (2006). *Biology wars: The religion, science and education controversy.* Washington, DC: The Pew Research Forum on Religion and Public Life. Retrieved July 11, 2007, from http://pewforum.org

Lee v. Weisman, 505 U.S. 577 (1992).

Lupu, I. C., Elwood, F., Davis, E., Masci, D., Tuttle, R. W., & Berz, S. K. (2007, May). *Religion in the public schools.* Washington, DC: The Pew Research Forum on Religion and Public Life. Retrieved July 11, 2007 from http://pewforum.org

Lynch, S. N. (2007, May 31). Police find Gilbert teen innocent in bomb scare. *East Valley Tribune.com.* Retrieved July 11, 2007, from http://www.eastvalleytribune.com/story/90694

Marks, A. (2007, June 1). Arabic school in N.Y.C. creates stir. *Christian Science Monitor.* Retrieved July 12, 2007, from http://www.csmonitor.com

Matsumura, M. (1999). A new tactic for getting creation science into classrooms? *Reports of the National Center for Science Education, 19*(3), 24–26.

Mauro, T. (2001). *High court turns away question: Is prayer at school events constitutional?* The Freedom Forum. Retrieved July 11, 2007, from http://www.freedomforum.org

Minnesota Department of Education. (2007). *Charter school locations.* Retrieved September 22, 2007, from http://education.state.mn.us/MDE/Data_DataDownloads/Maps/Charter_School_Locations/index.html

Moore, J. R. (2005). The role of Islam and Muslims on American education: Critical issues in teaching and curriculum. *Curriculum and Teaching Dialogue, 7*(1/2), 155–165.

Moore, J. R (2006). Islam in social studies education: What we should teach secondary students and why it matters. *Social Studies, 97*(4), 139–144.

Nahi-Tobias, C. S., & Garfield, E.N. (2003). An Islamic school responds to September 11. In S. Books (Ed.). *Invisible children in the society and its schools* (2nd ed., pp. 13–33). Mahway, NJ: Lawrence Erlbaum.

Nord, W. A. (1995). *Religion and American education: Rethinking a national dilemma.* Chapel Hill: University of North Carolina Press.

Nord, W. A., & Haynes, C. C. (1998). *Taking religion seriously across the curriculum.* Alexandria, VA: Association for Supervision and Curriculum Development.

Ostling, R. N. (1999). American's ever-changing religious landscape [Electronic version]. *Brookings Review, 17*(2), 10–13.

Palmer, P. J. (1998–1999). Evoking the spirit in public education. *Educational Leadership, 56*(4), 6–11.

Pew Forum on Religion and Public Life. (2002). *Americans struggle with religion's role at home and abroad.* Washington, DC: Author. Retrieved July 10, 2007, from http://pewforum.org/publications/surveys/religion.pdf

Pew Research Center. (2006, August 24). *Many Americans uneasy with mix of religion and politics.* Washington, DC. Retrieved July 15, 2007, from http://pewforum.org/surveys/

Public Broadcasting System. (2007). *Evolution: A journey into where we're from and where we're going.* Retrieved July 15, 2007, from http://www.pbs.org/wgbh/evolution/index.html

Religion in the Public Schools. (1995). *Religion in the public schools: A joint statement of current law.* Retrieved July 15, 2007, from www.ed.gov./Speeches/04-1995/prayer.html

Riley, R. W. (1998). *Secretary's statement on religious expression.* Retrieved July 15, 2007, from http://www.ed.gov/Speeches/08-1995/religion.html

Santa Fe Independent School District v. Doe, (99-62) 530 U.S. 290 (2000).

Scherer, M. M. (Ed.). (1998–1999). The spirit of education. *Educational Leadership, 56*(4).

Schwartz, W. (1999). *Arab American students in public schools* (ERIC Digest, No. 142). New York: ERIC Clearinghouse on Urban Education (ERIC Document Reproduction Service No. ED 429 144).

Selman v. Cobb County School District, No. 02-2325 (N.D. Ga. Jan. 13, 2005).

Sewall, G. T. (1999). Religion comes to school. *Phi Delta Kappan, 81,* 10–26.

Seymour-Jorn, C. (2004). Arabic language learning among *Arab* immigrants in Milwaukee, Wisconsin: A study of attitudes and motivations. *Journal of Muslim Minority Affairs, 24*(1), 109–122.

Shabbas, A. (Ed.). (1998). *Arab world studies notebook.* Berkeley, CA: Arab World and Islamic Resources and School Services.

Sizer, T. R., & Sizer N. F. (1999). Grappling. *Phi Delta Kappan, 81,* 184–190.

Smith, C. Denton, M., L., Faris, R., & Regnerus, M. (2002). Mapping American adolescent religious participation. *Journal for the Scientific Study of Religion, 41,* 597–612.

Somalia. (2007). In *Encyclopædia Britannica.* Retrieved September 22, 2007, from Encyclopædia Britannica Online: http://www.search.eb.com/eb/article_37734

Southern Poverty Law Center. (2001). Tolerance in the news: Americans vs. Americans. Retrieved July 15, 2007, from http://tolerance.org/news/article_tol.jsp?id=275.

The Higher Ground Academy. (2005–2006). *Annual report.* St Paul, MN: Author.

The Pluralism Project. (n.d.) Statistics by tradition. Harvard, MA: Harvard University. Retrieved July 10, 2007, from http://www.pluralism.org/resources/statistics/tradition.php

U.S. Department of Education. (2004). *Innovations in education: Successful charter schools.* Retrieved September, 2007, from: http://uscharterschools.org/pub/uscs-docs/scs/full-print.htm

UNICEF (2005a, June). *Back to school campaign.* Retrieved September 24, 2007, from http://www.unicef.org/somalia/education_1372.html

UNICEF. (2005b, December). *For Somali children, every minute in school counts.* Retrieved September 22, 2007, from http://www.unicef.org/somalia/education_2432.html

UNICEF. (n.d.). *Somalia education.* Retrieved September 20, 2007, from http://www.unicef.org/somalia/education_56.html

Wallace v. Jaffree, 472 U.S. 38 (1985).

Weiss, A. M. (1995). The society and its environment. In P. R. Blood (Ed.), *Pakistan: A country study* (pp. 75–146). Washington, DC: Library of Congress.

Williams, P. W. (2000). Plus ça change: Has American religion changed during the past century? *Cross Currents, 50*(1–2), 264–276.

Zehr, M. (2007, July 12). Textbook written for U. S. Muslims. *Education Week* [serial online], *25*(37), 7.

Index

Native Hawaiian and Other Pacific Islanders, use of term, xxv. *See also* Asian-Pacific Islanders
New poverty, 150
No Child Left Behind Act (NCLB), 20, 22–23, 39, 174, xx
Non-Christian religions, 249
Nondenominational churches in U.S., 248
Nonverbal communication, 57, 119, 120
Nutrition, inadequate, 155

O

Office of Management and Budget (OMB) race categories, xv
Onteora Indian, case of, 128–37
Oral history, 34
OXFAM, 264

P

Paradigmatic mode of knowing, 68
Parents
  education level of, poverty and, 151
  expertise of, 72
  females in mathematics and, 199–200
  involvement of, 47–52 (*See also* Family involvement in schools)
  of mixed race children, 105
Parents, Families, and Friends of Lesbians and Gays (PFLAG), 229, 232, 238
Parent Team (PT), 50, 51
Partnerships, building. *See* Family involvement in schools; School-family-community partnerships
Pedagogy, equity, 24
Peer influence on female performance in mathematics, 202–3
Pentecostal/Charismatics in U.S., 248
People for the American Way, 251
People of color, use of term, xv
Personal racism, 171
Personal Responsibility and Work Opportunity Reconciliation Action (PRWORA), 156
Phonology, 120

Physical differences, racial identity and awareness of, 102
Plan of action, developing and implementing, 71, 74–75
  in migrant student case, 91–94
Plyer v. Doe, 7
Positionality, 204
Poverty and socioeconomic class, 146–68
  brain development and, 154–55
  composition of the poor, 151–52
  culture of poverty, 149
  current facts on, 148–53
  definitions, 154
  educational progress of diverse learners in high-poverty schools, 20
  expectations and realities of, 146–48
  hidden rules about, 149
  homeless families and children, 153
  impact on school-aged children, 154–55
  migrant families, 81
  migrant families and, 152
  of minority students in special education, 158–64, 170, 171
  obstacles to involvement of families in, 53
  schools' role in dealing with, 157–58
  state and federal provisions and, 155–57
Practical knowledge, 66, 69
Practice and theory, chasm between, 69
Prayers in school, student, 252, 261
Prejudice, 48, 250. *See also* Discrimination
  reduction, 25
Prereferral service, 171
Presbyterians in U.S., 248
Preschool years
  programs for gifted students in, 178
  racial identity in, 102
Preservice teachers, 75. *See also* Teacher preparation
  attitudes and beliefs concerning cultural diversity, 40
  knowledge levels of, 40
  math and science background of, 195
Principals
  demographics of, 10–11
  role in developing teacher leadership, xxiii

Teachers
  attitudes, beliefs, and behaviors about
    females in mathematics, 197–98
  demographics of, 10–11
  developing leadership, xxiii
  gay, 226
  at high-poverty schools, 20
  inclusive classroom and, 175
  leadership, 75
  modeling by, 70
  preservice, 40, 75
  religion and, 254
  student teacher, case involving, 109–11
Teaching cases. *See* Cases
Temporary Assistance for Needy Families
    (TANF) program, 147, 148, 156
Theory and practice, chasm between, 69
Thinking, critical, 70
Title I schools, 47
Title IX, 194, 227, 228
Toys, gender-typed, 196–97
Tracking, educational progress of diverse
    learners and, 21–22
Training, sexual orientation issues and, 229.
    See also Teacher preparation
Transformational ministry, 227
Transgendered students
  See Gay, lesbian, bisexual, and transgendered
    students
Translators, need for, 57–58, 59
Two-way bilingual programs, 127

U

Underachievement, traditional school
    curriculum and, 27
Underrepresentation of minorities, in gifted
    and talented programs, 176–77
UNESCO, 263, 264
UNICEF, 263, 264

Unitary school districts, 113
United Nations, human rights issues,
    international migration and, 4
United Nations Conference on Population
    and Development (1999), 4
Universal Design for Learning (UDL), 175

V

Values and beliefs
  framing stage of decision making, 73
  mutually shared, xxiv
Values education, 258
Verbal communication, 57
Visa Lottery Program, 8

W

Wallace v. Jaffree, 252
Welfare provisions
  impact of reforms, 155–57
  state and federal funding for, 155–57
Wesleyans/Methodists in U.S., 248
White privilege, 108
Whites
  racial identity development in, 102–4
  use of term, xxiv
White students, scores of
  in mathematics, 18
  in reading, 16
  in science, 18
  in writing, 17
Women, in Muslim society, 259, 260–61
Writing
  educational progress of diverse learners
    in, 16
  proficient level in, 19

Y

Youth violence, 206